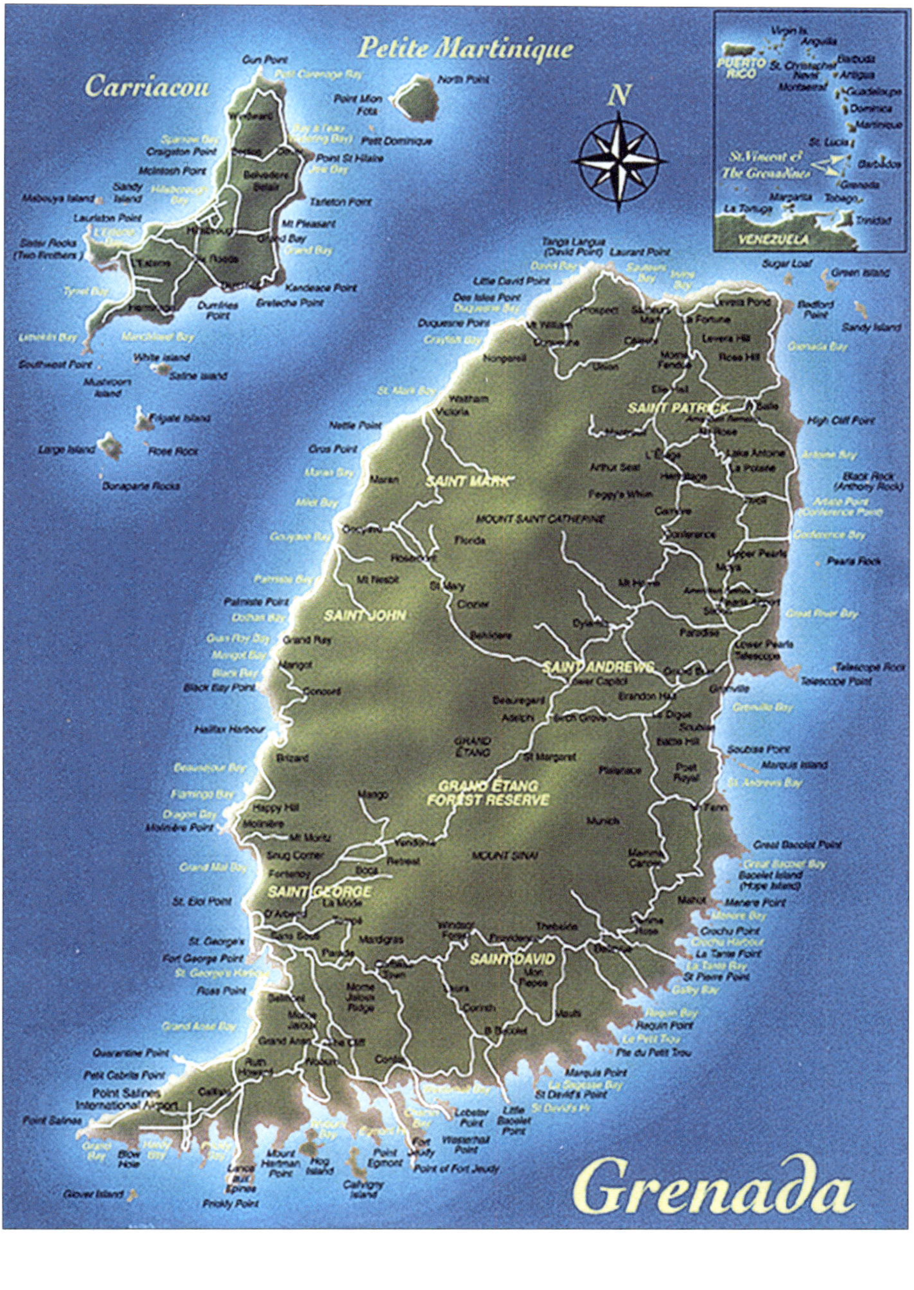

Grenada
Carriacou
Petite Martinique
N
Gun Point
North Point
Point Mon Fota
Petit Dominique
Craigston Point
McIntosh Point
Mabouya Island
Sandy Island
Lauriston Point
Sister Rocks (Two Brothers)
Tyrrel Bay
Windward
Belvedere
Bellair
Hillsborough
Mt Pleasant
Grand Bay
Tarleton Point
L'Esterre
Kendeace Point
Gretecha Point
Dumfries Point
Harvey Vale
Lauriston
Limlair
Lehekin Bay
Southwest Point
White Island
Saline Island
Mushroom Island
Frigate Island
Large Island
Rose Rock
Bonaparte Rocks
PUERTO RICO
Virgin Is.
Anguilla
Barbuda
St. Christopher Nevis
Antigua
Montserrat
Guadeloupe
Dominica
Martinique
St. Lucia
St. Vincent & The Grenadines
Barbados
Grenada
Tobago
Margarita
La Tortuga
Trinidad
VENEZUELA
Tanga Langua (David Point)
Laurant Point
Sugar Loaf
Green Island
Little David Point
Bedford Point
Sandy Island
Levera Pond
La Fortune
Levera Hill
Rose Hill
Prospect
Sauteurs
Mt William
Nonpareil
SAINT PATRICK
High Cliff Point
Walltham
Victoria
Nettle Point
Gros Point
SAINT MARK
Black Rock (Anthony Rock)
MOUNT SAINT CATHERINE
Florida
Gouyave
Rosemont
Mt Nesbit
St Mary
SAINT JOHN
Pearls Rock
Palmiste Point
Grand Roy
Mt Horne
Belvidere
Dyer
SAINT ANDREWS
Lower Capitol
Telescope Rock
Telescope Point
Black Bay Point
Concord
Beauregard
Grenville
Halifax Harbour
Birch Grove
La Digue
Soubise
Soubise Point
Marquis Island
GRAND ETANG
St Margaret
Brizard
Paradise
GRAND ETANG FOREST RESERVE
Happy Hill
Molinière
Molinière Point
Mt Moritz
Mango
Munich
Vendome
Snug Corner
MOUNT SINAI
Great Bacolet Point
Great Bacolet Bay
Bacolet Island (Hope Island)
SAINT GEORGE
St. Eloi Point
La Mode
Menere Point
St. George's
Fort George Point
St. George's Harbour
Windsor Forest
Thebaide
Crochu Point
Crochu Harbour
Providence
La Tante Point
SAINT DAVID
St Pierre Point
Morne Jaloux Ridge
Mon Repos
Corinth
Ross Point
Requin Bay
Requin Point
Grand Anse Bay
Quarantine Point
Grand Anse
Petit Cabrits Point
Pte du Petit Trou
Point Salines International Airport
Marquis Point
St David's Point
Calliste
Point Salines
Lobster Point
Little Bacolet Point
Woburn
Westerhall Point
Blow Hole
Lance aux Épines
Mount Hartman Point
Hog Island
Point Egmont
Point of Fort Jeudy
Glover Island
Calvigny Island
Prickly Point

# TRIALS *of a* TRIAL LAWYER


DERICK F. SYLVESTER

CBA, LLB (UWI), LEC (HWLS)

*Attorney at Law, Grenada*



H

HANSIB

First published in Great Britain by Hansib Publications in 2021

Hansib Publications Limited
P.O. Box 226, Hertford, SG14 3WY, United Kingdom

info@hansibpublications.com
www.hansibpublications.com



ISBN 978-1-912662-19-7
ISBN 978-1-912662-34-0 (Kindle)
ISBN 978-1-912662-35-7 (ePub)

A CIP catalogue record for this book
is available from the British Library



Production by Hansib Publications Limited

Printed in Turkey

**www.hansibpublications.com**

DEDICATION

*My Grandmother Norma Sylvester-Morain the beacon of light and hope in my life, who guided, protected and taught me the values I hold so dearly today. And, for instilling in me Christian values. Job well done, "thou good and faithful servant."*

## ACKNOWLEDGMENTS

This work would not have been possible without God's grace, guidance and His constant protection over my life.

I am grateful to the following since without their individual contributions this work would not have been completed.

My brother Andre Sylvester, whose dedication and support throughout my life has enabled me to fulfil my dream including, becoming a lawyer and publishing this book.

Dr. Francis Alexis QC who unhesitatingly and unreservedly accepted my request to edit, provide guidance, direction and write the Foreword. Winston B. Coard who edited, and wrote one of the reviews. Dr. Trevor Layne MD and Delano Viechweg who painstakingly read the manuscript and provided their individual reviews.

Sabina Gibbs, Attorney-at-Law, for her invaluable assistance in securing and delicately preserving some of the newspaper articles used in this book. Rickol Julien for the design of the front cover of this book. Besha Ottley, Lecturer at T.A. Marryshow Community College (TAMCC), for her expertise in Information Technology (IT), general advice and guidance. Desiree Stephen past Chief Personnel Officer of the Public Service Commission (PSC) for her support throughout the process.

Dr. Francis Alexis, for securing Hansib Publications for publishing this work. Andy Johnson of Andy Johnson Photos (andygjohnson@outlook.com) for his professional expertise in providing the photographs for the front page and the inner back page of the book.

To my family for their support and patience throughout this process, and to the staff at Derick F. Sylvester & Associates, your daily support and encouragement was a constant source of inspiration.

# CONTENTS

# FOREWORD

*Trials of a Trial Lawyer* by Derick F. Sylvester relates autobiographically how his primary school resolve to be a lawyer was made a reality, with emphatic success. That was on sheer determination; fully utilising available educational opportunities; driven by spiritual faith that help cometh from our Creator God, instilled in Derick by his maternal grandmother.

The story starts at rural Corinth, St. David, Grenada. There, in the early 1970s, Derick grew up with his grandmother, humbly. There was a two-bedroom wooden house. It had outside amenities for baking, bathing and 'bluting by day; with a kerosene lamp for light by night, by which Derick did homework from the Corinth Government Primary School.

Late 1978 Derick joined his mother and stepfather at their home at suburban Morne Jaloux, St. George. At least this home had electricity and television; with the Morne Jaloux RC Primary School nearby. But that interlude was brief. Back to Corinth. Thence, when he could afford it, he commuted to Wesley College Secondary School, some ten minutes' walk from the City Centre in St. George's.

With saved earnings from working as a Government road checker in St. David and an international telephone operator with Cable & Wireless in St. George's City, Derick invested in a minibus. His savings grew.

Derick signed on to the University of the West Indies (UWI) first year law programme, at the UWI Open Campus in Grenada. Next, he entered the UWI Cave Hill Campus, Barbados, completing the LLB. He then headed to the Hugh Wooding Law School in Trinidad & Tobago, where, with a loan, he completed the professional course for the LEC for admission to practise as a lawyer.

Derick was duly admitted to so practise before the Bar of the Supreme Court in Grenada.

The true mission of the noble profession of a practising lawyer is that, acting on instructions from his or her client, he or she helps the law, or the courts, indeed society, in its pursuit of having justice prevail over injustice, fairness over unfairness, equality over inequality, good over evil. This is all about human development.

This book presents the numerous cases in the courts, and other ways, by which Mr. Sylvester has been adhering to that mission. He records that, among his many other achievements, he was the first lawyer in Grenada to have his client plead guilty to a charge of murder, in 2009. That he could do because of the ruling by the Privy Council in 2002 that the mandatory death penalty for murder contravenes the constitutional protection against inhuman or degrading treatment.

This book, in many places, presents unique insights and information. Such is the coverage of the resentencing of persons convicted of murder in the Maurice Bishop Murder Trial. That is in Chapter 17, one of its four chapters on that Trial.

Many a trial lawyer serve society across a wide spectrum of activities. Included among the constitutional and statutory posts held by Mr. Sylvester was that, in which he served rather efficiently for two consecutive three year terms, of Chairman of the Public Service Commission of Grenada.

Mr. Sylvester tells of his life's trials to date with admirable frankness; with his passion for the law. Quite profound are his comments on the impact of crime and criminal law on offenders, victims, families and society; in human terms.

Mr. Sylvester unfolds his mission in his words, at a very lively pace. His style is direct, engaging, absorbing. Never is there a dull moment in the narrative. His presentation is certainly reader-friendly. Once you start reading the book you cannot put it down until you finish it.

The book is an encouragement to the reader that, no matter how daunting the trials along life's way, one should press on with making one's dreams a reality; through perseverance, discipline, self-confidence. Where there is a will there is a way, with faith in God.

On all the above virtues of the book, I most enthusiastically commend as invaluable the writings of Derick Sylvester in his *Trials of a Trial Lawyer.*

**Francis Alexis**
*1 July 2019*
*St. Paul's*
*St. George*
*Grenada*

CHAPTER ONE

# LESSONS YOU NEVER FORGET

*"The influence of each human being on others in this life is a kind of immortality."*
SIR WINSTON CHURCHILL

## MY GRANDMOTHER: NORMA SYLVESTER-MORAIN

Amidst the quietude in the village of Corinth in the parish of Saint David, on the eastern side of Grenada, nestled a two bedroom house made of pitch pine wood covered with galvanise sheets. The house was about 20 by 25 feet with a singular wooden two piece door for an entrance, which opened inward, with a hasp and staple for locking. At the front there were two wooden steps to enter the house. Neatly positioned in the living room was a wooden table complemented by wooden chairs. These were used not only for dining but also to unbend the hardship of the day. Electricity was as present as the sunshine at night, thus a kerosene lamp with a glass shade and a wick would normally be lighted. The glass shade was inscribed in the middle with the comforting words "home sweet home". I remember the joy that my eyes never hid, when the lamp was lit at nights; for the setting sun was a symbol of impending darkness. The stories of 'jumbie', 'la diablesse', 'flying horse' and 'flying men' called 'loup-garou' that only came out at nights for children weighed heavily on my mind.

Directly behind the living room was the kitchen and to the right was my grandparents, Ashley Morain and Norma Sylvester-Morain room. My grandfather was the alpha male in the family. Next to their room was another room occupied by me. The ply wood partition in the house did not reach the top of the ceiling, although the house was only ten feet high. On entering the house, one took approximately ten to twelve steps to walk from one end of the house to the other. The logs for cooking were gently placed in the yard; a subtle reminder of our humble

*My grandfather, Ashley Morain, was the alpha male in the family*

beginnings. The yard was my playground and a copper filled with water was my swimming pool. I was equipped with my flotation device. My grandmother would not allow me to go into the 'pool' without first ensuring it was safe for me to do so. That was the caring and loving granny, about whom I have much more to say later in this book.

This was always a soothing experience, as I waddled my way in the water and enjoyed every minute of the waves. The luxury of having a swimming pool created a blissful oasis even if momentarily.

The house was later subdivided by making the kitchen smaller and adding another bedroom. The only space available was walking to the left side and the bed was positioned on the right. The outside bathroom was located away from the house, it was a galvanised enclosed structure with no roof, about 3 feet by 4 feet.

The supplemental kitchen for baking was built about 20 feet away with a 'mud oven' that baked the best tasting bread. Log wooden pallets were used to insert the bread in the oven after it was preheated with wood for hours and removed when it reached the desired colour. When butter was placed in that bread and served with hot local chocolate, the taste was indescribable; and my mouth waters even now as I think of it. My grandmother's baking in that mud oven was the best I have ever had.

*Equipped with flotation device and stepping into my 'swimming pool'*

## OUTSIDE FACILITIES

The outside 'pit latrine' was even further afield, it was the practice that the use of both facilities had to be done before outside was dark. With no electricity, the darkness was blinding, so much so that you could not see your hands or other body parts and if you had company you relied on the spoken word to determine the proximity of the other person. On one occasion during the day, while having a shower outside, I felt an instant blow to my head and immediately I felt warm and saw a red substance. Blood started pouring from my head, I was filled with shock and terror. I immediately looked up because there was no roof. A 'chenet' tree was resting against the bathroom but no one was in sight and fear engulfed me even further. It was believed that a 'jumbie' attacked me in the bathroom. There were other houses with cousins, aunts, uncles and extended family members about a hundred meters away. However, this attack had all family members reeling, as no one knew what had caused such a vicious unprovoked attack on an innocent boy.

The house was filled with unmeasured love, security and a state of tranquillity that even in the face of scarce financial resources and other

*Left to right: My grandmother, Norma Sylvester-Morain, my cousin, Saul Sylvester, and my grandfather, Ashley Morain*

challenges my grandmother was able to smile with compassion. My grandmother no doubt had loved me as her own and treated me that way. She was never afraid to show it, sometimes to the discomfort of other family members. She was the mother of eleven (11) children and I was like her twelfth. Most of her children were adults and had moved on and out. She took to prayers and was destined to find out who had attacked her 12th child. Then one day, approximately three (3) weeks after the 'jumbie' attack, my aunt's daughter confessed that she was throwing stones to pick a mango and one accidentally struck me in the head. She immediately ran away realising what had happened because she was too scared to speak. The relief this brought to me was exhilarating and the physical pain paled on my discovering that I was not attacked by some evil force; destined to 'deal' or 'sell' children for the devil, as we were led to believe.

My grandmother had hundreds of dried coconuts in the yard, the same had to be peeled with a cutlass or machete so as to remove the outer layer or skin, the hard shell would then be cracked, and a specially designed knife bent to a 'C' shape was used to remove the white hardened fruit or kernel of the coconut. The kernel would then be grated, with a specially designed zinc sheet, sized and nail driven in a circular motion to facilitate the grating of the kernel into very fine strips. Thereafter, the strips were rinsed with water repeatedly, until the white milky kernel was drained of its white juices then strained and placed in plastic buckets for a day or two, a process called 'setting'. This was a form of fermentation to separate the oil from the water, which was used to wash the stripped kernel. The oil would then be removed from the top of the bucket and placed in a pot. This process was called 'skimming', a very precise use of a small container, to remove the oil and place it in a pot for boiling. Three stones would be carefully chosen and placed together in the shape of a triangle and a large aluminium pot would be placed over it, the 'raw oil' poured inside the pot, and sticks and pieces of logs would be lighted under the pot. The fire was fed repeatedly with the logs until the colour of the oil turned golden brown, or kept on the fire until the desired colour was achieved. The process of cooling resulted in the oil remaining there for hours and thereafter strained with a fine cloth, bottled manually and taken to the Grenville market every Saturday morning, for the purpose of sale.

I remember the dedication and industry of my grandmother as she dealt with her daily tasks; she did it with grace and always said, "There is pride in honest work". It was my desire to grow quickly so I could alleviate her of all the manual labour. Even though she never complained, sometimes I saw the tiredness and fatigue emanating from her whenever she paused or took a sip from her favourite enamel cup. Aluminium pots, enamel cups, coal pot iron were the wares of choice.

## PRAYERS

The memory of seeing my grandmother exert physical labour without complaint has amazed me to the present day. Oh how she carried her burdens with grace and humility. She was soft spoken, prayerful and had a strong belief in God. Being a Christian, she instilled in me values such as; honesty, decency and cleanliness, which I hold dear to the present day.

Prayer was a nightly routine, and the prelude to going to sleep was thanking God for his many blessings, guidance and protection to see another day. The first prayer I was taught by my grandmother goes like this:

*In my little bed I lie,*
*Heavenly father hear my cry,*
*Lord protect me through this night,*
*And bring me safe till morning light*

There would be the nightly routine, when my grandmother would ask me to say a silent pray. This I did without fail, my silent prayers were what a child would normally ask for, like toys, food and to always play. I enjoyed flying kites so much, I wanted to do so forever. But as I grew older, my prayer trajectory changed. During the morning it was the Catholic Church ritual that was never broken. The Sunday afternoon routine of going to 'Brother Bestly' Gospel Hall church was a rule. Brother Bestly was a short man, very polite, friendly and respected as a spiritual leader in the community. He is even to the present day. My grandmother's house was located on a hillside, we had to walk downhill to cross a ravine to the main road, and then a northerly direction took you to the church. I could stay in my grandmother's house and see the church, it was the place of Sunday evening worship. Failing to go to church was equivalent to 'spiritual betrayal' and being ungrateful to God for his plenteous mercies towards us.

Now, as an adult, I understand and appreciate fully what my grandmother did to ensure she instilled Christian values in my brother Andre Sylvester and me. Going to church was not a task or a duty. It was a necessary path towards human existence and growth, for my failure to attend church was equivalent to being deficient in one's upbringing, and the challenges of life we would not have been able to face. My grandmother never failed in that duty and she has been the female who had the most impact on my life, for which I am ever grateful.

Education was very important to my grandmother. She always reiterated that school was important. I enjoyed no better sport than attending school, receiving corrections, and 100% in exams. Anything less would lead to a torrent of tears, as I complained to my grandmother I did badly. On numerous occasions my grandmother would sing Slinger Francisco 'Mighty Sparrow's' song for me to hear and it goes in part like this:

*Children go to school and learn well,*
*Otherwise later on in life you going to ketch real hell,*
*Without an education in your head,*
*Your whole life would be pure misery you better off dead,*
*For there is simply no room in this whole wide world,*
*For an uneducated little boy or girl,*
*Don't allow idle companions to lead you astray,*
*To earn tomorrow you got to learn today...*

This song stayed with me and I am sure it will remain. The message was clear, the hard work I endured and the poverty I experienced as a child, I decided was not going to follow me into adulthood.

## SELLING COCONUT OIL

As I grew older I became adept in the coconut trade as I went to the field, collected the coconuts and assisted my grandmother. I even went to the Grenville market with her every Saturday, as was the routine, to sell the bottled oil. I would normally take the bottle of oil and walk around the Grenville market to the outskirts in the fish market area and sell one bottle of oil 750 ml or 26 ounces for five dollars ($5.00). I was very respectful as I was trained by my grandmother, since an obscene or harsh word would lead you to hell's damnation. On numerous occasions while trying to sell coconut oil to adults as a child I would be met with criticism, insults and disparaging comments. This never daunted me. From that moment, I learnt that I would treat every human being with dignity despite their riches, social standing, colour, race or class. Adults can be cruel to children and sometimes treat them as insignificant creatures. I have had my fair share; but I was destined to let nothing hinder me.

Since a child, I had an insatiable appetite for fairness, and I hated injustice. I knew becoming a lawyer, police, judge, magistrate, prison officer or being in any profession to correct, or at least try to lighten, society's wrong, was my calling. One day I prayed to God to, "get big quickly" (my childish prayer) so I could prove to the world that this little 'oil selling boy' would make his grandmother proud and remove her from the Grenville market, every Saturday. She had to wake from her bed every Saturday at about 4 am to get transport either in the form of Emrol Harris also known as 'DJ Harrow' bus or 'Pem' truck to get to the market early. All this was done in the name of making an honest and decent living.

I looked forward to my fresh beef soup on Saturday nights, with christophine (chou-chou), carrots, dumplings and local seasoning. The taste of my grandmother's soup was unequalled to any I have tasted before, during or after her existence. On Sundays the breakfast menu included roasted bakes cooked on fire wood, fish cakes, blood pudding, or salt fish souse and cocoa tea or bush tea (for example black sage, lemon grass, mint, bay leaf and numerous others). She would always insist on eating local and state the benefits of doing so. All the plates were enamel and there were special glass wares in a cabinet locked securely to be used on special occasions, for example, Christmas or if there was an overseas visitor.

Respect, discipline, honesty and fear of God were some of the ideals instilled in me. "Honesty is the best of policy"; "Friends bring you go, but do not bring you back"; "The evil that men do live after them"; "Thief from thief make God laugh"; "Every day the bucket go to the well one day it will drop"; "99 days for the thief but one day for the watch man"; "Showing off is an expensive thing"; and "Pray in and out of season that you will catch the right season". These were words reiterated by my grandmother and ring in my ears every day.

As I look back on my life, I understand and appreciate what my grandmother has done for me both in terms of my education and life lessons. She was not lettered and always said the reason for her not attending school, was due to her mother's financial position, which caused her to stay home to take care of her siblings. However, she saw the need for education, and recognised it was the only avenue out of poverty.

The art of being neat, clean and tidy was mastered by me, through the artful teachings of my grandmother. "Cleanliness is next to Godliness", she would say. By the age of four (4) I was taught to use a coal pot iron, a metal iron heated over burnt wood in a coal pot; this was used to press my school clothes. So that, I was always clean and sharp on my way to school. I wore that khaki pants with blue shirt, black belt, black socks and shoes with pride and gusto.

The discipline at school was just a continuation of what I received at home. Upon entry into school both hands had to be out stretched for inspection; to ensure nails cut short and clothes well worn. Any shortcoming was met with the instant attack of a wooden ruler on the defective parts. I was not perfect, but never a beneficiary of correction as a result of untidiness. This has remained with me to the present day.

## FIRST DAY AT PRIMARY SCHOOL: ST. PETER'S R. C. SCHOOL

My first day of primary school, I was well decked off and I arrived early. Mr. Victor Ashby was the Principal of St. Peter's R.C. School in Corinth in the parish of Saint David. The school's name has since been changed to Corinth Government School. I was taught by Teacher Denise, who later became Mrs. Denise Ashby, the wife of the then Principal. The school was wooden with concrete flooring, nestled at the top of Baillies Bacolet Hill, a hill I knew all too well, having travelled it almost daily with coconuts from my grandfather's garden or that of the neighbouring uninhabited lands. At the start of assembly the chairperson asked for a volunteer to come on stage and sing a song. Without hesitation I rushed to the stage, what song I was going to sing? I could not care less! I knew a lot that my grandmother sang. I was so small, that I was lifted and placed on top of a wooden desk. I looked around at the crowd and instantly loved all eyes on me. I smiled, when I received a nice childish tap from the chairperson who asked, "What are you going to sing for us today?" I instantly said 'Yellow Bird'. I was given a few seconds to compose myself and I started singing:

*Yellow bird up high in banana tree*
*Yellow bird you sit all alone like me*
*Did your lady friend leave the nest again?*
*That is very sad, makes me feel so bad*
*You can fly away, in the sky away*
*You're luckier than me.*

I received a rousing round of applause from the staff and students and I became a celebrity for the day. Thereafter, I excelled academically and attained some popularity from my class mates. Other than being the smallest in the class, I avoided fights, confrontations and breaking school rules. It was abundantly clear to me, if my grandmother had to come to school, I would receive a good beating and it would be for a good reason. I was lucky to never have an infraction.

## SIR ERIC GAIRY GOVERNMENT OVERTHROWN

On the 13th day of March 1979, while at home with my grandmother, very early in the morning as was normal, she played her transistor radio on the usual local radio station. The normal programming was interrupted with the words, "Attention! Attention! Attention! People of Grenada, the Government of the criminal dictator Eric Matthew Gairy has been overthrown." My grandmother was visibly perturbed, as she was a staunch supporter of Uncle Gairy, as he was affectionately called by his supporters. He was the leader of the Grenada United Labour Party (GULP). The theme song of his political party always rang in my grandmother's house. She would speak of how much he had assisted the workers on the plantation to get a decent wage and better working conditions.

Being a child of tender years, I was unable to comprehend the magnitude of the turn of the political events that were unfolding. Later, in my adult life, I better appreciated and understood its full import.

## GOING WITH MY MOTHER: MARIA SYLVESTER

One day I returned home from school and my grandmother looked pensive, I knew right away something was wrong. She maintained a calm smile and quietly said, "Your mother has returned from Trinidad and she would like to have you with her. You will be relocating to Morne Jaloux with your stepfather, as your mother wants you to be with her."

*With my brother, Andre (left)*

My heart sank, I became mad, and I wondered why she would even allow that. To have me removed from her presence was more painful for her than it was for me. Yet still, she comforted me by saying, “You would visit every weekend and on holidays.” I was going to live eight (8) miles away. In those days transportation was scarce, which made the 8 mile journey seem oceans away. At that time, my mother only had two children, Andre my younger brother and myself.

My brother Andre was resilient as a child; even though he was one year my junior, he was taller than me and he was very quiet. Sometimes I would refer to him as ‘Andre the giant’. However, he had a contained aggressive side, that was only unleashed in the extreme of circumstances. It was an unwritten rule that, “You should never hit his brother or say anything bad about his mother.” These were red lines.

My stepfather would normally visit. He was a taxi driver, he had a bright green Datsun car 260C, registration number H6023; I remember every detail of that car as if it was yesterday, when it came to uproot me from my grandmother’s house and sped to Morne Jaloux. My clothes were packed and the ride was approximately 30 minutes. I looked back until I lost sight of the village. There was no motorable road to my grandmother's house. It was a foot path to get to the main road and one had to jump and skip over a ravine to reach the main road. That ravine flowed heavily when it was raining; logs of wood were placed to allow us to cross. I have learnt to walk gingerly on moving logs so as to avoid a plunge into the ravine. This log walking skill was mastered, so much that I no longer walked on the unstable logs but ran. In the event of a mishap, I would have succeeded in the mission of crossing.

After all the bags were packed in the car, I examined my stepfather's face as he gave a taxi driver's smile and he said "All aboard!" as he drove southward. I saw places for the first time as my journey with my grandmother was mostly north to the Grenville market. The drive to the south was nostalgic, as I pondered on what this new life would bring, leaving my school friends and villagers behind. I had loved all the elderly people in Corinth, starting from Ms. Catherine, Ms. Bella, Ms. Zeltina, Ms. Rita, Ms. Faith, Ms. John, Cousin Gertude, Ms. Braveboy, Ms. Grant, Ms. Sharon, Ms. Fleming, Ms. Francois and many more. And it was without doubt that my love for them was reciprocated. My heart was filled with joy at seeing my biological mother, but grave sadness for leaving my grandmother. The thought of returning every weekend was appealing then, but not having the usual grandmother's home cooked food was troubling both my brother and me. The bigger perturbation was the fear of the unknown, having no idea of what our life was going to be like.

Now as an adult I understand and appreciate fully what my grandmother did to ensure she instilled the Christian values in my brother and me.

My mind was less disconcerted by the cornering of the Datsun 260C as it swerved upwards to Marian gap. I instantly recognised the change in the neighbourhood. It seemed well manicured. Most of the houses were concrete, having wall fencing and or planted flowers. It was in that instant I recognised it was an urban or suburban part of Grenada. The car pulled to a stop and the taxi driver said, "We have arrived!" My brother and I took a deep breath and we thoroughly examined the surroundings, through childish eyes and with mixed emotions. This was the village of Morne Jaloux that would become my place of abode for the next four (4) years.

The car came to a halt on the left side of the road, there was a concrete structure, about 30 feet by 30 feet; with a downstairs which was unfinished, having no windows. Three concrete steps led downwards with a walkway of about 10 feet, then we were greeted by a very small seated area and the entrance door was to the left. There was no hasp and staple. It was a silver lock handle that turned downwards, very smooth and the two sided door had glass embedded on both sides. Upon entering I saw the living room area with a chair set and a door leading to a bedroom that later became that of my mother and stepfather. To the right was the kitchen and another bedroom followed. This became the bedroom of my brother and me. A table top stove was housed in the corner of the kitchen with two burners, a gas cylinder and a refrigerator.

The house had galvanised roof and it was lined with plywood so you could not see the galvanise from the inside, unlike in Corinth. I wondered then, whether I would hear the patter of the rain, as it fell on the roof. A sound that I enjoyed so much, since it always sent me to sleep. I entered the bedroom and there with a warm embrace for me was my mother Maria Sylvester. She invited us to the bedroom to unpack and a quick introduction as we were marshalled to our routine thereafter.

There was a dog in the yard that later became our responsibility and two pigs which were kept further away from the house, as if to disassociate from its owner. There was a continuous steep decline at the back of the house. That area later became our playground for us and the neighbours. To the left was a concrete house owned by the Brathwaites, I had the benefit of having two teachers from that house. To the right were our first friends we made at Morne Jaloux, Junior and Judy who lived next door. They were about our ages at the time and we attended the same school in the area.

My brother and I settled down quickly to our chores of cooking, cleaning, feeding the dog, feeding the pigs, going to the shop, washing, ironing and any other tasks assigned to us. My mother was a continuous worker and found tasks to do as the minutes went by.

## NEW SCHOOL: MORNE JALOUX R.C. SCHOOL

The primary school in my new locality was the Morne Jaloux Roman Catholic School. That it was a Catholic school was a welcome relief, as I was a Roman Catholic, and I dared not stray from my grandmother's religious teachings, lest I betray her. The school was located about three minutes' walk from our home even two minutes with speed.

My first day at the new school was tense since my brother and I were in different classes, I was one class ahead. I was six years (6) old and my teacher Ms. Indy-Ann Antoine, who became my favourite primary school teacher, ensured I was settled in nicely. A proper introduction and my unforgotten grandmother's training; respect, attitude and cleanliness impressed her. I was placed in standard two (2) and within a week I was promoted to standard three (3). I was an avid reader and the discipline planted within me both at home and school in Corinth placed me in good stead to be at the top of the class. Quickly, I assimilated into the school system making friends, but yet grieving for the ones I left behind. In retrospect, I have realised how resilient children can be and there is indeed 'A Special God for children'.

School was a welcome relief from my many home chores. Vacation was an unwelcomed guest as my home tasks were ever unfolding. The promised weekly visits to our grandmother's home were sporadic. Communication was impossible as there were no phones in our residence. Monday to Friday was school and on Saturdays my grandmother went to Grenville market, the trip I missed so much. In addition, on Sundays there was no public transportation. Walking from Morne Jaloux to St David would have taken us approximately two to three hours one way, a return trip would take about four to six hours. So this was not done until we grew a bit older, braver and bolder.

My stepfather, being a taxi driver, was hardly ever at home. He came at nights, and was present only for short intervals during the day. His communication with us was minimal. Andre and I had several conversations about our future with our mother, grandmother and two neighbours Ms. Melda and Ms Rita, who both assisted in nurturing us when our mother was not at home.

It was my desire to be a lawyer even though the idea seemed like a mere illusion because financially I knew there was no way I would be able to afford it. Despite knowing this, I held on to this dream as a kid waiting for Santa Claus to descend from the chimney. I prayed and deliberated on the idea of going to university. One day when I was asked at school what I wanted to do when I grew up, because I was asked by my favourite teacher, I simply responded "teacher". She smiled gloriously, either because she knew my response was to make her happy or she felt she had a positive impact on me. Both answers were true, but the desire inside my bones to become a lawyer would overwhelm me, so many times. When the black and white coloured television was purchased by my stepfather, and Perry Mason movies were on, my eyes were glued to the screen. I looked at every motion and noted every syllable from the mouth of the well-spoken, intelligent and savvy lawyer. There was an antenna planted on a long bamboo pole on the side of the house, connected to the television to enable better viewing reception. Whenever the television screen went blank I would rush to readjust the antenna to enable better viewing. I would guess the plots, the killers and the scenes in Perry Mason movies. Later, I read every related novel I could have borrowed or placed my hands on. At that time, I knew no one who was a lawyer and my desire to be a lawyer was more to ensure justice and fairness was done to all, both adults and children.

## BISHOP SYDNEY CHARLES

Church was a pious and solemn occasion when all the children sat at the front. I walked to church every Sunday and my mother ensured that was maintained, the walk was about ten (10) minutes. When we arrived Father Sydney Charles, the parish priest, later Bishop Sydney Charles, would forever remind us that God is the creator of the universe and we must love our neighbours as ourselves. This advice was nothing new to me, just a reiteration of the teachings of my first teacher, priest, mentor, educator and counsellor, my grandmother.

There was soon to be an addition to the family when my mother became pregnant and later gave birth to Deloris my sister, whom I had the benefit of assisting in caring, nurturing and providing brotherly care while either my mother did chores or was absent for short periods. I learnt the skill of plaiting hair, corn row and single plaits. My stepfather later became the father of five children with my mother, for whom my love is unwavering.

## WRITING COMMON ENTRANCE EXAMINATIONS

School became a welcome routine, and as I grew older my love for academics grew stronger. The mantra, "Education is liberation, education is a need, not a want," propelled me forward. Time flew by quickly, I was almost ten years and Common Entrance preparation was the new rigour. Common Entrance was the singular national annual exam to be had by all primary schools. The successful applicants got a place at a secondary school where after a five year matriculation GCE (British based) and or CXC (Caribbean based) examinations were held. The morning of the Common Entrance examination, there were arranged transportations to take all the students in standard six to Tanteen, St. George's. The same location with the Institute for Further Education (IFE) and Grenada Technical and Vocational Institute (GTVI) now collectively called TAMCC (T. A. Marryshow Community College). We were all seated at our respective desks with pencils, awaiting the 9:00 am start time. As I gazed around the room, I saw all my class mates anxious and nervous as lambs to the slaughter. I was sweating profusely. As is customary, I prayed the night before; the morning when I got up and all the way to Tanteen. I felt sure my grandmother was praying for me, so I knew all would be well. Her faith was like nothing I have seen, that even in the face of adversity she would calmly say, "Leave all in God's hands, He is in charge, not man, man would reign but for a while". Those words held true and I saw its manifestation even when I became an adult.

My thoughts were quickly interrupted by the invigilator giving strict instructions about talking, cheating, using the bathroom and general examination rules. When the sheets with the questions were passed around, again I prayed and I delved into it as a cheetah with its prey. Time flew by quickly and when I was finished with the exam it was the first time I raised my head from that paper. I entered the room praying and I left praying, thereafter I prayed every day about the exam results, until they were published.

## WHAT A WALK

Much happened in quick succession while waiting for the examination results. I awaited the moment when we had to visit our grandmother on the weekend and my brother and I walked to St. David from Morne Jaloux via Calivigny. It was an arduous journey, we had no money for bus fare, and hunger enfolded us that day. It was a painful journey, we walked for miles on roads that seemed to have no end. Our legs were so short, that the distance from telephone pole to telephone pole seemed like a marathon. Finally, we got to a junction, the road was divided into a 'Y' and we had absolutely no idea whether we should go left or right. I later learned that this was the 'Red Gate roundabout' and the left went to Perdmontemps back to St. George's from whence we came, and the right was about a mile away from my grandmother's house. It was already getting dark and we were in a fit of hysteria, my brother was always braver than I. He said, "I believe we are almost there." We waited a bit and we saw an elderly gentleman walking towards us. I had never felt so happy to see another human being. We rushed to him and asked for directions to Corinth. Then he said, "Aren't you all 'Ashley' grandchildren?" I instantly felt like a celebrity. "Yes!" we said. "What are you all doing on the road this hour?" he asked. I said, "We are going by our grandmother." He gave us directions to Corinth, bid us farewell and looked visibly concerned. That was the kind of care and attention I had grown accustomed to at my grandmother's house. We departed on our journey. Later, we learnt that the gentleman was an overseer at the nearby plantation where my grandfather once worked and he was nicknamed 'Brigadier'.

When we arrived at my grandmother's house we were hungrier than when we left. The journey was tiring and exhausting. For children, miles of road seem like an eternity. I swore I would never walk that route again and I have kept that promise. As I entered the yard of the house I went searching for my grandmother and I said, "Mummy, Mummy," the name by which I always referred to her. I saw her coming out of the house with her usual sweet smile and calm disposition, as if she was expecting us. We received a sweet embrace, sweet because it felt so good I could have tasted it. The love I felt immediately soothed my aching feet, stomach and head. "Are you hungry? What's wrong?"

"This time of night you all come up here alone?"

"Where's your mother?"

"Why your stepfather didn't drop you all up?"

The questions were fast and furious, I assured her we were ok and all was well. She did not believe me one iota, even though I said I was not hungry. I was fed that night as if I was travelling the next day and would not see her again. Indeed I was travelling the next day. The night my brother and I told her of our experiences in Morne Jaloux and she sternly promised to take us back to live with her. I never thought I would have heard such stern words emanating from my grandmother, who always seemed to relent to my mother's demand for my presence; today was the exception. I thought about all the friends I made at Morne Jaloux and my favourite teachers, Ms. Indy-Ann Antoine, Ms. Brathwaite, Mr. Leslie Austin and others. Even though I had grown to assimilate into the Morne Jaloux culture, school was my place of solace. Soon I would be attending secondary school after the results were released and the city of St. George's would be my nesting place for the next five (5) years.

## BACK TO MY GRANDMOTHER

I returned to Morne Jaloux with a sense of pride, composure and zeal as if I returned with an army behind me and an outrider ahead of me. My grandmother's words and commands rang through my ears. I settled into my routine of work, chores and instructions, before I could relay my grandmother's request, my mother stated we were all moving back to St. David to live. I automatically knew that my place of abode was already well settled and immediately I felt a sense of sadness, as I was leaving a place I had grown accustomed to. This quickly changed to relief that I was returning to a place where my grandmother's love abound.

The night came and I packed, due to return to Corinth. However, my stepfather's transportation was not forthcoming. I was forced to remain another night and day. I returned to my grandmother's haven, where I would remain until I left for university in September of 1997. There was neither telephone nor modern form of communication then, commuting was the fastest means of carrying messages.

## RELIEF ON PASSING COMMON ENTRANCE

The results for Common Entrance were released and I breathed a sigh of relief as I had passed the examinations. Sadly, though, my brother, who was one year behind, had to continue his primary school life at Corinth Government School. I cannot imagine the process of reacclimatising he had to go through, as he had to make new friends and hope the ones he left would reacquaint themselves with him.

"Der Der"...I heard my grandmother calling me, that was my pet name sometimes. "Congratulations for passing the Common Entrance". I got a lecture from my grandmother about St George's School, bad friends, alcohol and every possible distraction that could be brought to bear on me at school. I remember these warnings, "Be careful with friends for they don't always mean well, not even the devil knoweth the mind of man", "don't cut your nose and spoil your face" and repeating, "cleanliness is next to Godliness". These words were reiterated, and served to properly school me in the do's and don'ts, it aided with my academic transition.

## WESLEY COLLEGE SECONDARY SCHOOL

The school selected for me was the Wesley College Secondary School, it was a Methodist school and I was ready to embark upon my journey to become a lawyer for many reasons.

At my grandmother's house I was back in my usual bedroom, the 'home sweet home' lamp welcomed me and seemed to shine brighter than the electric lights I had grown accustomed to at Morne Jaloux. My Grenville routine continued, and I assimilated into my usual coconut task. When I returned to Corinth, Mr. Victor Ashby, was now the Principal of the Grenada Boys' Secondary School (GBSS), a prestigious boys' school in St George's. My hope was elevated for a transfer as I felt I was well known to him at the primary level albeit my four years away at Morne Jaloux. It was agreed that my mother and I would attend at the GBSS to see Mr. Ashby to request a transfer. When we got to the school, my mother went into the Principal's office and spoke to Mr. Ashby. I was soon called in and the answer was in the negative. Later, I got to realise that everything occurred for a reason.

I was an avid reader, I read every sign, bottle, paper, and bill board; anything written which I could put my hands on. When I was leaving the GBSS compound, I saw written in bold on a notice board which I memorised:

> *Never be contented with failure because success is all you should aspire to.*

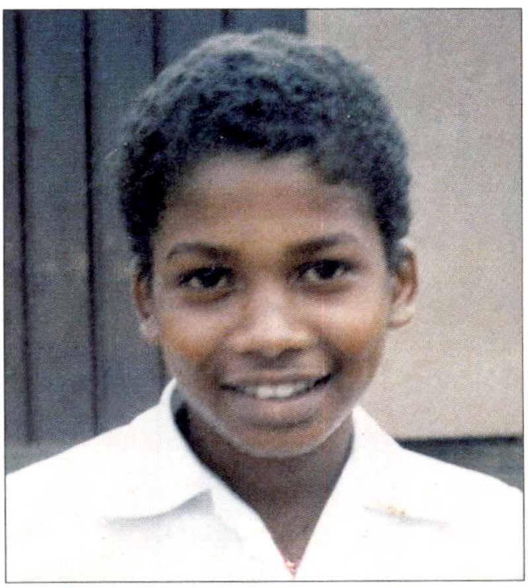

*At Wesley College Secondary School in 1983*

I kept these words close to my heart and wrote them in my first purchased Grenada Constitution that I used at University and I have in my possession even today. That was one of my many mantras.

My first day at secondary school in September of 1982, I was well adorned with brown shoes, socks, pants and belt; white shirt and the school's badge inscribed with the insignia, 'Virtute et fide Vincimus', Latin which means , 'By Virtue and Faith We Conquer'. I was met in assembly by Mr. Kapur, the Principal, who delivered the charge to us students. He was a man of Indian descent, gentle and respectful, who urged the importance of education. The school was located on Lucas Street, an extremely busy street in the city of St. George's; the physical building was housed one step away from the main road. The vehicular traffic made teaching a work of art and song; the teacher had to pause from speaking and writing, whenever a vehicle passed. As fate would have it, that busy street later became the home of my law office.

## PROTESTING SCHOOL SITE DURING THE REVOLUTION

My five years in secondary school was very interesting. It had its challenges. I started secondary school in 1982 at the height of the Grenada revolution that spanned March 1979 to October 1983. The form five students were militant, vocal, expressive, had a strong sense of pride and political identity. While a freshman in form 1W (the forms were grouped into 1W and 1C. (W for Wesley and C for college), the student organisation was headed by Reginald Lord, who was very well spoken, and possessed leadership qualities. I admired him and thought of him as the 'Maurice Bishop' of Wesley College (Maurice Bishop was the Prime Minister at the time and very popular with the masses). He and other students of the senior forms organised a demonstration to have the school relocated because of the constant noise from vehicular traffic. This was my first experience of challenging authority. The fear that came over the faces of the teachers and the Principal, as the plan started growing in momentum! For any opposition in those days was met with 'heavy manners', arrest, detention and imprisonment without charge. But Comrade Reginald Lord and others organised their troops with placards, and school was forced to close as we marched through the street of St. George's shouting and chanting different slogans demanding a new location for the school and better conditions of study including library facilities.

The response to our protest was swift. The government of the day in short order arranged a new location for our school at River Road, St. George's, just about ten minutes' walk from the city. That school is at the same location to the present day, thanks to the militancy of Comrade Reginald Lord and others. I have always admired Reginald and felt he would one day enter the political arena; however he remained employed by the Government of Grenada and our paths crossed on many occasions thereafter.

## ODD SPOTS

I was always the smallest in my class and extremely quiet. My grandmother would provide me daily with meals in a 'flask' specially designed to keep the food hot. I always dreaded the idea of going to school with a plastic coated container with a heat contained interior. On one occasion I had fig (cooked green bananas) and salt fish. The flask fell and broke, and the food spilled on the floor. I was taunted by the children in the class for, despite the duration, it felt like forever. As a child, I was ignorant and was concerned a lot about image, perception and what people thought of me, a perception that no longer intimidates or hampers me as an adult. I tried to abstain from bringing food on the occasions when I could have. Despite this, my grandmother would always provide. There were occasions when it was financially difficult, and I knew, because coconut oil sales were bad. My grandfather was mainly doing farming which provided food for us periodically. He was a man with multiple visiting households in the same village of Corinth so there was some constraint on his part. But in fairness to him, he always ensured food was provided, he had 'fish pots', a very skilled way of catching fish in the Bacolet River, close to the location where he farmed.

Money was scarce and my commute to school was with a distant family member who had a bus in the village. His name was Augustine Smart alias 'Gus', which was the name placed on the bus, registration number H955. Gregory Isaacs songs were played daily on that bus, such as, 'Night Nurse'. It was the same cassette, day in and day out, in those days cassette players were the order of the day. There was an occasion in school during a period when my grandmother was financially strapped, I went to school famished. The vendors were selling snow ice (small frozen sweetened milk or juices tied in plastic bags) for 25 cents. It was the practice that persons would put the 25 cents in a bowl then take the snow ice. I was so hungry, that I waited until many students were buying, then I went and imitated my deposit of 25 cents and took a snow Ice. The vendor turned and said to me "You did not pay!" I told her I did and she relented. The night I asked God for forgiveness and I got 50 cents that week (I do not remember from where or whom) but I went back and boldly showed the vendor my money and I deposited it. Little did she know, I had two 25 cent pieces and I took one snow ice, which meant I paid for the one I took previously. My conscience would not allow me to sleep at nights so I had to correct that wrong. From that moment I have learnt that hunger can lead to desperation and a desperate man would do anything. I have learnt a lesson to always feed the hungry from that day forth. This may have been the foundation for the charitable outlook which engulfed me when I started working and earning sufficient to sustain my grandmother and me.

## LEARNING TO RIDE BICYCLE

Secondary school life was a blessing as it was a means of escaping the physical labour at home, I embraced the opportunity. I had a quest for academic knowledge, even though I was constrained by my financial circumstances. I wanted to experience everything. It was at secondary school I learnt to ride bicycle. A student named Glen Viechweg from Darbeau, a village neighbouring the secondary school, came to school with a bicycle; he would frequently allow me to practice riding his bicycle, until I became proficient. I enjoyed the physical activity.

## LEARNING TO SWIM

It was during my secondary school life that I also learnt to swim. I had a class mate Francis Baker of Woburn, who was my closest friend. He was a proficient and experienced swimmer. On one occasion we went to Grand Anse beach, a Saturday morning, I was taught to 'dog paddle'. It was a forward pull movement of the hands under water and the constant flipping of the feet until the body remained above water. I continued until I conquered the dog paddle and graduated to long arm stroke. On one occasion, as little boys would be adventurous, we embarked on an outward journey of swimming into the ocean, from Grand Anse beach. We continued to swim without looking back until we could see the Carenage harbour to our right which is located near the capital of St. George's. As care free teenagers we each had goggles examining the underwater. Lo and behold, we decided to look to the shore line and we were shocked to the point of near panic as to our distance from the shore. We were seeing persons on the beach about the size of one inch nails and we immediately decided to swim back. It was agreed that we would take our time so as not to get cramps or panic. This we did arduously.

I could feel the abject terror that embraced me when I saw the distance and the possibility of no return encircled my thoughts. Despite the perilous journey, we returned to shore. It was at these moments in my life, as I look back, I become more aware that God has preserved me for a purpose. For we were not expert swimmers; I was a novice, and the physical exertion to return to shore, mixed with adrenaline, made us persevere and complete the swim.

## SECONDARY SCHOOL GRIEF

On one occasion there was a sporting activity in the Tanteen playing field and numerous children were there. I was informed that a student of the Wesley College had a physical altercation with another. His name was Alton Henry. It was alleged and later proven true that he used a ratchet, and inflicted a fatal stab wound on another student. This caused me extreme sorrow as Alton was one of our star cricketers and was generally a good athlete. The death of another student and the stigma it brought on the students of the brown uniformed school left immense emotional pain. Since you always felt the students from other schools were looking at you as belonging to the school where the murderer evolved. During my secondary school years, morality and the norms, mores and values of community living were present at school.

## PREMONITION

During the latter part of December 1987, I kept having terrible dreams and I told my grandmother something bad would happen to me. She said, "Son, just keep praying, for all is in God's hands." I prayed incessantly but still felt bothered. On the 1st day of January 1988, I told my grandmother, "Mummy, this year would be a bad year for me." She asked, "Why?" I said, "Because I just feel it in my bones that something bad will happen." I saw that usual disturbed look on her face, likened to when she was speaking to me about society's ills.

One morning during the first week of January 1988, my grandmother requested that I run an errand. I was always an obedient child, never rude or disobliging. I said mummy, "I do not want to go anywhere". She said, "Just run quickly and come back", adding "don't be long!" So I took an empty rice bag as it was drizzling and I inserted one corner of the bag inside the other forming a cone shape and used it to cover my head. I departed downhill, crossed the ravine and entered the public road speeding northward to my destination. While about two minutes walking, I heard a vehicle approaching from behind with unusual speed. In those days, vehicles were infrequent on the road, especially Sundays. I decided to move further left while looking back to see what was coming. I received a very heavy blow to my right shoulder, the impact was so hard I heard my bone crack. I was struck with such impact that I fell to the ground. I felt immense pain to my shoulder, indeed to every part of my body. I never knew such excruciating pain existed. I saw Brian Thomas, a fellow villager and said to him; "Bryan go and tell mummy, I am dead". I heard him shout to the top of his lungs, "Ms. Norma, Ms. Norma!" As my grandmother's house was within hearing and seeing distance of the main

*With a broken hand in 1988*

road, he shouted, “Derick say he dead!” I lost all consciousness at that moment. Just before losing consciousness, I resigned myself to death.

I opened my eyes as I was jolted by the feeling of immense pain. Then I realised I was in a vehicle. In the corner of my eyes I saw the village Pastor, Benedict Newton. While going in and out of consciousness I saw a stocky gentleman holding a steering wheel, and empathetically insisting that he was sorry, the road was wet and what sounded like gibberish at the time. Then the chaos of screams, moans, bawling and demands to take me to the hospital quickly followed. I slipped into unconsciousness once again as the pain was unbearable. I awoke at the General Hospital, my surgery was carded for the 9th January, I was told it was a major surgery since the head of the humerus was fractured. The surgery was done on the 9th January 1988. I felt the same amount of pain as at the accident. I slept and woke in pain for approximately three weeks before this pain subsided. I wondered daily what I was being punished for. When I asked my grandmother she said, “Never stop praying”.

While at hospital I met a nurse named Donna Campbell who was gentle and graceful. The way she treated me caused me to memorise her name. She always made time to speak with me, a true epitome of what a nurse should be. Years later, I had the opportunity to retire her from the public service when I became Chairman of the Public Service Commission and I also represented her family company, Campbell Estates Limited.

## FIRST ENCOUNTER WITH MY FATHER

It was at the General Hospital in 1988, that for the first time I saw my father, Lashley Salfarlie in person. My mother kept a photo of him, where he was reading a newspaper with a side view, so I memorised it for the purpose of recognition if I were to ever meet him. However, given the circumstances under which we met, conversation was the least on my mind. I saw an average height, Indian man walk into the hospital. He looked stately, professional and walked with a sense of confidence. I immediately knew who it was as the mental picture remained in my head. He said “I am your father and I heard an announcement on the radio that you were in hospital and that I should come quickly”. I was unaware that my father was in Grenada at the time. How my mother knew my father was in the island still amazes me to today. I later learnt she placed an announcement on the radio that he should contact the hospital urgently regarding his son. We chatted for a bit, then he left. I tried not to show the extent of the pain I was enduring. Later, I was sent home and cared for by my grandmother. The level of pain I had from the fractured humerus of my right arm was affecting my left. There were occasions when I was confused and disoriented.

## FIRST FINANCIAL EARNINGS

When I got home, I later learnt that the driver of the car was Milton Gabriel from Perdmontemps in St. David, he lived about four (4) miles away from my home and was well known by my father, who was a lawyer for many years. He was driving a Daihatsu Charmant registration number P 8746, a blue car at the time. My father was instrumental in ensuring a civil suit was filed. He departed the state thereafter, Ashley Bernadine, another lawyer, handled the matter to completion. The proceeds from the judgment was my first financial earnings.

I had to stay away from school for some time; but as examinations were fast approaching, I was forced to continue school with the cast on my hand. I asked my grandmother for money to take some photos, which

*Third from left in the front row at Wesley College Graduation in 1987*

I wanted to keep. The time soon came and I sat my exams. By virtue of my age, fifteen years at graduation, I repeated another year at form five. There was no way I could have afforded the Institute for Further Education (IFE) where advanced level subjects were pursued. So, I devised a plan that I would seek employment, do my advanced subjects privately, and thereafter apply for a scholarship to proceed to university. That journey was a difficult one; I met with many obstacles, but I persevered.

## FIRST JOB: ROAD CHECKER

On the final day of secondary school, as is customary, all the graduates would wear white shirts inscribed with the names, mottos, advice, insignias of their fellow students and friends. Thereafter, the students would 'lime' in the city of St. George's, as a means of making a statement, which indicated the end of their secondary school life and the elevation to a new stage of their academic existence. On the final day, I was walking through the city thinking about my future, job, university; my mind was racing. While walking on Halifax Street in the city, I went uphill then down to Scott Street, I was thinking to myself, what's next? My nightly prayers encircled me as I recall my grandmother's words, "Put God first, for He is the Alpha and the Omega". As I was going downhill I saw a sign to my right, about 8 feet high on which was printed; Ministry of Construction, with a telephone number inscribed. I crossed the road and walked into the alley way and headed to the first desk I saw. I had my inscribed shirt, as I requested to see the Manager. I was told that his name was Mr. Roy De Coteau a man whom I later grew to respect and admire. I was escorted to a room wherein sat a short gentleman, wearing a pleasant smile. He said, "Young man, what can I do for you?" I instantly felt at ease, as he had a fatherly disposition both in his voice and mannerism. I told him, my name was Derick Sylvester, a recent graduate from Wesley College Secondary School and that I was looking for a job so I can continue my studies. "Do you have anything available?" He responded jokingly, "Young man, you are as little as a pin, who would employ you?" Then he smiled and asked me my age. I responded, sixteen. He looked at me and said, "On Monday morning go to Public Works Department in St. David and ask for Patrick Francis. Tell him I sent you to him, and to give you a job, or he can call me". I said, "Thank you Sir". He then said to me when I was leaving, "Do you know where it is?" I said, "Yes sir, I will find it; thank you." That name Patrick Francis, stayed with me and I could not wait to meet him. Later I had the opportunity to file a civil suit for Patrick Francis when an assailant amputated his hand with a machete over a farmland dispute.

On the Monday morning in or about June 1988, I went to St. David's Public Works Department to meet Patrick Francis. He was a man about 6 feet tall, muscularly built. He looked at me and said, "You are so little." And I thought to myself, you are so big! But I smiled and said "Mr. De Coteau sent me, he said you will help me and he said to give me a job". I wanted to place the ball squarely in his court and let him know he was the man with the authority. He said, "Ok, you could start work today?" I said, "Yes!" still in shock. He said, "We need a checker and I will introduce you to the staff, Paula Celestine, Martin Isaac and there are others who aren't here, Gabriel Henry and Terry Cox."

My time with the Public Works Department was well spent. I was paid fortnightly. I attended evening classes, pursuing advanced level studies while I worked to earn money. My job took me to all the roadways and alleys in St. David, since the workers I supervised were responsible for road repairs. I had to document their presence, absence, measure work done daily, document same and prepare pay sheets.

I grew to love and respect all the workers. They had a genuine love for people, showed friendship and camaraderie that I admired. I spent eleven months with the Public Works Department, saving as much as I could. I installed electricity in my grandmother's house and it was a relief. My uncle was an electrician; he did the electrical installation and bit by bit I ensured our economic condition improved. I started writing numerous applications to different places seeking other employment, all to no avail.

## INTERNATIONAL TELEPHONE OPERATOR

I did not give up. Then one day, I wrote to Cable and Wireless. I now had a telephone contact as my place of work being 1-809-444 6242 (now 473 444 6242); I used it on the application. I received a call from the Human Resource Department of Cable and Wireless, requesting my presence for an interview. I jumped to my feet and went to the Cable and Wireless building, which was located on the Carenage in the City of St. George's. As I entered, the secretary escorted me to an office, where a gentleman sat with his secretary. The interview was short and informative, the interviewer's name was Michael Regis. He told me he was from St.

*Former Cable and Wireless Building on the Carenage, St. George's, in 1991 (later housed High Court Number 3)*

David and was happy that I was from the same parish. He said jokingly, "I have been accused of employing only St. David people but if it's only St. David people applying, they cannot blame me", while he gave a mischievous smile.

I was hired as an International Telephone Operator (ITO) with Cable and Wireless Ltd and it was in that job that I was able to amass the financial backing which assisted in purchasing a bus for my brother Andre, to conduct and later drive. This was his lifelong dream to be a bus driver, he remained that to the present day.

During my years at Cable and Wireless, I pursued advanced level studies to completion. Thereafter I pursued studies leading to a Certificate in Business Administration (CBA) via the University of the West Indies Distance Teaching Experiment (UWIDITE) with Mona Jamaica 1992 to 1994.

Thereafter, I embarked on my first year law programme via UWIDITE from the years 1994 to 1996. My work at Cable and Wireless entailed a shift system normally working from 7pm to 7am. While at work I was

*Left to right, standing: Terrence Joseph aka T.I. (deceased), Carolann Penny, Dunbar Gooding, Ermyntrude Noel aka Minnie (deceased), Claudette Campbell and me, crouching*

provided with a head set and a computerised system for processing overseas calls to every country in the world. I used the slow period at nights, to study. In the operators room there were twelve cubicles. However at nights from 10pm only one person operated the computer system until 7 am.

My supervisor at the time, Claudia Simon, was a patient and loving individual who guided me during my adolescent years. Our paths later crossed when I started attending the Calliste Roman Catholic church where she is a member.

During my years at Cable and Wireless from May 1989 to September 1997, I applied every year for a scholarship at the Department of Personnel and Management Services (DPMS) which was located on the Carenage. Despite my annual application, to study in various fields, I was rejected.

## OPERATING A BUS

While I was at Cable and Wireless, I purchased a bus registration number HA743. Inscribed at the back of it, 'Positive Life', which I periodically drove.

During the carnival celebrations my brother and I would operate the bus for the entire day from 6 am to 6 pm, just stopping to shower and change. On one occasion we made $1,500.00 after paying for gas, which was synonymous to lottery winnings in those days. I knew God was really propelling me forward, as my eyes were fixed on attending university.

As a marketing strategy in order to maximise profits for my exit to academia, I installed cassette players, with twelve inch bazookas, equalisers, twitters and amplifiers in the bus, since this attracted commuters.

## READY BUT MADE TO WAIT

It was September 1996. I completed the first year of the law programme at the University of the West Indies open campus in Grenada, but I was not then accepted to the Law Faculty at Cave Hill in Barbados as the spaces for Grenadians were limited to two students per annum. It was a

*Named 'Positive Life' inscribed at the back*

*With high school friend Ken Joseph (aka KJ), right, in 1992. This was the first car I owned*

painful twelve (12) month wait for September 1997. That year I continued saving both from my work and the operation of the bus. During my years in Cable and Wireless I got a phone installed in my grandmother's house and this pleased her a great deal. Later, I purchased a stove and refrigerator. This was very useful since my grandmother developed diabetes and the refrigerator was used to store the insulin for her daily use.

## THE CALL CAME

In or about the year 1996 I was promoted as a Statistical Officer in the Marketing Department at Cable and Wireless. I was at my desk during the month of September 1997, when I received a call from Ms. Greenidge in Barbados; a voice I was all too familiar with by my numerous calls to her during the previous year. She informed me that I was accepted to the UWI Faculty of Law, Cave Hill, Barbados to study law commencing September 1997.

When I got home and I told my grandmother she was overjoyed. However, a sense of sadness was visible in her eyes. She was getting older in years and I was the provider and cognisant that my departure would take its toll. But, by that time my mother was residing in a house constructed next door in close proximity. Despite that, I knew my absence would create a void even though she was elated for me. On Sundays I would take her to church which was her delight. Her sight was failing then, from being stricken with diabetes and glaucoma. I had purchased a Daihatsu charade to travel to work registration number P6357 which I later sold and replaced with a newer model Daihatsu Charade registration number P5821.

## OFF TO UWI LAW FACULTY

My grandmother said to me, "Go with God, for He is your strength and guide". Other family members could not understand why I was leaving since they felt I had a good paying job. But the passion to study law was insatiable, was like an unexplainable internal propulsion that grew as I got older.

*Pictured in 1997 with the second vehicle I owned*

I was very shy as a child and I was told by many that my miniature physical attributes would not make me a good lawyer as I was not argumentative, loud, tall or aggressive. A perception people had from listening to lawyers.

I eventually sold the bus and amassed sufficient funds to cover university expenses. Then my brother bought his own. I ensured he was now on a path to achieving his goal of being a bus driver, that was his desire since at school; and I was now on a mission to accomplish mine. My bags were packed. I bade farewell to my grandmother. At the time, I felt both her joy and pain because of my departure. I was so eager to leave; but I did not want to appear to be happy to leave her. It was indeed my desire to return and make a better life for my grandmother. I left in a very sombre mood as I looked back at my village of Corinth disappearing in the distance. I spoke to my good friend Lochinvar Mc Donald, who told me, I would be a great lawyer. I bade Lochinvar farewell; unfortunately, he departed this life before I graduated as an attorney. When I returned for his funeral I was tasked with the responsibility of reading his eulogy.

The LIAT ATR plane exited the Point Salines International Airport (now Maurice Bishop International Airport), in September 1997. I embarked on a journey to complete my law (LLB) degree in Barbados. The life changing experience had begun.

CHAPTER TWO

# BAPTISM BY FIRE

*"We may encounter many defeats but we must not be defeated."*
MAYA ANGELOU

## LANDING IN BARBADOS

I sat on the plane, looking over the beautiful island of Grenada, contemplating all that I had left behind; my family, life, good paying job, business and friends. For the very first time I doubted myself, wondering deeply whether I made the right choice or were my family members correct in saying I should have remained. I was jolted to reality when I thought about my childhood, my innate desire to be the voice of the voiceless. I eliminated all doubts when I remembered one of my teachers at secondary school Mr. Martineau saying, "In life the only constant is change".

In an instant, I heard the interruption of my thought by the words, "Flight attendants prepare for landing, ladies and gentlemen we are about to land at the Grantley Adams International Airport. Please ensure all seat belts are securely fastened". I heard the landing gear and the screeching of the tyres on the tarmac, the descent was quick. I knew I was in the island of Barbados, bound for the University of the West Indies; no turning back.

## PROSPECT HALL, ST JAMES

Upon clearing security and immigration, I secured the services of a taxi to carry me to my destination-Prospect Hall, St. James; which would be home for the next few years. During the journey, I passed the sign which read, 'Welcome to St. James' I knew I was in Prospect Hall. The house was a single storey with three bedrooms. I lived there with two other

Grenadian students. It was an apartment referred to as 'The Grenadian Embassy', as it was handed down from generation to generation of Grenadian students. I was merely following the path laid down for me.

I immediately acclimatised to Barbados' culture, food, accent, people and life. That, I had no problem with. I sought to make good friends, stay away from bad company, at this I was successful. I called my grandmother as soon as I landed; I assured her all was well, she was elated. To her, I was in a distant land out of reach, just being able to hear me was a blessing. I ensured she heard my voice at least twice to three times per week, no matter how busy I was. I would head to the tuck shop, use the pay phone there or buy a phone card to call. I ensured the telephone at home was always working; my contacts at Cable and Wireless ensured that even though payment was late the phone was never disconnected.

## THE LECTURE HALL

The lecture hall was located to the back of the campus on a slight elevation. The other faculties were on a lower plane, this was my first observation. The library was well stocked; I appreciated that, as law books were scarce in Grenada. The seating in the lecture hall was arranged in descending order, with the lecturer positioned at the front bottom of the stage so as to enable everyone to properly focus on him or her. I was eager to commence. The programme started with a lot of work. That I enjoyed. I had to acclimatise quickly, as it was my first time on campus; in the second academic year, having completed year one of the University of the West Indies (UWI) Law programme in Grenada. I adapted quickly, got close to the students from Grenada and the other countries whose friendship I garner to the present day.

## PURSUING LAW DEGREE (LLB)

The two years at the University of the West Indies, Cave Hill Campus, flew by quickly. I met a few great Barbadian friends who assisted me with acclimatising to the country's culture; I had an extensive tour of Barbados when I was away from school. A bicycle was gifted to me; it was registered and licensed, bearing number L2223. I was amazed since, in Grenada at the time, registration of a bicycle was unheard of. It was orange and black in colour. I used it to travel to school at nights.

*University of the West Indies, Cave Hill Campus, Barbados, May 9th 1999. Doctor's office, students' guild, cafeteria and Sherlock Hall are in the background.*

There was one occasion when the volume of work overwhelmed most of the students in final year. I started questioning my presence on campus. I was speaking to Erica Cummings, a final year law student from Trinidad and Tobago; she said, "Just think of the future benefits that your children and grandchildren would have; knowing their father, grandfather or even great grandfather was a lawyer, the effect on your family and society". She said these words during a light moment downstairs the waiting area outside the law library, we were immediately jolted to reality. The course work was completed; the final exams were ahead of us. In 1999, I successfully completed the UWI degree of Bachelor of Laws (LLB).

As I reminisce on my academic life I recall the lecturers at Cave Hill who made a positive impression on me. They were Tracy Robinson, Jeff Cumberbatch, Randolph McIntosh (deceased), Rahim Bacchus (deceased), Margaret Demerieux (deceased), Hugh Rawlins (who later became the Chief Justice of the Eastern Caribbean Supreme Court), Sampson Owusu, Dr. Albert Fiadjoe and Gilbert Kodilinye.

I returned to Grenada every semester break. I could see my grandmother's health condition deteriorating. On one such visit I started getting concerned for her wellbeing. At that moment, I questioned whether I had made the right decision to leave her. But she reminded me that I had. She was proud of me. I returned home in July of 1999, having completed the degree of Bachelor of Laws.

## OVER TO HUGH WOODING

I registered with the Hugh Wooding Law School in Trinidad and Tobago for the semester commencing September 1999. It was an automatic acceptance upon satisfactory completion of the UWI law degree programme. It was now time for another phase of the legal journey in my life, this time to the Republic of Trinidad and Tobago. The mission was to complete the Bar exam and receive the Legal Education Certificate. The duration of the course was two years, to be completed in May 2001. The Hugh Wooding Law School was perched on Gordon Street. I lived in a rented apartment together with another Grenadian student Lisa Telesford. On the said compound were other law students including; Francis Paul, Kim George, Giselle Whiteman and Debra Burnette. Francis Paul, Lisa Telesford and I were in the same programme. We had all completed the law degree at UWI, Cave Hill.

## INTERNSHIP

After my first year at Hugh Wooding Law School, it was an academic requirement that a period of ten (10) weeks internship had to be completed at a law firm. An assessment of the intern performance had to be submitted in a sealed envelope to the school. I made oral and written requests to attorney at law Anselm Clouden, he accepted without reservation. He was very willing to teach with open discussions on topics of law, I recall how excited he got when a new authority on the law was published. I saw his passion for law and was convinced I had met someone whom I could identify with.

My period of internship was an eye opener, as I learnt a lot about the procedural aspects of the law. However, during my period of internship, Mr. Clouden was due to travel out of state, one of his secretaries accosted me with verbal non-pleasantries about a legal matter relating to the office. It was an uncivil manner of speaking to me, so much so, that I ignored her and decided to put pen to paper. I wrote a detailed report addressed to Mr. Clouden. I provided it to him on his return. I felt that if I was in training to represent and defend persons, then I should first be able to defend myself in a professional and dignified manner. Upon his return to office, I was approached by him, despite the fact that I did not respond to the defaulter verbally or in any other manner, a long discussion ensued about the contents of my response, which was merely a reproduction of

*In front of Anselm Clouden's Office on Church Street, St George's*

what transpired. In any event, I did not relent on the complaint. It was resolved that we should resume work. My time soon came to return to Trinidad for my final year at law school.

## GRANNY GONE HOME

It was August 2000, by then my grandmother was totally blind, had one leg amputated. Everything just seemed to happen so fast. Then her speech became slurred because of a stroke she succumbed to. Thereafter, she transposed my name from Derick to Daddy, on other occasions Jonathan, depending on what words her brain would allow her to speak. Some days she was lucid, others she was not. In September of 2000, she was hospitalised in the female section of the General Hospital, the same building where I was when I had the vehicular accident. When I arrived, the tears were hard to contain but, I did not want her to hear any emotions in my voice, so I immediately swallowed hard and enquired as to her wellbeing. She smiled and assured me all will be well. I was amazed at how clearly distinct she was, except that she appeared lethargic. I left that day knowing that the end was near; she faced the final curtain of her life. A life well lived, a job well done.

Very early the next morning the news of my grandmother's passing came. My heart sank, my chest became heavy, and I felt an aching in my stomach. The emotional pain transformed into an unforgettable physical aching that overwhelmed my every being. In as much as her death was imminent, nothing can prepare you for the pain of the death of a loved one. It is faith in God that one has to rely on to be comforted in times like these. The day of the burial soon came; I was tasked with the responsibility of reading the eulogy, which I did with pride, pain and gusto for the life she lived. She was my knight in shining armour, the person who understood me most. She was interred at the Corinth cemetery. The final chapter in the life of the greatest human being I have ever known was closed.

The time soon came for me to return to the Hugh Wooding Law School (HWLS) in Trinidad to pursue the final year. The months flew by quickly; it was a mixture of pain and joy. The latter because my goal was being accomplished; the former because I knew when I returned home the house would be devoid of my grandmother.

The 26th day of May 2001, was my final exam at Hugh Wooding. I returned to Grenada soon thereafter; I embarked on a new phase of my life. At that time I was financially depleted, I expended all the cash I previously accumulated. I was therefore in a precarious position. Further, there was the issue regarding a place to live, my grandmother's house was no longer vacant or available; also, my mother's house was filled to capacity because at that time I had five other siblings, who were children of my stepfather. That excluded my brother and me. So, I embarked upon finding a place to live and employment. The tranquillity which I hoped for on my return home was absent.

My father was then residing in Grenada; we were now in constant contact. We developed a bond that grew with each passing moment, if not discussing law, then life, his experiences, generally giving me advice. He always spoke about his years in England while studying law. He conveyed his challenges, how he was able to overcome obstacle after obstacle. Having to juggle family life with school, then later working at a factory, because he could not find a job.

Later, I secured a rented apartment for $300.00 per month, for the thought of homelessness was a bitter pill that I was not prepared to swallow. I settled into an apartment in Beaulieu.

October 2001 approached quickly. The date for our admission ceremony to the bar was carded for the 19th October 2001 at 9:00 am. The admission was a formal ceremony wherein a senior attorney at law had to present the new applicant. A presentation was made in open court pursuant to a filed petition, with supporting affidavits outlining the academic and other achievements of the applicant. The court then had to ensure the legal and ethical requirements were satisfied, if there were no objections, the oath was taken. The new attorney was then given an opportunity to address the court. With eager anticipation, I awaited the moment. Thereafter the certificate of enrolment was issued, which granted the licence to practise law.

It was a proud moment for the Grenadian trio, Lisa Telesford who later became Registrar of the Supreme Court of Grenada; Francis Paul who entered into private practice; and myself. We were admitted to the Bar after we each took our individual oaths. Irene Stephney a citizen of Guyana was also admitted to the Grenada Bar on the same occasion. We all developed a close affinity to Irene both at university in Barbados and Hugh Wooding Law School. She was gentle as she was humble, always cheerful; we relished her presence with us. The presentation of the Petition before the court for Lisa Telesford and me was done by my father Lashley A. Salfarlie.

After I took the oath, it was time to address the court, which comprised of a dual panel; Justices Othniel Sylvester and Ian Mitchell. I gave the court the assurance that I would strive to maintain the ethics, integrity and dignity of the legal profession. "My admission to the bar should not be seen as a mere expression of the above, but a solemn undertaking to be strictly observed on my part as codified in the OECS code of ethics. I am prepared to shoulder the mantle of the undertaking and responsibility". This was documented in a newspaper article of the week ending 26th October 2001.

During my period of internship with Anselm B. Clouden, I wrote a multiplicity of articles in the weekly newspaper on legal topics. The flamboyant Clouden who had an affinity for television interviews, carried me along with him on each episode after the court hearings. It was time to send out applications as the possibility of employment was now at the top of my list, graduation was in November 2001 in Trinidad. So it was just a few months to put the machinery in place. I utilised the contact of my father who was in the state at the time. He assured me he spoke to a female attorney, who had agreed to offer me employment. I was elated and thanked him profusely.

# Three new Grenadian Lawyers

Three Grenadians were among four new lawyers called to practice with the Grenada Bar Association of Lawyers, (GBAL) last Friday.

The four young lawyers were admitted by High Court Judge Justice Othniel Sylvester during a ceremony held at the number one High Court in St. George's.

The four attornies Derek Sylvester, Francis Paul, Lisa Telesford and Irene Stephney of Guyana took their oath in the presence of acting Senior High Court Judge Justice Ian Mitchell, President of the (GBAL) Ruggles Ferguson and several other members of the legal fraternity and specially invited guest.

Speaking at the function Justice Sylvester called upon the new lawyers to be humble and warned them against arrogance, something which retired senior resident High Court Judge Justice Lyle St. Paul from time to time told young lawyers getting into the profession.

The Judge who has been sitting in his Grenada jurisdiction for more than six months urged the lawyers to develop a respectable attitude to the court.

He also used the opportunity to provide some guidance for the new-comers asking them to allow humility to be their watch words.

Sylvester who was represented in that claim by Attorney at law Mr. Lashley Sylvester thanked all those who supported

*The Grenadian trio newly admitted to the Bar*

him through different stages of his study and training.

The young attorney in his remarks gave the two Judges and his colleagues at bar table the assurance that he will forever strive to maintain the ethics, integrity and dignity of the profession and that his admission will not be seen as a mere expression but a solemn undertaking to be strictly observed on his part as stated in the OECS code of ethics.

"Respectfully my lords, I am prepared to shoulder the mantle of the above undertaking and or responsibility", said Sylvester who also indicated that he entered the profession solely to learn and practise law and that the guidance and assistance provided to him by his colleagues would be much needed and as such they should not be seen as a rival but a colleague.

"Though our system of adjudicating is adversarial, this means we will be opposed to each other on legal issues as time goes on, but let us maintain an atmosphere of professional respect and courtesy to one another in and out of court, always ensuring that justice is done", said the lawyer.

He called on his professional brothers and sisters and all those associated with the legal fraternity to join together and stand firm in the law as they go forth to practise in an atmosphere of professionalism and utmost integrity and pray that God give them all the strength, courage and wisdom to practise law in honesty, integrity dignity and good faith.

Telesford who was also represented by Mr. Lashley Sylvester acknowledge that she has entered a realm where honour, dignity and integrity reign supreme and as such she will like to publicly commit herself to uphold the code of conduct that permeates the profession.

According to Telesford she realises that her duties and responsibilities have now become alot more onerous as her first and most paramount duty is to the court and not her clients or members of the legal profession.

She expressed the need for her learned colleagues not to see her as a competitor but as a partner in a cause, a cause which is honourable and just and the type which ultimately brings justice and peace to the nation.

Like Sylvester the young female attorney lavished praises on God and all those who helped her in every step towards her success.

(Continues on pg 20)

*(Newspaper) Grenada Today, 25 October 2001. (Inset photograph) Outside High Court No. 1 on the day of admission to the Grenada Bar, 19th October 2001, with Lisa Telesford and Francis Paul.*

*Back row, left to right: Tamara Sylvester (cousin), WCPL #344 Agatha Sylvester (Aunt), CPL #688 Ryan Mc Donald (family friend). Front row, left to right: Matthew Sylvester (uncle), me and Maria Sylvester (Mother) 19th October, 2001 after my admission to the Bar.*

My first day with the female attorney was a welcoming experience. She greeted me very professionally. Her advice and candour was appreciated. She encouraged me to practice ethically; not deviate on a path that would destroy the nobility of the legal profession. I assured her I would honour the profession while looking forward to practise.

My first experience with legal arrogance was on my first day of work. I was the driver of a Mitsubishi lancer car registration number PC 847, a used car I had purchased to commute to work. I had parked the car in the parking lot downstairs, as the law office was on the first floor, the ground floor housed the law office of Derek Knight QC, whom I knew little of at the time. At lunch time as I was descending the stairs to get my car, I realised the entrance gate for the parking lot was locked with a padlock. This caused me to grow curious, but I dismissed it believing it was a means of added security. I immediately enquired at the law office downstairs where I spoke to the receptionist, I told her I was the driver of the car. She was quietly amused, as she requested I hold on, while she spoke to Derek Knight. Knight came out from a room, appeared to be in his seventies, slightly hunched, looking physically depleted and asked, "Who are you?" I told him I was a lawyer with the law office upstairs. I respectfully requested to be allowed to depart for lunch. He said to me, "I was not informed that you were coming to work anywhere, I locked

**Certificate of Enrolment**

**GRENADA**

**IN THE SUPREME COURT OF GRENADA**

**(ORIGINAL JURISDICTION)**

Claim **No.** GDAHCV2001/0671

IN THE MATTER OF THE WEST INDIES ASSOCIATED STATES SUPREME COURT (GRENADA) ACT CAP 336 OF THE LAWS OF GRENADA, 1990

AND

IN THE MATTER OF THE COUNCIL OF LEGAL EDUCATION CAP 71

AND IN THE MATTER OF AN APPLICATION BY DERICK FIELDS SYLVESTER TO BE ADMITTED TO PRACTICE AS AN ATTORNEY-AT-LAW OF THE SUPREME COURT OF GRENADA AND THE WEST INDIES ASSOCIATED STATES

**I,** ROBERT A.N. BRANCH.................................... Acting Registrar of the Supreme Court of Grenada and the West Indies Associated States

***Do hereby certify that*** DERICK FIELDS SYLVESTER was this day admitted to practise as an Attorney-at-Law of the Supreme Court in Grenada and duly enrolled.

GIVEN under my hand and seal of the Supreme Court of Grenada aforesaid this 19th day of October in the year of Our Lord Two thousand and One.

.........................................
**ROBERT A.N. BRANCH**
Acting REGISTRAR OF THE SUPREME COURT OF GRENADA. AND THE WEST INDIES ASSOCIATED STATES.

*Licence to practise law with the seal of the Supreme Court*

*With my father, Lashley Salfarlie, on the day of my admission to the Grenada Bar, 19th October 2001*

my gate, I am not opening it until 4:00 pm today! Please return at that time!" I was flabbergasted, I was taught about professional courtesy and respect for lawyers. This behaviour baffled me greatly, I was troubled. I immediately returned to my employer's law office and spoke to her. She telephoned Knight who did not relent. I departed at 4:00 pm sharp for he was punctual as he said he would. On occasions thereafter, I witnessed from the upstairs in my office numerous altercations with Derek Knight QC drivers who parked their vehicles in the lot to run errands in the financial institutions nearby and on their return, finding the gate was locked. They suffered like fate. There were occasions when the police were called. However, Knight was always belligerent and obstinate. I learnt early in the profession how not to treat my colleagues and fellow humans.

My father had given me a set of law books, *Halsbury's Laws of England* (3rd edn) together with numerous other legal practitioner's texts. I had them all shelved in my new office as I was destined to make that office my home. However, I was not cognisant that this would be short lived. The female attorney's practice was solely civil, I had the good fortune of learning many things from her. She was open to edify, she exuded a subtle legal confidence that I admired greatly. My first court matter was a magisterial civil claim, I was fully prepared. I examined every section of the Magistrates Act; Magistrates Judgments (Appeal) Act; Civil Procedure Act and every other section of the law dealing with any possible issue that may arise from the opposing attorney.

I left chambers well attired with my books in a brief, as I embarked on my first legal escapade. On entering the Magistrate's Court No. 1, I reflected on the many times I accompanied attorney Clouden to court as a law student and sat at the Bar table. He would usually request permission from the then Chief Magistrate Patricia Mark to allow me to sit at the Bar table for the purpose of note taking. But today, I was not a note taker, I was actually in the driver's seat. I was overwhelmed realising I now had a client to represent. I was anxious, nauseated, yet another part of me was eagerly awaiting the moment. The Chief Magistrate appeared from the door in the back of the room, seated at an elevated position. As was customary to start the court session, the police orderly shouted, "All stand, the St George's Magistrate's Court is now open!" This startled me, I leapt to my feet. I recalled, an attorney at law entered the room, it was Lisa Taylor. She had no idea how happy I was to see an attorney as I was alone at the Bar table. On numerous occasions, I have seen Clouden

*At the desk of my first law office*

and Chief Magistrate Mark engage in heated legal arguments. Given that I was his accomplice note taker, I was worried that some wrath may befall me, but it never did. Magistrate Mark was gentle, respectful and professional in her dealings. I admired her judicial disposition.

Lisa Taylor then in a very gentle manner said to me at the Bar table, "Welcome! I wish you well just work hard and you would be alright". I felt an instant relief. I was further relieved when she stood and introduced me to the court. The gratitude I felt for Taylor's introduction was likened unto the release of a ton from my shoulders. The civil matter was part heard, therein I started my legal journey.

Graduation ceremony was due in the Republic of Trinidad and Tobago in November, 2001, I was looking forward to it. As it was the climax after two years of demanding study, moot trials and assignments. However, one day while at work, it was a Friday, the final day of the month, the female attorney called me into her office after receiving my month's salary in the form of a cheque. I sat down, there I was thinking that I would be the recipient of words of commendations for my hard work and industry, because I was always punctual and diligent. She said to me in shortened version, that I could no longer work with her in the office, that day would be my last day with her. I instantly felt my heart stop, then it raced, I was stupefied as I sat in bewildered amazement. I felt like I was hit by a speeding truck, the motor vehicular accident I had at the age of sixteen could not have compared to that instant dismissal. The only words that could have been released from my buccal cavity, was thank you. Then I departed.

The pain that filled my heart for the next few months before I was employed again was indescribable. The mystery to me was not being on the bread line, but not knowing the reason for dismissal. I would later discover that the legal profession is not what it appeared to be on the outside. I was thrown into the legal furnace, facing baptism by fire.

One day while I was sitting in my rented apartment, I received a phone call from an attorney. He enquired whether I was working, I knew he would normally call or infrequently visit the chambers where I once worked. I was a bit startled, but I spoke to him. He further enquired why I was not working. I told him I did not know the reason; I was instantly dismissed. He then retorted that the information he had, was that another attorney and I were about to open a new law firm in the city, that was the reason for my dismissal. I was in total shock, I told him I never had such a discussion with anyone relating to such ambition. I felt at home with the female attorney, as we had open discussions, or at least, so I thought. I had no plans to leave any time soon, even if I did, not without notice. The attorney exclaimed that he was very unhappy with the state of affairs and wanted to know whether I would return to work with the female attorney. I unhesitatingly answered in the negative. Many questions remained unanswered about that incident to the present day. I felt my trials were insurmountable as I was learning more about the intricacies of the legal profession.

One day while I was thinking about the possibility of employment, I thought of the lawyers whom I knew had an amicable and approachable disposition. The first person who came to mind was Ruggles Ferguson. So I telephoned him, identified myself, we had a fruitful conversation. He invited me to his office for an interview. The interview was short, I was offered a position as an attorney at law in the firm Ciboney Chambers. This was a welcoming experience as the lawyers in the firm were respectful and hard-working. There existed a spirit of camaraderie.

It was at Ciboney Chambers that I continued my legal journey. I was exposed to the preparation and conduct of civil, contentious and non-contentious matters. Mr. Ovid C. Gill, now deceased, who is the father of Chief Magistrate H. Tamara Gill, was a skilled legal drafter in that firm. He taught me the art of being succinct. He disliked verbosity and complained whenever letters were badly written from other lawyers. He would call me into his office and say, "Look at this letter. This is how you should not write!" His message was clear. I learnt drafting;

*Edwin Heyliger QC (deceased), left, and Ovid C. Gill (deceased)*

conveyances, vesting deeds, mortgages, pleadings and other legal documents from his tutelage.

By this time my legal appetite had grown, my passion to practise filled my innermost being. There were occasions when I would get to work at six (6) in the morning, in order to meet deadlines or prepare submissions for court. It was at Ciboney chambers that my practice of law began to take shape, together with the attorneys who worked along with me. They were; Edwin Heyliger QC (deceased), Ovid Gill (deceased), Ruggles Ferguson, Nazim Burke, Jacqueline Sealy Burke, Peter David, Ferron Lowe, Francine Foster, Camille Gooding and Francis Paul.

## CHAPTER THREE

# LEARNING THE LEGAL CURVE

*"The heights of great men reached and kept were not attained by sudden flight, but they, while their companions slept, were toiling upward in the night."*
HENRY WADSWORTH LONGFELLOW

The blessing of a permanent job had rested comfortably with me, my future as a lawyer was normalised. After a few months working at Ciboney Chambers I was in a better position to make wise economic decisions. I was in a rented apartment. I spoke to my mother, who lived in St. David, about the possibility of constructing an additional room and garage.

I was trying to avoid a mortgage, because I was aware that financial responsibility came with interest. During my Certificate in Business Administration programme I had an Accounts Lecturer who always said, "Interest is the price you pay for not having money." I had a student loan to facilitate the completion of my final year at law school, secured from the Grenada Development Bank.

This would not have been possible without the assistance of two employees of the bank Thera Grant and Hazel-Ann Lewis, who never relented in their quest to ensure the loan was secured for me to complete my final year. They were invited as 'special guests' at my admission ceremony.

Later, I got an estimate for the quantity of electrical materials needed for the room and garage from my uncle, a licensed electrician. My other family members who were employed in the construction sector assisted with the material estimate. I urged them to be very accurate with their estimates since wastage had to be minimised. I utilised my business skills, every month I purchased some concrete blocks, steel, nails, wood, sand and gravel. Cement purchase was reserved for last. I subsequently purchased the electrical and plumbing items. After all the materials were on site, every weekend I would organise what is called a 'maroon', where my mother provided meals, mostly oil down and fish broth. I purchased the

*Flanked by workers of the Grenada Development Bank, Thera Grant, left, and Hazel-Ann Lewis after my admission to the Grenada Bar on 19th October 2001.*

drinks. Members of the community provided labour at no charge. On completion of the day's work we would then have a sumptuous meal with drinks.

During the year 2002, the additional bedroom was completed within approximately six to eight weeks of its start date. I then relocated from Beaulieu to my mother's house in St. David. The house was located on a hill side overlooking La Chausseur, a stone's throw away from where my grandmother's house was once located. That house was demolished after my grandmother's departure to the other life. My grandfather who was stricken with age relocated with one of his daughters.

My mother and I had a wonderful relationship. I was cared for in the same way that my grandmother cared for me. In many ways she was my grandmother's replacement, albeit at a different time in my life. She cooked, cleaned and provided meals daily. She never wanted me to buy food for lunch as it was her belief that her meals were the best and cost effective. I benefitted immensely. I therefore had sufficient time to focus solely on the practice of law, the law being a jealous mistress, a phrase I have heard so many times, I got to experience it first-hand.

My passion for the law caused me to merge with the Ciboney Chambers family, as a neatly fitted puzzle, so much so that they became my kith and kin. The normal hours of work for the administrative staff was 8:00 am to 4:00 pm, however, that rule did not apply to me or most lawyers at the firm. Despite having to drive from the eastern parish of St. David I soon became one of the early birds at work. I was given a personal key for the chambers as my hunger and thirst to get the research work done became obvious.

## A JUDGE OF GENTILITY AND WISDOM

Justice Brian Alleyne was one of the judges who was resident in Grenada at the time, he was Dominican, had a subtle gentility commensurate with his wisdom and experience. Even when unfair criticism was levelled at him he treated every lawyer with respect, senior and junior alike. This was a quality I revered in him. He was resolute and wise; even when he ruled against the state in matters wherein he was criticised he continued with his task unabated, coupled with pious Solomonic grace. He was an Extraordinary Minister of Holy Communion at the Catholic Church.

My grandmother's desire was for me to be a priest. She was instrumental in giving me my second name 'Fields'. I was given the story many times, it was confirmed true, that there was a Bishop in Grenada named, 'Bishop Fields', who died in church when a huge bell fell on him. This incident occurred around the time I was born when I was given the second name Fields. My mother gave me the first name 'Derick' which means 'gifted ruler'.

I grew accustomed to Justice Alleyne and his respect for the Bar. I looked forward to appearing before him as Counsel. He appreciated when an attorney was prepared and had their work well presented with submissions. I made it my duty to ensure I lived up to his professional expectations. There were occasions I went to court and heard Judges reprimanding lawyers at the Bar for not having submissions. Questions were put to them such as; "Where is your authority on the point? What section of the law supports your case? Pursuant to what section of the law was this application made?" It was my desire that any question to be addressed to me, should be a discourse on the interpretation of the law, not on legal ineptitude.

In March 2002, the news broke that Justice Brian Alleyne was due to depart the jurisdiction to be transferred to St. Vincent. There was a deafening silence as there was nothing we could have done to prevent this move. This sentiment was recorded in a speech delivered by Ruggles Ferguson the President of the Grenada Bar Association:

> "...We remain unanimous in our attitude to your impending departure: We do not wish to see you go. If we were to have our way, we would not allow you to leave Grenada, unless of course for the purpose of elevation to higher office.....the Grenada Bar Association's attachment is not based on any personal attachment developed over your tenure in Grenada but rather it is rooted in the tremendous respect you have earned for yourself as a selfless, fearless Judge who upheld the rule of law with a keen sense of justice without fear or favour."

Justice Alleyne later became Chief Justice (Ag.) of the Supreme Court (ECSC). The above echoed the general sentiments of the Grenada Bar Association. This was documented in more detail in the *Grenadian Voice* newspaper issue of March 30th, 2002.

Justice Alleyne's final sitting as a High Court Judge in Grenada culminated with the closure of the Assizes on 26th March 2002, with 51 cases being traversed. Justice Kenneth Benjamin was the replacement judge for Alleyne J. and served in that capacity for a number of years before he departed our shores for greener pastures. Sir Brian Alleyne SC, KCN, subsequently retired as Chief Justice of the Eastern Caribbean Supreme Court (ECSC) after having attained retirement age.

Ciboney Chambers was a magnet for a number of cases. The clients came in fast and furious. Numerous clients files were opened daily, the matters ranged from Civil, Criminal, Admiralty, Contentious, Non-contentious, Commercial, Insurance, Administration, Matrimonial and every other type of matter. The firm was engaged in general practice, Grenada has a population of one hundred and ten thousand, so specialising would not have been a wise economic decision. Ovid C. Gill was the most senior practitioner, who handled the conveyances, mortgages and also dealt with numerous court matters. He was the 'Legal Hercules' of proper drafting.

Ruggles Ferguson focused on every area of the law, he had no reservation as to time. He was a military style practitioner, on occasions

*Sir Brian Alleyne SC, KCN. Sir Brian left several gems in criminal jurisprudence. Thus, in a leading case on bail applications, Re. Teddy Mc Donald, Grenada Civil Suit # 77 of 2000, Sir Brian said:*

> *"The sections [regarding bail] must be interpreted ... as requiring a fair and proper procedure, free from arbitrariness, and which recognizes the presumption of innocence and the fundamental right to personal liberty. The interpretation must be liberal and generous and "ensure the full benefits of the constitutional provisions are enjoyed.*
>
> *"In my view this presupposes a right to be admitted to bail ..."*

# Lawyers regret departure of Justice Alleyne

After serving as a Judge in Grenada for the past five and a half years, Justice Brian Alleyne bade farewell to members of the Grenada Bar Association on Tuesday.

During a Special Sitting at the number one High Court persons in legal profession expressed what most they will remember him for.

Wishing him well in his future endeavours, Attorney-General Senator Raymond Anthony said that he found the Judge to be always approachable and willing to assist. "You have set a precedent for others to follow," Anthony said.

President of the GBA, Ruggles Ferguson said that it was a sad day for the Grenada Bar. "In a profession well known for its differences on so many issues — even in instances where the difference does not really make a difference — we remain unanimous in our attitude to your impending departure: we do not wish to see you go. If we were to have our way, we would not allow you to leave Grenada, unless of course for the purpose of elevation to higher office," he said.

Ferguson said that the GBA's position is not based on any personal attachment developed over his tenure in Grenada but rather it is rooted in the tremendous respect he has earned for himself as a selfless and fearless Judge who upheld the rule of law with a keen sense of justice and without fear or favour. "You sought always not just to mechanically apply the law, but also to ensure that equity and justice prevailed," he said.

*Justice Alleyne takes his final group photo with the Grenada Bar*

Describing his exemplary qualities as "hard work, discipline, scholarship, a high level of personal organisation, courage, commitment and an ability to grasp complex legal issues and to creatively apply the relevant principles of law," Ferguson said that Justice Alleyne, who will be transferred to St Vincent, was always cool, calm and collected. "Your humility and simplicity in the face of your undoubted authority as a Judge of the High Court, speak volumes of your strong character, self-confidence and self esteem."

Justice Alleyne is among the few who would have had an opportunity to serve in all branches of the state. A Dominican by birth, Justice Alleyne was a former member of that country's Parliament. He is also a former Attorney-General and a former Leader of the Opposition and a Senior Counsel in private practice for several years. "Indeed you have served in all branches of the state — the executive, the legislature and the judiciary. Rooted in the ways of the world, you are now using those invaluable experiences in your impartial dispensation of justice for the benefit of all," Ferguson said.

Reading a prepared text Ferguson said that among other things the Judge will be remembered for his "sterling contribution to the development of our jurisprudence and to the interpretation of several crucial aspects of the law......We shall remember the life you gave to the constitution, confirming in no uncertain terms that it is the supreme law of the land, never for one moment bending to the pressures and to the whims and fancies of the agents of an aggressive executive."

The Sitting which was attended by a wide cross section of the Bar, including newly installed Judge Kenneth Benjamin; Senior lawyers Derek Knight; Anselm Clouden and Lloyd Noel, was also addressed by lawyer Carol Bristol, QC; Acting Director of Public Prosecutions, Christopher Nelson; Dr Francis Alexis.

In his final message, he told the lawyers that after listening to their words, he finds it hard to respond. "But, I must tell you, I truly appreciate the period of time I spent in Grenada......I really enjoy working with you," he said.

*The Grenadian Voice, Saturday, 30 March 2002*

# END OF HIGH COURT SESSION

*Murder accused Stephan Sandy and Aldin Phillips on their way to the assizes*

*Three accused men under Police escort at the assizes*

March 26 was the final day of the first criminal assizes for 2002.

It ended with a record number of 51 cases being traversed to the next assizes which will start on June 4.

Among the cases pushed back were several murder cases involving a resident of Clozier, St. John's, Lincoln Mereigh, as well as one with Teron Francis of St. David's, and Stephan Sandy, and Curlan Frazer.

A number of other cases ranging from manslaughter, to stealing, were also forwarded to the June sitting.

The just ended assizes was notable for the conviction of 23 year old Kyron Mc. Farlene of Hillsborough, Carriacou who was charged in connection with the March 18, 2000 brutal slaying of Swedish couple, Renie and Eva Lindval.

It also brought an end to the stint on the island of High Court Judge, Justice Brian Alleyne of Dominica who lasted five-and-a half years on the bench.

Justice Alleyne is expected to take up duties in neighbouring St. Vincent and the Grenadines.

In his final remarks to the court, the jurist thanked the members of the Royal Grenada Police Force (RGPF) for the important role they played throughout the assizes, as well as the members of the court support staff.

Justice Alleyne also used the opportunity to remind the members of the media, especially the regular court reporters, that they are educators of the public and to recognise the limit beyond which they should not go in covering court matters.

The closing of the assizes also witnessed the traditional report from the Commissioner of Prisons on the numbers of persons held in custody at the institution.

The court was told that as of March 26 the total number of inmates at the Richmond Hill Prison stands at 313.

The report, presented by Superintendent Lincoln Telesford, indicated that there are 246 convicted male persons and 11 females at the prison.

Supt. Telesford announced that 10 male are currently awaiting trial while 30 others are held on remand.

He also said that there were 28 prisoners serving life sentences. These are 10 on Death Row, with the latest two being Archbishop Edmund Gilbert of the Baptist Faith, who was sentenced to death in connection with the murder last year of 14-year old Robbie-Ann Jeremiah.

*Grenada Today, week ending 5 April 2002*

the lawyers would enquire jokingly whether he slept. For he would leave the office late at nights and return very early. I never enquired of him, as I knew it was all said in good fun. Peter David was engaged mainly with criminal matters I admired his cross examination style. He always said, "Never ask a question, to which you do not know the answer." I was able to marinate his style of cross examination with that of Anselm Clouden and Ruggles Ferguson to come up with my own style. I loved cross examination, at short notice I would take files, and attend court whether civil or criminal. I became the legal grass hopper. I traversed almost every court in Grenada. Sometimes the work would overwhelm me but I was able to rest, recuperate and 'hit the road running'. This was the phrase I epitomised at Ciboney Chambers.

## THE LINDVALS MURDER TRIAL

In March of 2002, there was the murder trial intituled Regina v. Kyron Mc Farlene, wherein Ruggles Ferguson, Peter David and myself represented the accused in the matter of the double murder of a couple, on the sister island of Carriacou. This sent chills throughout the tri-island state. There was a call for justice from every quarter.

After the completion of the preliminary inquiry, the matter proceeded to trial. It was at the trial stage I was involved in focusing on the legal

## Mc Farlene murder trial

*Reine Lindval*

*Eva Lindval*

*Kyron Mc. Farlene*

The couple were found with their throats slit on Paradise Beach in Lauriston, Carriacou a few meters from the island's only airport.

Lindval was found with his throat cut and a number of marks on his body which led police to suspect that he was beaten by the attacker.

His wife's half naked body was discovered about 102 feet away in nearby bushes with her throat slit also.

Acting Director of Public Prosecutor (DPP), Christopher Nelson is leading the State's case against the murder accused who a few years earlier was also a suspect in another murder incident.

In opening remarks before the mixed 12-member jury, Nelson told the court that although the case for the crown is based on a great deal of circumstantial evidence it is indeed very serious in nature and that their undivided attention is of great importance.

Mc. Farlene is represented in the matter by defense counsels Peter David and Derek Sylvester from Ciboney chambers.

A total of 17 witnesses, including two Swedish nationals, one being the Lindval's son, as well as four medical Doctors, a secondary school teacher from Carriacou, a Jamaican Pathologist and a number of local Police officers are expected to give evidence in the trial which could finish sometime next week.

*Grenada Today, 15 March 2002*

submissions regarding prejudicial and probative evidence, hearsay, how the court should treat an alleged accomplice as a witness for the prosecution, admissibility of a confession statement and *voir dire* (trial within a trial) hearings. The above and more were explored in the case. My focus was solely researching and learning the law. I imbibed the legal submissions with tenacity and listened to their presentations. I was amazed how the practice of law was so different from the study of it. Despite my doing mooting at Law School, the real live trials were adrenaline infested. I relished it. I love the adrenaline rush, the research and preparation for trial.

# MC FARLENE TO HANG FOR MURDER

23 year old Kyron Mc. Farlene has been sentenced to death by hanging by high court judge, Justice Brian Alleyne after a 12-member jury returned a guilty verdict against him on a charge of murder.

The jury reached its verdict on Monday in connection with the March 11, 2000 incident in which the bodies of two Swedish tourists were found on Paradise beach in Carriacou with slit throats.

When the matter started last Tuesday, the court heard that Mc. Farlene, the prime suspect in the matter had slaughtered the Swedish couple who came to the island on vacation.

The crown called seventeen witnesses

Kyron Mc. Farlene

*Front page, Grenada Today, week ending 28 March 2002*

A total of approximately seventeen witnesses were called by the prosecution; and the defence led their case. The accused was convicted by the jury before Alleyne J and sentenced to death by hanging.

The incident occurred on the sister island of Carriacou, drew immense public attention and was reported in the papers weekly until the accused was convicted and sentenced. The death penalty was delivered in dramatic fashion; the pronouncement had a chilling effect in the court room. The last execution in Grenada was in the 1970s.

An appeal was filed. However, success on that appeal required a monumental feat; that was not to be achieved. Conviction and sentence were unaltered by the Court of Appeal.

## OFFICER NOT GUILTY OF INDECENT ASSAULT

In April 2002, a police constable who was attached to the St. David's Police Station was charged with the indictable offence of indecent assault. He was suspended from the Royal Grenada Police Force, with half month's pay pending the outcome of the trial.

I questioned the constitutional legality of depriving a man of 50% of his salary in the face of the right to the presumption of innocence. Why should a man suffer the deprivation of 50% of his salary for a mere allegation? I embarked upon my research of the Police Act, Police Subsidiary Regulations and the Public Service Commission Regulations to prepare for trial.

Later, in my professional life, it became clearer to me that the accused had sufficient safeguards in that he could make application for his full salary through the Public Service Commission, providing cogent reasons for the request. For example, family commitments, mortgage payments and other expenses or dire circumstances warranting full payment. Also, the interest of the public was better served by the accused being placed on paid leave. In addition, the accused would receive a financial benefit if convicted since he would have received 50% salary during interdiction. He did not have to repay it.

My desire then was to figure out how to ensure justice was done, preserve the police officer's years of service, which was his major concern by not having a conviction. My Criminal Law and Evidence Tutor, Dana Seetahal, from the Hugh Wooding Law School, always stated, "A thorough lawyer would always examine the legal issues applicable to

POLICE OFFICER CHARGED FOR SEX OFFENSE

Police in Grenada have arrested and charged one of their own colleagues in connection with a sexually related offense.

Thirty-four year old Police Constable Lennox Simon of Douglaston in St John's, had the charge laid against him after a female resident of St. David's made a formal complaint to police investigators, against the junior officer.

The accused was later arrested and charged with the offense of Indecent Assault to a 26-year old female.

Police sources told *GRENADA TODAY* that Simon, who had spent a number of years attached to the Royal Grenada Coast Guard, was only recently transferred to the St. David's Police Station.

When contacted last Friday by this newspaper, the Police Community Relations Department confirmed that the officer is alleged to have committed the offense on March 28.

The accused reportedly denied committing the offense to his superiors and wa said to be shocked to learn that he wa being investigated and charged.

Simon was placed on bail and suspende from all active police duties, pending th outcome of the court case.

It is not clear when the police officer wi make his first court appearance.

Police Constable Lennox Simon

*Front page, Grenada Today, week ending 19 April 2002*

*Dana Seetahal SC*

*Pictured in the front row, third from left, with Lecturer Dana Seetahal, centre*

the case at hand, then methodically research, and present it as concisely and cogently as possible". Seetahal demanded a high level of preparation for her tutorials; I was the only Grenadian in her Tutorial Group. Therefore, I had no choice but to learn the laws for my jurisdiction thoroughly. Thus, in private practice I was well poised to demonstrate what I had learnt. I researched the limitation period for the offence, the particulars of the charge, the procedure for committal and every other technical area possible.

The preliminary inquiry proceeded expeditiously and the trial was conducted in the High Court before a nine-member jury panel. Every day of the trial seemed like eternity, because the fate of the accused was in the hands of the jury. On judgment day, I was relieved (I am certain the accused was) when the court orderly said, "Ladies and gentlemen of the jury, have you reached a verdict?" The answer was, "Yes." "Are you unanimous?" "Yes!" "How say you; is the accused guilty or not guilty?" The foreman paused looked at the accused and looked at me, which caused a panic attack. He smiled and said, "Not guilty." The accused was indeed delighted as he returned to work with his accumulated salary being paid to him. He was relieved not just for the verdict but for the stigma that had encircled him throughout, including the newspaper front page publication. He was vindicated, a new chapter in his life unfolded.

There were always discussions in chambers during the monthly and quarterly meetings, which were used not only to strategise the firm's financial future but also to hold discussions touching and concerning legal matters. The group of lawyers developed an appetite for legal challenges, the rights of the citizen and this sphere included civil as well as criminal issues.

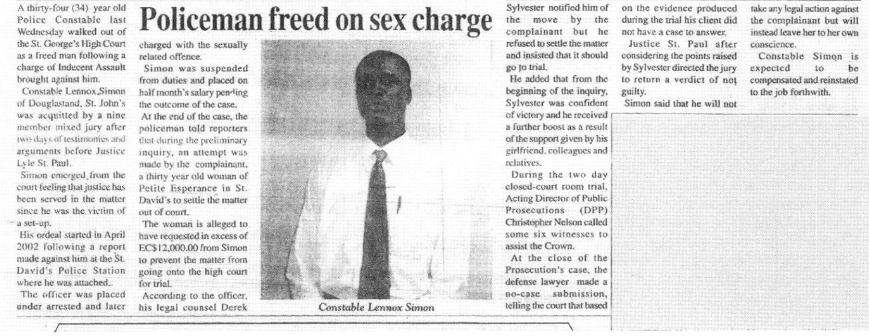

# Policeman freed on sex charge

A thirty-four (34) year old Police Constable last Wednesday walked out of the St. George's High Court as a freed man following a charge of Indecent Assault brought against him.

Constable Lennox.Simon of Douglastand, St. John's was acquitted by a nine member mixed jury after two days of testimonies and arguments before Justice Lyle St. Paul.

Simon emerged from the court feeling that justice has been served in the matter since he was the victim of a set-up.

His ordeal started in April 2002 following a report made against him at the St. David's Police Station where he was attached..

The officer was placed under arrested and later charged with the sexually related offence.

Simon was suspended from duties and placed on half month's salary pen-ling the outcome of the case.

At the end of the case, the policeman told reporters that during the preliminary inquiry, an attempt was made by the complainant, a thirty year old woman of Petite Esperance in St. David's to settle the matter out of court.

The womari is alleged to have requested in excess of EC$12,000.00 from Simon to prevent the matter from going onto the high court for trial.

According to the officer, his legal counsel Derek Sylvester notified him of the move by the complainant but he refused to settle the matter and insisted that it should go to trial.

He added that from the beginning of the inquiry, Sylvester was confident of victory and he received a further boost as a result of the support given by his girlfriend, colleagues and relatives.

During the two day closed-court room trial, Acting Director of Public Prosecutions (DPP) Christopher Nelson called some six witnesses to assist the Crown.

At the close of the Prosecution's case, the defense lawyer made a no-case submission, telling the court that based on the evidence produced during the trial his client did not have a case to answer.

Justice St. Paul after considering the points raised by Sylvester directed the jury to return a verdict of not guilty.

Simon said that he will not take any legal action against the complainant but will instead leave her to her own conscience.

Constable Simon is expected to be compensated and reinstated to the job forthwith.

Constable Lennox Simon

*Grenada Today, 27 June 2003*

## DREADLOCKS IN PRISON

The firm had represented four Rastafarians, including three citizens of St. Vincent and one Grenadian. Two of the Rastafarians grew their hair (locks) for the last twenty four and sixteen years respectively. They were at Her Majesty's Prison, after being convicted for possession of marijuana. It was the practice that upon entry into the Prison male inmates would receive a haircut.

A constitutional motion was filed in the Supreme Court after thorough research. The constitutionality of the Prison Authorities to cut the hair of Rastafarians was challenged on the basis of their right to the expression of their freedom of religion. We also argued that it was a discriminatory practice on the basis of sex, as females were not treated in like manner as per the Prisons Act. Seven grounds were filed with supporting cases from across the Commonwealth and other jurisdictions. It was gruelling including preparation, submissions and response to submissions.

The motion was filed on the 5th March 2002; the arguments were heard in June of the same year. On entering the court, the claimants received the support of the Rastafari community. They came to court in full show of force, approximately twenty of them, dressed in full religious regalia. They were all wearing scarfs, coloured red, green and yellow. They were respectful to us, I had no idea they were aware of the case or

***Dreadlock Rastas outside High Court after filing motion***

**Cutting dreadlocks in Prison could be unconstituitonal**

Rastafarians in Grenada are challenging Prison regulations that demand the cutting of convicted male prisoner's locks ( long hair) on entry to the prison. The matter, which is now being argued before Supreme Court Judge, Kenneth Benjamin, surfaced following the refusal of four convicted Rastafarian men to submit themselves to Prison Officers to have their hair and beard cut in accordance with Prison rules and regulations.

The four men: David Laidlow from St. Vincent growing his hair for the past 24 years, Keith Prentice from England growing his dreadlock for the past 16 years. Evans La Borde, seven years dread from St. Vincent and Saloman Charles from Grenada, four years dreadlocks, all contacted the Prison Commissioner through their counsel requesting a stay of the hair-cutting until they get clearance from the High Court on the constitutionality of the prison regulation.

Having being granted their stay lawyers Roggles Ferguson, Peter David, Derrick Sylvester and Frances Paul of Ciboney Chambers used almost the entire days proceeding challenging the unconstitutionality of the prison regulation. Lead Council for the Chamber, Ferguson, argued that the Prison regulations which mandates hair and beard cutting, contravene section 106 of the country's Supreme law - the Constitution.

Ferguson went further to say cutting the dreadlocks without their consent violates their right to practice there religion, a right given to them by the Constitution. Ferguson further said deadlock cutting by Prison Authority contravene the men's enjoyment of their conscience, including freedom of thought and religion and to manifest and propagate their religion and belief in worship practice and observance granted to them by section 9 (1) of the Constitution.

Prison authority's reasoning behind cutting dreadlocks is that is provide a health risk and security threat They also claim that dreadlock could be used as hiding place for dangerous weapons

In responding to such claim, Ferguson said this is highly speculative since none of his clients has been guilty of such occurrances.

The state is being represented in the matter by Jamaican Hugh Wildman, Special Prosecutor.

Judge Benjamin on Monday heard arguments from one side and Wildman is expected to reply at the next [illegible]aring date on June 13th. The Rastafarians' claim is being strong[illegible] [illegible]pported by the Naybengi tribe in Grenada, many of whom were present at Monday's hearing. It is also believed that a ruling in favour of the Ra[illegible]farians would have implication for similar matter in the ent[illegible] OECS region.

*Grenada Today, 7 June 2002*

## *Rastas files Constitutional motion against Prison Authorities*

The constitutional motion involving four rastafarian men serving sentences at the Richmond Hill Prison who filed motions preventing the prison authorities from cutting their beard and dreadlocks, got under way before High Court Judge Justice Kenneth Benjamin on Monday.

The claimants Vincentians David Laidlow and Evan La. Borde, Brition Lawrence Keith Prentice and Grenadian Solomon Charles alias "Buffie" on March 5th filed the motion through their lawyers requesting a stay on the cutting of their hair and beard pending the determination by the High Court.

The claimants are contending that their rights as guaranteed to them in sections 9 (1) & 13 (1) & 13 (2) of the constitution are being or are likely to be contravened (in relation to him for redress) in accordance with section 16 of the constitution.

When the matter begun *on Monday morning*, lead defense attorney for the claimants Ruggles Ferguson who was supported by two of his colleagues Peter David, Dereck Sylvester and from the Ciboney Chambers led off with the arguments on the basis of the seven points/grounds sighted in the motion.

The matter was heard admist the presence of more than twenty members of the rastafarian community whose presence was a show of force and support for what they said was a positive move by their rastafarian brothers.

With flags and scarves carrying their colours; red, green and yellow and their symbols of the Lion and the late Selassie I, the rastafarians sat quietly in court as they listened to Ferguson put forward his case.

However *GRENADA TODAY* on Monday afternoon managed to obtained a copy of the motion which read that the claimant Laidlow a member of the Rastafarian sect known as the Church of Haile Selassie I Theocratic Government', and pursuant to the beliefs and practices of the said church, has grown his hair or Rasta dreadlocks and beard for the past 24 years without cutting the same.

The second and third grounds spoke of the claimant on or the 26th day of April 2001 was arrested and charged for the possession and trafficking in a controlled drug (to with) Marijuana which he was found guilty of on or about the 1st day of March this year before Magistrate Ms. Patricia Mark and was fined the sum of $20,000 ECC payable in one month or in default to serve eighteen (18) months in prison.

The rastafarian brothers and sisters as the exited the Court House on Monday

He was later informed that as a convicted prisoner his hair and beard will be shaved by the prison authorities in accordance with their rules and regulations, but Laidlow's attorney immediately contacted the Commissioner of Prisons by letter requesting a stay of the beard and hair cutting exercise pending the determination by the High Court, ground four explained.

This newspaper learnt that the fifth ground of the motion deals with section 9(1) of the Constitution which speaks about the claimant's enjoyment of freedom of conscience and of religion, which includes his freedom to manifest and propagate his religion or belief in worship, teaching, practice and observance. This also includes that Claimant's freedom to practice his religion, and the freedom to grow his hair and beard in keeping with the teachings of the Church of Haile Selassie I Theocratic Government.

The sixth ground the four inmates are contending has to deal with section 104(2) of the Frison Regulations, Cap.254, Volume IX of the 1990 Revised Laws of Grenada which mandates that the hair of a female prisoner shall not be cut without her consent. Section 104 (1) however of the said Prison Regulations purports to give the prison authorities a discretionary power to cut the hair of a male prisoner, whether he consents or not, and notwithstanding his religious or other beliefs.

It is understood that Laidlow and his other three rastafarian brothers are of the view that section 104 of the said Prison Regulation therefore contravenes the spirit and letter of the Constitution in that:

(i) It makes provisions that are discriminatory both of itself and in its effect in contravention of Section 13 (2) of the Constitution.

(ii) It makes provision for the Claimant, being a male prisoner, to be treated in a discriminatory manner by the Prison Authorities wholly or mainly because of his sex, in contravention of Section 13 (2) of the Constitution.

The motion further explains in ground seven that Section 104 (1) of the Prison Regulations is unconstitutional, null and void and of no effect by virtue of Section 106 of the Constitution and that there is no basis in law for the Prison Authorities to cut, shave or in anyway interfere or remove the hair and beard of the Claimant without his consent.

It also points to the fact that the Claimant is being or likely to be deprived of his rights to manifest and practice his belief in the teachings of the Church of Haile Selassie I Theocratic Government in contravention to the spirit and letter of the Constitution, which makes the shaving and cutting or removing or interfering with the hair and beard of the Claimant by the authorities unconstitutional, null and void and of no effect.

Laidlow is seeking five (5) carefully outlined relieves in which the fundamental points raised call for a declaration that the cutting of his Rasta dreadlocks on the grounds of his conviction to serve a prison sentence will be unconstitutional in that it will be done in contravention of the his enjoyment of his freedom of conscience, thought and religion.

Also a declaration that the hair cutting exercise will be unconstitutional and in contravention of his rights not to be treated in a discriminatory manner by any person acting by virtue of any written law or in the performance of the functions of any public office or any public authority as guaranteed to him by section13 (2) of the Grenada Constitution.

A declaration that section 104 of the Prison Regulations, Cap 254 which purports to give the Prison authorities the right to cut without consent the hair of a male prisoner, but not that of a female prisoner, is unconstitutional in that it makes provisions that are discriminatory both of itself and in its effect and to an extent violates section 13(1) of the Constitution and by virtue of section106 of the said constitution *is null* and void and of no effect.

Laidlow is also asking for an injunction restraining the Prison Authorities at the prison whether by themselves, their servants or agents or otherwise from cutting, shaving or in any other way interfering with or removing his hair.

Mr. Laidlow is calling for all such orders, writs, directions as may be necessary or appropriate to secure redress for a contravention of the human rights and fundamental freedoms guaranteed to him in the constitution.

*GRENADA TODAY* understands that apart from Laidlow La. Borde has grown and never cut his hair for the past 7 yrs, Prentice for the past 16 yrs and "Buffie" for the past 4 yrs.

Government is being represented in the matter by Special Prosecutor Jamaican Hugh Wildman. The motion continues next Thursday June 13th, before Justice Benjamin.

*Grenada Today, 7 June 2002*

that they would come to court to show solidarity. They were respectful. On our way to court, they each gave their blessings to us lawyers by uttering, "Jah guidance, Jah Rastafari, Justice for Rasta, the Twelve Tribes of Israel and justice shall prevail."

The arguments went on for an extended period of time. Justice Kenneth Benjamin presided and allowed both sides to present their case. A stay of execution was granted preventing the Prison authorities from cutting the Claimants' hair until the determination of the matter. The Rastafarians breathed a sigh of relief.

This was an explorative relief for all the Claimants including the Rastafarian community. To date the injunction by Benjamin J remains in effect.

## CIVIL PROCEDURE RULES 2000 (CPR 2000) INSTITUTED

My legal experience grew with each passing day. Between and betwixt criminal trials I was drafting conveyances, drafting pleadings for civil matters, preparing for Coroner's inquiries and filing submissions. The new Civil Procedure Rules were instituted; it took some legal manoeuvring to ensure every facet of the rules was followed. The new Civil Procedure Rules 2000 was a blessing as it placed deadlines on matters and were now court driven as opposed to attorney driven.

The trials continued. It seemed as if it was a daily occurrence, for weekends were consumed with submissions and preparing matters for filing. The joy it brought me to see the law in motion, its application and applicability was amazing. Being able to pre-empt the opponent's arguments and finding supporting authorities to refute same was a continuous mission. My focus then was always on the task at hand. I would not be distracted.

## TOO YOUNG TO SWEAR

In June 2002, I was chosen to conduct the defence in the matter of Regina v. Raphael Sandy, for the indictable offence of indecent assault. I received the record of proceedings and thoroughly scrutinised the facts therein. I then directed my attention to the applicable law as my training demanded. I embarked upon an excursion to determine whether there were any legal issues which demanded a preliminary submission. This would normally be on a point of law. The matter was due to be heard before Justice Lyle St. Paul. He was always prepared to reward you and make concrete criticism, or as he would prefer to say corrections, when necessary.

I went to the office for the weekend researching every legal point, copying cases and preparing. I went thoroughly through the Criminal Code, Criminal Procedure Code, Criminal Procedure Code (Preliminary Inquiry Act), Jury Act, Evidence Act and the Magistrate's Act to ensure every procedure was followed.

The complainant was a child; on the face of the deposition she was unsworn. The oath was not taken by virtue of her inability, I assumed, to understand the nature of an oath. Further, there was no corroboration, simply put, independent supporting evidence that the crime had occurred, as was mandatory pursuant to section 203 of the Criminal Procedure Code. A light bulb went off in my head as I felt an instant relief. I prepared the submission, properly bounded and filed. I could hardly wait for court on the morning following, to hear the orderly say, "All rise, the St. George's No. 1 High Court is now open, sit please!"

Francis Paul another lawyer in chambers accompanied me at trial, the words rang out and Justice St. Paul empanelled the jury. I challenged jurors whom I felt may exhibit sympathy for children like elderly persons; I tried to secure a relatively young jury panel. I did not quite succeed but it was a balanced panel. The trial started with an address by the prosecution and the attempt to swear the complainant on oath. She could not have been sworn. That decision was made by the trial Judge. I then sought leave of the court to make a preliminary submission.

I was relieved as I went to the pith and substance of my submission. I saw the look on Justice St. Paul's face. I somehow knew he was thinking the prosecution was in trouble. I was taught to look for the legal issues and challenge same in every case. After my submission the Judge rose from the bench called the lawyers in chambers. Later, the jury was directed to return a verdict of not guilty.

The success in these trials was always filled with mixed emotions. For I was torn between my love for the law on the one side and my concern for the victims on the other side. It is amazing how one's upbringing could mould one's life. However, my grandmother always said, "The evil that men do live after them". There was a *patois* (creole) song she would sing, sometimes in English explaining, 'the effect of one's wrong, never goes away but stays with you to the grave'. However, I took solace in the fact that I stood by my clients' instructions.

RAPHAEL SANDY FREED ON SEX CHARGE

Former three time OECS Welter-weight Boxing champion, 29 year old Raphael Sandy is once again a free man, following a High Court decision in his favour on Wednesday.

Sandy who hails from the San Souci St. George's area, was the first Grenadian to win the Caribbean Boxing Champion title against Jamaica's Mark Fonté.

However, earlier this year he was slapped with a charge of Indecent Assault after it was reported to Police investigators at the Head Quarters of the Criminal Investigation Department (CID) in St. George's, that the boxer had assaulted a female minor.

The former OECS and Caribbean Boxing Champion, at the time of his arrest was accused of touching the private parts of a ten year old school girl from the River Road area, at about 7:30 a.m. one morning in January and as a result her parents instructed the lawmen to press charges.

It was reported that the complainant also told the police that the accused had held her down, in an attempt to have sexual intercourse with her eve though it was not clear how the victim, who is also a resident of River Road, managed to come into contact with the accuse.

When Sandy made his first appeared at the St. George's Magistrate Court before Magistrate Patricia Mark he was granted bail without any objection from the police.

However at the start of Sandy's High Court criminal trial on Wednesday morning, he told the court from the prisoners and accused docket, that he was innocent.

Because of the age of the victim, High Court Judge Justice Lyle St. Paul then carefully asked her a few questions to determine her capability of giving sworn testimony against the accused.

The well renowned jurist after completing his questioning concluded that the ten year old witness was

Raphael Sandy

*Front page, Grenada Today, week ending 28 June 2002*

## RAPHAEL SANDY FREED ON SEX CHARGE

•FROM FRONT PAGE

docket, that he was innocent.

Because of the age of the victim, High Court Judge Justice Lyle St. Paul then carefully asked her a few questions to determine her capability of giving sworn testimony against the accused.

The well renowned jurist after completing his questioning concluded that the ten year old witness was incapable of giving sworn testimony since the law requires that the unsworn testimony of a child must be corroborated in law.

Justice St. Paul then rose for a few minutes and met with defense lawyers Direck Sylvester and Francis Paul and Crown Counsel Nevline John in chambers to discuss the matter, where it was decided that the prosecution should stop the proceedings against the accused.

It is understood that Mr. Sylvester submitted to the Judge in chambers that the matter must be "nolle prosequi pursuant" to section 203 of the Criminal Code.

The nine member mixed jury which was already impaneled was instructed to return a verdict of not guilty against the accused.

Moreover, the presiding Judge commenting on the matter, said that the police should have investigated the matter properly prior to proceeding with it.

*Grenada Today, 28 June 2002*

## 24 year old charged for murder

A twenty-four year old mechanic of Richmond Hill, St. George, has been charged in connection with last Friday's fatal stabbing in the Richmond Hill area.

Information reaching the Fearless Weekly revealed that the Roya[l] Grenada Police Force has levied a charge of murder on Otis Baptiste as they attempted to find the truth surrounding the killing of anothe[r] Richmond Hill resident, thirty-four old Vernon Pascal.

Pascal, originally from Mt. Rich, St. Patrick, died after receiving [a] stabbed wound to the abdominal area late Friday evening.

INFORMER learnt that the incident stemmed from a heated argu ment between both individuals, which subsequently resulted in a fight

Sources said both individuals have had some form of confrontatio[n] in the past and therefore did not enjoy the best of friendship over th[e] years.

In fact, one individual said, last Friday's fight was not the first be tween the two men.

Baptiste appeared before Chief Magistrate, Patricia Mark on Thurs day as an indictable charge of murder was read out to him.

Baptiste is represented in Court by lawyers Peter David and Dere[k]

*Grenada Today, August 2002*

In August 2002, a young man named, Otis Baptiste who was twenty four years old at the time was charged with murder. The prison facility was so overcrowded it had caused both Peter David and me some consternation. We could not apply for bail in the Magistrate's Court as the law did not allow. The possibility of bail in the High Court was highly unlikely. But that changed after the decision in the case of Spence and Hughes. We were in a legal predicament and decided our only option was to expedite the preliminary inquiry. The newspaper reported the story, it settled on the front page of the Grenada Informer. In later proceedings he was represented by other counsel and convicted before a jury of his peers.

## REPRESENTING THE ALLEGED SHOOTER

In October 2002, the Criminal Investigation Department was on hyper drive to solve the murder of a female who was shot and killed in her Belmont home, during the hours of the night. The police later arrested and charged four men. I was chosen to represent the alleged shooter who was eighteen years old at the time, Kenton Phillip. Sheldon 'Dutch' Bain secured my services to ensure he was safely brought in to the police station, to this I obliged. This matter rattled the Belmont community. The nation's police officers were put on high alert, as there was an escalation in violent crimes during that era.

LOCAL NEWS

### WOMAN EXECUTED IN BELMONT.....Four South Men Detained

Police have apparently made a major breakthrough in connection with Monday night's slaying of 44-year old Omelia Roberts of Belmont, St. George's.

Informed sources told ***GRENADA TODAY*** that four persons from the Grand Anse area have already been held for questioning and a search is in progress for three others for the murder of the Vincentian-born woman who is a trafficker by profession.

According to a well-placed source, a team of police investigators are interrogating the suspects and taking statements from them with a view to laying charges against some of the detainees within the next 48-hours.

The source said that the police are looking for the suspects including the youngster who allegedly pulled the trigger and pumped the fatal bullet into the body of Roberts.

He stated that officers from the Criminal Investigation Department (CID) of the Royal Grenada Police Force (RGPF) picked up certain information on Tuesday which this in order to conceal their fingerprints. A family member told ***GRENADA TODAY*** that one of the attackers climbed through a window in the front section of the house to gain entrance into the building.

The window is about six to eight feet from the ground. The foot tracks of the person who climbed through the window was also visible on the wall leading to the window.

According to the family member, the intruder placed a gun to the head of one of Roberts' son and forced him to open the front door that was locked and protected with rat iron in order for the two other assailants to get into the house.

The family member stated that the gunman then demanded to be shown the room where the mother was sleeping.

He spoke of the gunman advancing to the room when Roberts who got up due to the commotion tried to prevent him from entering the bedroom.

He said there was a struggle before the trafficker was fatally shot by the gunman. There are reports that Roberts was gunned down in the presence of her little daughter who is around eleven years old. The bandits fled the house without getting any money

Another occupant in the house told this newspaper that she was inside another bedroom when she became aware of the confrontation.

"I was too scared to come out. I was afraid that they might do me something too", she remarked.

The young lady indicated that she heard a gun shot and then a noise from the trafficker lady when she was shot.

When *GRENADA TODAY* spoke with the husband of the deceased, he stated that his wife had been experiencing problems in recent weeks with someone she had been purchasing lambi from to take to Trinidad and Tobago.

The husband who was in Carriacou at the time of the slaying said that he did not know whether the killing was linked to a physical confrontation which his wife had last week in Port-of-Spain with another trafficker.

One of the surviving sons of the trafficker spoke of the mother complaining to him about receiving threats from a certain quarter in connection with monies owed on the lambi deal.

"The man had threatened to come into the house and kill everyone. My mother had stopped deal with him, she was doing business with another person. She had paid him most of the money owed. She only had $200.00 for him", the son said.

A police investigator confided to this newspaper that a few days ago the woman had placed a call to a senior officer at the CID in St. George's in order to see him.

He could not confirm whether the meeting took place since the officer is known to have fallen sick shortly after the report was made.

*The house where the trafficker was gunned down in Belmont*

*Grenada Today, 11 October 2002*

The men were brought to court amidst high public tension and scrutiny. It was a daunting task having to represent accused persons where the public outcry was so great in a small island state, but the professional confidence and legal training was enough to catapult me forward.

The preliminary inquiry was an emotionally challenging one. No one could tell as it was masked with professional fortitude. The children of the deceased gave evidence about the intrusion and the sound of the fatal shot. The complete scenario was just a sad one. A mother had lost her life. Four young men, two of whom were teenagers would likely spend an extended period of time in prison.

On completion of the preliminary inquiry, the matters were expedited to trial in the High Court, before a twelve member jury. My client's defence was accident. It was our case that the gun was allegedly used to scare the deceased into giving up her cash. There was an ensuing struggle and the gun went off. I ruminated on the defence of self-defence, even though I felt that it may have been a far stretch. The accused's defence was that he entered the house with a gun to rob the deceased and was forced to defend himself. Nevertheless, I placed it before the jury. Finally, I had no option but to submit there was no intention to kill. At that time in Grenada, for a conviction of murder to succeed the prosecution had to prove it was a crime of specific intent, meaning, that the accused intended to kill the deceased.

None of the above was accepted by the jury. All the accused men were convicted. The jury's deliberation was short. No amount of legal submission was able to persuade them. Each accused was convicted of murder and sentenced accordingly.

The accused, Kenton Phillip, was distraught. I had to console him on numerous prison visits. He was remorseful as he was regretful. He reiterated how one foolish mistake, being led by his peers was now costing him possibly the rest of his life behind bars, or death in prison. His parents were overwhelmed with grief. I had to play the role of counsellor, lawyer, social worker and pastor. I had to muster all my human emotions to show sympathy also remind them a life was lost and children were left devoid of their parents. The emotional part of the job was a difficult one, but my love for the law, humanity and passion for trials kept me going.

I felt compelled to file an appeal like all the other lawyers who were involved in the trial. Dr. Francis Alexis QC had represented Zoyd Clement, Anselm Clouden represented Elvon Barry and I represented

Kenton Phillip. Cajeton Hood represented Sheldon Bain who had escaped prison. He could not have been sentenced until he was later captured.

The appeals bearing numbers 5, 9 and 10 of 2002 were heard before Justices of Appeal Michael Gordon QC, Denys Barrow SC and Sir Hugh Rawlins. The multiplicity of grounds by each lawyer did not find favour with the court. The accident defence, lack of intention, and appeal against sentence were thoroughly presented before the court. The court reserved its decision. The convicted men were all hopeful, as would be most appellants in that situation. A glimmer of hope was better than none at all. My experience visiting inmates was such that a word of encouragement or advice about a possible positive outcome where appropriate was the difference between hope and despair. Most first time inmates I met were very remorseful and regretted their decision. I have come to adapt the adage, "Youth and wisdom are sometimes ill wedded companions."

Two months thereafter the written decision was delivered. However the appeal failed. The sentences were affirmed. The appellant Kenton's only hope remained with the Mercy Committee for a review of his sentence. There was really no basis in law to proceed any further with the appeal to Her Majesty in Council. I saw the effect first hand when young impressionable boys were led down a slippery slope by their peers. Life can be likened to a train ride, with stops, screeches, bumps, exits and entrances.

My experience has taught me that criminal trials are a circuitous roller coaster for all involved; the investigators, the accused, the victims, prosecutors, lawyers and the judges. No one can be discounted with the emotional turmoil each party goes through for different reasons. At the end of the day there are no winners in criminal trials. Experience has

# BAIN CHARGED WITH MURDER

Exactly one day after reputed gang leader, Sheldon "Dutch" Bain turned himself in to police officers attached to the Criminal Investigations Department (CID) in St. George's, the island's Chief Magistrate Patricia Mark remanded him to the Richmond Hill prison on a murder charge.

The 24 year old murder suspect of Green Street in St. George's was charged less than five hours after he showed up at the CID building last Wednesday as part of a deal allegedly struck with a St. George's vendor.

Bain is the fourth person to be charged in connection with the slaying of 45-year old Vincentian-born trafficker, Omelia Roberts who resides at Belmont.

When the murder suspect made his first court appearance last Thursday, he was closely guarded by law enforcement officials both to and from the court room.

The accused who has reportedly retained barrister-at-law, Derek Sylvester of Ciboney Chambers was read the charge of murder by the Magistrate who then remanded him to prison until November 4.

Three others, 17 year old Elvon Barry, 18 year old Zoid Clement and 20 year old Kenton Phillip appeared before the same magistrate two days earlier in connection with Roberts' murder.

Police are alleging that Bain played a major role in the October 8 shooting to death of Roberts in a mid-night robbery staged at her home.

GRENADA TODAY understand that "Dutch" was also a key player in the Ginger Crew gang of Coals Gap in St. David's.

Earlier this year he was accused of chopping another St. George's resident and also burnt his vehicle.

He was placed on EC$5,000 bail and became the State's main witness in the murder inquiry of Rawle "Southie" Gilkes who was found dead in an abandoned motor vehicle in the Point Salines area three years ago.

"Dutch" is believed to have passed on information to the police that the imprisoned bandit, Aldin "Aussie" Phillip was the person who shot Gilkes.

Police later brought a murder charge against Phillip who was deported from Trinidad and Tobago a few years ago after serving time for a number of offenses.

Sheldon "Dutch" Bain

*Front page, Grenada Today, week ending 24 October 2002*

taught me, when a crime is committed we are all losers. For vengeance, hate, animosity and anger do not heal the soul, only the peace of God can facilitate that. With the many criminal trials there were also numerous civil trials that were embarked upon. At Ciboney Chambers we mastered the skill of multi-tasking.

## BOND FOR FAMILY MAN

On one occasion, there was a client named Junior Cox, who was a family man with eight children ranging from two (2) to fifteen (15) years. He was charged with a co-accused who was a recidivist with twelve previous convictions. They were charged with the offence of robbery in the sum of $52,000.00. I was tasked with the responsibility to represent him.

I had the unenviable task of trying to save the accused, the sole bread winner of the family, from the prison gates. I embarked upon research into case law as it related to sentencing for robbery, both within and outside the jurisdiction. I researched Commonwealth cases. I was concerned as I pondered on the possibility that my client, albeit a first time offender, may have to be away from his family for a long time. The social devastation it would have on the family would be catastrophic.

I carefully prepared my submission on the facts of the case and the law. I also got numerous witnesses to speak to the character of the accused. A social inquiry report providing glowing statement about the accused was received. I spoke to the accused about his possible fate, since I operated on the basis of worst case scenario. I did not want to be greeted with any shock on the day of sentencing. The accused specifically requested that his family be present at the sentencing hearing. I told him that is normal and should be preferred. The impression I had was that of the accused's wife and siblings, maybe his mother, being present in court. But I was so wrong.

On the morning of the sentencing, when I arrived at court, the accused was well dressed as was expected. However his wife and seven (7) of his eight (8) children were present outside the precincts of the number one High Court. That court was an open court with four large doors. The Judge had a clear view of the outside. I went through the mitigation orally although it was submitted on paper. I presented the character witnesses and referred to the social inquiry report. At that time I knew the moment had arrived to speak about the accused family commitments. Justice Benjamin was the presiding Judge. I had appeared before him on

## Sentence handed down in 2002 Calivigy robbery

Two men charged in connection with the 2002 Calivigny robbery involving the disappearance of some $52,000 have being convicted and sentenced but the victims are outraged at judges ruling. Judge Kenneth Benjamin last week sentenced one of the two accused men, Anthony Rougier 27 to six years in prison with hard labour and place second to six years in prison with hard labour and Junior Cox 38 on a two year bond in addition to which , he was assigned to do community work around the South St. George School ground every Saturday for two years.

Both individuals pleaded guilty to the robbery with evidence made against them. According to evidence disclosed by the prosecution lead by Director of Public Prosecution Christopher Nelson the men masked themselves with cutlasses and attacked the Calivig-ny Island Project Main offices and demanded the staff to hand over all cases in their possession. Fifty-two thousand dollars sources said, monies that were already assigned as pay-ments to workers during the 2002 Christmas period was stolen. Through their lawyers both men expressed remorse for what had happen an apolo-gized to their victim. Rougier who was represented by Anselm Clouden told the court he has reached the turning point in his life after twelve previous convictions and promise to now walk on the straight and narrow path.

In the circumstances, he said six years jail with hard labour a reduction from what could have been a fifteen years jail term. Cox on the other hand represented by Derick Sylvester, convinced the Court that a prison term would seriously put into detriment the survival of his eight children ages 2 to 15. To justify his case for a non-custody sentence, Cox brought his common law wife with seven of his eight children in the premises of the court with his Lawyer pled on his behalf .

Cox was not let off the hook he was assigned to do community work on the South St. George School ground every Saturday or other places assigned to him by the Police. Cox is also placed on a bond to hold the peace for two years. Violation of which he would be brought back to Court for sentencing. From the 52,000.00 stolen only 16,780 was recovered.

*Grenada Informer, 2002*

numerous occasions. He was always concerned about family life. I came to that conclusion having listened to him in court.

When I submitted on the accused family, I notified the court they were present. I ventured to show the court his family who was outside. The wife of the accused and the seven of the eight children walked in with tearful expressions, as it was feared that their dad was about to be sent to prison. I looked at the Judge who was normally expressionless. I saw a remote glimmer of sympathy through the eyes behind his glasses. It was at that moment I felt a sigh of relief.

The court rose for a few minutes. The Judge emerged from his office with his decision on the said day. I always appeared calm under pressure but I was confident I did my best. The rest was left to the higher powers. The first accused was sentenced to seven (7) years. Immediately I felt the accused should receive a lesser sentence. Tears started rolling down the children's faces as they were out of the court but at least they heard the first sentence. The court then announced that the accused would be sentenced to two years. There was a pause. My heart sank as I immediately felt I had failed the accused. However as fate would have it, Justice Benjamin said, "Bond". Instant relief, words could not properly express what I felt then. The accused was placed on a two year bond with other attendant conditions. The newspaper reported on the hearing. It was indeed a relief.

Junior Cox, his wife and children were very appreciative. He has always sought my advice on many matters from that day forth. Later, I had the opportunity to meet his children as they grew older. The memories of that case have stayed with me. It was sad as it was emotional, but, through it all, lessons were learnt. My legal journey continued.

## NOT GUILTY OF RAPE

It was in October 2003, that I was tasked with the responsibility of representing Christopher St John, he was charged with the offence of rape. He was in an emotional state; the thought of prison was too much for him to conceive. I had to be his constant counsellor. The horror stories that emanated about prison were enough to cause him terror. Furthermore, he always protested his innocence.

The preparation for this trial was mentally exhausting, not because I was concerned about the verdict, but rather I feared the possibility of a young man being sent to prison innocently. What if the jury got it wrong? What if I fail this young man? What if the victim was telling the truth? I had to put aside the 'what ifs'. During the trial it became apparent that the accused's story was indeed credible and supported by other witnesses. This was a mild consolation as the destiny of the accused was with the nine (9) member jury panel.

# RAPE ACCUSED FROM ST. PATRICK

# FREED

**A St. Patrick's man, accused of raping an eighteen-year old woman, of the same address, in January this year has been set free.**

**The young man, Christopher St. John, of Mt. Rodney, St. Patrick, was arrested by officers of the Sauteurs Police Station in Janaury, 2003**

The incident took place on a beach in the St. Patrick area It was reported to the Police by a relative of the victim and St. John was subsequently arrested.

During a High Court trial which lasted three days, defense counsel, Derick Sylvester argued that the accused was innocent of the charges laid out against him and told the court that the matter before them was the result of a long lasting relationship that failed to secure the blessings of family members of the victim.

Information reaching the Fearless weekly revealed that the alleged victim in the matter also admitted having an affair with the accused, which was stifled due to family pressure.

On completion of argument from both parties, jurors assessing the evidence returned a not-guilty verdict after 11/2 hours in the jury room.

The decision came as a surprise to some, but was welcomed by the accused man, who threw his hands into the air saying "Thank You Jesus", before bursting into tears.

In an unrelated matter, Grand Anse residents, Rondella Stewart and Thaddeus Charles, both charged in connection with rape and indecent assault, had their matters completed at the No.1 Supreme Court last week.

Stewart pleaded not guilty to rape, while Charles pleaded guilty t o indecent assault. The evidence surrounding the charges was of some complexity, therefore, Judge Benjamin had Charles, one of the two, sentenced to 9 months in prison.

The victim in this matter admitted to promising to have sex with Stewart, but said Charles forced her into having oral sex with him. Derick Sylvester, defense counsel, represented both men.

*Front page, Grenada Informer, week ending 31 October 2003*

The pronouncement of the verdict soon came. The Prosecutor worked very hard and I am aware that we both gave the trial our all. We left no stone unturned, both by way of submissions and exposing the facts. The jury took ninety (90) minutes of the one hundred and twenty (120) allotted to them. The faces of the jurors I always tried to read, I thought I had mastered their facial expression. For a smile in the direction of the accused could mean, 'not guilty'. There were no smiles, no emotions and absolutely no reactions. I was thinking now I have to prepare a mitigation in aid of sentencing; prepare witness statements, request social inquiry report and continue counselling for the accused.

However, it was customary that the court room always got silent whenever a verdict was about to be delivered. You could actually hear a pin drop. When the question was posed, that I have heard too many times: "Mr. Foreman what is your verdict." He looked up and said unhesitatingly, "Not guilty." Then I heard the accused say with a loud shout, "Thank you Jesus" and started weeping uncontrollably. I was pleased for the verdict but had mixed emotions since the accused was sitting directly behind me. I knew not what to say to him. So, I remained calm until the judge asked him to stand; then discharged him. He left the court room with a burst of speed. These facts were reported in the weekly newspaper.

After the court was adjourned the accused was nowhere in sight. I could not believe that he did not stay to express his gratitude. I left the court feeling pleased that I had at least done my job. I quickly refocused on other trials.

The following morning I was standing outside of the office. I saw a young man walking with a '100 pound flour bag' on his head with his two hands holding either side of it. The bag was filled with items like fruits, vegetables and provision. This was an unusual sight. As a child, I would see people carrying their load on their heads to the Grenville and St. George's market. To my amazement it was the accused from the day before. He was smiling as he trod to the office with his bag full of ground provision and vegetables expressing his profound thanks. I was in utter surprise yet appreciative more so for the lengths he went to express his gratitude. For the young man commuted via a passenger bus from the north of the island to St. George's, walked from the bus terminal to my office; that sight I cannot forget. The depth of human gratitude could be limitless.

## BAIL FOR MURDER ACCUSED

A senior attorney once said to me, "Approach every case with the attitude that there is always a way out, you just have to find it'. When David Otway III was charged with the offence of murder, the legal team at Ciboney chambers kicked into high gear. The accused was a chronic diabetic, and a prolonged incarceration would more likely result in his death. Constant medical monitoring and tests were essential, including a regular supply of insulin.

The granting of bail for the offence of murder was a rarity. However, research was undertaken to assist the accused. I immediately canvassed medical reports together with the help of other attorneys including Peter David. We were destined to apply for bail. When filing the application all medical reports, legal authorities regarding bail where special and exceptional circumstances existed were placed before the court. Bail was granted. That was a great moment. It was indeed a team effort. The strength in collective representation shone throughout the legal process.

The prosecution department offered a plea of guilty to the lesser count of manslaughter. The accused accepted the plea. It was always a sigh of relief when accused persons showed a high level of regret for having committed an offence; the accused fell squarely in that category. His was continuously apologetic. As I have experienced so many times in my practice, accused persons would give anything to turn back the hands of time to make a different decision. Sadly, this is a luxury none of us has been afforded.

Due to the team effort at Ciboney Chambers with David leading the mitigation, the accused was given a non-custodial sentence with numerous conditions. It was more of a relief than it was a victory. For our primary concern was if the accused had received a term of years that could have been equivalent to a death sentence. I believe the oratory of David was succinct on the point as it was accepted by the Judge.

As I continued the practice of law, I got even more aware of the frailty of human existence. I sometimes wonder why we cannot all coexist in peaceful harmony. But then again, that would be a perfect utopia and in a world as imperfect as this, I could only keep hope alive.

During 2003, the island was shaken with the news of an alleged 'gang rape'. Eight men were detained, arrested and charged. The family members, especially the mothers, flooded the law office seeking representation. These were offences which were not only serious but

# HIGH COURT FOR GANG RAPISTS

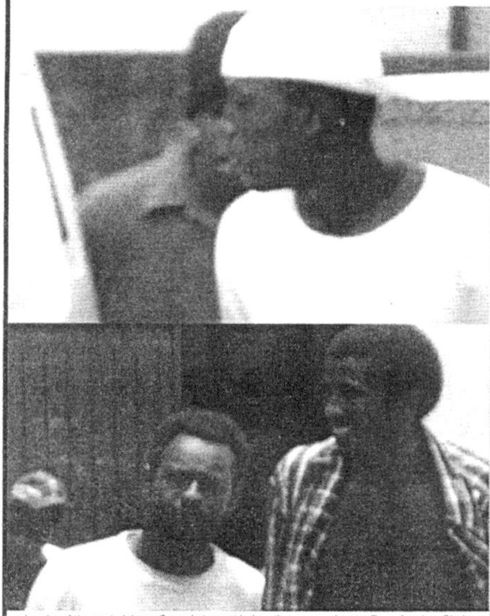

Chief Magistrate Patricia Mark on Monday committed the eight persons accused of gang raping a teenager to face a criminal trial before a judge and jury of the High Court in the October assizes.

Magistrate Mark handed down the decision after a lengthy preliminary inquiry which lasted for more tha three months and highlighted by a unsuccessful no-case submissio from a team of defense lawyers.

She informed the defendants tha she was satisfied with the evidenc provided by the Prosecution and tha

(Continues on page 3)

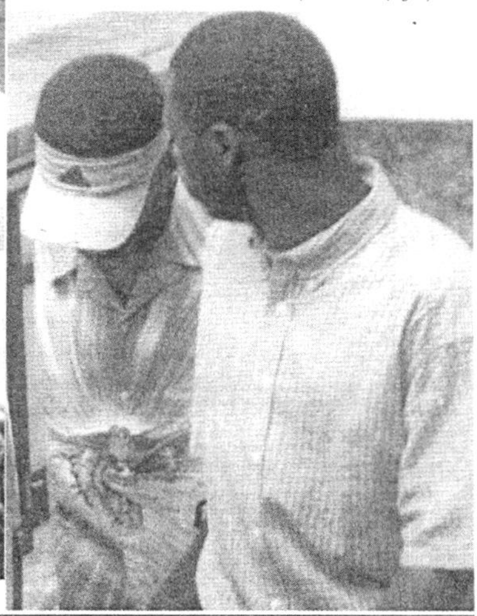

*Leader of the pack Johnny Connel along with the other accused rapist Ryan Antoine, Clarie Wallace, Brendon Briggs, Devon Charles, Edmund Phillip, Lyndon Williams and Keron Sandy*

*Front page, Grenada Today, week ending 29 August 2003*

# High Court for Gang Rapists

she was satisfied with the evidence provided by the Prosecution and that they have a case to answer in the high court.

The Magistrate also granted five of the accused persons bail in the sum of $15,000.00 EC with two sureties.

The lucky five are Ryan Antoine, Edmund Phillip, Devon Charles, Lyndon Williams, and Clarie Wallace.

The other three, Brendon Briggs, Keron Sandy and Johnny Connel who alone has thirty-three and Clarie Wallace in connection with the Morne Toute raping of a twenty-three (23) year old woman.

Wallace is being represented by former Magistrate, George Prime, while barrister-at-law, Anslem Clouden is representing Connel, Noel by Francis Williams.

Derek Sylvester of Ciboney Chambers is representing Antoine, Renaud, Williams, Sandy, Charles, Briggs and Phillip.

Meanwhile, a local women's organisation on the island is calling for stiffer penalties to be taken against persons on rape charges in light of a recent High Court decision where a River Sallee, St. Patrick's man was given a light sentence of three years in jail for the raping of a 9 year old school girl.

The victim is believed to have undergone more than three medical operations since the incident.

*Grenada Today, 29 August 2003*

had devastating effects on the victims. Society had low tolerance for such. I have learnt with each passing year that every factual story had three sides, the accused, complainant and the truth. I have endeavoured on all occasions to take my clients instructions and request the truth upon signing their statement.

In this case, the accused men's story in relation to the incident was on all fours. This case resulted in tremendous public discussion and the involvement of many non-governmental organisations. The women's organisations were very vocal in condemning the alleged actions. I remained silent on the issue as I had a professional duty to perform.

The matter was later concluded at the High Court without a conviction. The young men went on with their lives with lessons well learnt. Punishment to an accused is not only when he is imprisoned, but from the moment an accused is detained, arrested, charged and bailed. The stress is immeasurable, especially for a first time offender; but also with some repeat offenders. The idea of having to abide by stringent bail conditions, coming to court periodically, is a means of taking away one's life and placing it within the justice system. It is fitting to be reminded that the justice system was meant to protect both accused and complainant so as to ensure justice is not only done but seen to be done.

## MURDER IN CARRIACOU

In December 2003, I had the opportunity of appearing in the criminal matter of Regina V. Peter Duncan with Karl Hudson Phillips QC (now deceased). His cross examination skills, artful execution of the task at

**DUNCAN IS GUILTY OF MURDER**

The fate of 33 year old murder convict Peter Duncan of the sister isle of Carriacou will be determined by High Court Judge, Kenneth Benjamin and a 12-member mixed jury when the court convenes next month.

Duncan is expected to be sentenced for the death of 21 year old school teacher, Christopher Charles of Belair of Carriacou after he was found guilty of murder last Thursday at the number one High Court in St. George's.

Director of Public Prosecutions (DPP ),Christopher Nelson, told the Court during the 4-day trial that on February 13, 2002 the deceased was fatally stabbed in the chest by Duncan.

Charles received four stab wounds, from the accused while he was inside a shop. He died as a result of a stab to the chest which punctured his heart.

The Prosecution called seven witnesses including two medical doctors, Abubaka Mohammed and Professor Lazor Vigoa to give supporting evidence in the case.

Duncan who resided at Brooklyn, New York prior to the incident gave sworn testimony to the Court, claiming that the deceased had something in his hand and was swinging it at him.

Duncan was represented by a four-member defense team led by Queen's Counsel Carl Hudson Phillips, and included Rohan Phillip of Henry Hudson Phillip & Co, as well as Derek Sylvester and Peter David of Ciboney Chambers.

Most of the defense arguments were led by Hudson-Phillips who was successful in getting one of Duncan's statements thrown out.

It was the defense theory that the accused was provoked, acted in self defense and that the deceased met his death by an accident which could have been caused by something he (the deceased) had in his possession while engaged in the scuffle with the suspect).

The Jury took approximately two (2) hours before they returned the guilty verdict against Duncan.

Meanwhile, the mother of the deceased, Beverly Charles, in a telephone interview on Friday said that she was extremely happy about the outcome and felt that God had answered her prayers in ensuring that justice was done.

"I am not worthy to thank God for his mercy. I prayed to God every night. I was very sorrowful at the time my son was killed and God knew that my son didn't deserve to die the way he did. He knew the killing of my son was wrong and I had to go to him in prayer", she said.

When asked if she will call for the death penalty for Duncan, the grieving mother said: "No".

"I will not seek the death penalty because I have forgiven him and I have asked God to forgive him but at

*(Continues on page 38)*

*Front page, Grenada Today, week ending, 23 December 2003*

## DUNCAN IS GUILTY OF MURDER

*• FROM FRONT PAGE*

to God every night. I was very sorrowful at the time my son was killed and God knew that my son didn't deserve to die the way he did. He knew the killing of my son was wrong and I had to go to him in prayer", she said.

When asked if she will call for the death penalty for Duncan, the grieving mother said: "No".

"I will not seek the death penalty because I have forgiven him and I have asked God to forgive him but at the same time he should stay in the prison and work for the Government which should be his punishment", she added.

According to Charles, the time has now come for Duncan to get on his knees and ask God to forgive him for that great sin he has committed.

"He must humble himself and change his life by walking in the way of God", she said.

The distressed mother pointed out that she was very sorry for Duncan's mother knowing that she did not send him to do what he did to her son.

She said the the mother of the accused must also accept the fact that what her son did was wrong and justice had to be served.

*Grenada Today, 23 December 2003*

## MURDER CONVICT GETS 7 YEARS

Peter Duncan - gets a light sentence

A High Court Judge in Grenada on Wednesday handed down a seven year jail sentence on murder convict Peter Duncan for the February 2002 killing of Carriacou school teacher, Christopher Charles.

Justice Kenneth Benjamin passed judgement on the accused who was found guilty of murder last December at the conclusion of the October criminal assizes.

Duncan, 33, is said to have stabbed Charles four times about his body, during an altercation inside a shop in down town Hillsborough.

The court was told by a medical doctor that the deceased had sustained a stab wound in the area of the chest which punctured his heart and as a result he succumbed to his injuries.

The court was also asked to believe that the instrument used to commit the offense was sharp and was in the possession of Duncan.

Director of Public Prosecution (DPP), Christopher Nelson during the trial called seven witnesses which included two medical doctors, Abubaka Mohammed and Professor Lazor Vigoa.

During the trial, Duncan gave sworn testimony to the court in which he claimed that the deceased had something in his hand swinging at him and that they both had a scuffle

(Continues on page 4)

*Front page, Grenada Today, week ending 6 February 2004*

hand indicated to me, it was only experience which could have taught him his craft. I relished every moment of the research, the presentation of the submissions to the court, the succinct nature of the issues, together with a calm confidence, was admirable. Years of experience shone through the colour of his gown as it had transformed from black to darkened brown.

A statement of the accused was excluded from the evidence at trial, due to the fact that the accused was labouring under an injury at the time the statement was taken. The admission by the witnesses during cross examination was so compelling that the court was duty bound to exclude the accused statement.

Despite the accused was convicted of murder at the High Court. An appeal was filed in the matter. It was argued by one of the lawyers on the original team. The appellant succeeded. The conviction was quashed. The legal lessons were put into practice during future trials.

Karl Hudson Phillips QC stated that preparation is key; this includes thorough research, understanding of the law and issues. He also stated you should know the other side's case just as yours and probably better. I came to realise very early that law is a continuous process of learning. It is a trajectory with no end, but a process of exponential growth.

## EXTRADITION LOOMING

The possibility of deportation for extraditable offences is a dark thought for any accused. The family members, and friends, normally descend into a state of frenzy and panic. In December 2003, four young men faced the possibility of extradition to the United States of America for alleged involvement in drug activity. I came to the realisation that there

*Front page, Grenada Today, week ending 31 December 2003*

## Four Caught in U.S Cocaine Sting

Four Grenadians are facing possible extradition to the United States to face illegal drug charges in the U.S capital city of Washington, D.C.

The four are Ralph Blackman of Woburn, St. George's, Andrew Mc Burnie and Ricardo Lewis of La Mode, St. George's, and Deron "Dapper" Thomas of Morne Toute, St. George's.

Informed sources told GRENADA TODAY that the U.S government has made a formal request to the Government of Grenada for the nationals to be handed over to their jurisdiction for trial.

A well-placed source said that the locals along with another person, currently in U.S custody, were indicted by a Grand Jury on April 15, 2003 for conspiracy to import and distribute several quantities of cocaine into the United States.

He indicated that the Grenadians fell victim to a sting operation conducted by the U.S Drug Enforcement Agency (DEA) in an undercover operation during the period 2000-2003.

He spoke of the DEA liking the men to the importation of several quantities of 5 kilos of cocaine on numerous occasions into the United States.

Speculation is rife that the Grenadians are accused of shipping more than 60 kilos of cocaine into the United States in recent years.

The four made their first appearance before Chief Magistrate Patricia Mark on December 23, one day after they were picked up by local law enforcement officials based on the request made by the United States.

Barristers-at-law Peter David and Derek Sylvester of the law firm of Ciboney Chambers have been retained to look after the interest of the detained Grenadians.

The magistrate remanded the four to the Richmond Hill prison until their next court hearing on January 9.

Of the four, only Blackman has run afoul of the local law. He has a number of matters pending before the Magistrate court which are regarded as "trivial".

The source said that the Office of the Director of Public Prosecution (DPP) is prepared to withdraw the proceedings in favour of the extradition request by the United States.

Washington is making the request for the extadiction of the four Grenadians under a 1998 treaty signed between Grenada and the United States to cover a

*Grenada Today, 31 December 2003*

## Four locals face drug trafficking charges in the United States of America

**FOUR Grenadian men suspected for being involved in drug trafficking to the United States have been labeled as wanted in the U.S. to answer drug charges.**

The four – Ralph Blackman, Devon Thomas, Ricardo Lewis and Andrew Mc Burnie, have already been picked up by local law enforcement officers following a request from the U.S. Drug Enforcement Agency, to have the man extradited to the United States to be tried for possible drug trafficking charge.

According to information reaching INFORMER, the decision to have the men stand trial in the U.S arose out of alleged transaction made in 2000 to an under cover Drug Enforcement Agent.

Based on information received, the man who is now likely to be the main witness in the case against the Grenadian had been in Grenada for a period of time in 2000 and was tightly linked to the men who now face the hot seat.

The four men appeared in court on Tuesday, December 27th before Chief Magistrate Patricia Mark to first undergo an extradition hearing, the only thing now standing between them and standing trial in the United States.

The Grenada Court, through a preliminary extradition, must first determine

*Front page, Grenada Informer, week ending 2 January 2004*

are some accused who learn life's lessons from a singular infraction but there are others who repeat it. My experience has shown that crime leaves a trail of destruction; the pain remains with both victim and accused, sometimes lasting a life time. Regret is no stranger to the equation.

In December 2003, the lives of four young Grenadian men were tilted in the balance. The representation afforded gave them a second chance at life. This was a life lesson they never forgot.

The case was heard before the Chief Magistrate, then a motion was filed in the High Court and finally determined by a single Judge of the Court of Appeal.

The primary objective for the practice of law should be passion for justice, fairness and equality. It is a constant; any deviation and one would lose sight of the true objective. For human beings anywhere and everywhere should have an insatiable appetite for equality and justice. For any society without laws, tyranny would reign supreme.

CHAPTER FOUR

# WHEN THE BOUGH BROKE

*"I cannot change the direction of the wind, but I can adjust my sails to always reach my destination."*
JIMMY DEAN

When offences occur between family members, it always has a lasting effect, especially in instances where one of the members succumbed to their injuries at the hands of another. I have had occasions of representing family members against each other. It plants a seed of discord between them. Far too many times families are divided, dismantled and sometimes the emotional wounds never heal; the scars last a lifetime.

## MURDER IN LA DIGUE

In March 2005, in the village of La Digue in the eastern parish of Saint Andrew a twenty seven (27) year old female was charged with the offence of murder, by causing the death of her uncle who was fifty five (55) years old. It was a day of mourning for the family members. The accused had her fair share of grief. Despite the circumstances that would have led to the incident, the taking of another's life has a lasting effect on the perpetrator.

I went to visit the accused, at the Grenville Police Station. It brought out the usual emotional battle of having to face an accused whose life was about to take an immediate decline, with the deprivation of liberty. After speaking to the accused, seeing her youthful look coupled with her pained expression was disconcerting. But I remained the professional that I was trained to be. I started taking instructions nonetheless. Upon completion, I came to the conclusion that bad things do happen to good people. The circumstances which led to the incident indicated that the accused was indeed a victim in this instance.

I had a brief discussion with the investigating officers. On leaving I was convinced that the accused would be charged. The options were murder, manslaughter or manslaughter by negligence. Within forty eight (48) hours, I was in receipt of a phone call by one of the family members, who stated that that the accused was charged. It was confirmed when I received the charge sheet that she was charged for the offence of murder.

It was a Monday morning. I drove to the Grenville Magistrate's Court and made an appearance before Magistrate Oforiwa Augustine. The court had no jurisdiction to grant bail. The accused was remanded to Her Majesty's Prisons. The pain for the family was as raw as a fresh wound.

The thought of the accused remaining behind the walls of the prison was difficult for the family, given they were cognisant of the circumstances which led to the incident. They transferred their burden to my shoulders. I was tasked with the responsibility to apply for bail in the Supreme Court. I embarked upon the preparation of the legal documents, preparing numerous character statements and other evidence in support of the application for bail. The court had to be satisfied that the accused would not abscond, interfere with witnesses, that she would show up for her trial and numerous other conditions had to be satisfied. I had to ensure that whatever evidence I placed before the court was not capable of rebuttal by the prosecution. The accused had no prior convictions, which was a relief. A measure of leniency would normally be given to that category of accused. The female prison at the time housed between ten (10) to twenty (20) inmates. It was adjacent to the male

## ST. ANDREW'S CONNECTION

# Murder in La Digue

A twenty-seven year old female from the village of La Digue in St. Andrew has been arrested and charged in connection with the death last Saturday morning of a fifty-four year old man, believed to be her uncle, from the same village.

According to reports reaching the *Fearless Weekly*, the victim, Ledon Lessey, was pronounced dead on arrival at the Mirabeau Hospital on Saturday after sustaining a number of stab wounds to the chest.

Sources told **INFORMER** that Lessey was involved in a physical fight with his twenty-seven year old niece, Donna Lessey, when he sustained the injuries.

It is not clear, sources said, what triggered the fight. However, we learnt that upon entry into the house by one of the occupants, Ledon was seen sitting on his niece administering physical blows.

Moments after, we were told that Ledon collapsed and had to be rushed off to hospital, but expired before reaching there.

After being taken in by Police for questioning, Donna was subsequently charged in connection with the killing and made her first court appearance Monday at the Grenville Magistrate's Court.

Still in its infancy stage, the matter was adjourned until March 29th. Donna will be represented by Defence Counsel, Derek Sylvester.

Meanwhile, she is being remanded to the Richmond Hill Prison until such time.

Having consulted several persons in the La Digue area, many of them expressed shock, but were not surprised over what had transpired.

One individual disclosed to the INFORMER that the young mother of two must have had enough from the source of years of abuse. As a matter of fact, INFORMER learnt that several complaints had been made to the Grenville Police Station by the young lady in respect to abuse meted out to her bover a period of time.

*Grenada Informer, 4 March 2005*

prison which was bursting at its seams, housing in excess of four hundred (400) male inmates.

Bail was granted to the accused by the Supreme Court. It was a day of great jubilation, filled with sunshine for the family. I treated these moments as an epoch in my legal growth.

The Director of Public Prosecutions (DPP) was fair as he was fearless. He conducted his task not on the basis of wins or losses but what the justice of the case demanded. The accused benefitted from the above when the DPP filed and served a *nolle prosequi* or a discontinuation of the criminal matter. This was a relief for the accused, family and friends. It was indeed a great day for justice since substantiating the charge would have been difficult.

Criminal matters involving family members is a bitter pill to swallow. It destroys the very moral fabric of our society. The family is the bedrock upon which our society rests, to destroy its foundation is equivalent to societal suicide.

There were instances in my practice when I questioned the veracity of my clients' instructions. There were occasions when I had to be persistent in order to get from them truthful instructions.

In one instance, an adult complainant, on a charge of incest, did not wish to continue with the proceedings. The accused was charged and remanded to prison. The matter was discontinued before provision of the witness statements. The accused was overjoyed. The sense of relief the accused felt resonated in his physical appearance. It was a state of instant relief.

## Incest accused walks free

A Tivoli St. Andrew's man accused of committing incest with his daughter a few years ago, walked out of the Grenville Magistrate's Court last Thursday, a free man.

The accused freedom came not because he did not commit the crime, one officer said, but because his daughter, the victim, declined to offer any evidence in the matter.

At the time of his freedom the accused was on remand at the Richmond Hill prison, awaiting the preliminary inquiries into his trial to begin. The daughter of the accused who told the court that she was twenty years old, said that she did report the matter to the police after the incident occurred.

However, she told the court that she did not want to continue with the matter. The accused was represented by Attorney at law, Dereck Sylvester.

*Grenada Informer, 25 November 2005*

## HIGH SEAS CHASE

When matters of a criminal nature occur on the high seas it is always a prosecutorial task to ensure the incident occurred within the territorial jurisdictional of the state. The process of charging alleged perpetrators on the high seas must be thoroughly researched. The statements from the alleged witnesses must coincide. In criminal trials the fact finding tribunal must feel sure of the guilt or innocence of the accused in order for there to be a fair and impartial trial.

In or about April 2004, eight (8) South American nationals were detained by the Royal Grenada Police Force on the high seas. The intercepting of the vessel led to their arrest. The investigation was swift. Three of the men received bullet wounds. There was a forty eight hour period in which to detain and charge the suspects, in accordance with the laws of Grenada. The men were all Spanish speaking except one. The police secured an interpreter. I proceeded to the South Saint George Police Station (SSGPS) to consult with them.

I was a frequent visitor to the police station for the purpose of executing my legal duties. When I entered, the police knew why I was there. I was rarely delayed or obstructed from consulting with my clients. I hastily went to consult with them. They were all bundled together in a room. They appeared frightened out of their wits. It was their first time to Grenada, an English speaking country. They did not know what to expect. I explained our law to them as detailed as I could have. After a myriad of questions I departed the police station to return the following day.

After leaving the police station that night, I spent time researching the law on jurisdiction, the territorial sea, maritime boundaries, offences committed on the high seas, with cases from every jurisdiction on the point. The Halsbury's Laws of England and numerous other texts were my pillow that night. At the dawn of day, I returned to the police station. The police investigators were hard workers, very diligent. I knew I had to be prepared to face serious legal arguments if the matter proceeded to court. The exact location of the commission of the alleged offence was important. However, if it was a charge of conspiracy or an inchoate (incomplete) offence, then the accused statement would be of major relevance to the charge, so as to properly substantiate it.

There were no charges laid as yet. I awaited the impending forty eight (48) hours, while at the same time being plagued with many calls

POLICE SHOOT THREE VENEZUELANS

FULL STORY ON PAGE 3

Eight of the Venezuelans who were taken into custody by the police

Media consultant Troy Garvey (r) and ASP Griffith (l) addressing members of the local media

One of the injured Venezuelans at the hospital

The police took away these five drums with gasoline from the pirogue used by the arrested men

*Front page, Grenada Today, week ending 23 April 2004*

from the family members of the eight (8) men. The forty eight hours elapsed. An application for *habeas corpus* was in the process of being filed for their release. However, I was informed by the investigators that the men would be released and preparations were being made for their departure. I was asked by the accused to accompany them to the coast guard base as they were uneasy about being escorted by the police to their boat. I insisted that our police force was laden with honourable men who upheld law and order. They would do nothing to harm them. Yet, they begged and pleaded for my presence. After discussion with the coast guard officers it was agreed I would join the coast guard team who sailed alongside their boat. They were escorted out of the territorial waters. They were elated by my presence. They were all smiles the night of their departure. Despite their injuries they boarded their small craft, except the one who was seriously injured, he had to remain. He departed at a subsequent date.

One of the memories that stood out in my mind was the bravery of the men, approximately eight of them entered the small craft, with its bow pointing extreme north and the back of the boat was extremely close to the sea level. It amazed me that these men would be travelling to Venezuela in a boat that size. To embark upon a journey in a vessel that size, at such a distance is to my mind humanly incomprehensible.

I recalled being on the Coast Guard vessel travelling alongside the men in their craft. They appeared so comfortable. They were all settled in their respective corners on the boat; the captain stayed at the back by the engine. The boat was opened to the elements of the weather, when we were miles out at sea, we bid them farewell. Their last words rang out to me as I waved. They smiled and said, "Adios abogado."

## Police Shoot Three Venezuelans

*The go fast pirogue which was intercepted by the Local Coast Guard*

The Royal Grenada Police Force (RGPF) could press charges by today (Thursday) against a group of Venezuelans allegedly caught illegally within the island's territorial waters on Saturday night.

Media Consultant Troy Garvey told GRENADA TODAY on Wednesday that the men from the oil-rich South American republic could face charges within the next few hours.

However, Garvey could not give specific details of the charges and whether or not the police had acted illegally by holding the suspects for more than 48 hours without charge.

"I will have to look into it and get back to you", Garvey told this newspaper.

During the operation, three of the eleven Venezuelans who were taken into custody were shot by members of the Coast Guard.

The police are working on the theory that the suspects were involved in illegal drug trafficking.

This newspaper was told that the Venezuelans were taken into custody after their 360 HP "Go-Fast" pirogue, was intercepted in territorial waters approximately 10 miles south-west of Point Salines.by a party of officers engaged in night patrol.

Commander of the Coast Guard division, Assistant Superintendent Osmond Griffith told reporters during a press briefing on Monday, that his men had observed the vessel proceeding in a North-Easterly direction towards Grenada.

The pirogue was moving at close to 30 knots when the police allegedly attempted to stop the boat using Standard Operating Procedures (SOP's).

ASP Griffith said the Coast Guard instructed the occupants to stop the boat but this was ignored when they attempted to evade the patrol boat by accelerating the speed on the pirogue.

He pointed out that the Coast Guard gave chase and the suspects were seen dumping a number of packages into the water. The police say they suspect the packages to contain illegal drugs.

The senior police officer also reported that the Venezuelans attempted to ram and sink the Coast Guard.

Commander Griffith said that the officers on duty were forced to fire at the engines of the pirogue and in the process disabled one of them.

The senior police officer disclosed that three of the suspects were shot in the operation and later taken to the General Hospital in St. George's for medical attention.

One of the suspects was shot in the leg, another in the back and the other in the area of the shoulder.

ASP Griffith said that no illegal drugs or fishing equipment were found during the operation, except a number of containers containing approximately 300 gallons of fuel.

Coast Guard officials searched the seas where the packages were allegedly dumped but found nothing.

When asked if the police had notified the office of the Venezuelan Embassy in Grenada about the incident, ASP Griffith said that this was being handled by the Ministry of Foreign Affairs.

He declined to give further information on the grounds that counter narcotics operation procedures are very sensitive and could compromise their investigations.

Meanwhile, GRENADA TODAY understand that the arrested men have requested the services of local attorney-at-law, Derek Sylvester who is attached Ciboney Chambers law firm in St. George's to look after their interest.

When contacted, Sylvester said he was advised by police investigators that charges are still to be laid against any of his clients.

*Grenada Today, 23 April 2004*

# POLICE FAIL TO MAKE CASE....

## *As Venezuelans Are Freed and Sent Home*

One week after the Coast Guard unit of the Royal Grenada Police Force (RGPF) had detained ten Venezuelans and one Guyanese on suspicion of illegal drug trafficking in Grenadian waters, the men were released from custody without being charged.

The suspects were allowed to leave the island on Friday night to return to their homeland after police investigators decided not to press charges against them.

Legal sources told this newspaper that it was a difficult job for police to lay charges since nothing illegal was found on the Venezuelans who left on board their 28ft go-fast boat.

It is reported that the non-nationals were assisted by Coast Guard officials to repair the disabled engine and ensuring that they had everything they needed to make it back to their homeland.

The Venezuelans, in the presence of their legal representative Derek Sylvester, departed from the Prickley Bay base of the Coast Guard located at True Blue in the south of the island.

However, one of the detained men, Angel Luis Zorrilla who is believed to be in his mid-fifties was not able to join his colleagues on the return journey since he is still recovering from a bullet wound to the back.

Three Venezuelans including Zorrillia were shot by Coast Guard personnel who tried to disable the engines of the go-fast boat after it allegedly attempted to ram the local Coast Guard patrol boat during the incident on April 17 in the area of Point Salines.

Sylvester told this newspaper on

*(Continues on page 19)*

*Derek Sylvester the attorney for the Venezuelans who were detained by the Royal Grenada Police Force*

*The men after they were released by the Police*

*Front page, Grenada Today, week ending 30 April 2004*

## SLAYING IN GOUYAVE

Any lawyer who practices criminal law in a small island as Grenada is almost certain to encounter harsh criticism from the public. They are needed by the accused, sometimes viewed with contempt by the complainants and their families. The task was never an easy feat. It was therefore important to focus on the ethics of the profession.

In July 2005, the nation was rocked with the murder of a thirteen year old, allegedly killed by a twenty one year old. The radio call-in programmes exploded with callers demanding increased punishment, vengeance and expeditious trial. I had the opportunity to assist the accused at his first court appearance. The juvenile nature of persons who are accused of vicious crimes is sometimes irreconcilable with the type of offence. This was such a case. A young boy looking rather frail, appearing almost helpless was accused of committing such a horrific act. This was just mind boggling.

The trial continued. The accused was represented by other counsel.

*Front page, Grenada Today, week ending 22 July 2005*

**Brutal Murder in Gouyave**

A 21-year old farmer of Maran, St. John's, Norris Bedassie has been charged by police for the brutal murder on Friday of Neilroy "Tatie" Mendes of Central Gouyave Estate, overlooking the fishing village of Gouyave.

The badly mutilated body of 13-year old Neilroy was discovered Saturday by a member of the search party that went looking for him after he failed to show up home on the previous day.

Bedassie appeared before Chief Magistrate Patricia Mark in the St. George's Court on Wednesday and was remanded to the Richmond Hill prison until July 29.

He was represented at the brief court hearing by barrister-at-law, Derek Sylvester of Ciboney Chambers.

Neilroy's distraught mother, Velma Mendes told *GRENADA TODAY* that she is anxious to lay her hands on the murder suspect in order to get satisfaction for the death of her loved one.

"I want justice for myself. Give me five minutes with him and I will get justice. I don't want anybody to touch him, just leave him up to me", she remarked.

The mother said that she had lost a son who was a key member of the family despite his youthful age.

She stressed that she could have depended on him to do a number of tasks around the house like putting up hurricane shutters, and help in washing clothes.

She told this newspaper that her son left home around 9.00 a.m on Friday to look for feed for his rabbits located in the back of the house.

She said that he was expected to return home within half-an-hour but failed to show up.

According to Ms. Mendes, she at first thought that he had gone off with another group of youngsters from the village in search of mangoes.

She said that when the youngsters came back and Neilroy was not with them she became real concern about her son.

She spoke of the 13-year old often going with his pet dog in the bush in search of rabbit feed.

Ms. Mendes said that the dog eventually came home without Neilroy and she alerted others in the small village who quickly formed a search party and went out looking for the missing schoolboy.

She said the police were also contacted but the family did not get any help of substance from the lawmen who indicated that they needed to wait for 24-hours before they could get involved in a missing person's case.

She pointed out that just before nightfall a member of the search party saw the dog in the yard and indicated that he had seen the animal a few hours earlier patrolling a certain part of the hilly area.

He promised to go back to the area next day when it was much brighter. The youngster did and stumbled on the mutilated body of Neilroy whose body was littered with a number of chop wounds.

Ms. Mendes said that she felt that the suspect was involved in the alleged murder of her son since she was familiar with that family who owned most of the lands in Bo-Plan Estate where the body was found.

Neilroy had passed this year's Common Entrance exams as a student of the St. John's R.C School and was looking forward to going to the St. Rose Modern Secondary School in September for the new school year.

*Grenada Today, 22 July 2005*

## HURRICANE IVAN'S TRAIL OF DESTRUCTION

There are always administrative issues to be dealt with where the court is concerned. They may not be addressed as quickly as expected. There are occasions when the public intervenes and the issues are quickly resolved. Historically, getting things done can be attributed to some form of protest; either speaking up, silent march or other forms of resistance. In September 2004, the island was struck by a severe hurricane named 'Ivan'. It left a trail of destruction on the infrastructure, psyche, moral and economic well-being of the country.

This impacted the court system severely. Approximately three months after the passage of hurricane Ivan the St. David Magistrate's Court was still out of commission. This led me to issue a public clarion call to the relevant authorities to give priority to the justice system. I made a public call for the reopening of the St. David Magistrate's Court. This call was heard and acceded to. It enabled the reopening of the court, the wheels of the administration of justice continued to spin.

It brought me great pride to be able to make a public pronouncement on behalf of the people in the parish where I was nurtured. The encouragement they gave to me daily was a show of their appreciation for someone whom they had known, if not all, then most of their lives. The joy of being able to give back to my community, no matter how small, brought a sense of pride.

## *Call for reopening of St. David's court*

*Attorney-at-law Derek Sylvester*

A practicing Grenadian barrister-at-law, is calling for the immediate reopening of the St. David's Magistrate's Court.

Attorney Derek Sylvester made the call last Friday after receiving several complaints from his clients especially those residing in the parish of St. David.

He told reporters his clients who have matters pending before the court have expressed the desire to have those cases completed rather than having to wait too long for justice to be done.

Sylvester said that the Magistrate's Court which is located downstairs the St. David's Post Office suffered minimal structural damage as a result of the damages caused to the building by Hurricane Ivan on September 7.

The lawyer lamented the fact that more than three months later no attempt has been made to address the problem especially as it relates to the court which is a very important pillar in any democratic society.

Sylvester said there are several places in st. David that can be used to temporarily house the Magistrate's Court as was done in the case of the Post Office in the parish.

"The court sits twice weekly and is responsible for the hearing of juvenile matters on the third Monday of each month, the granting of liquor licenses to persons, the revision of the jurors' list, as a coroner and for all civil and criminal magisterial matters", he remarked.

According to the defense lawyer there are several criminal matters pending before the court and according to Section 101 of the Criminal Procedure Code, a person on remand for a summary offense must be brought to court within 11 days upon remand and where such offense is indictable he or she must be brought to court within 21 days.

"The mere fact that the court is closed means that all the legal procedures that the law speaks about are not being adhered to", he said.

The young practicing attorney said based on the Magistrate's Court Act, cap 177, Magistrates are creatures of statue and operate jurisdictionally and as such any civil or criminal matter that are presently before the Magistrate in that jurisdiction cannot be heard in another jurisdiction.

"With the magistrate court being closed for so long it creates serious legal obstacles where persons cannot access the administration of justice....", he said.

"....It is apparent that justice is sleeping in St. David's. Issues such as bail applications for persons on bail or on remand who may need to travel for urgent or other important reasons, although such applications can be made before the high court, there will be obstacles that will arise", he added.

Longstanding Magistrate Lloyd St. Louis is the person who was in charge of that district which is referred to as the Eastern District at the time of Ivan.

Sylvester said he believes there are hundreds of matters pending before the court which are cause for concern and it is very important for the Ministry of Legal Affairs to look into the matter.

He indicated that he plans to put forward certain motions whenever the court reopens since the rights of a number of his clients especially those on remand are allegedly being violated.

Sylvester noted that the president of the Grenada Bar Association (GBA), Ruggles Ferguson commented on the matter a few weeks ago and brought the matter to the attention of the local high court judge.

*Grenada Today, 2005*

## DEATH BY DANGEROUS DRIVING

It is a driver's nightmare to collide with a pedestrian even if he could not have foreseen or avoided the collision. Pedestrians who are inebriated can sway into oncoming traffic without warning or notice, especially in small islands like Grenada where sidewalks are rare.

In April 2005, a young man was detained by police officers in connection with the offence of causing death by dangerous driving. It was a sad day because both the deceased and the accused were known to each other. They lived in the same village of Beaton, in St. David. I was called by the family members of the accused, to visit him at the police station. I was prepared since I had dealt with similar matters before. When I arrived at the police station he was distraught, in a state of shock and grief. Not only was he in an emotionally devastated state, in that he

### Evans charged with Manslaughter

Police have arrested and charged a Beaton, St. David's man with manslaughter following a fatal incident last week.

Reports reaching GRENADA TODAY revealed that the accused, Jerrad Evans was taken into police custody in connection with the death of 39 year old Shurlan Anthony Paul of the same address.

According to reports, the deceased, and two of Evan's uncles, were involved in an altercation on the day in question, which resulted in the deceased inflicting a stabbing wound to the arm of one of the men.

This newspaper was told that following the stabbing incident, a number of persons in the area assisted in quelling the disturbances.

Later in the day, one of the men's nephews allegedly confronted the deceased and spoke to him with respect to the stabbing incident.

It is alleged that the victim when confronted may have used words which may have angered the accused and as a result the accused slapped the victim who immediately fell and knocked his head.

It is believed that the deceased who is known to be a heavy drinker later died due to internal head injuries.

Meanwhile on Wednesday afternoon, Paul was laid to rest following a funeral service held at the La Qua Brothers Crematorium in St. George's.

In other related police news, investigations are nearly complete into an incident which occurred in the Fort Jeudy area on Monday night.

According to information obtained by our news desk, a team of police officers reportedly gave chase to a 22 year old man in a stolen vehicle.

It was reported that sometime on Monday evening, Kevon Paul of Boca in St. George's had visited the Fort Jeudy where he stole a motor vehicle along with a few items belonging to the owner of the vehicle.

The officers in an attempt to capture the fleeing suspect were involved in a high speed chase and within minutes they were able to bring an end to the ordeal and capture the suspect who was taken into custody.

A police spokesman said that Paul will be charged for the incident but did not give specifics of the likely charges to be laid against him.

*Grenada Today, 8 April 2005*

was unsure of his fate as the prison gate was staring him in the face, but also the fact that his fellow villager died at his hands. I went into counselling mode. I explained the legal process to him. As difficult as it was, I tried to console the accused, who was a young man probably in his early twenties.

The grief of the witnesses was evident throughout the preliminary inquiry. The evidence was taken at the Magistrate's Court. Then, the accused was committed to stand trial at the High Court. It was my duty to determine whether there was any legal point to be raised in an effort to have the matter dismissed without trial. The only issue which arose was the mandatory legal requirement for the service of the 'notice of intended prosecution' on the accused.

However, upon the instructions I received from the accused he was served with oral notice of intended prosecution. There was no stone left unturned by the prosecution. The matter was therefore trial ready. The pain and trauma for the accused lasted until the matter was completed without his incarceration. The accused was satisfied with the outcome of the case. However, he found himself in an emotional and psychological prison. The memories of taking a life under these circumstances was devastating for him to live with.

## DEATH AT THE HANDS OF A TEENAGER

On the other hand when a teenager commits a murder, irrespective of the circumstances, it leaves a stigma of a depleted society. A human life is irreplaceable; its loss negatively impacts the whole society. Family members find it difficult to come to terms with natural deaths much less in these circumstances. Sometimes society's cry is for vengeance through the death penalty. However, none of these could heal the wound of a life being lost.

In July 2005, a nineteen year old was charged with the murder of a fellow villager. The pleas of self-defence, provocation, lack of an intention to kill and accident, were proffered. Even if successful, the allegation leaves a scarred conscience and possible criminal record if convicted. It is only after crimes are committed that accused persons are sometimes ordered to attend counselling programmes.

The reintegration of a murder accused into society after they served their time in prison, is but the start of renewed incarceration. They now have to face possible rejection from the family of the deceased, society and sympathisers. There is also the stigma associated with a conviction.

MURDER ON THE CLIFF

Dead after receiving a chop to his neck

Onlookers at the scene of the killing

*Front page, Grenada Informer, week ending 15 July 2005*

Most persons would be very reluctant if not fearful about employing a convicted murderer. This is especially so in a small close knit society. Obedience to the law is advantageous not only to the perpetrator but to the society at large.

The practice of law is coloured with bitter sweet moments and memories. It becomes very difficult if a lawyer has to represent someone in a criminal matter who is close to that lawyer. I was involved in the commencement of the Preliminary Inquiry. The Accused later pleaded guilty to the offence of manslaughter at the Supreme Court. I never wanted to represent persons who were class mates, school friends or close acquaintances. A conviction could be difficult to fathom especially when it leads to an extended prison term.

## REPRESENTING SCHOOL MATE

During 2005, I was approached by the family members of a former school mate. We attended the same secondary school. I recalled he was in yellow house; one of the very popular students at school. Upon a retrial, he was convicted for rape and sentenced to seven (7) years in prison. I was not aware then that he was charged or convicted. I was asked to conduct the appeal. However, despite my reluctance, he specifically requested my representation.

I made a formal request via the usual means to visit Her Majesty's Prison. I sought an appointment to see the appellant. I secured a copy of the record of the trial proceedings, to determine whether there were arguable grounds of appeal. Upon entering the main gate of the prison, further inside, was the entrance to the reception. I then proceeded to the usual area prepared for lawyers' consultation with their clients, and awaited the appellant.

While waiting for some time I got a bit bored. I stood at the door looking around the remand section of the prison. The consultation area was a small section in the remand yard. There were inmates present. Two prison officers emerged from the general prison carrying someone. I was of the impression that an inmate was being taken to the hospital, since the person was merely skin and bones. His eyes were sunken into his head, his bones were pronounced. He appeared malnourished. I was still awaiting the appellant. It felt like forever.

While the prison officers were about to pass the door where I was standing, I saw them turn in my direction. I was astounded, I almost asked, what's wrong? One of them said, "This is the appellant." I could not help, but exclaim, "What is wrong? Is he sick? What's the nature of the illness?" He could not even smile, but whispered softly, "Derick!" Then I regained full composure. I had to struggle during the interview to receive instructions. Trying not to appear disturbed, I maintained normal conversational tone. This was the most difficult prison visit I had up to that point. He was a young man who appeared to be on the verge of death. As far as I could have determined it appeared as if he had already resigned himself to death. He told me he was sentenced to seven (7) years in prison and he had spent approximately three years. He did not think he could make it.

I left the prison with the record of proceedings. The days ahead I knew would be challenging. Every night I read the trial transcript. I went through the record numerous times. However, I could not find any arguable grounds for appeal.

Then I decided to petition the Prison authorities for the release of the appellant on medical grounds. There were numerous administrative hurdles to have the appellant released on medical grounds. This proved futile. However, the appeal court which is an itinerant court for the OECS Islands, was due in a matter of a week or two. I visited him again at prison. He wanted me to give him the assurance that I would have him released. I assured him I would do my best. He looked no better than when I saw him last.

Before I departed, I read the trial transcript; there was a discussion about him having a criminal record. It was confirmed he had. However, there was no direction, correctly so, by the trial Judge on his good character, which included a direction on credibility and propensity. He assured me he had no criminal record. That the record referred to a different person, who carried the same name. I wanted to check the record with the criminal records office myself. The next day I embarked upon the search. He was correct. He had no prior convictions. Therefore, a good character direction was mandatory.

The jubilation I felt was like one thousand fireworks being released around me all at once. I was happy, as I delved into the preparation of the submission for the court of appeal. The preparation was expeditious, documents were prepared at alarming speed, as the eight (8) bundles were filed and a copy served on the DPP's office. I awaited the appeal hearing. The day came swiftly. The accused was brought into court. He sat all skin and bones. He appeared much more famished than when I saw him last.

The appeal was successful. A retrial was ordered. Bail was immediately granted by the Court of Appeal. However, another trial was not acceded to by the State as it would have been his third. The accused was released that day. His inability to walk did not prevent him wearing a broad smile upon his release.

# Accused rapist may WALK FREE

*A La Mode resident accuse d of raping a young woman in 2002 could soon receive freedom in totality from a seven-year jail sentence.*

Troy Simon through his lawyer Dereck Sylvester on Monday had judgement in their favour from Appeal Court judges who ordered a retrial to his already lengthy trial.

The judges on Monday upheld argument, forwarded by defence lawyer Sylvester, challenging the presiding High Court judge's failure to address the Court on Simon's good character.

In the circumstances an immediate retrial was ordered and Simon who had already spent three out of his seven year prison term, was placed on $5,000 bail with one surety.

Following the allegation of rape made against him, simon was brought to trial in 2001. Jurors after lengthy deliberations could not reach a verdict and therefore, the panel was declared a hung jury.

A retrial was had in 2003 and Simon was convicted and sentenced to seven years in prison.

Monday's decision mean that Simon would be tried for the third time on the same matter. However, there are indications that the State would not be seeking a retrial in the matter.

If this is so, Simon would be made a free citizen. Worthy of mention was the fact that Simon had to be carried into the court room rather than walking into the room.

Words were that Simon was unable to walk, having contracted a disease while in prison, reducing his weight in the last three months from 165 lbs to 65 pounds.

Simon's lawyers attempted to have him released from prison on medical grounds, but sources said, Chief Medical Officer, Carlene Radix, failed to submit any medical report, making it impossible for Health Minister, Hon. Ann Antoine to act.

INFORMER further learnt that Simon's disease is an unusual one and doctors are yet to make any specific identification.

*Front page, Grenada Informer, week ending 9 December 2005*

## POLICE INVESTIGATOR CHARGED

It is normal in our society for accused persons to be ordinary members of the public. However, when accused come from within the rank and file of the police force it has serious social consequences. For instance, it can lead to a breach in the public trust and a general lack of confidence in the ability of the police force to carry out its mandate in a fair and efficient manner. It brings the whole organisation into disrepute, can lead to irreparable damage to the psyche of the other officers.

In January 2006, a police officer who was attached to the Criminal Investigation Department (CID) was charged with six indictable offences including; house breaking, possession of fire arm and ammunition. This

# SCANDAL ROCKS RGPF

## As Detective threatens to name names

**Officers attached to the Criminal Investigation Department of the Royal Grenada Police Force made a major break through with an outstanding matter and arrested and charged Joseph Tillock of La Tante in St. David's. At the time of his arrest, Tillock was a member of the Royal Grenada Police Force attached to the C.I.D. in St. George's.**

**Tillock appeared in Court Tuesday, but was not granted bail.** • *See Page 15* •

*Front page, Grenada Informer, week ending 27 January 2006*

rocked the foundation of the CID and the RGPF, as the officer charged was an excellent investigator. He was well known to me. On numerous occasions I had the opportunity to cross examine him in relation to evidence he gave in court. However, the roles were reversed in this case, he was now the accused.

On the day of the hearing, it was a spectacle for the media; the public thronged the court. It was difficult for the officers who once worked with the accused to now detain one of their own. It was regrettable. He was remanded to prison. However, it was difficult as he would now face

## No bail for Detective Constable Joe Tillock

*CHIEF* Magistrate Patricia Mark on Tuesday denied ranting bail bond to Police Constable Joseph Tillock, now facing six indictable charges ranging from housebreaking and stealing to possession of fire arms and ammunition.

Director of Public Prosecution, Christopher Nelson relying on what he dubbed a strong case against the now suspended officer, convinced Magistrate Mark, that granting bail to Tillock at this time would only hindered the process of investigation. into a number of matters facing Tillock.

In addition to creating the risk of flight for fare of the stiff penalty facing the defendant if found guilty.

Although Nelson's claim was adequately refuted by defence lawyer Derick Sylvester, who was prepared to have his client surrounded, all relevant travel document if flight was an issue Magistrate Mark opted to remind the officer until February 13th. She however, reminded the defence team that they have the right to apply for bail before the judges.

Tillock 26, a resident of I Tante, St. David, who served at the Criminal Investigation Department faces, two charges of housebreaking and stealing, were according to prosecution, he allegedly broken into the exhibit room of the CID in August of 2005 and stole among other things a quantity of cocaine valued in the region of $135,000.00 E.C.

In addition to the cocaine, it is alleged that Tillock also took two 38 revolvers. Additionally, Tillock also faces two counts of fire arm possession and two counts of possession of ammunition.

Sources told INFORMER, two guns including a quantity of ammunition were found in a locker at the CID allegedly belonging to the officer on Thursday, January 19.

Inside sources told INFORMER that officers came down Tillock following a hint given to them by one of the officer's former lover, who felt that her life was in danger after repeated threat on her life by the officer.

Following that hint, we were told that Head of the CID ordered an intense investigation before Tillock's name came up as prime suspect.

Sources told INFORMER that apart from pointing to items missing from the CID exhibit room, the lawmen investigation also uncovered one of the guns that were missing from the Grenville Police Station in 2005.

Tillock who was at the time attached to the Grenville Police Station when that gun was missing, was then transferred to the CID Department in St. George's.

Although one might describe the move as a physiological victory for the Royal Grenada Police Force, sources told INFORMER that Tillock who has been suspended with immediate effect by Acting Commissioner of Police, Winston James, has since hinted to other officers that he is not going down alone.

Sources told the Fearless Weekly that Tillock has expressed a willingness to disclose the name of other officers involved in the items stolen at the CID exhibit room.

Acting Commissioner James in a release to the Media called for a through and decisive investigation into the matter. The 26-year-old who joined the RGPF in October of 1998 faces excess of forty years in prison on all six counts if found guilty,

*Grenada Informer, 27 January 2006*

LOCAL NEWS

**POLICEMAN ON CRIMINAL CHARGES**

*from front page*

Suspended Police Officer attached to the Criminal Investigations Department (CID), Joseph Tillock has been denied bail on charges of being in possession of illegal guns and ammunition.

Tillock who is from La Tante, St. David's was charged with two counts of Possession of Firearm, two counts of Possession of Ammunition; and Housebreaking and Stealing.

A police source said that Tillock is also being investigated in connection with the disappearance of a quantity of cocaine that the Royal Grenada Police Force (RGPF) had confiscated late last year from a passenger attempting to board a plane bound for the United Kingdom.

The Police Constable made his first court appearance Tuesday before Chief Magistrate Patricia Mark.

His legal Counsel, Derek Sylvester made an application for bail but it was opposed by Director of Public Prosecutions, Christopher Nelson and denied by the Chief Magistrate.

Tillock was remanded to the Richmond Hill Prison until February 13, when he is due to make his next court appearance.

Police insiders told this newspaper that Tillock became a suspect when the locker of a Sergeant of Police was broken into and his service revolver stolen at the Grenville Police Station.

"We heard that he was around and a decision was taken to search his place", he remarked.

According to the official, the search resulted in the recovery of the stolen gun under Tillock's bed at the CID in St. George's.

He was allegedly in the process of trying to get someone to smuggle the gun out of CID when the officer swooped down.

The search party then decided to inspect the Constable's Locker when another weapon was allegedly found there.

It is said to bear the same description and serial number as the missing gun from CID in St. George's.

An official statement issued by the police force said that at the time of his arrest, Tillock was attached to the C.I.D. in St. George's.

According to the release, the suspended police officer was first detained on

CONTINUES ON PAGE 04

CONTINUES FROM PAE 03

Thursday (January 19) and formally arrested and charged on (Saturday) January 21.

It said: "The house breaking and stealing charges are linked to the unauthorized removal of items from the Police exhibit storage room in August of 2005 and the disappearance of a service revolver from the Grenville Police Station.

"In August of 2005 a quantity of Cocaine, monies and two firearms were stolen from the exhibit storage room.

"Officers of the C.I.D. are continuing their investigations and other drug related charges could be filed against Tillock

"Tillock was enlisted in the Royal Grenada Police Force on the 5th October 1998 and his two recent postings were at the Grenville Police Station and the C.I.D. in St. George's. He is a Constable of Police.

"The Office of the Commissioner of Police has ordered the immediate suspension of Tillock pending the outcome of the legal proceedings", it added.

Acting Commissioner of Police, Winston James has instructed the Officers handling the Tillock investigation to be thorough and decisive with the matter.

"This matter has seriously compromised the integrity of the Force, and the arrest of someone within our Ranks makes it even worse", he said.

"That's why it is imperative that we handle this professionally and ensure that all involved are brought to justice", he added.

Speculation is rife that Sylvester was representing Tillock on behalf of another Attorney-at-Law, Peter David who was at the Grenada Trade Centre participating in the 2006 Budget Debate.

When contacted, David said he heard that some people were trying to contact him in the matter but he will not be able to get involved since some of the items allegedly stolen from the Police Exhibit room belong to one of his clients.

*Grenada Today, 27 January 2006*

numerous inmates whose cases he investigated and were incarcerated. I contacted the prison authorities, informing them of the state of affairs, requesting additional arrangements for security to ensure his safety. The commitment was given.

I hastily applied for bail which was granted by the High Court.

It was a constant reminder during trials, that to err was human. Sometimes one had to be in another person's position to actually understand what motivated them. The practice of law exposes one to a better understanding of human nature, sometimes sympathy is generated not only for the victims but also the accused.

In the continued pursuit of justice, members of the legal profession are placed in a position where they have to seek to protect the nobility of the profession and ultimately the community in which they serve. Sometimes, the desire to explore all the legal technicalities available for the benefit of accused persons result in condemnation by the same citizens who would one day ultimately benefit. The cause of justice is never an easy one. In an adversarial system there are so many nuances at work, one has to be forever vigilant, focused, ethical, and most of all, professional in one's dealings.

## POLICE INVESITGATOR'S TRIAL CONTINUES

The trial continued with the police officer from the Criminal Investigation Department, who was remanded at Her Majesty's Prison. Since he would have been instrumental in securing the ultimate incarceration of many of the inmates, I knew his time on remand would be a difficult one. The Magistrate refused to grant bail after strong opposition from the prosecution. The grounds for their opposition were multi-pronged. Despite the legal constitutional retort I had for every ground, it did not find favour with the Magistrate.

Justice Davidson Baptiste was a sitting Judge on the island at that time. He was intimidatingly tall, humble, professional and disciplined. He had a respectful disposition towards lawyers. He epitomised the nature of service to humankind; a statesman. I prepared the bail application for the accused. The prosecution was afforded the usual opportunity to object. Bail was granted by Baptiste J. It was during the week of my birthday in February 2006. It was a great birthday gift. The family of the accused man was extremely concerned for his well-being during his incarceration. He was granted bail in the sum of $30,000.00 with two sureties.

Policemen are normally held to a higher standard than ordinary members of the public. This is due to the fact that they are placed in

**Suspended CID cop gets bail**

JOSEPH Tillock, the twenty-six year old police officer, who received marching orders from the fold of the Royal Grenada Police Force last week, following allegations which led to his facing six charges of criminal activities, finally got bail.

The suspended CID Officer was forcefully denied bail on several grounds including the possibility of his not turning up to attend trial, given the serious nature of the charges against him.

Tillock has now been granted bail of $30,000 with two sureties by High Court Judge Davidson Baptiste.

*Front page, Grenada Informer, week ending 3 February 2006*

SHAME AND SCANDAL IN RGPF

as 3rd officer charged with offence

Charged for stealing and possession of arms and ammunition Police Officer Joel Horsford

Much-respected Commissioner-of-Police Winston James means to weed out the wrong doers within the Royal Grenada Police Force regardless of who they may be.

Police Officer Joseph Tillock is charged for theft of money, arms and drugs

*THE* Royal Grenada Police Force (RGPF) has suffered another psychological blow as another of its members (the third in two months) is being brought down on criminal charges.

The latest Frederick "Ballar" Noel, a member of Prime Minister Dr. Hon. Keith Mitchell's Persoanl Security Unit, was officially charged last Friday with causing grievous harm.

Officers at the Criminal Investigation Department executed the charge at the CID on Friday last, some five months after the offence was committed.

Sources told INFORMER that move to charge "Ballar" came as a result of pressure brought to bear on the office of the Director of Public Prosecutions by the victim of a shooting incident and his Attorney, an offence for which Ballar was the prime suspect.

The incident occurred in the village of The Bocas in St. George in September, 2005. According to information circulating at the time, another Noel was shot in the arm, while enjoying a cool evening with his girlfriend in a parked vehicle in The Bocas area.

Sources told INFORMER, the incident was love-related and that Officer "Ballar" was later called in to assist the police in their investigation, being the main suspect.

At the time of the incident, we were told, the young lady involved, sensing danger, fled the scene, leaving Noel to face the bullet.

INFORMER learnt that the delay in the execution of the charge was deliberate as attempts were made to have the matter settled out of Court.

Nevertheless, we were told that failure on Ballar's part to take corrective measures to have the matter settled, in fact, outran the patience of the victim and his lawyer, and therefore the present move is one in search of justice against the officer.

Noel was therefore charged under section 207 of the criminal code and has been placed on $5,000 bail. He would be represented by defence council Dereck Sylvester and is expected to make his first court appearance on March 27.

If convicted, Ballar could spend a maximum 5 years in prison.

Meanwhile, Joseph Tillock and Joel Horsford, two Police Officers depicted above were charged in Jan. an Feb. with stealing. They are also on bail.

*Front page, Grenada Informer, week ending 17 February 2006*

a position of trust. Their responsibility is to protect and serve the citizenry. They must therefore lead by example. The same principle applies to every member of the legal profession. The entire police service can be brought into disrepute whenever there is an allegation, truthful or otherwise, for it is the perception that is brought to bear on that august body.

## LAWYERS TAKE A STAND

In February 2005, there was growing opposition to the proposed appointment of a certain attorney to be appointed as Attorney General in the State of Grenada. The lawyers ensured their voices were heard unanimously. The Grenada Bar Association, including the President, the Bar executive, rebuked the alleged appointment. Numerous letters were sent to the Trade Union Council, the Grenada Chamber of Industry and Commerce (GCIC) and non-governmental organisations.

The Bar Association had its Annual General Meeting (AGM) on the 31st January 2005. A decision was taken, that effective 1st February 2005 all courts in the country were to be boycotted. The lawyers were noted for championing the cause of their clients. Now it was time to champion their cause. The administration of justice would benefit. The lawyers assembled at the Supreme Court Registry, in a show of force, expressing their discontent. It was the coalition of attorneys for a common cause as no other. The lawyers were not prepared to relent.

The opposition to the attorney's appointment grew stronger with each passing day. There was no sign that the authorities would change their minds; silence was clearly a sign of their indignation at the lawyers' request. The protest to prevent the appointment intensified.

The opening of the criminal assizes was boycotted by all. There was a total of eighty four (84) cases. The task of the sitting Judge was a tiring one. He was diligent. Despite the administrative pressure which would have befallen him by virtue of the boycott, it was hoped that he understood the cause.

The lawyers' struggle increased with each passing day. The pulse of the legal profession was nearing boiling point. The letter to the Trade Union Council was met with approval and solidarity. There was no turning back now. This was a difficult time for lawyers, as clients whose matters were adjourned caused concern for them. Many of them expressed their understanding, which was a catalyst for our struggle.

The support continued to grow. Two Queen's Counsels, Carol Bristol and Derek Knight (both deceased), supported the Grenada Bar Association. They made their positions known. The Bar was in unison. During the demonstrations, the continued protests became obvious that

## *Lawyers seek to intensify struggle*

*The protest action by lawyers in Grenada could intensify in the coming days.*

*The Grenada Bar Association (GBA) has written to the powerful trade union movement on the island to solicit its support in the ongoing battle between government and lawyers over the controversial appointment of Jamaican barrister Hugh Wildman as the island's next Attorney-General.*

*The island was almost brought to a standstill in 2000 as trade unions called "sympathy strikes" to support teachers in their dispute with government over salary increases.*

*The government was forced to back down after the Conference of Churches of Grenada and other civic groups intervened.*

*Following is the text of a letter dated February 3, 2005 which GBA President Ruggles Ferguson wrote to the TUC President, Derek Allard on the impasse:*

*The President*
*Grenada Trade Union Council*
*St. George's*

*Dear Sir,*

I write in my capacity as President of the Grenada Bar Association (GBA), and in connection with the GBA's effort to prevent Mr. Hugh Wildman whom it is very widely considered wholely unfit, to be appointed to the highest legal position in the due Administration of Justice in the State of Grenada - that of Attorney General of Grenada.

Mr. Hugh Wildman is a Jamaican National and he first came to Grenada in about 1994 when he held the post of Director of Public Prosecution (DPP) - taking over from another Jamaican National

*Grenada Today, 11 February 2005*

# GROWING OPPOSITION TO WILDMAN

The Grenada Bar Association (GBA) is taking its case against the appointment of controversial Jamaican lawyer Hugh Wildman as the island's Attorney-General to a number of civic groups in the country.

The lawyers have despatched letters to the Grenada Trade Union Council, Conference of Churches of Grenada, Grenada Chamber of Industry and Commerce and Grenada Employers Federation among others.

On Wednesday, a five-member GBA team met for the first time with Legal Affairs Minister Elvin Nimrod to discuss the current impasse in light of the decision by lawyers to boycott all court matters until the Wildman issue is resolved.

The GBA delegation was led by its President Ruggles Ferguson, and included barristers Anslem Clouden, Lisa Taylor, Lloyd Noel and Reynold Benjamin.

Apart from Nimrod, the government side included Solicitor-General Avril Trotman of Guyana who is the wife of Speaker of the House of Representatives, Lawrence Joseph, and Permanent Secretary in the Ministry of Legal Affairs, Nordica Mc Intyre.

During the one-hour-and-a half hour meeting, Nimrod listened to the concerns of the lawyers and agreed to take them to Cabinet for consideration.

The GBA took the issue to the nation on Tuesday night when President Ferguson addressed Grenadians about their specific fears and concerns about the move by the Keith Mitchell-led government to hand the Attorney-General post to Wildman.

Following is an edited version of the speech.

At its Annual General Meeting on January 31st, 2005, the Grenada Bar Association took the unusual and unprecedented decision, effective the following day (February 1st), to boycott all courts in the State of Grenada, including the Magistrate's Court, Master's Chambers and High Court to protest the impending appointment of Hugh Wildman as the new Attorney-General of Grenada.

The Bar was clear and unanimous in its view that Hugh Wildman was not a fit and proper person to hold the high constitutional office of Attorney General, and

(CONTINUES ON PAGE 19)

Hugh Wildman - not sure of landing t[…] A.G post

Lawyers show unity and strength in the yard of the Supr[…] Court Registry in their battle with government over th[…] Wildman appointment

*Front page, Grenada Today, week ending 11 February 2005*

# Lawyers boycott all Courts to protest Wildman appointment

*Ruggles Ferguson and Reynold Benjamin speaking to the press*

*Lawyers filing out of the #2 High Court after addressing Justice Benjamin*

*Hugh Wildman*

**Protesting the Government of Grenada's recommendation that Jamaican lawyer Hugh Wildman be appointed to the post of attorney-general the Grenada Bar Association (GBA) boycotted all courts in Grenada on Tuesday and continued the boycott on Wednesday and Thursday.**

Criminal and civil lawyers alike attended the opening of the February Criminal Assizes at High Court #2 to let Justice Kenneth Benjamin know of their intended action.

President of the GBA, Ruggles Ferguson, as well senior members Lloyd Noel and Reynold Benjamin, addressed Justice Benjamin.

Ferguson said that the decision to take this action against the judiciary system was agreed upon unanimously by members of the GBA during their annual general meeting, which took place on Monday evening. They plan to stay away from all courts: the Master's, Magistrate's and High Courts.

Among their reasons for protesting, said Ferguson, was the fact that they were not officially informed or even told that Hugh Wildman had been recommended by the Government of Grenada to be attorney-general; in fact, they had not even been consulted in the matter.

Mr Ferguson said that the GBA has had many problems with Mr Wildman since their first experience with him in 1994, when he was Director of Public Prosecutions, and do not think he is suitable for this new position.

He recounted several occasions when Wildman's behaviour in the court was "shocking".

Ferguson also cited statements from regional and international courts regarding Wildman's behaviour, including one from the Privy Council in the failed DIPCON matter which said, in effect, that he showed utter disregard for and disrespect to the court.

Making Wildman attorney-general would place him as the de facto head of the bar and an ex officio member of Cabinet with the power to influence the policy-making process for Grenada, which is unacceptable to the GBA, said Ferguson.

Mr Benjamin called this move by government "a slap in the face for the legal profession," since government knows how the GBA feels about Wildman.

This sentiment was also echoed by Dr Francis Alexis, who said in a press release that Prime Minister Dr the Rt Hon Keith Mitchell "has shown himself to be extremely insensitive" in considering Wildman as attorney-general.

Benjamin also said that the GBA's experience with Wildman over the years has caused them not to have any respect for him, and "how can one become a leader if he does not have any troops?"

Mr Noel said that the boycott is in no way intended to disrespect the court, but rather is to preserve the integrity of the justice system, a point that was reiterated by Ferguson and Benjamin.

Hugh Wildman has not yet become attorney-general; according to Mr Ferguson, he was supposed to have occupied that position effective Tuesday, but that had been delayed due to a technicality with the current Attorney-General Raymond Anthony.

Speaking to The Grenadian Voice, Permanent Secretary in the Ministry of Legal Affairs Ms Nadica McIntyre said that there is no guarantee yet that Mr Wildman will be the next attorney-general, since the matter is still before the Judicial and Legal Services Commission. It is not known when the commission's recommendation will be released.

The GBA president said that the boycott will continue until the association is satisfied that government will not put Mr Wildman into that office; he further added that the association will not recognise Wildman in that position if he is appointed.

When questioned about Anthony's removal from that position, Ferguson said that while there had been complaints against him before, the association had not had problems working and meeting with him; neither was there any problem with his character.

He also said that while they had not been officially notified that Anthony was being appointed attorney-general, in the past, they had been well aware of new appointments beforehand; with Wildman, it was purely by accident that they found out about him being recommended.

The GBA also said that they would be happy to provide their own recommendations to the appropriate authorities "when the time is right."

Hugh Wildman first came to Grenada in 1994 under the National Democratic Congress' government, when he served as DPP until 1995. He returned to Grenada in 1998 to serve as DPP again, but again was put out of that position. He has continued to serve in Grenada since then as Police Advisor and Special Prosecutor, his current position.

Meanwhile, the opening of the criminal assizes continued without lawyers present.

Eighty-four cases are on the list, a large number of which had been traversed from the last period of assizes due to prisoners being held in St Lucia.

Five defendants pleaded guilty to their charges; the jurors were sworn in and instructed on their duties by Justice Benjamin.

*Front page, The Grenadian Voice, week ending 5 February 2005*

**GRENADA TODAY**
**Established in June 1990**

*Grenada Today is published by Grenada Today Limited*
*P.O. Box 142, St. John's Street, St. George's, Grenada*
*Email: gtoday@caribsurf.com*
*Phone: 1 (473) 440-4401/6592*

**EDITORIAL**

# We agree with the bar

**GRENADA TODAY** would like to associate itself with statements issued by the Grenada Bar Association in challenging the appointment of controversial Jamaican lawyer Hugh Wildman as the next Attorney-General of Grenada.

Our editorial is adopted from excerpts of a speech delivered to the nation on Tuesday night by President of the local bar, Ruggles Ferguson on MTV:

We say: enough is enough. We have a duty to protect and promote the rule of law; to protect the integrity of the office of Attorney-General; to ensure that the institutions of the justice system remain effective and serving the public interest; to ensure that these institutions are not compromised for the benefit of a few.

A few days ago the Government of Grenada issued a statement expressing surprise at what they describe as "the confrontational stance" of the Grenada Bar Association.

We ask: Who is really taking a "confrontational stance"? And how can they be surprised about the Bar's opposition to Wildman given the history of the relationship over the years?

How could they be surprised when the GBA, since 1994 - approximately 11 years ago has been consistently exposing the wild and reckless exploits of Wildman to all concerned, including the Government, the Judicial and Legal Services Commission and the people of Grenada?

How could they be surprised when in 1994 - as far back as 11 years ago -the GBA has been calling on the Government and the JLSC to revoke his appointment as DPP?

How could they be surprised when in 1999 the GBA publicly and vehemently opposed all efforts of the Government of Grenada to re-appoint him as Director of Public Prosecutions, even going to Court in an effort to do so?

How could they be surprised when in 1999 the GBA boycotted the Criminal Assizes in protest over his appointment as DPP?

How could they be surprised when the GBA has consistently and publicly condemned his unprofessional, unwarranted and sickening public attacks on Judges when they rule against him and the Government of Grenada?

What would have been surprising - and indeed shocking - would have been the failure of the Bar to respond to this proposed appointment in the strongest and clearest terms.

Who is really taking the confrontational stance? Is it the Government or the Grenada Bar Association? We say the evidence is overwhelming to show that it is the Government of Grenada that has always been taking the confrontational and provocative stance on the Wildman issue.

They are the ones who have consistently and publicly defended his conduct - defended him when he attacked Judges, defended him when he attacked lawyers.

Who are the ones, who, without notice to the Bar, but with full notice and knowledge of the Bar's position on Mr. Wildman, attempted to foist him upon us as Attorney-General, and effectively head of the Bar, as of February 1st?

We ask you the public to Judge for yourselves. We have to protect and promote the independence of the Judiciary; to defend our Judges from unwarranted attacks from agents of the executive; to speak out for the Judges who cannot speak out for themselves, save and except through their Judgments; to ensure that the separation of powers implicit in our constitution is maintained and that the Executive, Judiciary and Legislature are truly recognized by all as separate but co-equal arms of the State.

We cannot sit idly by and allow Judge after Judge who rules against the Government to be attacked and decried by the likes of Mr.Wildman and others.

Essentially, we have two options. Either we sit back, relax and allow the appointment of Wildman to take place and to cause further chaos and confusion in the legal system; or we stand-up and fight an effective and decisive battle to stop the appointment.

We have chosen the latter. Stopping the appointment of Mr. Wildman is in the best interest, not of ourselves, but of the people of Grenada who are the beneficiaries of the justice system.

To allow the appointment of Wildman will be to bring the justice system into further disrepute; to engage in unending and costly battles with the Government; and to exist in a state of constant crisis and confusion.

For the avoidance of doubt on the character and other traits of Mr. Wildman, we asked the JLSC to seek further information from current and former members of the Bench who would have interfaced with him, both in Grenada and Jamaica, where he worked previously.

We recommended names such as Justice Stanley Moore, a former High Court Judge in Grenada and now a Justice of Appeal of the Supreme Court of Botswana; Justice Brian Alleyne of our own Court of Appeal; Justice Errol Thomas, former Attorney-General and now a High Court Judge based in Antigua; Justice Malcolm Holdip, former Director of Public Prosecutions in Grenada and now a High Court Judge in the Republic of Trinidad and Tobago; Madame Justice Charmaine Pemberton, former Judge of the Eastern Caribbean Supreme Court and now a High Judge in the Re[illegible] Trinidad and [illegible] and Chief [illegible] Lensley Wolf[illegible] Supreme C[illegible] Jamaica.

We have com[illegible] ed our decisi[illegible] concerned, i[illegible] the Chief [illegible] Judges of th[illegible] Court and Magi[illegible]

We have re[illegible] adjournments t[illegible] ters in which [illegible] are involved, [illegible] the resolution [illegible] matter.

We have also [illegible] ed a sub-comm[illegible] the Bar [illegible] to find practic[illegible] tions to urgent [illegible] of clients that n[illegible] during the bo[illegible] the court - p[illegible] that will n[illegible] require prompt [illegible] tions to the c[illegible] urgent relief [illegible] injunctions or p[illegible] orders.

The GBA sta[illegible] and resolute in [illegible] sition to Mr. W[illegible] appointment [illegible] Attorney-Gener[illegible]

We call [illegible] Government to [illegible] honorable st[illegible] withdraw the [illegible] mendation to h[illegible] appointed.

We are of the f[illegible] that this is the [illegible] to bring about [illegible] tion of the curre[illegible]

*Grenada Today, 11 February 2005*

# Knight and Bristol support their colleagues

Two of Grenada's senior practicing lawyers, Queens Counsels Derek Knight and Carol Bristol have thrown their full support behind the Grenada Bar Association (GBA) in its on-going protest with government over the pending appointment of controversial Jamaican lawyer Hugh Wildman as the island's next Attorney General.

The two lawyers who have been practising for over 40 years each in the legal profession indicated that Wildman is not the best suited person to holder that high judicial office.

Knight, a former government minister in the 1970's, was approached by reporters for comment when he was spotted Friday outside the Number One High Court in St. George's observing the protest by lawyers.

"In my view Wildman is not the best person suitable to hold that office", said Knight who was casually dressed and not in lawyers robes.

He went on to say: "Many people believes that the Attorney General role is only to advise the Government, but such concept is wrong. The Attorney General in any country has a responsibility to the people of the country and it is part of the Attorney General's obligations to ensure that the people of Grenada get a good run for their money.

"If there are matters that affect the people as a whole it is the duty of the Attorney General to get involved and see what assistance he or she can make for them and I doubt Mr. Wildman will be in a position to do that for the people of Grenada.

The veteran lawyer pointed out that he is not a member of the Bar Association but commended his colleagues, noting that it was the first time he had seen the Bar coming together in such numbers like they did on the Wildman issue.

*Queens Counsel Carol Bristol*

*Queens Counsel Derek Knight*

Knight was in full admiration for the lawyers for the stand taking on the issue in light of the fact that Wildman in recent times had cost the Government millions of dollars in lost court cases.

He questioned whether the Jamaican lawyer was the most suitable person to be vested with the powers of Attorney General in Grenada.

He added that the Judicial and Legal Services Committee (JLSC) which is to make the appointment, is an independent body and its obligation is to see that the most fit and proper person get appointed to the post.

Like Knight, Bristol who is another long standing local jurist said that he is in full support of his colleagues on the decision to oppose the appointment of Wildman.

According to Bristol, the Attorney General is the principal legal adviser to the Government and the people of Grenada and not to any political party.

He stated that the holder of such office must be a person of integrity and from what he has heard and observed, Wildman is clearly not a suitable person to be made Attorney-General of Grenada and far more important to be made head of the local bar.

Bristol made mention of an incident in court involving a Court Order served on the Police to prevent the law enforcement agency from deporting some foreigners out of Grenada.

He charged that despite the Court's order, the people were deported and Wildman who is known to be a legal adviser to the police, knew about the existence of the order.

"I don't see how a person who ignores the order of the Court can give the people of Grenada proper advice", said QC Bristol.

*Grenada Today, 11 February 2005*

## TUC backs the lawyers

*STATEMENT OF SOLIDARITY WITH THE GRENADA BAR ASSOCIATION IN ITS OPPOSITION OF THE APPOINTMENT OF MR. HUGH WILDMAN TO THE POST OF ATTORNEY GENERAL OF THE STATE OF GRENADA.*

*February 8th, 2005*

*The President*

*Mr. Ruggles Ferguson*
*Grenada Bar Association*
*c/o Ciboney Chambers*
*H.A. Blaize Street*
*St. George's*

*Dear Sir,*

The Grenada Trades Union Council (GTUC) - an affiliate of the Caribbean Congress of Labour (CCL) and the International Confederation of Free Trade Union (ICFTU) - adds its voice to the growing chorus of prominent persons objecting to the appointment of Mr. Hugh Wildman to the post of Attorney General in the State of Grenada.

In joining this objection the GTUC relies on the great wisdom of your organisation and is mindful of the plethora of rebuking comments made by courts both in Grenada and the Region about the said Mr Wildman.

Particularly our attention is drawn to the comments made by one Mr. Lawrence Rowe in an email to the former CEO - 1st International Bank of Grenada, Mr. Van Brink, and the subsequent comments made by a High Court Judge in the United Kingdom when a matter came before his court for consideration.

It is clear to us, and so too must it be all right thinking persons that Mr. Hugh Wildman is not a fit and proper person to occupy the post of Attorney General and we demand the immediate and full revocation of any such consideration.

Please be assured of our continued support and solidarity.

*Respectfully*

*Ray Roberts*
*General Secret*

*Lawyers in the yard of the Supreme Court Registry*

*Grenada Today, 11 February 2005*

## *Some lawyers are 'the real threat'*

***The Grenada government has decided not to bow to the demands of the Grenada Bar Association (GBA) and pull back on its nomination of controversial Jamaican barrister-at-law, Hugh Wildman to become the island's next Attorney-General.***

***The position of the Keith Mitchell-led New National Party (NNP) government was outlined last Friday night by Minister of Legal Affairs, Elvin Nimrod in a national address.***

***Following is an edited version of the address:***

The Government has exercised its legal and constitutional right to propose a candidate for appointment to the post of Attorney General, subject, of course, to the approval of the Judicial and Legal Services Commission.

However, the Government has been vigorously and radically challenged by some members of the Grenada Bar Association regarding the choice of the candidate, Mr. Hugh Wildman.

In demonstrating their opposition to the Government's choice of the candidate, members of the Bar walked out on a sitting of the Assizes, boycotted the proceedings, and partially shut down the operations of both the civil and criminal court system.

This system, it must be noted, was established by our Constitution to protect the legal and constitutional rights of you, the citizens of this great Nation.

The Government of Grenada strongly condemns this radical and inappropriate use of industrial action by some members of the Bar Association for several reasons.

Not only is such action a direct challenge to the legitimate authority of the Government, but it is also depriving you, the citizens, of your constitutional rights to your day in court.

When you are denied access to the justice system, what does this tell us about those who should be representing you in court? It tells us that their political agenda surpasses their responsibilities and commitments to their clients.

The Bar Association has protested the proposed candicacy of Mr.

*Former President of the GBA - Reynold Benjamin*

*President of the GBA - Ruggles Ferguson*

Wildman for the post of Attorney General to His Excellency the Governor General, Sir Daniel Williams, the Minister of Legal Affairs, your humble servant, the Judicial and Legal Services Commission and to

culties in the choice of Mr. Wildman as a proposed candidate for the post of Attorney General of Grenada.

In a recent communication to the Government a well renowned and highly respected jurist from

***which he started, is as committed to efficiency, and has the same appetite for knowledge of the law as he had when he first came to the Bar, then in so far as his capability as an Attorney is concerned his appointment as***

fact that it is within Government's legal constitutional righ propose a candidat its choice for appo ment to the post Attorney General, notwithstandi Government's own cere belief that I

*Grenada Today, 25 February 2005*

## *Some lawyers are 'the real threat'*

*A group of lawyers meeting with local reporters in the yard of the Supreme Court Registry*

• FROM PAGE 8

Association. We acknowledge, in some instances, some behavioural indiscretion on the part of the candidate. This, it must be noted, is not uncommon by many practitioners in the legal profession.

On the other hand, the Government has considered its responsibility to obtain the best legal advice in the conduct of the administration of justice, since the Constitution provides that the Attorney General is the principal legal advisor to the Government.

Moreover, it is imperative that Government has an Attorney General who is sufficiently trustworthy to meet the criteria of the Constitution of Grenada.

I refer to Section 59 (2) which states: and I quote "That the Attorney General shall be an ex-officio member of Cabinet".

In other words, the Attorney General, as a member of Cabinet, is privy to all deliberations of Cabinet. It follows that Cabinet must have total trust and confidence in the Attorney General.

It is therefore essential that Government has the ability to nominate the person of its choice.

After due deliberation and careful consideration of the facts and circumstances surrounding this matter, including the documentation and concerns presented by the Bar Association and Government's interest in enhancing the administration of justice, the Government saw no compelling reason or reasons to withdraw the nomination of Mr. Hugh Wildman for the public office of Attorney General.

However in a spirit of compromise and in an effort to find an amicable solution to the legal stalemate, the Government had agreed to propose a short term contract for Mr. Wildman, with certain conditions that would help guide Mr. Wildman in carrying out his duties.

On Wednesday, February 16, I met with members of the Bar for a second time, as promised, and communicated Government's decision.

Specifically, I expressed Government's willingness to appoint Mr. Wildman on a six-month contract, in the first instance, instead of the normal two year contract.

This would provide an opportunity for both the Bar and Government to assess the performance of Mr. Wildman and to make any necessary changes.

*The protesting lawyers as they marched through the streets of St. Geor on Wednesday*

The outright rejection by the Bar Association of Government's offer of a reasonable compromise compels one to wonder whether those members of the Bar do not have an agenda other than the concerns they have put forward.

We need to remind ourselves that in 1999 it was the same members of the Bar Association who used the same allegations to launch a vicious protest against Mr. Wildman when he applied to be admitted to practise as an Attorney in the Courts of Grenada.

Needless to say, that those same baseless allegations were dismissed by the Judge and Mr. Wildman was admitted to the Bar of Grenada.

In our opinion the real threat to the proper administration of justice in our Country comes not from the appointment of Mr. Hugh Wildman as Attorney General, but from the drastic and radical action by some members of the Bar in withholding critical legal services from their clients.

Ladies and gentle Government is co dent that Mr. Wild will conduct him with the greatest de of competence commitment and devote his conside energy and talen serving the citizen this Nation.

I thank you for li ing and let us pray good sense, so judgement and res for our Constitution love of our Cou will prevail.

This is essential a continue on the l and arduous journe reconstruction development of Nation.

*Grenada Today, 25 February 2005*

lawyers united can be a force to reckon with. There is strength in numbers. It is best to stand up and speak out, for if this was not done, it would have been equivalent to acquiescence. I have never seen the lawyers so united; it was a breath of fresh air.

A Grenada Bar Association (GBA) delegation of Ruggles Ferguson, Dr. Francis Alexis QC and others met with the Judicial and Legal Services Commission (JLSC) in St. George's. The intended Attorney General was also present.

The Trade Union Council (TUC) did not hesitate to support the lawyers. The coalition of all the supporting forces against the proposed appointment of the intended Attorney General was becoming more powerful by the day. The General Secretary of the Trade Union Council penned a letter of support, adding fuel to the flame.

BATTLE LINES ARE DRAWN

.......The Wildman Issue Getting Nasty

Ruggles Ferguson - President of the Bar

Governor General - offered a proposal

Elvin Nimrod - The ball is in his court

FULL STORY ON PAGE 3

The Lawyers as they staged a protest action outside the Supreme Court Registry

*Front page, Grenada Today, week ending 18 February 2005*

The ignition of support was far and wide. Despite that, there seemed to be no indication as to the State's position. Continued silence could have meant the lawyers were being ignored or was it a period of tranquil reflection.

The editorial of a weekly newspaper gave credit to the lawyers struggle and supported us fully. This was generally unheard of. This type of struggle was rare; the support from numerous quarters in the society was commendable.

The State was undaunted in their quest. Battle lines were drawn. The Minister of Legal Affairs in a national address stated the attorney was competent for the job. He tried to convince the public that lawyers had a political agenda which was in priority to their responsibility and commitment to their clients. He echoed numerous other allegations. There was a proposal to have an initial six (6) month contract for the appointment of the Attorney General. However, it was not accepted by the Bar Association. This was a legal debacle. There was no end in sight.

# BATTLE LINES ARE DRAWN

Lawyers in Grenada will spend the weekend pondering on their next move after rejecting proposals from the State for the conditional appointment of controversial Jamaican lawyer Hugh Wildman as the country's next attorney-general.

The lawyers are into the third week of a boycott of all local courts to protest the impending appointment of Wildman to the top judicial post on account of his behaviour and demeanour over the years.

Informed sources told ***GRENADA TODAY*** that President of the Grenada Bar Association (GBA), Ruggles Ferguson is presently briefing lawyers on communication received from official quarters on the Wildman issue.

This newspaper was told that Governor-General, Sir Daniel Williams informed Ferguson on Monday that he was offering a compromise for Wildman to be given a nine-month probation and not the customary 2-year contract.

During the meeting at Sir Daniel's private home at Westerhall, St. David's, the Governor-General

lawyers, if the bar was to agree to the offer and Wildman signed his contract under the conditions outlined then one year later he can behave as he likes and nothing could be done since he can claim that he signed the contract under duress due to pressure from the Bar.

This proposal for a nine month contract for Wildman was reportedly restated to Ferguson on Wednesday by the Keith Mitchell-led government which deliberated upon the issue at Monday's weekly Cabinet sitting.

The lawyers had initially met with Sir Daniel on February 1 to ask him to intervene and stop the appointment and on February 8 with Legal Affairs Minister Elvin Nimrod.

The senior government minister assured the lawyers that he would take their concerns to Cabinet.

A source close to the lawyers said that they are not prepared to accept the proposal on the grounds that Wildman is just not fit for the post.

Wildman is not fit and he is just not fit", said a lawyer close to the talks.

He stressed that the battle lines have now been drawn between the lawyers and government "and they can expect us to come out vigorously because we are not willing to compromise".

"They (government) should prepare themselves for all sorts of things", he added.

A three member GBA delegation headed by President Ferguson is expected to travel to St. Lucia tomorrow (Thursday) to share their concerns on the Wildman issue with the Chief Justice of the OECS Supreme Court, Adrian Saunders and members of the St. Lucia Bar.

Ferguson will be accom-

*Grenada Today, 18 February 2005*

The lawyers were perceived as the real threat, but the allegations did not daunt the continued protest.

One of our Senior Lawyers Lloyd Noel (now deceased) who wrote weekly articles sought to explain in one of his articles, why the attorney was not fit for the position. The article was headed, 'Competence Plus Character to Breed Confidence'. He gave reasons for opposing the appointment.

# COMPETENCE PLUS CHARACTER TO BREED CONFIDENCE

LAW AND POLITICS

*by Lloyd Noel*

The objection by the Grenada Bar Association (GBA), to the proposed appointment of Mr. Hugh Wildman as Attorney General (A.G.)" of Grenada if not handled properly, could have far reaching and serious consequences for the Rule of Law, and the Administration of Justice in these Spice Isles.

A News Release from the Ministry of Legal Affairs, in the absence from the island of the Minister, Hon. Elvin Nimrod who was in Jamaica at the time, speaks of Mr. Wildman being "eminently qualified for the Judicial and Legal Services Commission (JLSC) to recommend his appointment to the Governor General."

The said release further stated - that the ministry "reiterates its confidence in Mr. Wildman", and still further, "that it is expected that he would competently advise Cabinet and will sit as an ex officio member of Cabinet."

Judging from the tone of the release as a whole, it leaves one to seriously wonder who in fact wrote it.

But be that as it may - the fundamental principle in substance, when considering Public Officials to fit into the expected calibre of such a high office as that of Attorney General, must always be competence or qualification, as well as good character and conduct, to justify confidence and reliability.

None of these on its own would suffice, it must be a combination of all the elements.

The Attorney General is the principal Legal Adviser to the Government - in every aspect of Government's operation and Administration.

He or she is also considered the head or leader of the Local Bar, and in well run Government Administrations the Attorney General's Department work hand in hand with the Bar Association in promoting the Rule of Law or due process, and in the execution of the Administration of Justice.

It must follow, therefore, that the person holding that very high and prestigious office - must be qualified with much more than a mere Certificate from Law School.

Whether or not Mr. Wildman has been "extremely successful" in the conduct of matters he had to deal with as D.P.P. or Special Prosecutor, according to the release, is a matter of opinion.

But that is not the issue, in this struggle to bring back and maintain some ethical standards of decency, and dignity, and propriety, in the highest offices in our suffering land.

What is at stake in the GBA's objection, is the very persistent and deplorable behaviour and unbecoming conduct of Mr. Wildman - inside and in the precincts of the Court; as well as his attitude to the job in hand, and his derogatory statements and gutter-type insulting remarks about Judges who rule against him in court, or Lawyers who demonstrate to the Judge and Jury, or the Court of Appeal, that his constant barkings are very much louder than his bite.

There are so many instances of documented proof of his "wild" behaviour, that one of his country men, who is a lawyer and well aware of his reckless behaviour as a Lawyer, has described him to me as "wild" in name and in nature."

And the irrefutable evidence, from Judicial pronouncements at the Court of Appeal Level in Jamaica, is readily available for the Minister of Legal Affairs and the Prime Minister to scrutinise, before going off on a tangent.

In the case of "Gregory Johnson against the Crown" in Jamaica - reported in Volume 53 West Indian Reports, in 1996 - the Court of Appeal of Jamaica was hearing an Appeal from Mr. Johnson, against his conviction and sentence for a Murder that took place in September 1991.

At the trial before the Judge and Jury in the High Court of Jamaica, Mr. Wildman was the Prosecuting Counsel for the Crown.

During the trial, Mr. Wildman made many improper and unfounded allegations against the Defence Counsel, who was a Queens Counsel (Q.C.)on numerous occasions. And he did so openly in front the jury, and with such bad taste that it prejudiced the fair trial of the Appellant.

The Court of Appeal opined - "suffice it to say that such outrageous conduct before a Judge and Jury was quite improper and should not have been allowed to occur."

They quoted from an English Law Lord to add .... "Counsel entrusted with the public task of prosecuting accused persons, should realise that one of their primary duties is to be absolutely fair to the accused."

The Court of Appeal added much more admonitions to Mr. Wildman, about the dignity of the Court and the integrity of opposing Counsel that should never be compromised.

Even the Senior Counsel for the State, who was supposed to be on Mr. Wildman's side, he frankly admitted that he could not defend Wildman's conduct, nor could he refute the fact that the trial Judge had failed to control him and curb his conduct.

The Court of Appeal held that "having regard not only to the inadmissible evidence that was admitted, but also to the reprehensible conduct of prosecuting Counsel" - the Appellant had not been afforded the substance of a fair trial and his conviction and sentence were quashed and he walked away a freeman.

The above pattern of behaviour of Mr. Wildman in our Courts is history, and every time a Judge tried to control him that Judge got castigated.

He behaved so badly during his first stint as D.P.P. in 1994/1995, that he was asked to leave by Dr. Francis Alexis, then Attorney General, after a very short time in the job.

And although he was given a second chance, when he was brought back by the current Regime, he has not shown any semblance of change or remorse.

If anything, he has moved further away - in that as a Government Legal Officer he filed a Law Suit against a Sitting High Court Judge, accusing him of bias and seeking a Declaration that Justice Brian Alleyne, now a Court of Appeal Judge of the OECS Supreme Court, should not be allowed to hear any case in which he was involved.

Needless to say, like in the Jamaica Court of Appeal, he was thrown out of Court - and Justice Othniel Sylvester who heard his "Bias Case" described his indiscretion as "frivolous, vexatious and an abuse of the process of the Court."

And when the case from which he made those accusations of Justice Alleyne, the Dipcon Engineering claim against the Government of Grenada, went to the Privy Council in London - his action against the Judge surfaced, and the Law Lords commented that Justice Alleyne was very correct in the way he deal with Mr. Wildman's behaviour.

Against that background, and there are many more instences duly documented and readily available in the GBA's bundle of evidence, it leaves one to wonder what standards the Ministry of Legal Affairs and the Government are looking for in a new Attorney General, when their release of February 3rd stated .... "He has been extremely successful in the overall conduct of matters with which he has been entrusted. He is committed to the pursuit of Justice."

If his outrageous and reprehensible - behaviour, towards his fellow Jamaican National Gregory Johnson, is anything to go by - then I dread what would happen to Grenadians should he achieve that exalted position of Attorney General.

Even as recently as 2002/2003, when I defended Dunstan Henry, in the Murder case brought by Wildman in the usurpation of the DPP's function; after the Jury quite properly returned a not guilty verdict in favour of Mr. Henry.

A member of the Jury swore an Affidavit to say, that Mr. Wildman was heard to say that "Dunstan Henry was guilty, but the Judge, and the Prosecution Witnesses (the Police) and the Doctor, conspired with the Defence against him, that is why he lost the case. The whole System in Grenada is crooked."

All those instances of unacceptable and grossly inappropriate behaviour on Mr. Wildman's part, have been forwarded to the relevant authorities for consideration.

The GBA Committee, responsible for coordinating the struggle on behalf of the general membership, had a very useful meeting with the Governor General on the day we walked out of the Assizes, and he appeared very concerned when he was provided with the documentary evidence in support of our contention in opposition to Wildman's appointment as Attorney Genefal of our Tri-Island State.

At the time of writing this Article (Saturday/Sunday) I was informed that the Minister of Legal Affairs, through his Permanent Secretary, had requested a meeting with the Committee and that was carded for Wednesday 9th February at the Ministry.

By sheer coincidence, in the very week (3rd February) that we were mounting the opposition to what is considered a backward step - in Caribbean jurisprudence at this time in history, another group of Lawyers and other concerned citizens in Jamaica - had just received the news, that their Appeal to the Privy Council, against the passage of Three Bills in the Jamaican Parliament - that in effect were Amending the Constitution, and bringing into being the (CCJ) Caribbean Court of Justice as the Final Court of Appeal in Jamaica, to replace the Privy Council in London - had been successful, and those Bills were declared null and void.

The effect of that ruling would be widespread, for other CARICOM States with a similar Constitution to Jamaica.

It would also have a dampening effect, on the proposed coming on stream of the "Caribbean Single Market" in Guyana later this month.

And as for the CCJ itself, the proposers have to go back to the drawing board and pay much more Legal and Constitutional attention to the protection of people's rights and freedoms - in the wake of ever-increasing political and governmental misbehaviour across the Caribbean.

Many of us have been saying that the proposals for the CCJ, in its Appellate Jurisdiction, are wide open for future abuse and far more entrenched provisions must be included to guard against that possibility.

And the P/C is saying - that because the people's rights are so very important, they cannot simply be taken away without having in place the functional protection of a Constitution to guard against - such Governmental misbehaviour in the future.

We in Grenada have not reached that stage as yet, but the battle lines are clearly drawn by that decision.

In the meantime, we have to ensure that those appointed to advise Government on such critical issues - do have what it takes to do so - because Certification, without Character and good conduct accreditation, is certainly not enough to satisfy the required standard.

*Grenada Today, 11 February 2005*

The Newspaper reported on the issue with gusto, as it was unlikely that such strong opposition would be meted out against an attorney. The report was entitled, "Battle lines are drawn". The strike was into its third week. With each passing day it seemed like the flame of support for the lawyers was increasing. On the 18th February 2005, the Newspaper headline was glaring. Everyone waited with anticipation as to how this growing problem in the fraternity would be resolved.

The Grenada Bar Association decided to take the matter one step further. A delegation was formed to meet with the Acting Chief Justice, Adrian Saunders, who later became President of the Caribbean Court of

# Lawyers meet Chief Justice

In their continued defiance to Jamaican born Hugh Wildman proposed appointment as Grenada Attorney General the Grenada Bar Association is taking their struggle one notch higher.

A special delegation from the Bar led by President Ruggles Ferguson left the Island earlier today (Friday) for St. Lucia to apprise the acting Chief Justice Adrian Saunder and Appeal Court Judges on the matter and the stance taken by the Grenada Bar.

According to information reaching the GRENADA INFORMER the team which also include Anslem Clouden and Renold Benjamin are expected to bring the regional body up to date and justified their position by providing among other things, the reasons for not attending Court for opposing Wildman's appointment as Grenada's Attorney General . The acting Chief Justice is expected to be among appeal Court Judges assembling in St. Lucia on Friday for a special sitting to bid farewell to Justice Saunders who would be taking up a new position on the Caribbean Court of Justice.

The Grenada Bar Association has since met with a number of civil society bodies among them Trade Union groups, conference of churches and N.G.O's.

They have also had discussion with Governor General Sir Daniel Williams all with a view of justifiying their action .

Strike action opposing Wildman is now in its second week.

*Front page, Grenada Informer, week ending 18 February 2005*

# NATIONAL STRIKE IS COMING

Grenada could face a one-day shutdown of all sectors of the economy very soon as protesting lawyers continue their battle with government on moves to appoint controversial Jamaican barrister Hugh Wildman as the island's next Attorney-General.

Informed sources told ***GRENADA TODAY*** that the Grenada Bar Association (GBA) has called on the powerful Trade Union Council (TUC) for solidarity in its four week old struggle with the Keith Mitchell-led New National Party (NNP) regime.

The government has restated its position that the proposed appointment of Wildman as Attorney-General "is a correct one based on the established criteria for appointment to this post".

According to a well-placed source, the lawyers and the trade union leaders held an important meeting Wedesday at which the main talking point was the involvement of labour in helping to force government's hand on the Wildman the issue.

He said that if the TUC gives its blessings to the proposed one-day strike it could see the Technical & Allied Workers Union (TAWU) effecting a shutdown of all air and seaports in the country, as well as disrupting key utility services such as electricity, water, telephone and port services.

The source indicated that teachers are most anxious to take part in the strike action in order to send an early warning message to the Mitchell government with regards to their current dispute on the State's proposal for a wage freeze for the next two years.

The Grenada Union of Teachers (GUT) is insisting that it wants the final payment of the last 3-year industrial agreement and has given the administration until month-end to fullfil its obligations to them.

The source also dropped hints that the government could get a serious blow with plans for the one-day national strike if the Public Workers Union (PWU) gives the green-light to civil servants to join the battle.

He said that the call for strike is a very sensitive one since the TUC will have to engage in some kind of a dialogue with interest groups like the Grenada Chamber of Industry and Commerce (GCIC) and the

**(Continues on page 3)**

*Front page, Grenada Today, week ending 25 February 2005*

**Government's nomination of Jamaican Hugh Wildmar**

# REJECTED BY RJLSC

**Lawyers return to Court**



*Front page, Grenada Informer, week ending 4 March 2005*

Justice (CCJ) to ventilate the issues surrounding the administration of justice in Grenada. The news media relished the story. Once again the lawyers were headlined.

A national strike was now looming. None of the parties to the dispute was budging. Government held unto its position. The Bar Association together with its supporters did the same. A national strike was not in the best interest of any party. The disruption in the utility service sector alone would have been a nightmare. For another week the lawyers' struggle headlined the newspaper as the protest remained unabated.

During the month of March 2005, the request for the appointment of the Attorney General was finally rejected by the Judicial and Legal

# Wildman rejected by R.J.L.S.C

The Regional Judiciary and Legal Services Commission (R. R.J.L.S.C.) has rejected Government nomination of Jamaican born Hugh Wildman as Grenada's Attorney General.

News of the rejection of Wildman's nomination hit the streets early Tuesday, one day after he appeared before the Commission and one day after members of the Grenada Bar Association together with members of the Trade Unions Council and civil organizations had taken to the streets walking with placards opposing the nomination.

In addition, it coincides with a defiant one month total boycott of all court proceedings, by members of the Bar to show their disapproval with the nomination.

Lawyers contended then, that given Wildman's past conduct he was not suitable to occupy such a high office and therefore Government should withdraw the nomination.

Government, on the other hand, equally firm on the stand taken contended that Wildman was the best man for the job, and is the only individual with whom they could work comfortably.

After several weeks of verbal exchanges and discussion with various interest groups on the part of the lawyers, the matter was referred to the Regional Judicial and Legal Services Commission for the final decision which was in fact handed down on Monday after discussions with all parties involved.

Moments after the disclosure, Minister of Foreign Affairs, Elvin Nimrod , in a press conference said Government views this news with disappointment and regret considering Wildman was seen as not being qualified for the position of Attorney General.

Nevertheless, Nimrod said, given Government's law abiding stand, they would respect the R.J.L.S.C. decision.

Nimrod further went further on said that it must be noted that throughout the entire ordeal, Government acted with restraint and discipline while awaiting on the R.J.L.S.C. This decision he said was in stark contrast to the behaviour of some members of the Bar Association who took drastic and rapid measures instead of waiting.

Not withstanding the Commission's decision, Nimrod said, Government is of the view that the ruling set a dangerous precedent in that it does not only give the impression that the Lawyers were rewarded for their irresponsible behaviour, but also denies the Government of its right to appoint the best man for the job of Attorney General in Grenada.

In a similar manner, members of the Bar Association also held a press conference on Tuesday after hearing the news, and according to president Ruggles Ferguson, this comes as no surprise as according to him the bar was of the honest view that the Commission had sufficient evidence to return the kind of ruling that they made.

Ferguson, however, regretted that the matter had gone to the extreme

According to him, Government should have acted earlier to prevent such happenings. Government, Ferguson added, instead chose the path of high handedness and allowed the matter to be decided on by the Commission.

Ferguson was accompanied by Former Attorney General Dr. Francis Alexis and a former Bar President.

In responding to question of conduct of Lawyers during the one month boycott Alexis responded that bad conduct was initiated by Wildman and no one else and therefore Government should have been embarrassed to even raise the question of conduct on the part of Lawyers.

Meanwhile, the position of A.G is now vacant as Government, according to Nimrod, had paid off Raymond Anthony for the remainder of his contract.

Reports are that that man received one hundred thousand dollars in compensation.

Lawyers returned to their normal duties on Tuesday 1st March 2005 almost one month after their protest started.



*Grenada Informer, 4 March 2005*

HUGH WILDMAN IS REJECTED!!

After weeks of protest by lawyers, the Judicial and Legal Services Commission (JLSC) has refused to accept the nomination of controversial Jamaican lawyer Hugh Wildman as the next Attorney-General of Grenada.

The rejection is a bitter blow to the ruling New National Party (NNP) Government of Prime Minister Dr. Keith Mitchell which had put forward the recommendation of Wildman for the top judicial post.

Speaking to reporters on Tuesday, Legal Affairs Minister Elvin Nimrod who was disappointed by the decision said the ruling by JLSC simply means that the protesting lawyers were able to convince the body to make that particular ruling.

The lawyers objected strongly to Wildman landing the job on account of his attitude and behaviour over the years.

Nimrod was asked to comment on whether the government was thinking of having its own way on the appointment by offering Wildman a position in the Senate to allow him to occupy the post of Attorney-General in a political capacity.

He said: "The Constitution of Grenada states that the post of Attorney-General can either be that of a Public Officer or a Minister. So you would understand that the government can exercise that right (through the Senate) under the Constitution to bring him (Wildman) in as Attorney General as a Minister, which is the fall back position".

"Our options are not limited. The Prime Minister has the right to make recommendations for Senators, to revoke appointments and make new appointments....if he feels that he wants to do that", he added.

While political observers do not expect Wildman to be appointed through the Senate, the feeling in some quarters is that if the government goes that route then the likely casualties are Senators Nigel Stewart or President of the Senate, Leslie-Ann Seon.

Minister Nimrod also sought to clear up the status of the post of Attorney-General by stating that the current holder Raymond Anthony has no contract for the job with government.

"The government has done all that it has to do in terms of terminating the post of Attorney General in so far as Mr. Anthony in concerned", he said.

Nimrod pointed out that Anthony's appointment was on a contractual basis and it would have ended in November but government decided to exercise its right to terminate the contract at an earlier stage.

He said the termination of that contract took effective last Wednesday and technically the office of Attorney General is vacant.

"The Government has tendered a cheque to Mr. Anthony, compensating him for the unexpired term of his contract that is up until November and in addition for accrued vacation leave. So he has gotten his money", he remarked.

When asked about the actual amount paid to Anthony, Minister Nimrod said that this was "privileged information and I will not like to disclose the amount of money he received".

(Continues on page 3)

*Hugh Wildman - suffered a most humiliating defeat*

*A protest march of the victorious lawyers who led the crusade to influence the judicial commission not to look in the direction of controversial Jamaican barrister-at-law, Hugh Wildman for the AG post*

*Front page, Grenada Today, week ending 4 March 2005*

Services Commission. The headlines in the newspapers displayed the story with so much zeal, there were radio call-in programs, and the television carried the story. It was the talk of the town. This brought an end to a long saga. I recalled each passing day as if it would never end.

In one issue of the *Grenada Today* newspaper it was reported that the Minister of Legal Affairs had intimated that the rejection of the attorney's appointment as Attorney General by the Judicial and Legal Services Commission was only one avenue of appointing him since the Government had other political options. He could first be appointed as a Minister, then as Attorney General. The constitution allows for the post to be either that of a public officer or Minister.

The suggestion of appointing the same person as a political Attorney General would have been met with more resistance, as a victory in the first round was seen as added impetus to continue the struggle if it was warranted. This suggestion did not materialise. The struggle was like a lengthy trial where adrenaline kept you going. The victory nullified the pain of the long arduous task.

Thereafter, the court resumed its normal functioning. It was business as usual. The wheels of justice continue to spin unabated.

## CHAPTER FIVE

# LEAVING THE NEST

*"Only those who will risk going too far can possibly find out how far one can go."*
T.S. ELIOT

While at Ciboney Chambers, the myriad of cases, legal discussions, and the cohesion of the attorneys formed a beautiful legal tapestry, all destined to ensure that we fulfilled our duty first to the court, then to our clients. The thought of embarking on my own practice was then prominent in my mind, as I felt legal growth was imperative to my development. On one occasion, I took the opportunity to broach the subject with my Principal at Ciboney Chambers. My previous experience of dismissal for me 'allegedly' considering moving into my own practice was foremost in my mind.

Human beings are so varied in character. The manner in which persons behave is probably based on their personal experiences or life lessons they learnt along the way. For this reason I tried to understand, instead of condemn; appreciate instead of denigrate. My Principal was professional and diplomatic in all his dealings; a gentleman who looked out for our well-being.

I engaged him in a discussion of my plans to one day leave the firm. I was amazed at his receptiveness to the idea. I thought it necessary to alert him as he was extremely good to me. I wanted to ensure the professional relationship continued. He was very supportive. I explained my intention to provide sufficient notice when that time came. I further assured him that I would be willing to assist with the completion of any matter subsequent to my departure.

I then engaged my father in discussions regarding opening my chambers. It was agreed we would have a shared tenancy arrangement. The next mission was securing office space in close proximity to the courts in the city of St. George's. It was not very difficult then, as there were a few places available. The rental cost was a deterrent. Soon enough, we secured an available space with two offices, kitchenette and all the amenities. It had a beautiful view of the ocean and the city. We then decided to open our practice during the year 2004. Unfortunately, hurricane Ivan struck the island during the month of September that said year, resulting in large scale devastation. The plan was delayed for another year.

This was a blessing in disguise as I was able to give my then employer additional notice. Many of the law firms in the city suffered immense devastation both to their buildings and filing structures. Even the Supreme Court Registry which was the administrative engine of the courts, suffered tremendous loss. The roof of the No. 1 High Court was blown away completely.

One year later, on the 1st September 2005, after the registration of my business Derick F. Sylvester and Associates, the law firm opened its doors. I vividly recall the first client who walked through the door. That memory has been permanently etched in my mind. It was a great feeling. The thought of now having the sole responsibility of dealing with clients' legal issues was a constant reminder that I had to work towards continued excellence. The law practice came with great financial, legal, administrative and social responsibilities. I took with me the words of Ovid C. Gill (deceased) who always said, your motto must be: "The difficult you do right away but the impossible takes a little time." He encouraged excellence in every form. He would be disheartened whenever he received badly drafted documents. I took this lesson from him. I owe him a debt of gratitude. He was a lawyer, teacher, father, adviser to all the lawyers at Ciboney Chambers. He was wise as he was humble.

## MENTOR DEPARTED: OVID C. GILL

I recall how sad it was when Mr. Ovid C. Gill departed this life. We had lost a respected and admired teacher in the law. Indeed Mr. Gill left a remarkable legacy in the legal profession and the lives of those he touched. The weekly newspaper Grenada Informer dated Friday 1st May 2009, chronicled his life as succinctly as they could have, and reproduced hereunder.

I continued on my legal journey. My quest to ensure I fulfilled my duty to the court and ultimately the society at large. As onerous as it

## Profile of Ovid C. Gill

Ovid C. Gill was born in Grenada in December, 1929. He received his primary school education at Wesley Hall School under the headmastership of Mr. H. Graham, (later Sir Samuel Graham) from which school he graduated with the Cambridge Senior School Certificate in December, 1943. At the age of 14, he taught at the Belmont Primary School then situate at Springs (St. George) for about three years and was then transferred to Wesley Hall, whose headmaster was then the late Mr. John Morris of Barbados, later to enter into politics and to become a Parliamentary Representative for the city of St. George's. While teaching at Wesley Hall , Ovid sat the Cambridge School Certificate as a private candidate in December, 1947 and achieved grade 2 certificate, with exemption from the London Matriculation examination. In fact he left his teaching job at Wesley Hall and joined the staff of and became articled to Mr. Samuel Graham, who was then practising as a Lawyer in the Chambers of Renwick & Payne in Church Street, St. George's. Mr. Graham left his law practice around 1954 when he was appointed a Magistrate in St. Lucia and Gill's articles were then transferred to Mr. A. O. Payne of the law firm of Renwick and Payne.

During his clerkship in Renwick & Payne, he applied for and was appointed in May 1956 Legal Clerk to the Legal Advisor to the Central Agricultural Rehabilitation Committee, a committee which was established after Hurricane "Janet" in September, 1955 to assist farmers and other land owners with the rehabilitation of the properties damaged by the hurricane. He resigned from that position in December 1957 to pursue law studies with the tutorial firm of Gibson & Weldon of London England. In December, 1958 he passed the Intermediate Examination of the English Law Society, graduated in 1960 with the passing of the Final Examination, and was admitted to practice as a Solicitor of the Supreme Court in January 1961. He then entered into private practice in Grenada and practised as such for about 19 years from January 1961 to September 1980 when he left for Barbados to join the staff of the Caribbean Development Bank as Legal Counsel.

During the period of his practice in Grenada he acted as Solicitor for the Grenada Development Bank formerly the Grenada Agricultural and Industrial Development Corporation and also acted as Magistrate of the Easter District (Grenville and St. David) in 1962. He was also a member of the Public Service Commission and Public Service Appeal Board during the 1960's and 1970's, and also a Member and Chairman of the Grenada Telephone Company during same period. In 1978 he was President of the Lions Club of St. George's. In June 1983 he was admitted as a Solicitor of the Supreme Court of England, and in November 1991 was elected as a member of the Law Society of England. As Legal Counsel with the Caribbean Development Bank, from October 1980 to December 2000 he worked on several projects, both public and private sector, which the Bank financed for Grenada. These include the Western Main Road project, the Frequente and Seamoon Industrial development projects and the La Source Hotel project. He later received an award for distinguished performance of his duties as Legal Counsel at CDB. He retired from the CDB after serving there for two decades, returned to Grenada in December, 2000 and joined the staff of Ciboney Chambers as a Consultant, a position which he occupied until his death.

*Grenada Today, May 2009*

was, I relished every moment. The period of transition for me was smooth. I hit the ground running. I was in the trenches daily, a phrase used by defence lawyers to indicate their daily court battles. The day of my departure from Ciboney Chambers was bitter sweet, but the professional relationship engendered continued. The transition was seamless. I was cognisant that with this move came significant responsibilities.

## PRIME MINISTER'S SECURITY CHARGED

There was an incident which occurred involving a member of the Prime Minister's personal security detail. The individual was charged for grievous harm due to an alleged shooting. Not only does an incident of this nature taint the accused, but also the organisation. On that occasion, bail was granted in the sum of $5,000.00 with one surety.

There were numerous times during my practice when my professional resolve, resilience and ethics were tested. Nevertheless, I was relentless in the face of any attempt to manipulate me in the execution of my professional legal responsibilities. The newspaper articles were always reporting on issues within the legal fraternity in relation to law enforcement officers. Since this was always a hot topic which generated much interest.

Curious enough, one day, I received a call from a particular legal officer who instructed me to challenge the authority of the Director of Public Prosecutions (DPP) on the basis that he was unlawfully appointed. Further, the individual instructed me to challenge other issues in the case of the PM's security. I politely invited the lawyer to conduct that challenge; however he explained the professional dilemma in which he found himself.

It was then that I had to decide whether the dog would wag the tail or the tail would wag the dog. I chose the former. In short, I refused to be drawn into the fray.

Another attorney sought to challenge the legal authority of the Director of Public Prosecutions in relation to the instructions given to me, but suffice it to say it did not get very far.

BALLA FIRES AT DPP....

As NNP Tries To Bring Down Nelson

STORY ON PAGE 2

r Nelson — attempts being made to undermine him as DPP

Hugh Wildman - offering legal advice to "Balla"

Derek Sylvester - refused to be drawn into the fray

*Front page, Grenada Today, week ending 24 February 2006*

## PP threatened with 'personal legal action'

*Christopher Nelson*

***A lawyer in the well-to-do area of Lance Aux Epines has been retained to represent Frederick "Balla" Noel, one of the bodyguards of Grenada Prime Minister Dr. Keith Mitchell.***

***Balla has been charged with causing grevious bodily harm after shooting a male resident of the Bocas, St. Paul's in September 2005 over a quarrel with a female companion.***

***The newly retained lawyer is Venescia Francis-Banfield who recently returned home to practise law after living in Britain for a number of years.***

***One of the first acts of the lawyer is to challenge the authority of Director of Public Prosecutions, Christopher Nelson to file the criminal charge against the P.M's bodyguard.***

***Following is the full text of the letter which was obtained by the GRENADA TODAY newspaper:***

13th February, 2006.

Mr Christopher Nelson,
Director of Public Prosecutions,
Church Street
St. George's

Dear Sir:

I act on behalf of Corporal 403 Frederick Noel of Telescope, St. Andrew's.

You are aware that my client was charged on the 10th February, 2006, on your instructions, with the indictable offence - to wit: Grievous Harm contrary to section 207 of the Criminal Code.

My client has instructed that the above charge was preferred in the name of the Commissioner of Police but was done through Inspector 13 Earl Dunbar of the Criminal Investigation Department, St. George's. The preferment of a charge made unknown to the Commissioner of Police.

I am therefore instructed that you permit my client to have sight of the following:

(a) Your authority for preferring the said charge; and

(b) A copy of your instrument of appointment to the post of Director of Public Prosecutions

This matter comes up for hearing on Tuesday, 21st March, 2006 and in the circumstances, I would appreciate if the relevant copies of the above requested documents could be made available within 7 days of the date of this letter.

I am further instructed that failure to produce these documents within the time stipulated would leave my client with no alternative but to take personal legal action against you, including a complete withdrawal of the charge preferred against him.

Venescia Francis-Banfield

cc: Inspector 13 Earl Dunbar
CID, St. George's.

The Commissioner of Police
Police Headquarters, St. George's

*Grenada Today, 24 February 2006*

## ristopher Nelson reacts to the 'Balla' move

*Christopher Nelson - under pressure from NNP operatives*

Director of Public Prosecutions (DPP) Christopher Nelson is not taking lightly a threat made to institute "personal legal action" against him in the Frederick "Balla" Noel shooting incident.

In an exclusive interview with ***GRENADA TODAY***, Nelson acknowledged receipt of a threatening letter that was sent to him by Balla's new attorney-at-law, Venescia Francis-Banfield whose address was given as Lance Aux Epines, St. George's.

According to Nelson, he is giving "serious consideration" to the letter in terms of how best to respond to it since "I have been threatened personally with legal action".

He did not rule out the possibility of seeking legal advise on the matter from lawyers both inside and outside of Grenada.

"Even if you are a lawyer, one would have to seek advice from counsel", he remarked.

Nelson disclosed that he had informed the relevant government officials on the island about this latest development in the case.

He did not identify the officials but legal sources said that the DPP had written letters on the issue and sent copies of the Balla letter to the Permanent Secretary in the Ministry of Legal Affairs, as well as the Minister of Legal Affairs.

The DPP's office had suggested several months ago to the Royal Grenada Police Force (RGPF) that both Balla and the civilian should be charged for the incident that took place outside a home in the Bocas area of St Paul's in September 2005.

Nelson has been performing the duties of Director of Public Prosecution since February 1, 2000.

Legal sources told this newspaper that the Balla letter is insinuating that Nelson's contract as DPP is no longer valid and that he acted illegally in bringing the indictable charge against the PM's bodyguard.

*Frederick "Balla" Noel - going after DPP Nelson*

According to a source, the Court of Appeal had ruled on a similar issue in a matter involving former DPP and current high court judge in Trinidad and Tobago, Malcolm Holdip when the Keith Mitchell-led New National Party (NNP) government moved to replace him in the post.

The Justices ruled that Holdip was entitled to remain in office at the expiration of his two-year contract since it was the intention of the framers of the constitution to ensure that the Office of the DPP and high court judges are far removed from the dictates of the political directorate.

Nelson admitted that it was the first time since assuming the post that he had received such a threatening letter of personal prosecution from anyone.

"It's the first time that I have received such a letter or any query or challenge to my authority to give the police instructions, advice or directions in relations to a criminal matter", he remarked.

When asked if he felt that controversial Jamaican attorney-at-law, Hugh Wildman was behind the move to undermine his authority as DPP, Nelson said: "Your guess is as good as mines".

"I don't know the facts. What is facts is that a letter was received from this lawyer (Francis-Banfield) on behalf of her client (Balla)", he added.

Nelson was also asked to comment on his relationship with Wildman whom he replaced as holder of the office five years ago.

He said: "I get along with everyone who wishes to interface or interact with me personally or professionally".

However, Nelson was also quick to point out that he held no animosity towards Wildman and had worked with him on matters involving the State.

He said that the two of them are members of "a particular committee established by law" but "our social lives do not cross paths".

"However, I will be extremely disappointed if that individual has anything to do with the legal moves being made against me", he added.

Since arriving in Grenada over a decade ago, Wildman has been engaged in several heated exchanges with local lawyers.

In the latest encounter, the Bar Association of Grenada was successful in a move to get the Judicial and Legal Services Commission (JLCS) to turn down a move by the Mitchell government to appoint Wildman to the post of Attorney-General.

*Grenada Today, 24 February 2006*

## Derek Sylvester: 'I was not fired"

Attorney-at-law, Derek Sylvester is denying claims made in certain quarters that he was fired by Frederick "Balla" Noel, the personal bodyguard of Prime Minister Dr. Keith Mitchell for failing to obey instructions.

Sylvester represented "Balla" for only a few days after Police charged the bodyguard in connection with a shooting incident last September that left a resident of San Souci, St. George's suffering injuries from a gun shot wound to the hand over a lover's quarrel.

Well-placed legal sources told ***GRENADA TODAY*** that the lawyer is insisting that it was he who refused to continue working for Balla based on the instructions that the P.M's bodyguard was giving him in order to conduct the case.

Balla was charged with causing "Grevious Bodily Harm" to the San Souci man who was in the company of a female that is suspected to be one of the lovers of the P.M's bodyguard.

A source quoted Sylvester as saying that he asked Balla to seek help from another lawyer since he could not agree to the course of action to be pursued in the case.

"What I know for a fact is that Balla told Derek (Sylvester) that (Hugh) Wildman) wanted he, Derek to challenge the authority of the DPP (Director of Public Prosecutions, Christopher Nelson) to file the charge against him.

***Attorney-at-law, Derek Sylvester***

"Balla was saying that Wildman wanted Nelson to produce his letter of appointment as DPP since he (Nelson) was believed to be in the post without any good standing at all.

"Derek refused to do that (challenge the status of the DPP) and Balla went back and told Wildman that Derek was refusing to do it. Wildman then sent back Balla to Derek. And this is what Balla said to Derek: "Wildman wanted to know which side you (Derek) was on".

According to the source, Balla informed Sylvester that Wildman was not too sure whether the said Sylvester was on the side of lawyers attached

*Grenada Today, 24 February 2006*

## Derek Sylvester: 'I was not fired"

***CONT'D FROM PAGE 10***

George and Nazim Burke, who is the current holder of the St. George North-east seat in parliament.

The Jamaican-born Wildman is a Special Prosecutor with government and also serves as Legal Advisor to Cabinet.

According to the source, Sylvester became fed-up with the approach of the Balla camp and asked him to get another lawyer to handle the matter for him in court.

.The source said that the Balla camp then decided to hire the newly admitted Venescia Francis-Banfield to conduct the case on behalf of the P.M's bodyguard.

Legal sources confided in this newspaper that Francis-Banfield who is new to the jurisdiction might have been approached to do the job since most other lawyers on the island would be hard-pressed to take such action against the local DPP.

Over the years, the Mitchell government has often used local attorney, Michael Sylvester to institute legal action against persons considered as its opponents.

In recent weeks, Sylvester has not been able to attend to court matters due to ill health.

*Grenada Today, 24 February 2006*

## P.M Security Man finally Charged

Speculation is rife that attempts are being made to scuttle a charge brought against Frederick "Balla" Noel, one of the most prominent security officers attached to Grenada Prime Minister Dr. Keith Mitchell.

Balla was charged last Friday in connection with a shooting incident which occurred since last September at the Bocas in St. George's.

The Royal Grenada Police Force (RGPF) finally brought the charge against Balla five months after the shooting incident sent shock waves throughout the country.

Police insiders confided CONT'D ON PAGE PAGE 03

*Front page, Grenada Today, week ending 17 February 2006*

# P.M Security Man finally Charged

*CONT'D FROM FRONT PAGE*

The Royal Grenada Police Force (RGPF) finally brought the charge against Balla five months after the shooting incident sent shock waves throughout the country.

Police insiders confided to this newspaper that Director of Public Prosecutions (DPP), Christopher Nelson had recommended months ago that charges be brought against both the police officer and the civilian due to the nature of the encounter.

Balla is said to have shot the other man in the hand over an apparent lover's quarrel late at night.

The man from San Souci, St. George's spent severla days at the St. George's General Hospital receiving treatment for the gun shot wound to his hand.

The police officer alleged in his defense that the man pulled out a knife on him and he was forced to shoot in self-defense.

An official police report said: 'Frederick NOEL, Police Officer, residing at Telescope, St. Andrew's, was arrested formally charged and cautioned for the offence of causing Grievous Harm. Committed on the 2.9.05".

Informed sources told ***GRENADA TODAY*** that high-level legal moves are already being made to get the matter thrown out of court on the grounds that "Balla" was improperly charged by the Criminal Investigation Department (CID).

According to sources, documents to this effect have already been served on an Inspector of Police attached to the CID.

Hours after he was officially charged, Balla retained the services of barrister-at-law, Derek Sylvester to look after his interest.

According to government sources Sylvester was approached in the absence of the barrister-at-law normally used by the State for these matters, Michael Sylvester who is ill at the moment.

These sources indicated that government officials were forced to sack Derek Sylvester for allegedly failing to conduct the case based on instructions given to him by Balla.

"What I was told is that Balla informed Derek that (name of foreign lawyer withheld) wanted him to conduct the case along a particular line.

"He (foreign lawyer) wanted Derek to file a motion in the high court challenging the authority of the DPP (Director of Public Prosecutions) for bringing the charge against him.

"When Derek refused to do that, Balla then fired him. I understand that they (government officials) are looking for another lawyer right now to represent Balla.

Legal sources told this newspaper that Nelson is not liked in government circles.

In the recent budget debate, Prime Minister Mitchell sought to link Nelson as "a friend" of the main opposition National Democratic Congress (NDC) during a heated debate with Opposition Leader Tillman Thomas.

Balla is considered as a loyalist to Prime Minister Mitchell after he openly stated that he is prepared "to take a bullet" for the Grenadian leader.

*Grenada Today, 17 February 2006*

# Balla Appears in Court

**The man who says that he is prepared to take a bullet for his boss, Prime Minister Keith Mitchell, appeared in court for the first time on Tuesday for shooting a civilian over a lover's quarrel**

It was a heated exchange in court Tuesday as one of the key Security Officers attached to Prime Minister Dr Keith Mitchell made his first court appearance before Chief Magistrate Patricia Mark.

Frederick "Balla" Noel was charged last month in connection with the shooting of a San Souci, St George, resident on September 02, 2005, at the Bocas in St George's. The victim was shot in the hand over a lover's quarrel.

"Balla" was accompanied by his attorney-at-Law, Venescia Francis-Banfield who clashed verbally with Director of Public Prosecutions (DPP), Christopher Nelson.

The very heated exchange was sparked off by a request made by Francis-Banfield for full disclosure by the prosecution of all documents pertaining to her client and the incident.

Court sources told this newspaper that Nelson was incensed by a statement made by the

CONT'D ON PAGE 03

*Front page, Grenada Today, week ending 24 March 2006*

# Balla Appears in Court

*DPP Nelson - gave a tongue lashing to Balla's female lawyer*

*CONT'D FROM FRONT PAGE*

Court sources told this newspaper that Nelson was incensed by a statement made by the female lawyer which suggested that the DPP might become a party to the case and that legal action could be taken against him.

According to a well-placed source, the normally cool Nelson lashed out at his female colleague and reminded her that she is a rookie lawyer in the business.

He spoke of Nelson telling Francis-Banfield who was admitted to the local bar a few weeks ago that she could proceed to take legal action against him on behalf of "Balla" if she so wished.

"Balla" on the instructions of Government's Legal Advisor, Hugh Wildman of Jamaica had earlier approached defense lawyer Derek Sylvester to question the status of Nelson as DPP and advice the police to institute criminal charges against him.

Sylvester was reluctant to proceed against Nelson and Francis-Banfield was then retained to represent Balla.

The Keith Mitchell-led government is known to be opposed to Nelson continuing to perform the role of the island's DPP.

During his presentation to the 2006 Budget Debate, the Grenadian leader branded Nelson as "as friend" of the main opposition National Democratic Congress (NDC).

"Balla", a resident of Telescope, St Andrew's, was arrested and charged on February 10 for the offence of Causing Grievous Harm.

The matter has been adjourned until April 7.

*Grenada Today, 24 March 2006*

## MEDICAL PERSONNEL UNDER INVESTIGATION

In our society professionals are normally held to a very high moral standard. However, the medical profession was brought under tremendous scrutiny when a female patient attended at the general hospital to do a minor surgery. The medical personnel allegedly sought to violate her privacy by an act of indecent assault.

I received a telephone call from the complainant, who explained to me what transpired. I immediately instructed her to make a formal report with the Criminal Investigation Department, which she did. The accused was a Cuban citizen who was working in Grenada. Grenada and Cuba shared diplomatic relationship which was about to be disrupted as a fiasco was on the horizon. The Cuban was brought into the CID office on Hillsborough Street, where he was questioned. He was subsequently released pending further investigation.

The Complainant was not only distressed, but also angry that nothing was seemingly being done. So much so that she was willing to subject herself to a lie detector test. She demanded the accused complete one as well. However, the days passed by. The investigation continued. Soon it

*Front page, Grenada Today, week ending 26 May 2006*

became obvious that the possibility of charges being laid was growing dimmer, for sexual allegations of this sort are so difficult to prove. The accused was never charged. He departed the State.

The editorial of the Grenada Today in its May 2006 publication highlighted the incidence of the increased number of cases of alleged sexual assault, not only among professionals but also the general increase in reported cases of a sexual nature which plagued our society.

## Cuban Male Nurse being investigated

A St. David's mother of two embroiled in the sexual molestation accusation against a Cuban male nurse on the island would like the Royal Grenada Police Force (RGPF) to thoroughly investigate the matter and take the appropriate action.

The young lady confirmed this to *GRENADA TODAY* on Tuesday in the presence of her attorney-at-law, Derek ... ter what I have to do, I would stand up for her. I want them (government) to know that she is not a dog and nobody will run over her. You better believe that", he said.

The boyfriend felt that the Keith Mitchell-led government was engaging in double standard on the issue.

"If it was a poor Grenadian man who did it (sexual molestation), they would have crucified him", said the boy friend who has two young ones with his girlfriend.

Meanwhile, well-placed sources told this newspaper that a senior government official called CID giving instructions to the effect that the Cuban suspect should not be prosecuted by the police over the allegation made against him.

When questioned Tuesday by local journalists, Jamaican-born Legal Advisor to Cabinet, Hugh Wildman denied that he had made any such call to the police.

Wildman said that he is not fully aware of the incident and is not involved in the matter whatsoever.

On completion of their investigations, the police are expected to submit the case file to the Director of Public Prosecutions (DPP) for further instructions on the matter.

*Grenada Today, 26 May 2006*

## Police To Question Cuban Doctor For Sexual Molestation

"As I laid down on the bed, he (the Cuban doctor) bent over and put his tongue into my private parts", said the young woman from Bailes Bacolet, Bacolet. (FULL STORY ON PAGE 03)

## Patient Sexually Assaulted at Hospital

Grenada police are planning to question a Cuban doctor at the St. George's General Hospital for the alleged sexual molestation of a female patient on Monday.

The woman who is from Bailes Bacolet, St. David's confirmed to *GRENADA TODAY* that she had made a formal complaint to the Criminal Investigation Department (CID) about the behaviour of the doctor who reportedly used his mouth on her private parts in the Theatre Room.

It is the second embarrassing incident involving a member of the medical profession in the country within recent weeks.

Last month, another Cuban-trained doctor who is a member of the main opposition National Democratic Congress (NDC) found himself embroiled in another sexual molestation case.

Hospital sources confirmed to this newspaper that officers of the CID visited the General Hospital on Tuesday to speak with nurses about the alleged incident.

According to the woman's story, she went to the hospital to do surgery under the guidance of Dr. Jorge Dominquez and that another Cuban doctor (name withheld) allegedly interfered with her while preparing her for the operation.

She said that the Cuban doctor was taking information from her for Dominiquez who was the surgeon assigned to perform the surgery.

The young woman was already been dressed in the gown for surgery when the Cuban doctor alleged made the sexual advances.

She said: "He started off by touching me, telling me that I had nice legs and lips. As I laid down on the bed, he (the Cuban doctor) bent over and put his tongue into my private parts. While he was doing this, I kept telling him if he knew what he was really doing.

"I also said to him if he is not afraid that he would get fired (for what he did), and he said to me, " I would get f...ked before he gets fired", she added.

The woman informed our News Desk that she decided to inform Dr. Dominquez about what had happened to her in the presence of his Cuban colleague.

She said that after the surgery was done she was waiting to see Dr. Dominquez but did not manage to see him.

She spoke of a nurse informing her that the Surgeon (Dominquez) was in the Operating Room and "would not come out soon".

The St. David's woman left the hospital compound with her little daughter who had accompanied her for the surgery for St. George's to get something to eat since she had not had anything for the entire morning.

She said that on reaching home, she informed her boyfriend of what she had experienced at the hospital with the Cuban doctor who interfering with her most private parts.

She indicated that her boyfriend was "mad" when he heard what actually happened and suggested that they should go back to the hospital to confront the Cuban doctor who violated her rights.

The woman said that the doctor was still on the premises and when she confronted him he denied the allegation.

"He (the doctor) started to tell me if is money ah want, I would not get because he is working for the government and he does not have any money.

The woman said that the nurses who were present also denied that such an incident could have happened since they were always in and out of the room when the Cuban doctor was preparing her for surgery.

They asked her why she did not scream out when the doctor was sexually molesting her.

"I was so ashamed at what was happening to me that morning inside the room", she told this newspaper.

The woman's boyfriend immediately called barrister-at-law, Derek Sylvester on the cell phone and he instructed them to go immediately to CID and make an official complaint.

Sylvester who spoke to *GRENADA TODAY* said that once the police decide to prosecute the Cuban doctor, he intends to approach the Director of Public Prosecutions (DPP) to give him the go-ahead to take charge of the court proceedings and to prosecute the matter himself.

The police are expected to interview the Cuban doctor by Wednesday or Thursday.

*Grenada Today, 19 May 2006*

## LAWYERS SPEAK FOR THE JUDICIARY

The judiciary is not in a position to respond to attacks or speak to issues concerning them, for the ethics and ethos of the legal profession would not allow it. Therefore, it is incumbent on a strong Bar Association with independent lawyers who have that sense of fairness and fearlessness to speak up irrespective as to the effect on the political directorate, to defend the judiciary.

During the year 2007, the Carriacou Magistrate's Court was devoid of basic facilities for magistrate, lawyers and clients alike to enable the court to function effectively. Nazim Burke (another attorney) and I led a campaign calling on the State to rectify the situation as quickly as

**"Carriacou Court appalling - No toilet facilities "... Nimrod treating Kayaks like animals..." say Burke and Sylvester**

Two well-respected Attorneys have described conditions at the Carriacou Magistrate's Court as deplorable, sickening, inhumane and appalling and are calling on the Attorney General, Elvin Nimrod, to act swiftly to improve the state of the facility so that it will be comfortable and pleasant to all concerned.

Both Nazim Burke and Dereck Sylvester, emerged from the Court last week Wednesday looking extremely fustrated at the condition they are being forced to put with at the court.

Burke, a Carriacouian, went futher by saying that for Nimrod to be the Attorney General and Parliamentary Representative for Carriacou and have the court in such shabby state in his constituency shows that he treats Carriacouians and Petite Martiniquians as animals.

"Nimrod must learn to treat the people of Carriacou and Petite Martinique as decent citizens of this country and not like animals, in the condition in which they are forced to attend court", said Burke.

He said he is appalled at the conditions.

"Look at the condition at which the Magistrate has to hear cases, Lawyers have to represent their client and under which the public have to function in court", said Burke.

He added that the officers of the court are trying their best under these trying circumstances.

But it is really deplorable that, in the court house in Carriacou, there isn't a washroom where the Magistrate can use, no toilet facilities, nowhere to wash her hands, no air-condition.

"When you look at the desks Lawyers have to work to take information , ask questions, we are really quite embarrassed", added a firm tone from Burke.

"And we are even more embarrassed that the Minister for Carriacou and Petite Martinique Affairs, who is also the Attorney General of this country, cannot see it fit to represent his constituency and the interest of his constituency in a forceful way and to insist on his Government to ensure steps are taken to improve the conditions in his constituency; I mean I'm appalled," added Burke.

He added, "You need to build a court-house for the delivery of justice".

Burke, who is attached to Ciboney Chambers, pointed out that the court is being accommodated in the police station.

"These are two separate institutions and this was not intended to be a court-house but a police station.

"There is only a room being offered by the Police station to have court matters .

"This is deplorable", Burke noted.

Sylvester said it is appalling.

"There are no toilet facilities for the Magistrate, Lawyers, Prosecutors, orderly, court officers and I think that is very, very sad".

"In 2006 there is no toilet facilities".

"Also the internal and physical conditions of the court.

"I sat on a chair yesterday (Tuesday last week) and it was comical but I fell to the ground.

"I'm calling on the authorities to do what is necessary to ensure that the environment in which we work is properly maintained.

"Let's be fair, persons cannot be forced to operate under improper conditions and expects to perform at their fullest potential.

"So I'm calling on the powers that be to at least take some remedial action as it relates to the Carriacou Magistrate's Court", said Sylvester.

*Grenada Informer, 1 September 2006*

## Letter to the Minister of Legal Affairs

Re: Non-functioning Carriacou Magistrates Court

January 21st, 2008

Hon. Claris Charles
Minister of Legal Affairs
Ministry of Legal Affairs
H.A. Blaize Street
**ST. GEORGE'S.**

Hon. Minister,

**Re: Non-functioning Carriacou Magistrates Court**

It is with deep concern that I write to you on the current non-functioning of the Carriacou Magistrate's Court which serves both Carriacou and Petit Martinique. As you must be aware, this Court sits on the third Monday to Wednesday of each month, a mere three days per month.

In November 2007, renovations began on the compound which houses the Court and the Carriacou Police Station. When the Court sat in November, work had already started on the outside of the building. After that sitting, the staff of the Court was instructed to vacate the premises so as to allow work to begin on the inside. In compliance the two staff members secured the contents of the Court, including the court records, books and furniture which are now stored at the old Ministry of Carriacou and Petit Martinique building.

Since then, Hon. Minister, no alternative accommodation has been made available as a temporary facility while the renovations are being carried out which I understand should be completed by May 2008.

You would no doubt appreciate the serious implications for the administration of justice in Carriacou and Petit Martinique as a result of this totally acceptable state of affairs.

The unavailability of a facility for the sitting of the Court in December 2007 has resulted in the non-selection of jurors for the Assizes for the year 2008. The sitting for January 21st to 23rd has had to be cancelled, creating a backlog in the system.

Apart from the issue of Court sittings, there is no Court office which can give rise to a catastrophic situation.

The police as well as private citizens have no place to file actions, fines imposed by the Court cannot be collected, warrants cannot be prepared and executed, fixed penalty tickets for traffic offences cannot be paid, just to give you an idea of the host of problems which are arising.

It has been brought to my attention that arrangements are being made to rent certain premises to arrest this untenable situation. To date, these have not been finalized. In the meantime the people of Carriacou and Petit Martinique are being denied access to justice via the Magistrate's Court.

I urge you therefore, Hon. Minister, to deal with this state of affairs as a matter of urgency. There must be several options which are open to the State in finding a temporary facility for the Court.

I find it difficult to understand how such a situation can arise especially since the Attorney-General of Grenada is the Minister of Carriacou & Petit Martinique Affairs. Surely the people of our sister isles deserve better.

I look forward to your prompt action.
Yours faithfully,

Ruggles Ferguson
President

Cc.Hon Chief Justice. E.C.S.C
Attorney General
Chief Magistrate

*Spice Isle Review, week ending 24 January 2008*

possible. A press conference was held to bring the issue into the public domain. However, the Magistrate did not speak on the matter as he was not authorised to. We both felt he needed a voice to speak for him.

This brought some attention to the inadequacies present at the Carriacou Court. Thereafter the facilities were upgraded; the Court was able to function with some measure of comfort. The president of the Bar Association wrote the Minister for Legal Affairs demanding urgent attention for the court.

## CARRIACOU DRUG BUST

The task of a police officer in solving crimes is sometimes a very difficult one, especially with scarce resources or insufficient training. Forensic science has increased the ability of the police force to solve crimes. In some instances the knowledge of its existence acts as a deterrent.

Possession and trafficking in illegal drugs, with their symbiotic relationship to gang violence, is a scourge, if not a curse, on any society. An accused was charged for possession of and trafficking in cocaine and marijuana with a street value of $227,500.00 and $5,400.00 respectively. The drugs were found well concealed in leather sandals which were allegedly found on the accused's compound. It was reported as a major drug bust in Carriacou, the sister island of Grenada, where activities of that kind were at that time unheard of. Bail was granted to the accused in the sum total of $105,000.00; the trial was due to proceed.

Travelling monthly to Carriacou on the small airplane with Captain De Gale was always a daunting task, despite my interest in flying. I boarded the flight at the Point Salines International Airport now Maurice Bishop International Airport bound to Carriacou. After the flight landed, I took my usual taxi, Uncle Polo, who kept me updated on the happenings in Carriacou. He would explain to me the close knitted nature of the society.

The court house was on the main street in the town close to the bus terminus, so the influx of the public to hear cases was normal. The trial was heard before Magistrate Seales who had an appreciation for legal submissions, expert cross examination, as he would always say, "Your ethics must be intact". The trial started with the cross examination of the prosecution witnesses.

The statements of the witnesses were provided before trial. I had visited the scene where the illegal substance was allegedly found. I was confident that unless there was a drastic departure from the police's initial story, the case would be a difficult one for the prosecution. I cross examined both police officers, their stories did not add up. It was alleged by one of the witnesses that the accused after concealing the drugs in the bushes, made his way through a hole in a fence, close to where he had hid the drugs. The size of the hole was given, as well as a full description of the area where the drugs were found.

I had devised a plan to visit the *locus in quo* or site visit. Therefore when the prosecution closed its case, the defence was called upon to put its case, the application was made to visit the site. This caused some unease as it was unusual for a Magistrate then to accede to visiting crime scenes. This was mostly done at the High Court; however Magistrate Seales acceded to the request.

At the scene it became apparent that the hole in the fence was made by a dog which was tied on the side of the fence, and was visible when we visited. The hole was not large and very close to the ground. Further, the police officers showed where the drugs were to be found at different locations. There were many other inconsistencies. We then returned to the Court. Magistrate Seales adjourned for the preparation of a written judgment. It was the first time I had received an extensive written judgment from the Magistrate's Court. The accused was acquitted. This highlighted the fact that sometimes oral evidence was just not enough to present a thorough case.

## GENTLE GIANT DEPARTS OUR SHORES

Despite the many trials wherein I appeared as Counsel, foremost in my mind has always been my societal responsibility. I never got so consumed in the job that I forgot that aspect of it. Our judiciary has seen a fast turnover of judges. Sometimes they left our shores sooner than we would have wanted them to, but this was never left up to us lawyers, for if it was, Justice Davidson Baptiste would have still been in Grenada. In October 2006, it was time to bid farewell to him. It was difficult for

### Bar bids farewell to Justice Baptiste

*Members of the legal fraternity*

Members of the legal fraternity in Grenada assembled at a Special Sitting at the No 1 High Court on Tuesday morning to bid farewell to Justice Davidson Baptiste who left the island on Wednesday to take up a new posting as resident Judge in his homeland, Dominica.

The outgoing judge is being replaced by Justice Claire Wason-Henry of Antigua whose last posting was in Dominica.

Justice Henry who was expected to arrive on the island on Wednesday is due to start work next week Monday.

The removal of the Dominican jurist comes in rather controversial circumstances following alleged protest at the level of the Judicial and Legal Services Commission (JLCS) of his performance by the Keith Mitchell-led New National Party (NNP) government.

Justice Baptiste was branded as a "bias" person by government's Legal Advisor Hugh Wildman of Jamaica after the judge ruled in a case against him.

Wildman was seeking to overturn a decision taken by the JLCS itself not to appoint him to the post of Attorney-General of Grenada in the face of protest by local lawyers.

public criticism, but warned that judges cannot compromise on justice.

Speaking to reporters shortly after the sitting, the senior high court judge, Justice Kenneth Benjamin said that he was loosing a "brother" in such a short space of time.

And outspoken attorney-at-law, Anslem Clouden, a critic of the Mitchell government pointed out that anytime one starts tampering with judges the way is being paved for anarchy in the country.

Clouden said that it was sad to see Justice Baptiste leave but is taking comfort in the fact that he will continue to maintain the independence of judges and the judiciary.

He branded the judge's removal from serving in Grenada as a loss for the island, adding that he was indeed, "a great man, a great jurist", whose judgements can stand the test of time.

He sees the manner in which Justice Baptiste was being recalled from duties on the island as "a sad day for Grenada when we have an unbricled interference in the judiciary by the executive".

According to Clouden, the members of the local Bar are "all saddened" over the turn of events in Grenada in recent times is nothing but "a gross and crass erosion of the rule of law" by government's legal advisor when he made such "callus" statements in public against the judge.

He is fearful that Grenada under Mitchell's ruling New National Party (NNP) government is heading down a path without law and order.

Opposition Senator George Prime, a barrister-at-law himself also shared the sentiments of Clouden and described the departure of Justice Baptiste as a great loss for the country.

President of the Grenada Bar Association (GBA), Ruggles Ferguson who also spoke on the issue said that local lawyers are extremely concerned about the recent spate of attack on judges by officials of the State.

He said it is no secret that since Justice Baptiste took up post in Grenada from September 2005 he had been the centre of attacks following a number of rulings against the Mitchell government.

He described Baptiste as a "fearless judge" who rules in accordance with the law as he sees it.

Ferguson said that judges may be wrong in their rulings but there is no reason for anyone to go

*Grenada Today, 13 October 2006*

some of us who grew to admire and respect him. I do not think he was aware that he was sometimes referred to as a gentle giant standing above six feet. The members of the legal fraternity were aware of the challenges faced by Justice Baptiste but he never waivered in his commitment to serve. I believed then and was convinced later that Grenada merely moulded him for greater achievement which did come to pass. He now serves as an Appellate Judge in the Court of Appeal of the ECSC.

## BATON PASSED TO JUSTICE HENRY

Justice Clare Henry of Antigua and Barbuda replaced Justice Baptiste. She was a legal eagle paving the way for the continued development of our jurisprudence both in the civil and criminal law. In my view she was able to survive our jurisdiction with the help of her strong belief in God, her resilience and legal acumen. The sticker on her Nissan X-trail read, 'Life is short, pray long'. Justice Henry had a genuine concern for young people, their development and the impact they had on society. She was a judge who imparted knowledge and impacted all. In her clarion calls usually made during the Christmas season which was reported in a local newspaper at the close of the assizes, she urged those listening to:

"Ask for the blessing of the young people of the nation so that the peace of the season would engulf them so that they would avoid confrontation".

In sum Justice Henry's demeanour reminded me of a snippet of a poem by Max Ehrmann:

"Go placidly amidst the noise and haste and remember what peace there may be in silence. As far as possible, without surrender, be on good terms with all persons. Speak your truth quietly and clearly and listen to others, even to the dull and ignorant; they too have their story..."

### Justice Henry is concerned abou young people

*Justice Henry*

High Court Judge, Madam Justice Clare Henry has voiced concern over the large number of young people who are facing criminal charges in Grenada.

Justice Henry was at the time addressing the closing ceremony of the October 2007 Criminal Assizes.

She recalled that when she first began her law practice it was mainly mature people who were facing criminal charges.

According to the female judge, it seems as though the people committing serious offenses now are getting younger and younger.

She urged the jurors to ask for the blessings of the young people of the nation as they seek the peace of the yuletide season.

"Ask for the blessing of the young people of the nation so that the peace of the season would engulf them so that they would avoid confrontation," she told the court sitting.

The final case that was heard during the assizes resulted in a 19-year old youngster from La Poterie, St. Andrew's, Hercules Andrew being found guilty of the murder of 17-year old Skitta Edgar of the same village. At the time of the offence Andrew was 17 years old.

Justice Henry challenged the jurors to allow the experience that they would have had during the assizes to have a positive impact on their lives and that of their community.

The October Assizes ended with just over 50 percent of the cases on the cause list being completed.

The senior judge felt that it was a successful session, adding that the quality of the justice that came out of the assizes was the important thing and not the number of cases heard.

Eighty-two cases were listed on the cause list. Out of that number, 49 cases were completed and 33 traversed to the next Assizes which is scheduled to begin on February 5, 2008.

Thirteen sexual offenses were completed, while three were disposed of.

Out of the nine murder cases on the list only two were heard, while one of the manslaughter c was disposed of. of the 11 housebr ing and stealing c were completed.

The court learn as of Thursday December 2007 6:00 a. m. there 385 inmates conf at the Richmond Prison.

From that num there are 265 m and eight females are convicted. males and one fen on remand, 41 m awaiting trial, appellants, and prohibited im grants.

*Grenada Today, 28 December 2007*

## DEATH IN POLICE CUSTODY

The sister island of Carriacou was generally a peaceful, serene island with a population of about 5000, a single police station and hospital. A very close knit society.

On the 10th June 2001, a young man died allegedly while in police custody. The facts surrounding the death were inconclusive as to time, place and cause of death. This case sparked much public emotion. The media, including television and radio stations, were buzzing with discussions surrounding the death and the alleged cause or causes. Speculation escalated to boiling point.

There were no criminal charges laid. However, a coroner's inquest was ordered to enable inquiries into the death. Four police officers were brought in for the purpose of the inquiry together with numerous witnesses.

With a Coroner's inquest there must be a total of five (5) jurors who are persons from the community, normally selected from the jury list. I recall thinking how impossible it would have been to have a fair hearing in such an emotionally charged environment, let alone the society from whence the jurors came. But I had faith in the jury system.

### Six witnesses appeared at 'Tools' trial

Joseph's mother, Ohenia Sylvester and sister, Rose Sylvester.

They were cross examined by Attorney, Derek Sylvester, who is acting on behalf of the four police officers accused in the June 10, 2001 death of the 42-year old Joseph.

Appearing on behalf of the family was Nazim Burke of Ciboney chamber.

The court, which included a five-member jury and members of the family of the decease, heard several statementsfrom the witnesses.

Rose told the court that when she was told of her brother's death she came to enquire at the police station where she said he was locked up for the night.

While there, she added, she saw blood looking substance coming from the in-side the station.

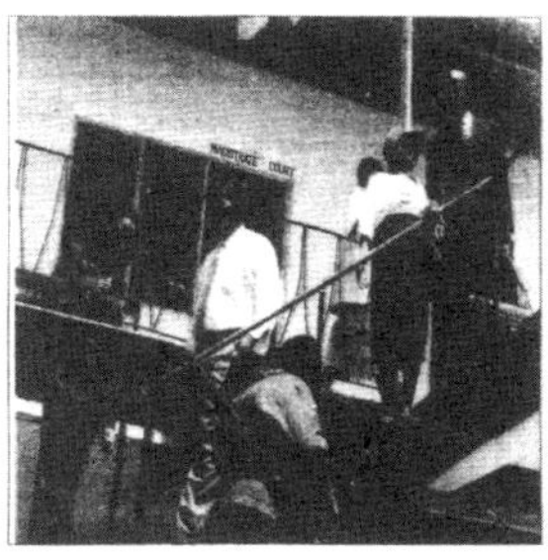

She told the court upon enquiring she was told by an officer that "a dog that died there".

She said she then questioned the officer "So all you locking up dogs now".

The police van, she told the court, also had blood looking stains.

She also spoke of being told by an officer that her brother died in the village of Caco.

She also told the court of her brother's body bearing marks.

However she, like all other witnesses was strongly cross examined by Sylvester.

*Grenada Informer, 30 June 2006*

There was some anxiety on both sides since the outcome of the Coroner's inquest could ultimately lead to the Director of Public Prosecutions laying criminal charges against the policemen. There was a total of twenty six (26) witnesses. The travel to Carriacou for that matter seemed unending, but I had an obligation to fulfil.

It was a sad case because a life was lost. The family of the deceased wanted to get to the bottom of what actually transpired. It must have been painful for the mother and other family members to lose a loved one. Further, not knowing what actually transpired. In addition, they would have been constantly bombarded with news about the deceased, whether true or false. It must have caused great anxiety while they travelled along a road littered with grief and sorrow.

The matter soon ended. I could not help but think there was no way the police officers would get a fair hearing. But on the other hand, I felt the jurors had an obligation, a sacred one at that. The hearing came to an end. It was inconclusive on a number of issues which could have grounded a criminal charge. The jurors listened. It was evident they answered the questions posed to them only by the evidence presented, for if they had deviated one iota, the outcome may have been different.

The hearing was a public one. Numerous members of the public including members of the deceased family were present at the Coroner's hearing. This was important in enabling the society at large to be dissuaded from pointing fingers and misstating the facts. Carriacou had to rebuild the trust of the police; and vice versa. This happened in very short order.

The outcome of the inquest was such that there was no evidence to indict the police officers.

## MAD MAX ON TRIAL

The law has piqued my interest since childhood. As I grew older my legal appetite expanded. After receiving my licence to practise, it exceeded my expectation, for the nature, category and types of matters I had to deal with were sometimes mind boggling, yet very interesting.

Clients with mental issues always caused me some anxiety, for two reasons. Firstly, the unpredictability of their actions. Secondly, I would ask or say something which would get them angry or trigger them off.

*Front page, Grenada Informer, week ending 27 July 2007*

There was an accused who constantly visited the police station confessing to the killing of his girlfriend and burying her. He was, however, known to have a mental condition. Consequently, he was not taken seriously. So he continued with his reports. On one occasion he went to the Criminal Investigation Department and made the report. He demanded to take the police to the site where she was buried; to the shock and surprise of the officers, the report was true.

I was tasked with the responsibility of representing the accused. Although I had some concerns for my safety, I decided to visit the accused. Upon meeting the accused, I noticed he was about six feet two inches tall, approximately 220 pounds. I was not expecting that giant. I knew he could have snapped my neck like a twig. But I was determined to show no fear. I sat with him where he was confined. I later learnt from him that he believed he was Jesus and had the ability to walk on water. I declined a demonstration. He also indicated that he had a monkey brain, among some other very interesting facts. Then he descended into speaking gibberish. When I tried to bring him back to English, my efforts failed; it appeared as if he was getting a bit upset, so I responded in gibberish. He seemed to understand me perfectly well. Years after I would still laugh at how I communicated with the accused in his language. I never understood myself but he seemed very happy that I was fluent in his language.

## Killer deemed unfit to stand trial

St. Andrew's man ...ged in connection ... the death and ...ial of his girlfriend September of 2005, ... been listed as unfit ... stand trial.

...ouglas Forbes, a ... well-known to ... administration at ... Mt. Gay Mental ...spital due to his ...quent visit to that ...ility for his mental ...blem, was ordered ...e detained at Her ...jesty's Pleasure for ...role in the death ... his lover, Ann-... Francois of St. ...drew.

High Court Judge, ...nneth Benjamin, ...nded down sentence ...ursday, moments ...er a team of Jurors ...d that Forbes was ...it to stand trial.

...heir verdict hinges ... strong medical ...dence from doctor, ...o examined Forbes ...ile in prison and his ... history of mental ...blems.

...he doctor described ...bes' condition as ...chotic, meaning he ...s not in sine with ...lity. Often-time, the doctor said, these persons are disillusioned, controlled by external forces and received external messages.

People like Forbes, the doctor said, experience their own reality different from the normal person.

The doctor further stated that Forbes is one case where anti-psychotic treatment has not helped after three years and therefore the likelihood of improvement look grim.

Dean Lawrence of the Prosecution, in her address to the Jury, stated that being able to mount a defense including advising Council is an essential element of coming to Court and based on the doctor's evidence, it seems unlikely that Forbes possesses those qualities.

Defense Counsel, Derek Sylvester, also endorsed the doctor and prosecution's claim that Forbes, a man who profess to be Jesus walking on water, having a monkey brain and giving his name as Rudolph Max...

among others, is not capable of advising in Council on the charge for which he appeared in Court.

Judge Benjamin, acting on Section 180 Sub-Section 1 of the Criminal Code, decided not to proceed with the normal trial, but instructed the jury to deliberate and returned a verdict on the suitability of the accused to stand trial.

Forbes was taken into custody for allegedly killing his girlfriend and burying the body. It was hinted at the time that he made his action known to the Police, but they failed to take him serious until Forbes took on his own and told his story to the CID.

He later took the police to the place where he buried his ex-lover.

The body was dug up and Forbes was subsequently arrested and charged in connection with the offence.

*Grenada Informer, 27 July 2007*

Then it became evident that medical intervention was necessary. An accused who cannot give instructions is every defence lawyer's nightmare. Thereafter, I approached the prosecution department. It was agreed that medical and psychological interventions were necessary. The medical evidence was presented before the Court. Justice Kenneth Benjamin presided. It became apparent that even in the absence of the medical evidence, the accused was a man unfit to stand trial. After the presentation of the medical evidence the jury had no difficulty in coming to a conclusion as to the fitness of the accused. He was deemed unfit and kept in confinement, at the pleasure of the State or until he became so fit to be tried.

## PRISON LIFE

I had numerous experiences with young persons who vowed never to return to the prison. They have kept their word because they realised that life in there was so different from the free world. There were inmates who would literally shed tears about the thought of returning to prison and others who did not. I recalled an incident while at the Grenville Magistrate's Court, an accused begged of me to support his plea of not returning to prison. There were inmates who found it difficult to acclimatise to prison life. These are the ones who would not return.

It is a resounding lesson to all that crime also destroys the perpetrator. In one of the pieces by Oscar Wilde he wrote:

*The vilest deeds like poison weeds*
*Bloom well in prison-air*
*It is only what is good in Man*
*That wastes and withers there*

When young men embark on a criminal enterprise with a gun, the result can be disastrous, and lead to death. In July 2007, two young men sought to rob a gas station, during which the attendant was shot dead. The trial

## Inmate wants freedom from conflicts at Her Majesty's Prison

A prison inmate who appeared at the Grenville Magistrate's Court last Monday, is appealing for freedom claiming that he does not want to return to the life of conflict in jail.

The young man who sports a dreadlocks, is on remand in connection with a number of criminal offences. He told the Court that he did not wanted to return. His matter is not yet completed but he is begging for freedom.

His sentiment was further endorsed by Barrister at law Derick Sylvester who was also present in Court. Sylvester gave examples of incidents of that nature which occurred in prison and has since become a serious concern.

He also pointed out that there was an instance where an inmate suffered a broken nose and has lost a number of teeth. Another inmate also raises the issue of an outbreak of chicken pox in prison.

*Grenada Informer, 12 May 2006*

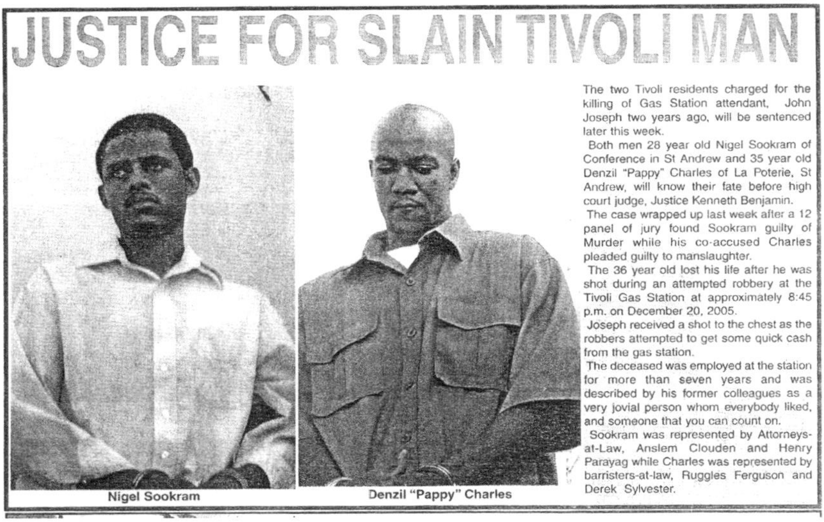

# JUSTICE FOR SLAIN TIVOLI MAN

The two Tivoli residents charged for the killing of Gas Station attendant, John Joseph two years ago, will be sentenced later this week.

Both men 28 year old Nigel Sookram of Conference in St Andrew and 35 year old Denzil "Pappy" Charles of La Poterie, St Andrew, will know their fate before high court judge, Justice Kenneth Benjamin.

The case wrapped up last week after a 12 panel of jury found Sookram guilty of Murder while his co-accused Charles pleaded guilty to manslaughter.

The 36 year old lost his life after he was shot during an attempted robbery at the Tivoli Gas Station at approximately 8:45 p.m. on December 20, 2005.

Joseph received a shot to the chest as the robbers attempted to get some quick cash from the gas station.

The deceased was employed at the station for more than seven years and was described by his former colleagues as a very jovial person whom everybody liked, and someone that you can count on.

Sookram was represented by Attorneys-at-Law, Anslem Clouden and Henry Parayag while Charles was represented by barristers-at-law, Ruggles Ferguson and Derek Sylvester.

Nigel Sookram

Denzil "Pappy" Charles

*Front page, Grenada Today, week ending 16 March 2007*

was premised on who the shooter was, even though legally the prosecution relied on joint enterprise; they both could have been convicted for murder. The jury is sometimes more inclined to bring a verdict of murder for the shooter and some lesser offence for the accomplice. However, I had seen many instances where the accomplice received the same verdict.

In the middle of the trial both Ruggles Ferguson and I accepted the prosecution offer of a plea of guilty to the lesser count of manslaughter for our client. The trial proceeded with the other accused. We decided trial was a risk not worth taking. Sometimes as a defence lawyer you let your instinct guide you; coupled, of course, with your client's instructions. The accused was sentenced on completion of the trial.

With trials, whether civil or criminal, medical evidence may be very crucial in determining liability, guilt or innocence. Within the sphere of human existence and one's profession there would always be mixed views or opinions, either coming from experts or lay people. For even science is not exact. It is normally determined by a greater or lesser probability.

In criminal trials the Court is always called upon to determine which expert would be accepted, the defence's or the prosecution's. On many occasions even before the matter rests with the jury, the lawyer has to determine which one of the experts was most likely to be believed; whether there was any deficiency in their respective medical reports, or a third expert may be necessary.

## THE IMPORTANCE OF MEDICAL EXPERT EVIDENCE

There were two matters where medical experts were called upon to help the Court determine the veracity of the prosecution's case. On one occasion prior to the laying of a charge, a two year old child died, the cause of death was conflicting. It was either drowning or an injury inflicted by an adult. The medical report of one pathologist was conclusive of an abdominal injury which could have also equated to a fall; the other merely ruled out drowning.

The accused was charged with the offence of murder which was later reduced to manslaughter at the Supreme Court, by the office of the Director of Public Prosecutions. This highlights the intricacies of medical evidence and its importance in determining culpability. Medical science does get it right, but like everything else there would tend to be a modicum of doubt. Hence proof in criminal matters requires that the prosecution must prove its case beyond a reasonable doubt, that the jury must feel sure of the guilt of the accused, whereas in civil matters, a balance of probability is all that is required.

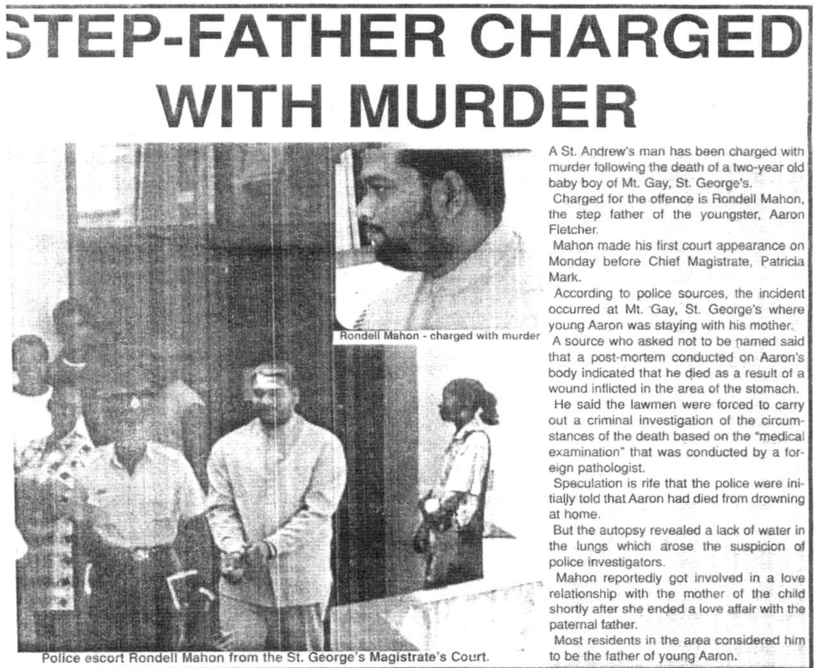

STEP-FATHER CHARGED WITH MURDER

Rondell Mahon - charged with murder

Police escort Rondell Mahon from the St. George's Magistrate's Court.

A St. Andrew's man has been charged with murder following the death of a two-year old baby boy of Mt. Gay, St. George's.

Charged for the offence is Rondell Mahon, the step father of the youngster, Aaron Fletcher.

Mahon made his first court appearance on Monday before Chief Magistrate, Patricia Mark.

According to police sources, the incident occurred at Mt. Gay, St. George's where young Aaron was staying with his mother.

A source who asked not to be named said that a post-mortem conducted on Aaron's body indicated that he died as a result of a wound inflicted in the area of the stomach.

He said the lawmen were forced to carry out a criminal investigation of the circumstances of the death based on the "medical examination" that was conducted by a foreign pathologist.

Speculation is rife that the police were initially told that Aaron had died from drowning at home.

But the autopsy revealed a lack of water in the lungs which arose the suspicion of police investigators.

Mahon reportedly got involved in a love relationship with the mother of the child shortly after she ended a love affair with the paternal father.

Most residents in the area considered him to be the father of young Aaron.

*Front page, Grenada Today, week ending 11 May 2007*

In another matter, an accused was charged for the murder of his wife. The first autopsy concluded cardiac arrest, the second autopsy concluded manual strangulation. The defence pathologist excluded the possibility of manual strangulation.

It was a test of the experts. The jury was left to determine the likely cause of death based on all the evidence presented to the court. Jurors are sometimes placed in a position which requires them to be almost medically Solomonic. There were three pathologists. Two from the Republic of Trinidad and Tobago, the other from Grenada.

The medical professional variation on the cause of death and apparent rivalry was evident throughout the trial. The pathologists were all determined to convince the court that their individual professional position was correct. In the end the prosecution's expert's theory was accepted by the jury. The accused was convicted of murder. The Court of Appeal upheld the decision.

Historically, crimes were generally against the person or property. However with the development in technology, there has been an explosion of cybercrimes, electronic fraud, ATM fraud and much more.

HUSBAND CHARGED WITH MURDER

Another murder has gripped the Tri-island State of Grenada pushing the murder total for the year to six.

Officers attached to the Criminal Investigations Department (CID) in St. George's arrested and charged 40-year old Nigel Abraham, a school teacher, for the murder of his wife Bernadette Abraham both of whom lived at Morne Delice, St Paul's.

Nigel made his first court appearance before Chief Magistrate Patricia Mark on Tuesday amidst a crowd of curious onlookers who gathered to get a first hand look at the man charged with murder in connection with his wife's death.

He is being represented by Attorneys-at-law Peter David of Ciboney Chambers and Derek Sylvester.

During the hearing, Sylvester told the court that he would like the matter to be dealt with expeditiously.

Residents of the area told this newspaper that the suspect was having rather strained relationship with his wife in recent months.

He was reportedly seeing a female employee at one of the departments at the St. George's General Hospital.

The body of 36-year old Bernadette was discovered by a neighbour at her home on June 23. She was a teacher at the St Paul's Government School.

Her husband, Nigel, a black belt karate expert, was formally charged after extensive investigations by members of the CID and findings of a

(Continues on page 3)

School teacher Nigel Abraham - charged with the murder of his wife

The deceased Bernadette Abraham

A section of the crowd that assembled outside the Magistrate's Court to get a glimpse of the murder accused

*Front page, Grenada Today, week ending 7 July 2006*

## Husband Charged With Murder

*• FROM FRONT PAGE*

June 23. She was a teacher at the St Paul's Government School.

Her husband, Nigel, a black belt karate expert, was formally charged after extensive investigations by members of the CID and findings of a forensic expert flown into Grenada from Trinidad and Tobago.

Police moved quickly to bring in outside forensic help after neighbours and family members started to make increasing complaints to them that they suspected foul play in the death.

An earlier autopsy conducted by a Grenadian medical doctor who was trained in Cuba had indicated that the female school teacher had died from a massive heart attack.

Well placed sources told this newspaper that the lawmen contacted a Pathologist from neighbouring Trinidad and

*Nigel Abraham*

day before her husband was picked up by local police officers and interrogated.

The husband allegedly told someone that his wife reported that she was not feeling well and had told him that she was going to see a doctor.

It is said that he went to work as usual and called back home to check on his wife but got no response to his phone calls.

There are reports that he called a neighbour and asked the individual to check on his wife, only to find out that she was dead.

It was also reported that when the couple's two children wanted to bid goodbye to their mother before leaving home for school they were stopped by the father who told them to leave their mother alone since she was not feeling well.

Director of Public Prosecutor (DPP), Christopher Nelson is appearing on behalf of the State in the matter.

Nigel has been remanded at the Richmond Hill Prison and is due to return to court on July 20 for the start of the Preliminary Inquiry into the murder case.

Sources close to the murder suspect confided in this newspaper that he is confident of proving his innocence of the charge in a free and fair trial.

The defense is said to be relying heavily on the conflicting conclusions by the two pathologists who examined the body of Bernadette Abraham.

*Grenada Today, 7 July 2006*

## SCHOOL TEACHER FOUND GUILTY

Bernadette Abraham, wife off Nigel, was discovered strangled to death; DD Christopher Nelson says he is not surprised at the verdict handed down by the jurors in this matter - Nigel Abraham wil be sentenced on March 18th 2008

*Front page, Grenada Informer, week ending 14 March 2008*

## School Teacher found guilty of strangling wife

*Defence Attorney Sylvester to call character witnesses*

Jurors at the Number one Supreme Court say former Primary School teacher Nigel Abraham is guilty of murdering his wife Bernadette Abraham, a former teacher at the St. Paul's Model School.

The team of Jurors, comprising ten women and two men, arrived at their decision after some two hours of deliberation in jury room midday last Thursday.

Bernadette died between the 22nd and the 23rd June 2006 at her home in St. Pauls.

After two autopsies done on her body, doctors came to the conclusion that Bernadette's deaths was not as a result of heart failure as earlier thought; instead it was as a result of manual strangulation.

Moments after releasing their findings, Bernadette's husband, Nigel was arrested and subsequently charged in connection with his

During the High Court trial that lasted just over two weeks the Prosecution team, lead by Director of Public Prosecution Christopher Nelson, called several witnesses to prove his circumstantial case against Abraham. Among them were the daughters of Nigel and Bernadette Abraham.

Highly emotional during their stint on the witness stand, having lost their mom and having to speak on matters that could also put their father away for the rest of his life, the children spoke of that dreaded morning 23rd June 2006.

The younger of the two daughters told the Court that having gotten ready for school she went into the room to bid her mom good bye but she did not respond and therefore she left for school.

She was careful to note that there was some evidence of blood in front her the sheet.

The elder of the two daughter said her dad told her that mom was not feeling well and therefore she did not entered the room, but stayed in the passage and saw her mom lying on the bed.

While in school the young lady said she got a call asking that she report to the office, and subsequently from her dad who told her that something had happened home but that she should remain in school until someone came to get her.

The young lady said she was later taken home by another teacher and on her arrival she met some neighbors at her home and her dad inside her room crying.

Shortly after completing her stint on the witness stand the young lady had to be taken off the Court room as she burst into tears.

The first medical person who arrived on the scene was a nurse from the casualty division of the General Hospital who accompanied the ambulance to the Abraham's home.

She told the Court she got there after 9am as a result of a call received at the hospital.

The nurse said she called Bernadette and there was no response. She tested for pulse and the rise and fall of the chest and there was none.

What was strange, the nurse said, was that she attempted to turn the body, but found the body unusually cold and that she was unable fact she said, the body turned like a statue.

The nurse said that she informed Nigel what the situation was and advised him to call the district doctor.

Bernadette was pronounced dead by the district doctor Tam Tam and like the nurse he found the body cold and joints unable to stretch.

Dr. Tam Tam concluded that Bernadette could have died some six to seven hours prior to his examination.

In his defense, Nigel told the Court in an unsworn statement that he loved his wife and would do nothing to hurt her.

He went on to say that on the morning of June 23rd he got up early after 3 a.m to prepare for school and while putting things together his wife got up and told him that she was not feeling well. He asked her if she wanted some hot tea. She said no, went to the bathroom and went back to bed.

Before leaving for school he said he prepared breakfast, went to tie his animal but before leaving the house for school he spoke to his wife and she responded.

He then went to school and while at school he called a neighbour to have them check on his wife, knowing that she was not in the best of health.

Shortly after speaking to his neighbor, he said he got a second call suggesting that all was not well and that he should come home.

Nigel told the Court that although they had their dark moments, he and his wife had a lovely relationship. They went to the beach together, took out mortgage together and things were looking up for them.

that his wife, at times take care of all the bills in the home when it was time for him to pay for his exams. "It would have been stupid of me," he told the Court, "to do anything that would have made me worst off".

The former teacher and martial art black belt told the Court the two years he spent on remand were by far the most stressful time spent in his entire life, not having his wife and his children by his side.

His final words to the Court were "I loved my wife, I love my wife, and I love my wife".

Among the fourteen witnesses called by the Prosecution to prove the case against Nigel was Trinidadian Pathologist Dr. Daisley who did the final autopsy on the body and concluded that Bernadette died from manual strangulation.

His conclusion was based on several observations including that of fingernail marking on Bernadette's neck, darken fingers, and other signs that are consistent with that of manual strangulation.

The defense team, lead by Attorney at Law Derrick Sylvester, refuted that finding and through one Dr. Devigney, said that Bernadette's death was natural.

At the end of the day however, the Jury went on the side of the Prosecution and found Nigel guilty as charged.

Moments after that pronouncement was made DPP Christopher Nelson told the Court that he would not be seeking the death penalty.

High Court Judge Claire Henry deferred Sentencing to March 18th at which time the Court requested a social services and a phosphoric report.

Defense Lawyer told members of the media that he would be calling character witnesses to speak on his client's behalf with regards to his next move. He said there are several options open to him; however he would be awaiting the sentencing before making his next move.

Asked whether he was surprised with the ruling, Sylvester said in the practice of law nothing comes as a surprise.

DPP Nelson, on the other hand, said he is not at all surprised with the dec[illegible] sion. The Prosec[illegible] tion, he said, had strong case despi[illegible] the fact that it w[illegible] based on circu[illegible] stantial evidence.

Nelson said t[illegible] evidence pointed only one directio[illegible] that death was n[illegible] natural and that was only the husba[illegible] that would have h[illegible] access to her du[illegible] ing that time and t[illegible] Jury followed th[illegible] and therefore this w[illegible] no surprise.

Thursday's rulin[illegible] could put Nigel b[illegible] hind bars for the re[illegible] of his life.

*Grenada Informer, 14 March 2008*

## School Teacher sentence to 15 yearsa in prison

Former primary school teacher, Nigel Abraham, will spend the next fifteen years of his life behind the Richmond Hill Prison bars for causing the death of his wife, a former teacher, by manual strangulation.

Abraham had the sentence of the Court slapped on him last Thursday by high Court Judge Claire Henry almost two months after Jurors found him guilty of murdering his wife Bernadette Abraham.

Bernadette's lifeless body was discovered by a neighbour who was at the time acting on the advice of her husband, Nigel Abraham, who simply wanted to make sure that his wife was ok, she having complained of not feeling well during the course of the night.

Having made the discovery, the neighbour raised an alarm, bringing to the scene not only scores of persons from within the neighbourhood but medical expert who subsequently carried out an autopsy that revealed Mrs. Abraham died from a massive heart attacked.

That finding was however quickly refuted when a second autopsy was ordered and suggested that Mrs. Abraham died from manual strangulation.

During his three weeks trial Abraham speaking from the dock on the advice of his lawyer Derrick Sylvester, told the Court that he loved his wife and would do nothing to hurt her.

Abraham told the Court that his wife

## Convicted Teacher Sentenced To 15 Years Imprisonment

Secondary School Teacher, Nigel Abraham has been made to pay for the grievous crime he committed in June 2006 in murdering his wife of 16 years, Bernadette.

The 43-year old teacher of St. Paul's, St. George's was found guilty on March 5 for the murder, and was due to be sentenced on March 18. However, sentencing of the convicted teacher was deferred for the June Assizes due to a request of a social inquiry report made by the defense council, Derick Sylvester to be done on his client by the Ministry of Social Development before sentencing is handed down.

High Court Judge, Madam Justice Clare Henry handed down a 15-year prison term on Abraham last week Thursday.

At the conclusion of the case, Director of Public Prosecution (DPP) Christopher Nelson gave early notice to the court that his Office was not seeking the death penalty.

Sylvester described his client as a model prisoner.

Abraham is currently engaged in teaching

*Above: Grenada Informer, 18 July 2008*

*Left: Grenada Today, 18 July 2008*

Keith Scotland, an attorney from the Republic of Trinidad and Tobago, and I had the responsibility of representing some non-nationals for money laundering, by the use of the ATM to facilitate financial fraud. The skills used to perpetrate the fraud showed a deep knowledge of the working of the computerised machine. They were convicted.

Soon thereafter, a technique referred to as the Lebanese loop was used to rob the ATMs. Despite the technique, the perpetrators were caught. Peter David and I represented the accused. Despite any possible defence, in the face of voluntary confessions, the plea of guilty was the only recourse. I learnt that trials should be encouraged always but one must always examine what were the calculated risks of trial. If the benefit outweighed the risk, then choose wisely.

The mysteries of criminal trials, the possible verdicts in the high court are dependent on the decision of nine sometimes twelve jurors; a system we refer to as the jury system. There are many arguments for and against

## Jail For Money Launderers

olice Officers attached the Financial ntelligence Unit (FIU) sited Flamboyant otel in Morne Rouge, t George's where they et and spoke with the otel manager, awrence Lambert.

According to Inspector rewen, Lambert led e officers to room umber 2?1 where they und both Conway and usaf.

When questioned both omen told the officers at they had 10,000.00 in their possession but a search of e room recovered a um of EC$61,000.00.

Also discovered were Vestern Union transfer eceipts, Republic Bank ithdrawal slips and arious bundles of ther bank drafts, along ith three laptop computers.

When taken to the FIU ffice, Conway and usaf confessed that hey were able to obtain the money from local commercial banks, through the use of various ATM Cards. They further confessed to having already sent $2,000.00 out of Grenada.

That money, according to the Police Prosector, was intercepted and did not reach its target place outside the island.

Yusuf was represented by Trinidadian attorney-at-law, Keith Scotland, while Conway was represented by local attorney Derek Sylvester.

Yusuf who obtained refugee status in Canada as a Permanent Resident, was on vacation in Antigua where she met up with Conway.

Moments after the sentencing, Scotland told a group of reporters it is likely they may appeal the verdict.

He said this is always an option available for someone who is incarcerated and is aggrieved by the sentence received.

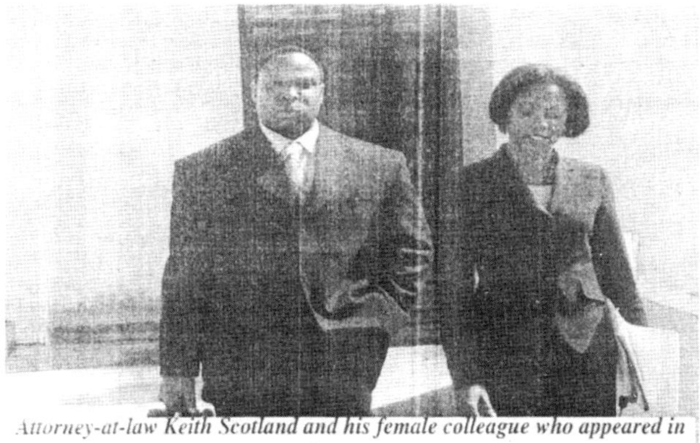

*Attorney-at-law Keith Scotland and his female colleague who appeared in the matter*

*Grenada Today, 2 November 2007*

# Trinis in court again!!!

*The three Trini tricksters captured on the day of their appointment before Chief Magistrate, Patricia Mark*

The three Trinidadian taken into custody for alleged fraud in connection with some ATM machines belonging to local banks are expected to make their second Court appearance Thursday before Chief Magistrate Patricia Mark.

Forty-nine-year old Kelvin Snagg, 44-year old Derek Maloney, and 23-year old Kristol Pereira have been charged with 11 counts of stealing.

The Trinis made their first court appearance last week Wednesday but were remanded to the Richmond Hill prison.

The police and the local banks have been praised by members of the public over the speec with which they moved to nab the culprits following investigations into a number of withdrawals from the Automated Teller Machines.

Reports are that the lawmen recovered thousands of dollars that the suspects allegedly managed to withdraw from some machines, including $18,000.00 from an account belonging to a German couple.

The trio arrived in the country on April 07 and within two days of their stay had allegedly tampered with ATM machines in both St George and Grand Anse.

It is believed that the suspects used what is known as the Lebanese Loop, an illegal device inserted into the card reader that captures the card, which the fraudster later retrieves, after offering to assist the affected customer and getting him/her to reveal their PIN.

The three accused T&T Nationals are being represented by Attorney-at-law Peter David and Derek Sylvester.

*Grenada Today, 2 November 2007*

it, even replacing it with trial by judges. Some are of the view that if the system is not broken then there is no need to fix it. However, no system is perfect; but perfection is to be pursued even though it may not be attainable.

I recall a distinct phase in my professional life when I had to reflect on the persons who really assisted me in my legal journey. My grandmother whose contribution was invaluable, my mother whose prayers never ceased, their mutual love nurtured me to who I am today.

While I was involved in a myriad of cases, one day I was approached by a local newspaper to tell more of my life story, to explain the reasons I wanted to study law. Initially, I felt it was a bit intrusive to get into my life but then I was a servant of the people. They had a right to know. I sat with the reporter from the *Grenada Informer*. I gave a brief story of what my life entailed and what I looked forward to.

DERRICK SYLVESTER:
The new kid in the legal fraternity who vows to make a difference

*"There is a fallacy out there that lawyers are dishonest and I have a duty in the practice to do whatever I can to reverse that belief, it matters not how small, but I believe that I should be able to do that by the nature of my practice. I want to make a mark in the legal profession of being one who is hard working, honest dedicated and love the law"*

[illegible]

In fact, Sylvester went further to say that he owes a debt of gratitude to partners at the Cyboney Chambers among them Peter David, Ruggles Ferguson, Nazim Burke and Leron Lowe for the assistance given to him in attaining the level of success he now enjoys.

In September 2005 Sylvester felt that the time had come to go alone and he took the bold decision to launch his firm Derrick Sylvester and Associate, a name which today continues to hold its own among leading law firms on the Island.

[illegible]

"It was never easy" Sylvester said "and I have a lot of people to be thankful to for helping me to climb that ladder of success and choosing the right path, key among them is my grand mother, a woman who was always there for me when the going got tough".

Why Law

"My desire to study law was always my quest to see justice prevailed and becoming engulf in the belief that lawyers had that ability to chart the course of human beings in history and wanting to be a part of that process of change".

[illegible]

"I should not be seen as a lawyer who is just there for taking clients money, my clients must respect me. I must be professional and therefore we must be free to communicate".

As an attorney, Sylvester said, "I want to leave a legacy, for my children and grandchildren. Derrick Sylvester, he said, must be remembered as honest, hard-working, dedicated, respectful, compassionate and most of all God-fearing".

[illegible]

"My focus for the new year is minized negativity and maximized"

"Never be content with failure because success is all one should aspire; and ignorance is the root to misfortune." This Sylvester said would always be his motto.

Attorney-at-Law Derrick Sylvester in Office

*Grenada Informer, 11 January 2008*

# MILLION DOLLAR DRUG BUST

The influx of illegal drugs can have a deleterious effect on the society. The police are normally called upon to perform a colossal task of surveillance, counter surveillance, intelligence which ultimately leads to detention arrest and interrogation.

I was instructed to represent an accused who was charged with possession of a significant amount of cocaine. In trying to apprehend the accused the police embarked upon a high speed chase which took them from Green Bridge in St. George's, through River Road, Tempe, Marrast Hill, Richmond Hill, Morne Jaloux, De Faux, Springs, and terminating in Jean Anglais.

The chase was abruptly halted when the tyres of the accused's vehicle were blown out by police bullets or the road terrain, depending on which version of the story you believed. In any event the accused was detained. The drugs were allegedly found some distance away from the parked vehicle. He was subsequently arrested and charged.

High speed chase ends in

$M DRUG BUST

FIU investigating internet lottery ar money scams

Some of the cheques that were recov

*Front page, Grenada Informer, week ending 28 November 2008*

## High speed chase ends in million dollar drug bust

A thirty-eight year-old (38) Belmont man, held in connection with last Thursday's high speed million dollars drug bust in the city of St. George's, has been denied bail.

Stephan Martin Alec appeared before Chief Magistrate Henry Paryag at the St. George's Magistrate's Court on Tuesday where two summary charges - namely possession and trafficking a controlled drug, were read to him in the presence of his lawyer, Derick Sylvester.

Alec pleaded not guilty to both charges and, through his lawyer, made an application for bail, which was strongly opposed by Police Prosecutor Andall, bringing to the fore several grounds for the Prosecution's position.

Among these, Andall stated, was the quantity of drug involved - some 53 kilos of cocaine with a street value of EC$4.5 million dollars, the likely penalty that can be imposed raises strong possibility that the defendant may not show up for his trial, given his trade 'sea man' makes it easy for Alec to leave the jurisdiction, fairs that he may interfere with the investigation.

The Police Prosecutor also hinted that Alec was convicted in two Caribbean countries for similar offenses, but that was condemned by Defense Council, telling the Court that these were matters outside this jurisdiction and therefore, as far as his client is concerned, he has a clean record in Grenada.

After listening the arguments from both sides, Magistrate Paryag told the Court although he has strong reservations about not granting persons bail, since they are presumed innocent until proven otherwise by the Court, the quantity of drugs involved in this matter is rather large and therefore, he is of the view that granting bail could be a risk.

Alec was therefore remanded to the Richmond Hill Prison until his next Court appearance on 16th December.

Although a summary charge was read to the defendant on Tuesday, there are strong possibilities that the lawman may elevate the charge to indictable.

Whatever the outcome, Alec faces, on summary conviction, EC$250,000.00 or five years in prison or both on each count if found guilty, and on an indictable conviction EC$500,000.00 or 20 years or both on each count if found guilty.

Alec was captured in a high speed police chase that ended in the Jean Anglais area in St. George.

Sources told INFORMER Alec refused to obey police instruction to stop in the River Road area. That raised suspicion and as a result, the police decided to pursue to speeding car.

The chase, we were told, ended when the officer shot the wheels of the moving car in the Jean Anglais area. The drug, contained in 55 packets, were subsequently discovered in the nearby bushes while Alec, the alleged driver of the speeding vehicle, who then attempted to flee on foot, was also caught in the said area.

During his address to the Court on Tuesday Sylvester said his client's right to council was seriously violated when officers at the Police Station denied him access to visit the detainee.

Sylvester said he was told that the investigating officer left instructions that visitors, including Council, should not be allowed to see Alec and this is a direct violation of the Judge's rules.

Police Prosecution responded by saying that the reason for denying Council's visiting rights was that the matter was still under investigation.

*Grenada Informer, 28 November 2008*

The matter was indictable, therefore the case was first heard at the lower court, wherein I represented the accused, before it went before a Judge and jury, at which stage the accused represented himself. However, at the appellate level I represented the accused. The value of the drugs being EC$4.5 million dollars aroused the interest of the media and public. The chase was also historic because normally in Grenada a chase would end much sooner. Interestingly, it was the accused's defence that he was an unlicensed driver. He therefore tried to evade the police, all to no avail. The version presented by the police was different.

It was common belief among the public that lawyers always carried the truth about their clients in their back pocket. They believed that by representing accused persons, this was an indication we condoned their action rather than condemned it. The former is the furthest from the truth.

At the High Court the accused was sentenced to twenty five (25) years imprisonment. At the appellate level the sentence was reduced to twelve (12) years imprisonment.

## PATRICIA MARK – CHIEF MAGISTRATE – RETIRED

Judicial officers have a heavy mandate, they are expected to perform excellently, be unbiased, noble and diligent. During their legal life, they must stay true to the law. In the process, individuals, organisations or even the executive may be aggrieved by their decisions. The sole avenue to ventilate that discontentment is by way of resort to the Courts to challenge actions taken against them. Lawyers and litigants alike have a duty to respect the judiciary and its judgments. Moreover, the ethics of the profession demand that members of the judiciary cannot speak publicly, to any legal matter on which they had adjudicated.

Patricia Mark, Chief Magistrate, was the first judicial officer I had appeared before as an attorney. I admired her professionalism as a judicial officer. She was polite, respectful and firm, a triad of qualities worthy of emulation. When it was time for her retirement, the Permanent Secretary in the Ministry of Legal Affairs wrote her, advising of her imminent retirement, stating the Ministry's intention to write to the Governor General that she be removed from the public service. The newspaper got wind of the story. It became a headline.

There was a constitutional challenge mounted against the procedural irregularity in the manner of the request. The legal challenge launched by constitutional expert Dr. Francis Alexis wherein the pith and substance

NNP MOVING TO FIR[E]
PATRICIA MARK

MINISTRY OF LEGAL AFFAIRS
COMMUNAL HOUSE
414 H.A. BLAIZE STREET
ST. GEORGE'S
GRENADA, W.I.

April 01, 2008

"PM6"

RECEIVED
3:00 p.m.
APR 0 ? 2008
MAGISTRATE'S COURT
SOUTHERN DISTRICT

Ms. Patricia Mark
Chief Magistrate
Magistracy Department
St. John's Street
St. George's.

Dear Madam,

It has been observed from the records that you attained the compulsory retirement age of sixty (60) years on 5th June 2003, and in accordance with the provisions of Regulation No. 43 of the Public Service Commission Regulations (SR&O 27/69), the Ministry proposes to advise His Excellency the Governor-General that you be retired from the Public Service on the Grounds of Age at the expiry of your vacation leave, that is, with effect from 3rd March 2009.

Should you desire to make representation regarding the proposed retirement, I request that you submit same in writing to reach me **no later than 30th April 2008.**

Yours sincerely,

Ruth Elizabeth Rouse (Ms)
PERMANENT SECRETARY (AG)

Cc: Chief Personnel Officer, Public Service Commission

Chief Magistrate Patrica Mark- not happy wi[th] approach being used to dismiss her.

Elvin Nimrod - taken to court to defend of the State.

*Front page, Grenada Today, week ending 11 April 2008*

was that the letter from the Permanent Secretary was an attempt to remove the Chief Magistrate from office; that it was the Governor General who, on the advice of the Judicial and Legal Services Commission, could send such communication to the Chief Magistrate. It became evident that lawyers, judges, magistrates at some time all needed lawyers.

Dr. Alexis QC had a legal reverence about him that made you listen and think. He was calm, humble and legally explicit. I admired his legal acumen and the grace with which he performed his duty. He was always helpful to lawyers, mounted his legal arguments with simplicity and humility. He represented Ms. Mark. The former Chief Magistrate got what was fair. Indeed both sides came to a mutually acceptable position.

The Attorney General responded to the claim, since it had caused great unease among the members of the Bar.

It was stated, that the procedure would be corrected. I contemplated that after one gave one's life of service to country and humanity, that it was only honourable, to ride off into the retirement sunset with a fanfare. But, in a world clothed with imperfection, fallacy and shortcomings, we could only do our best with utmost integrity and be judged by our own history.

The departure of a Judge or Magistrate, either by natural or unnatural means always leaves a sense of sadness, as a legal bond which was created is immediately severed. Legal disagreements are normal.

# Alexis: Leave Magistrate Mark alone

Grenada's leading Constitutional Lawyer Dr. Francis Alexis has issued a strong warning to the Ministry of Legal Affairs to decease from harassing Chief magistrate Patricia Mark.

Alexis comments came during a press conference last Thursday as he attempted to share light on the real issue surrounding Chief Magistrate and the Ministry of Legal affairs' decision to have her vacate the post.

Recognizing that the magistrate would have reached the age of retirement Alexis said that the approach embarked on by the Ministry to have her place on leave is totally wrong and flown in the face of the constitution and the right of the individual.

In a latter sent to the Magistrate, Alexis said she was informed of the Ministry's intention to advised the Governor General to remove of retire her from office.

Alexis said it must be noted that the Privy Council made it clear that any such removal falls within the protection of the constitution.

Alexis said having being retained by the Chief Magistrate to act on her behalf, he have since filed papers in the high court seeking a declaration that speak to the unconstitutional manner in which they intent to remove the magistrate.

Base on the content of the latter Alexis said there no way one can remove a member of the judiciary in the way the Ministry proposes to do.

Important to note, Alexis went on to say having recognized that they would have a made a mistake the Ministry have since wrote a second latter attempting to undo the damage done by the first latter, knowing fully well that subjudice a matter pending before the court and must first be decided by the court.

Alexis said to remove such individual for his or her post, the Regional Eastern Caribbean Judicial and legal Services Commission must be brought into the picture in such circumstances and should be the one giving the advise to the Governor General for such removal not the Government.

According the latter sent to thee magistrate she is

*Front page, Grenada Informer, week ending 25 April 2008*

# NNP moves against Chief Magistrate

*...er public officer has taken Keith Mitchell's ruling New National Party (NNP) government to court.*

*...latest is Chief Magistrate, Patricia Mark who is not happy with the methods being employed by the regime to remove her ...office (see front page story).*

*...Chief Magistrate who is from St. Paul's has retained fellow villager, Dr. Francis Alexis to take Attorney-General, Elvin ...ed to court to contest the decision that was taken to use the Permanent Secretary in the Ministry of Legal Affairs to write ...r about demitting office.*

*...k is contending that the Ruth Rouse letter is illegal since her appointment and removal from the service rests solely in the ...s of the Judicial and Legal Services Commission and not government.*

*...NADA TODAY was able to obtain a copy of the Chief Magistrate's affidavit in the upcoming court case:*

...TRICIA MARK ...int Paul's in the ...l of Saint George ...the State of ...ada, make oath ...ay that:

...the Claimant in ...laim herein.

I am the Chief Magistrate of Grenada. I was appointed to "the post of Acting Chief Magistrate,Grenada" with effect from 1 January 1994, by letter of 30 December 1993 to me from His Excellency the Governor-General of Grenada.

The appointment was made by His Excellency the Governor General, "acting in accordance with the advice of the Judicial and Legal Services Commission", as the said letter stated.

My acting appointment as Chief Magistrate was confirmed with effect from 1 June 1995, by letter of 14 June 1995 to me from His Excellency the Governor-General of Grenada.

The appointment was made by His Excellency the Governor-General, "acting in accordance with the advice of the Judicial and Legal Services Commission", as the said letter stated.

My appointment to hold office as Chief Magistrate was in conjunction with, in addition to, the other magisterial posts held by me.

I was first appointed as Magistrate with effect from 24 April 1984 as Magistrate, Eastern Magisterial District, and Additional Magistrate for the other Magisterial Districts, by letter of 4 May 1984 to me from the Chief Personnel Officer, Public Service Commission.

The appointment was made by His Excellency the Governor-General, "acting in accordance with the advice of the Public Service Commission", as that letter stated that appointment was confirmed and reconfirmed by similar letters of 20

August 1985 and 13 March 1987.

But at the time I was first appointed as Magistrate in 1984, and confirmed in 1995 and reconfirmed in 1987, still in suspension were provisions in section 88 of the Constitution of Grenada, Schedule 1 to the Grenada Constitution Order 1973, vesting the Judicial and Legal Services Commission with jurisdiction to give His Excellency the Governor-General of Grenada binding advice regarding the removal of Magistrates in Grenada

January 1992 respectively to me from His Excellency the Governor-General.

The appointments referred to in para 4.1 hereof were by His Excellency the Governor-General, "acting in accordance with the advice of the Judicial and legal Services Commission", as those letters stated.

I attained the age of sixty (60) years on 5 June 2003.

The Acting Permanent Secretary in the Ministry of Legal Affairs of Grenada by letter of 1 April 2008 to me, ("the said letter"), received by me that day, told me of the decision ("the said Ministry decision") that "the Ministry proposes to advise His Excellency the Governor-General that you be retired from the Public Service on the Grounds of Age at the expiry of your vacation leave, that is, with effect from 3rd March 2009".

The said letter added that "should you desire to make representation regarding the proposed retirement, I request that you submit same in writing to reach me no later than 30th April 2008".

I was required to proceed on what, at least in part, would be pre-retirement leave with effect from 5 May 2008 by letter to me from the Chief Personnel Officer, Public Service Commission, granting me 301 days vacation leave (total eligibili-

*Grenada Today, 11 April 2008*

# NNP Moving to Fire Patricia Mar

*Grenada's Chief Magistrate, Patricia Mark has taken court action against the Keith Mitchell-led government over its anxiety to remove her from office.*

*The Chief Magistrate has retained former Attorney-General, Dr. Francis Alexis who on Monday filed a lawsuit against the State which is trying to use the Office of the Governor-General to fire the judicial officer.*

*According to a top legal source, Dr. Alexis intends to argue that the impending move is illegal and that it is only the Judicial and Legal Services Commission (JLCS) that can make any determination on the status of the Chief Magistrate.*

*When this newspaper visited the Supreme Court Registry on Tuesday to get a copy of the writ which is a public document, our reporter was told by the Clerk on duty that the Registrar, Robert Branch had given instructions not to release it.*

*High-level legal sources say the NNP leadership has decided to move against the Chief Magistrate over her handling of the Criminal Libel case brought by Prime Minister Mitchell against Editor of GRENADA TODAY newspaper, George Worme.*

*Legal sources have said that the regime is annoyed with the Chief Magistrate for allowing defense attorney, Anslem Clouden to prolong with his cross-examination of the Grenadian leader who is still on the witness stand.*

*"We are getting the feeling that them big dogs and them (in the NNP) are upset with the Magistrate for not bringing a quick end to the cross-examination and sending the matter (criminal libel case) up to the high court as quickly as possible", one lawyer said.*

*"It is clear that they (NNP) would like to see Mr. Worme in jail and the Chief Magistrate is seen to be not co-operating with them and doing exactly what they would like her to do", he added.*

*This newspaper was able to obtain a copy of the CLAIM FORM that was filed by Alexis in the case involving Mark and the Attorney-General who is representing the State.*

*The document said in part: " The Claimant, PATRICIA MARK, Chief Magistrate of Grenada, of Saint Paul's in the parish of Saint George in the State of Grenada claims against the Defendant, the Attorney-General of Grenada, of the Attorney-General's Chambers of H.A. Blaize Street in the City of Saint George in the State of Grenada.*

*"that the decision by the Ministry of Legal Affairs of Grenada that, as the Acting Permanent Secretary of Ministry by letter of 1 April 2008 to the Claimant said, "the Ministry proposes to advise His Excellency the Governor-General that you be retired from the Public Service on the Grounds of Age at the expiry of your vacation leave, that is, with effect from 3rd March 2009", on which 1 April 2008 the Claimant was written another letter by the Chief Personnel Officer, Public Service Commission, granting her 301 days vacation leave with effect from 5 May 2008, contravenes section 88 of the Constitution of Grenada, Schedule 1 to the Grenada Constitution Order 1973, which, applying to persons holding such offices as the offices of magistrate, ordains that "the power to remove such persons from office shall vest in the Governor-General, acting in accordance with the advice of the Judicial and Legal Service Commission".*

*"Therefore, pursuant to section 101 of the Constitution, and in accordance with rule 8 of the Supreme Court (Constitutional Redress-Grenada) Rules 1968, SRO No.41 of 1968, and Part 56 of the Civil Procedure Rules 2000, the Claimant, having a relevant interest in the said contravention of the Constitution, applies to the Court for the following declarations and relief:*

(1). A declaration that the decision by the Ministry of Legal Affairs of Grenada to propose to advise His Excellency the Claimant Patricia Mark may not be retired from the office of Chief Magistrate on the basis of the said decision of the impending retirement from public office on the grounds of already reaching the mandatory age.

When questioned by a been done either by the Minister of Legal Affairs or Attorney-General.

The move against the Chief Magistrate took is due to take holiday leave on May 6.

Speculation is rife that the sitting Magistrate in Grenville, St. Andrew's, Jerry Seales is tipped as the long-term replacement for the Chief Magistrate.

Seales, a former executive member of the Grenada Labour Party ( is believed t close frien Attorney-Ge Elvin Nimrod.

*Grenada Today, 11 April 2008*

# AG responds to Patricia Mark

... the past few ... there has been ... and unwarranted ... and accusa- ... some members ... the bar that the gov- ... specifically the ... Branch, was ... to remove ... Chief Magistrate from office.

As Attorney General with some responsibility for the administration of the Magistracy, I wish to categorically deny such allegations as false and malicious.

I want to further state that the Executive Branch holds the highest regards for the integrity, professionalism and judicial competence of the Chief Magistrate.

As a matter of fact, it was contemplated that even though the Chief Magistrate may demit office by reason of attaining the compulsory retirement age, her services could be retained thereafter on contract.

The Chief Magistrate was appointed to her present post with effect from June 1, 1995 by the Governor General upon the advice of the Judicial and Legal Services Commission.

*Elvin Nimrod - defend the govt position*

*Patricia Mark - the outgoing Chief Magistrate*

Her letter of appointment stated in relevant parts: "YOU WILL BE SUBJECTED TO THE PROVISIONS OF THE PUBLIC SERVICE COMMISSION REGULATIONS, THE CIVIL SERVICE STAFF ORDERS, FINANCIAL AND STORE RULES AND OTHER REGULATIONS IN FORCE FROM TIME TO TIME. YOU WILL ALSO BE SUBJECT TO THE PROVISIONS OF SECTION 88 OF SCHEDULE 2 OF THE GRENADA CONSTITUTION ORDER, 1973".

Subject to Section 88 of the Constitution, the Public Service Commission may require an officer to retire from the public service at any age after such officer has attained the age of sixty years.

Section 42 Sub Sec. (2) relevant officer in writing of the fact of their attainment of the compulsory retirement age and advise the Public Service Commission accordingly.

On April 1, 2008, the Permanent Secretary in the Ministry of Legal Affairs wrote to the Chief Magistrate indicating that the Ministry proposes to advise His Excellency the Governor General that she be retired from the Public Service on the grounds of age at the expiry of her vacation leave that is with effect from March 3, 2009.

The Chief Magistrate responded to the Permanent Secretary's correspondence by filing a constitutional claim on the 4th of April 2008, wherein she asserts that the communication from the Permanent Secretary amounts to an attempt to remove her from office and that it is the Governor General who. Magistrate.

It must be noted tha Permanent Secretar the Ministry of L Affairs has since wr to the Chief Magis withdrawing the l letter and informing by letter dated Apr 2008 that the Pu Service Commis will be informed o Chief Magistrate ha attained the compul age of retirement.

The matter is under judicial consic tion and it is the gov ment's position tha government is me seeking to uphold rules, regulations laws of Grenada an action in so doing d n't and should no interpreted as an att to force the C Magistrate out of off

*(SUBMITTED B THE ATTORNE GENERAL IN RESPONSE TO AL GATIONS THAT T*

*Grenada Today, 23 May 2008*

## CHIEF JUSTICE BRIAN ALLEYNE RETIRES

During the month of March 2008, Chief Justice Brian Alleyne was due to retire. Many times I had appeared before him as Judge in the High Court and of the Court of Appeal. He was very prayerful, a devout Roman Catholic, infused with judicial experience. He rose to the level of Chief Justice (Ag.). He was fair and fearless. He faced his ample share of challenges in Grenada as was the case with many judicial officers. But the grace with which he executed his professional responsibility without complaint was admirable.

The sentiment from the Grenada Bar Association was in one accord: "Well done thou good and faithful servant".

In November 2008, Justice Denys Barrow, a legal luminary who once sat as a High Court Judge in Grenada and later elevated to the Court of Appeal, was demitting office. I had occasion to appear before

### ACTING CHIEF JUSTICE BIDS FAREWEL

Three year after his appointment as Acting Chief Justice of the Eastern Caribbean Supreme Court, Sir Brian Alleyne SC, KCN will no longer be sitting on the Bench, having attained the mandatory retirement age of sixty-five.

Sir Alleyne, a Dominican born who spent his earlier years in Grenada, a pass student of the Presentation Brothers' College, is now heading into retirement after spending some forty- two year of his life in the legal profession, during which he served in almost every capacity of the profession from Magistrate to Chief Justice.

Sir Alleyne also served as Attorney General of Dominica before returning to the profession as a Judge. He is expected to vacate the Bench later this year [illegible]

[illegible]

rod, Acting Director of Public Prosecution Ms Deon Lawrence, members of the Grenada Bar Association, members of the magistracy, the Court Registrar, past and present members of the Bench.

Also present was the wife of the soon-to-be retired Judge.

In bidding farewell to Judge Alleyne, Grenada's AG said the Government recognized the contribution made by Judge Alleyne toward the reformation of the justice system in Grenada and the wider Caribbean.

Nimrod said the Grenada Government fully supports Alleyne's vision for the establishment of a Hall of Justice in every member State and assured him that his effort in getting that project on stream would be highly appreciated.

"As you retire let me wish you all the best; thanks for all you have done and all the best in the future".

President of the Grenada Bar Association, Ruggles Ferguson, described the occasion as yet another historic occasion for the Acting Chief Justice albeit, one that comes with mixed reaction, having marked the end of forty-two year of outstanding contribution to the profession.

It is also a time, he said, of deep sadness over the stariban refusal to confirm the Judge to the full position of [illegible]

discipline, dedication, scholarship, and vision judicial wisdom, administrative and managerial skills embedded in the Chief Justice.

Ferguson said as head of the Grenada Bar they are ashamed to know that Grenada was party to that maneuver to prevent Judge Alleyne's confirmation to that position.

Ferguson said while the entire OECS without exception is saddened by the departure, there is joy in at least one Cabinet room in the OECS over the resignation.

It must be noted, Ferguson said, that Grenada as a nation hold a special place more positive than negative in the development of Judge Alleyne.

Those development, he said, span secondary school education right up to his early career development, spanning six of his seven years as a High Court Judge here in Grenada.

Grenada, Ferguson said, also holds not so pleasant memories of Judge Alleyne tenure as a legal professional.

Among those he hinted several public attacks by agents of the executive having been displeased with his ruling.

It was here in Grenada, Ferguson said, that High Court action was brought against Judge Alleyne, one that was thrown out by the Privy Council, and it was [illegible]

ber of the Executive refuse to sit in matters presided over by Judge Alleyne.

It must be noted, Ferguson said, that all of those attacks were treated with strong reserves by the Judge who showed in his ruling that he was above those behaviors.

Ferguson said the many historic judgment delivered by Judge Alleyne would long stand the test of time for years to come.

The President also commended the Government of Antigua for bestowing the honor of Knighthood on Judge Alleyne for his outstanding contribution to the Bar, the Bench and to public life.

Among all that his was able to accomplished, Ferguson said, Judge Alleyne also lead the way in organizing the 40th anniversary of the OECS Supreme Court.

The President noted however that what might last as the single most important legacy of that accomplishment was the Judge's commitment to translate into writing his vision to ensure that the first forty years of the Court was reduced to writing and available to all, a book written by Dr. Francis Alexis and edited by law Liberian of the UWI.

Ferguson said Judge Alleyne's retirement once again brings to the fore the issue of the retirement age of Judges [illegible]

repeat the call for an increase in the retirement age to seventy, while at the same time calling on the authority to act speedily in appointing a new Chief Justice.

The president called on the Judge to make good use of his retirement and see it as the opening up of new doors, but most of all do not allow his knowledge to go to waist since there are still room to make outstanding contribution in several arears.

Also making contributions during Monday's sitting were Mrs. Celia Edwards speaking on behalf of the Utter Bar and Mr. Carol Bristol speaking on behalf of the Inner Bar.

From the Bench sitting High Court Judge in Grenada Claire Henry said Judge Alleyne's [illegible]

He has accomplish his task with dignity.

In his response Judge Alleyne commended all who contributed towards his success, among them his first legal teacher his Dad Keith Alleyne, his mom, his wife, teachers of the PBC and many friends, among them Carol Bristol, former Judge Lyle St Paul, Denis Byron among others.

Grenada as a country, he said, played a significant role in his life.

Alleyne said despite the many successes the Court still faces many challenges. The civil procedure rules have been on the books for well over ten years, and the Court still faces heavy backlogged in the processing of criminal trials which contribute to the increase in crimes now [illegible]

territories.

It is his hope th[illegible] of the projects [illegible] would continu[illegible] several of those [illegible] would be dealt w[illegible]

Alleyne said th[illegible] needs to exami[illegible] state of its low[illegible] diciary, the Reg[illegible] Deputy Registr[illegible] Magistrate. Th[illegible] need to improv[illegible] status, performan[illegible] prospect.

The Court at all [illegible] need to have a [illegible] look, the infrastr[illegible] the place of busin[illegible] the like.

"To all who woul[illegible] impacted my life [illegible] thank you [illegible]

*Grenada Informer, 14 March 2008*

## Justice Barrow is stepping down

Although he has not yet reached the mandatory retirement age, Justice of Appeal of the Eastern Caribbean Supreme Court, Denys Barrow has decided to call it quits and return to private practice in his native homeland of Belize.

Justice Barrow who once served as Acting High Court Judge in Grenada leaves the Bench in December after serving the Eastern Caribbean Supreme Court for the past seven years.

During a special sitting of the Supreme Court of Grenada last week in honour of the newly appointed Chief Justice, Hugh Rawlins, and to mark the retirement of Justice Barrow, it was speculated that he was leaving for "greener pastures" in Belize as his brother, Dean Barrow is now the Prime Minister of that South American Country.

However, the Caribbean Jurist dismissed that claim saying that his decision to leave was made sometime ago.

"In terms of my future, I should tell you that my plans are quite modest. I seek no Office. I am very comfortable with the idea of going back into private practice", he said.

"The greenest of the pasture in Belize has always been there for me while I enjoyed the greenest of the judicial pasture in the OECS," he added.

The Judge, a father of four, pointed to a number of reasons based mainly on domestic matters for the decision taken to leave the Bench of the Eastern Caribbean Supreme Court.

"To move a mother from that matrix takes a bit of ego which perhaps a man of greater maturity at the time may have faltered at doing, but I claim the benefit of our youthfulness seven years ago when I made my first foreign (venture) and came out to the Eastern Caribbean as an Acting High Court Judge, and my wife was very clear that she is not leaving, she will come to visit me

Justice Denys Barrow

from time to time," he said.

"...It was always a sacrifice for her, and I always knew that I had the obligation not to demand for too long a period the continuation of that sacrifice. Gratitude and reciprocity require that I do the right thing, and therefore, I am happy to inform you that my reasons for leaving is principally domestic.

Another reason given by Justice Barrow is that he was now needed by his two daughters who are lawyers and operate his law firm in Belize.

Justice Barrow also had some kind words about the future of the court that he was leaving.

He spoke with confidence of Chief Justice Rawlins having the capabilities to reconstitute the Court of Appeal, and enhance the High Court in the jurisdiction.

The retiring Jurist challenged members of the local judiciary to make themselves available for possible appointments to the Court of Appeal since his going "creates room for others to come in."

"So members of the Bar, including the Grenada Bar, (please) respond to the need to give service on the Bench. So I do not take full responsibility for leaving the Chief Justice at this time because some of you must take responsibility for not offering to come on to the Bench at this time," he said.

Apart from Justice

*Grenada Today, 21 November 2008*

him. He was always intellectually challenging, stimulating, he engendered sharp wit. There was a special sitting of the Court to honour the contribution of this exemplary judicial officer as he was due to depart in December 2008. His contributions to the legal jurisprudence of the region are well documented. The attorneys who had the pleasure of appearing before him, including myself, will always remember him. For I learned at his feet.

In the same month, when Justice Barrow was departing our shores, Mr. Justice Hugh Rawlins was being appointed Chief Justice. This was cause for anticipated excitement, as he once lectured in law at the University of the West Indies, Cave Hill Campus Barbados, where I and many of my colleagues were students. Life was indeed unpredictable. While he sat as Chief Justice he was always happy to see his students appearing before him well prepared. For I knew he was filled with pride having contributed to the legal scholastic development of a generation of lawyers.

## A MOTHER'S NIGHTMARE

A mother's nightmare is to receive a call or to be notified that her child was either murdered or was accused of murder. In either case the grief would be immense. There were five (5) homicide cases, which occurred within close proximity of each other. It confirmed that youthful anger coupled with the use of a weapon is a dangerous brew.

In May of 2008, at a 'happy hour' activity at the Fish Market in St. George's where beers were being sold at $10.00 for three (3), young people congregated and indulged. It was a usual Friday evening activity or 'lime' as it was commonly called. With the infusion of alcohol, quarrels and altercations escalated easily, as persons lost their self-control.

A young man succumbed to an injury received at that activity. The accused was in shock after I spoke to him, when he learnt of the death of the deceased.

At that stage in my career it was difficult to deal with the mothers, fathers, family members and loved ones whose sorrow was so great, that it was much more difficult than the trials at court.

MURDER AT THE FISH MARKET

"I will miss him. He was a very good boy"

Those were the words uttered by Kathy-ann Cox who continues to mourn the loss of her 21-year old son, Akim, the latest victim of another senseless stabbing in the Spice Isle.

Akim's life was cut short on Friday night by a single stab wound to the chest delivered by an assailant who was part of the crowd assembled at the Car Park of the Melville Street Fish Market for the regular Friday night "Happy hour" lime.

See Pages 3 & 11 for full stories

Akim Cox - killed at the young age of 21

*Front page, Grenada Today, week ending 9 May 2008*

# Murder at the Fish Market

"He was a good boy".

That's how Kathy-ann Cox described her son, Akim who was murdered at around 11.00 p.m. Friday night in the latest spate of senseless killing by youngsters in the Spice Isle.

Young Akim, 21 of the Darbeau hills overlooking River Road in St. George's died as a result of a single stab wound inflicted on him at the Car Park of the Fish Market on Melville Street where he joined hundreds in partaking in the regular Happy Hour lime.

As Kathy-ann spoke to *GRENADA TODAY* newspaper, her own mother chipped in: "He (Akim) was nice to me. He was a loving boy to the family".

Akim, known by friends as ET is a past student of St. George's Anglican School known as Hindsey. He was a regular visitor to the Fish Market lime.

According to Kathy-ann, she and other members of the family were also partaking in the Happy Hour when Akim came up to her and held onto a beer that she was drinking and finished off the drink.

He soon disappeared from her, as he spotted a female companion and went away dancing behind her.

"I went to look for him and he showed me some girl of his and then I left and came up home", the mother said.

Kathy-ann indicated that later that night, she received a telephone call from a friend of the family who told her that Akim had been killed at the Fish Market.

"His friend Boyo also called and say, "ET" dead. Well I fall down on the ground and start-ed to bawl", she said.

The distraught mother left with other family members for the St. George's General hospital where she saw the body of Akim lying in the small mortuary.

Akim who is survived by five sisters and four brothers was expected to be laid to rest on Thursday at the St. George's Cemetery.

Kathy-ann made an impassionate plea to the youth of the nation to stop the violence and

*Grenada Today, 9 May 2008*

There was an incident at the bus terminus, when a passenger previously had a verbal disagreement with the bus conductor, returned and resumed the second phase of the altercation. The second incident resulted in his death, when a weapon was used to inflict a singular fatal injury to the chest.

The offence of murder, from my experience, is hardly ever a repeat offence. The society needs to be able to find alternative ways for youth to channel their strengths for useful purposes. I have always encouraged the young men whom I have had the opportunity to represent, to speak to their peers and other persons in the community, so as to aid in breaking the cycle of crime. There is a school of thought that stiffer penalties curb crime. I have not seen the statistics to support this. The debate continues.

In a third incident which occurred in the Grand Anse area commonly called 'Wall Street', where every Friday members of the public gather to wind down after a week of work. Alcohol is consumed in large quantities. Deep into the night patrons purchase food and drinks, having a merry time. On one occasion, two men were charged with inflicting a fatal

## ISORDERLY PASSENGER IS KILLED

Bus conductor Chris Modeste is charged with Manslaughter

Following a cooling off period from major crimes which engulfed the island in the earlier months of the year, Grenada was hit last Friday night with another unlawful death which resulted in the police bringing a charge of Manslaughter against a bus conductor.

The 22-year old Grand Anse resident, Nigel Keron Benjamin succumbed to a stab wound to the chest that he received from 19-year old bus conductor, Chris Modeste of Belmont, St. George's.

Informed sources told **GRENADA TODAY** that Benjamin boarded a bus in Grand Anse and started behaving disorderly and refused to pay the bus fare.

Benjamin was subsequently put off the bus by Modeste.

Sometime later that night, Benjamin confronted Modeste at the bus terminus and the two were engaged in an altercation.

An official police bulletin said that the deceased received a stab wound to the chest.

He died the following morning at the General Hospital in St. George's.

Modeste is now facing a charge of manslaughter.

He made his first court appearance at the St. George's Magistrate's Court on Monday and was placed on $10,000.00 bail with two sureties.

The accused who is being represented by attorney-at-Law, Derick Sylvester, has to report to the police station every Monday and Wednesday.

Modeste is due to return to court on January 6, 2009.

Meanwhile, Officers of the Criminal Investigation Department are ruling out any form of foul play in the death of Carl Smith of Darbeau, St. George's.

Smith, a construction worker, was found dead on Sunday morning in the River Road area.

A post mortem conducted on the 33-year old body determined the cause of death was an acute myocardial infarction.

Meanwhile, police have arrested a resident of south St. George to assist them with investigations into a report that the Food Depot in River Road St. George's was broken into and a number of items stolen.

The popular River Road establishment was broken into sometime during late Saturday night and early Sunday morning.

Police investigations are continuing.

…rl Smith - police ruled out foul play in his death

*Front page, Grenada Today, week ending 14 November 2008*

injury to the deceased. The prosecution's case was that of joint enterprise. Which of the two men inflicted the fatal injury was left to be determined at trial.

During the trial an application was made jointly by both lawyers, Ruggles Ferguson and I who represented an accused each, to visit the area where the incident had occurred to better appreciate the case as presented in court.

Both men were charged with the offence of murder. At trial they were both found not guilty of murder. One was acquitted altogether. The other was found guilty of manslaughter.

The fourth incident occurred in the northern parish of Saint Andrew, where a young male inflicted a singular injury to another resulting in his death. This was another example of two young men channelling their

## MURDER SUSPECTS BACK ON CRIME SCENE

*Kellon Andrews (wearing blue shirt) points to an area of the crime scene where Tobacco was killed. Also in the picture is Shane Donald, the co-accused of the murder. The men and their lawyers were accompanied by police escorts to Wall Street*

Two young men from St. George who are on trial for murder have been given the opportunity to visit the crime scene of that fateful February incident.

Kellon Andrews and Shane Donald who are accused with the murder of 40-year old David Alexis, also known as Tobacco, were accompanied by their lawyers Ruggles Ferguson and Derick Sylvester, respectively back to the famous Wall Street liming area in Grand Anse where the crime allegedly took place.

The two lawyers received the court's permission to take their clients to the crime scene under tight police security in order to take instructions on what had actually happened in the early hours of February 24, 2007.

At the commencement of the trial on Tuesday which is now being referred to as the Wall Street Murder Trial State Prosecutor Howard Pinnock told the Number Two High Court that the prosecution will rely on joint enterprise to prove its case as none of his 11 witnesses will be able to say which of the two men on trial inflicted the fatal stab wound.

Pinnock explained to the 14-member jury panel which includes the two alternates that where two persons go on a joint criminal enterprise with the intention to commit murder, no one

Cont'd on page 03

## MURDER SUSPECTS BACK ON CRIME SCENE

*Cont'd from front page*

can escape from the responsibility of the act that was committed.

One of the main State witnesses, Franklyn Scott gave a vivid account to the court that is being presided over by Justice Francis Cumberbatch of what took place at Wall Street.

Scott who is a radio Disc Jockey (DJ) said that at about 5:00 a.m. that morning Tobacco was engaged in a fist fight with another person when a white Toyota Corolla car driven by Donald showed up.

The vehicle was earlier parked on Wall Street in front of the Green Grocer building.

It was reported that the car went through the round-a-bout then pulled up and parked closer to the phone booth near to Wall Street.

Donald and Andrews emerged from the car, went to a van that was selling beverages, each took a bottle, broke it on the edge of the van and proceeded to Tobacco where they both attacked him at the upper part of the body.

According to Scott, the deceased man pleaded with his attackers to be left alone, and at one point escaped from them after receiving a stab wound, but in the process of running away fell to the ground.

The court was told that when Tobacco fell both Andrews and Donald trampled upon him.

The radio DJ said Tobacco escaped and again fell.

It was at this point that the eyewitness and a Corporal of Police came to the assistance of the wounded man in an effort to stop the bleeding.

Scott said at the two accused men then drove off in the car in the direction of Sugar Mill.

Later in the day, they were arrested in the Woburn area where the car was wrecked.

The Wall Street Murder Trial is expected to last for two weeks.

*Grenada Today, 7 November 2008*

# MURDER RATE CONTINUES TO CLIMB AS Telescope man knifed to death

Ricardo Edgar charged after making his first Court appearance

Dead is 38 year old Enoch Noel of Telescope St Andrew, the man commonly known in the Telescope and Grenville environment as Crapobone. Noel was pronounced dead on his arrival at the Princess Alice hospital last Wednesday night as a result of a fatal stabbed wound through his chest which punctured his heart. The fatal stabbing took place just outside a bar on the Ben Jones street in the town of Grenville just about five hundred yards from the Grenville police station, and seventy-five yards from the St Andrew's Methodist primary school.

Noel, a tradesman by profession and father of two, was having difficulties to cope with his daily life following the end of his relationship with his girlfriend many years ago. Although he was considered to be a trouble maker who cares less on one hand and a bad man on the other, there were times when he is not under the influence of alcohol thus displaying a badjohn mentality, but he would be spotted even on street corner crying over the end to his past relationship and not afforded the opportunity to see his children. Bone grew from a man of humble upbringing to frustration and there are times he even challenged the police for fight. Part of his life was spent in prison while there were occasions when he was hospitalized. Just about a month ago Noel had an altercation with another man from the village on whom he inflicted a burst head. The man retaliated and gave Noel a severe chop on one of his hand. Noel was then hospitaslized for over two weeks in a critical condition. He was later discharged from hospital with the bandages to the injured hand. On the evening Noel was killed he is reported to have had an altercation with another man earlier that morning, to whom he inflicted a number of wounds to the man's head. The injured man is reported to have visited a medical centre and Sought medical attention while Noel is reported to have continued on the rampage molesting other persons. He was seen in the town of Grenville during the course of Wednesday in confrontation with a number of persons and at one point a heated argument led to him kicking over a table, not knowing that his final moments were counting down. About 7.30 pm on Wednesday evening Noel was approached by the young man with whom he had an altercation earlier that day, who seemed to have come to take revenge for his earlier injuries. Within moments Noel was seen walking away from the front of the bar to the other side of the road where he collapsed directly tat the foot of an electric pole. Subsequently he was rushed to hospital but was pronounced dead on arrival, while one Richardo Edgar was later detained by police. Meanwhile Richardo Edgar, a citizen of Venezuela but resident of Grenada, appeared at the Grenville Magistrate's Court last Friday charged with murder. The charge was read to him but he was not allowed to plead. He was represented by Attorney at law Dereck Sylvester. The matter was adjourned to the 23 rd July

Enoch Noel the deceased

*Grenada Informer, 11 July 2008*

# Probation for Grand Mal resident

Former Wesley College Student, Kevin Francis has been given a three-year probation to keep the peace.

The Grand Mal resident received the sentence last week Thursday from Madam Justice Claire Henry at High Court Number One after pleading guilty to a charge of manslaughter.

The teenager was charged with the lesser

*Ryhym Rodney – lost his life tragically*

the 15-year old Rodney provoked Francis who was 14 years old at the time.

Both youngsters were reportedly embroiled in a confrontation in various areas of the school.

The court learnt that Rodney locked the youngster's neck and managed to get him into the toilet facility where a fight ensued.

From the toilet, the two boys continued the fight in a classroom from where the Grand Mal resident escaped and managed to obtain a knife, which was used to make the deadly blow.

Rodney was rushed to the St. George's General Hospital where he was pronounced dead on arrival.

*Grenada Today, 11 July 2008*

youthful energies in the wrong direction. On most occasions, the accused and deceased have children and other family members who are left to suffer the agony and shock of losing them. If only both sides could stop and think, more lives would be saved. There are many incidents where the crime is encouraged by passers-by, friends, onlookers and acquaintances, who disappear when death or serious bodily injury occurs.

The fifth incident was that of a youthful teenager having armed himself with a knife, used it on another who was physically assaulting him. A stigma is attached to those young men who commit those atrocities.

## LAW OFFICE CONSTRUCTED

Time surely flew by quickly. The year rolled by and every year seemed like yesterday. My father and I had shared office space. I had decided then that it was time to construct my own building. I solicited the assistance of a Real Estate Company to assist me in securing a suitable location. A lot of land was found with a dwelling house situated on Lucas Street in the city of St. George's, commonly called 'Lawyers Street' as there were approximately sixteen (16) to eighteen (18) law offices along that street.

In July of 2009, the demolition works commenced, after a series of interviews with numerous contractors. The office was constructed within four months. On the 1st November 2009, the three storey office was completed. Another phase of my professional life had begun. I therefore relocated from Church Street to Lucas Street in the city of St. George's.

*Law office of Derick F. Sylvester & Associates located on the upper floor.*

CHAPTER SIX

# SOLO FLIGHT

*"One does not discover new lands without consenting to lose sight of the shore for a very long time."*
ANDRE GIDE

The practice of law, and my love for it, propelled me along the legal journey with ease. Of course there were occasions when I had to ponder on my future in the legal profession. I wondered many times, whether law was my only calling. Was I consumed by my jealous mistress? As the law was normally referred to. The answer was always in the affirmative. There were occasions when I had to confront difficult legal decisions and cases. At other times test the boundary of the law. In Grenada, prior to the Privy Council decision of Spence and Hughes [UKPC] 12, delivered on the 11th March 2002, the death penalty for murder was mandatory: once an accused was convicted of murder, the penalty of death applied.

However, in 2009, there was an accused who was charged with causing the death of his common law wife. Diminished responsibility was not a defence in Grenada. The sole crux of the case was that of a mitigation to assist in sentencing. No one had ever pleaded guilty to murder in Grenada prior to this matter, under the Spence v. Hughes dispensation when the charge was read; he entered a plea of guilty. The court accepted it. The compilation of pre-sentencing reports and character witnesses was prepared.

In the interest of ensuring he got the benefit of a discounted sentence now that the mandatory death penalty was no longer an option, it was imperative to ensure that the pros outweighed the cons. The court normally gives a huge discount in sentencing when there is a guilty plea at the first available opportunity, and the accused is a first time offender, among other mitigating factors. The decision to plead guilty to murder post the Spence and Hughes decision eventually turned out to be the correct one. At the sentencing hearing the accused received a sentence

# Hands Gets 17 Years

*Davidson "One Hand" Paul – got 17 years for the killing*

A 17-year prison sentence has been imposed on Tempe resident Davidson Paul who is popularly known to many as "Hands" for committing a crime of murder.

Hands, 36, was charged with intentionally causing the death of his living companion, 40-year old Marie Lawrence by unlawful harm on July 28, 2008 at the house that they shared together in Tempe, St. George's.

The sentence is to run from the date he was placed on remand last July.

Hands created history in the local criminal jurisdiction when he pleaded guilty to that capital offence on February 17.

However, sentencing was reserved for the June Criminal Assizes.

Evidence produced by Crown Counsel, Dionne Lawrence-Pivotte state that Lawrence's daughter Esther Lawrence overheard a conversation between her mother and Hands relating to money.

The court learnt that during the course of the conversation, the deceased woman asked Hands to leave the house.

The court report said he made two trips taking his clothes away, and when he returned to make the third trip he was armed with a cutlass.

Lawrence went into the bedroom, and was then followed by Hands where an altercation begun.

They eventually came out onto the verandah where the murder victim sat on a chair.

The court heard that it was at that moment Hands launched the deadly assault on Lawrence.

She first received a cut on her left elbow and her side.

The daughter's statement said her mother tried escaping but Hands chopped off the left wrist and at that time she fell down the steps.

The murder convict continued his assault while Lawrence was lying on the ground by chopping her on the left side of her neck.

He then reportedly told the younger Lawrence, "sorry for killing your mother, you will have a better life."

Counsel for the defendant, Derick Sylvester told the court his client has expressed remorse for what had taken place.

Sylvester said Hands' action was precipitated by the use of alcohol and the use of derogatory words used to him by Lawrence.

The defense counsel called three character witnesses, one of whom was Opposition Senator Kennedy Roberts.

Hands did volunteer work for Roberts during last year's election campaign in the constituency of St. George's North East which was won by Finance Minister Nazim Burke.

Sen. Roberts said although Hands is helpful when he consumes alcohol, "he does not behave in an appropriate manner."

According to the opposition senator, the murder convict curses a lot, but he never encountered him in any violent behaviour.

Sen. Roberts told the court he has had the occasion to counsel, his political activist on his alcohol consumption.

The presiding judge, Madam Justice Clare Henry said Sen. Roberts statement was of great assistance to her.

However, Justice Henry who described the murder as brutal found that the killing was committed with intent.

She said although the court notes Hands remorse for the crime, she cannot lose sight of the fact that this was a most serious offense. She said there is a need for a general deterrent to other persons who might be inclined to use knives and cutlasses in settling disputes.

"A strong message must be sent that life is sacred," she said.

Justice Henry ordered that the murder convict be given counselling for alcohol abuse, and anger management.

*Grenada Today, 3 July 2009*

of seventeen (17) years. He was also ordered to seek counselling for alcohol abuse and anger management.

The pivotal lesson learnt in this matter was that sometimes a trial should be embarked upon, as it is better to ventilate the legal and factual issues. When, however, the facts and the law are against you, the decision to enter a guilty plea might be in the best interest of the client. A balancing exercise must be conducted.

With the dispensation of justice, the number of cases as opposed to the limited number of judicial officers is always cause for concern. On occasions there were two judges who sat in the criminal jurisdiction; with a few hundred cases pending; therefore not much could be done in one Assizes sitting. The criminal Assizes were held three times per year, commencing February, June and October. These sittings were of two to three months duration. The then Chief Justice Hugh Rawlins issued a practice direction for the extension of the criminal court sitting or what is referred to as continuous assizes.

This was a welcomed relief for accused, criminal practitioners, judges and lawyers. Justice Clare Henry always saw the need to expedite the legal process. She was always concerned with the administration of justice and its smooth functioning. This was vocalised by her once the occasion presented itself. She will be remembered for her dedication to duty and her professional posture in dispensing justice.

## Continuous hearing of criminal matters

*High Court Judge Clare Henry - speaks of continuous sitting for criminal matters*

*Inmates at Richmond Hill Prison - making their way to court*

The Supreme Court of Grenada in its criminal jurisdiction will from the New Law Year in October begin to have continuous sitting of criminal matters.

This was disclosed by senior High Court Judge, Madam Justice Clare Henry as she wrapped up the June Session of the Assizes.

Justice Henry said the new rules as laid down by Chief Justice Hugh Rawlins will now allow for longer sittings of up to six weeks, and according to her, there will only be a break to change the jurors.

As a result of the new rules, the October Assizes will commence one week earlier, October 6, and from 2010, instead of the usual start of the first session of the assizes of the year commencing in February, it will now begin in January.

The female High Court Judge said the continuous sitting of the court will help alleviate the backlog of cases.

Of the 73 cases on the cause list of the June Assizes, 31 cases were traversed.

The lion share of the 42 cases completed were done by Court Number Two that was presided over by Justice Lyle St. Paul who was brought out from retirement to serve as the third High Court Judge from the February Assizes.

However, the retired judge's seven-month contract came to an end on conclusion of the June Assizes. It is not clear whether he will be granted another contract.

The court learnt that there was a slight reduction in the prison population as of July 30.

At the close of the February Assizes on March 31, the Acting Superintendent of Prisons, Derek John reported that the prison contained 413 inmates.

However, in his report to the court on July 30, John said as of that date, the prison population stood at 400 inmates, with five of them being females.

Thirty-five of the inmates are on remand, 31 awaiting trials, 16 are appellants, and three are judgement debtors.

Upon inquiry by Justice St. Paul about what facility there is for juvenile offenders, John said there is no separate wing for the young offenders, except for a small quarter in the remand section of the prison.

The Richmond Hill Prison is the only State-run correctional facility on the island.

Just recently criminal attorney Anselm Clouden spoke of the need to have juvenile offenders committed to an institution other than the Richmond Hill Prison.

Clouden urged the Tillman Thomas-led National Democratic Congress (NDC) Government to act quickly to put measures in place to prevent juveniles from mixing with what he called "hard core criminals" at the prison.

*Grenada Today, 21 August 2009*

## FINANCIAL MELTDOWN

There was a financial culture in Grenada, where persons invested through companies which were set up for the purpose of receiving deposits with guaranteed interest rates much higher than the banks. This resulted in many deposits being made by Grenadians including; life savings or substantial deposits. The volatile nature of these investments, which were normally channelled through overseas markets, led to the eventual collapse of some of these financial institutions, resulting in the appointment of judicial managers by the Eastern Caribbean Supreme Court (ECSC) on petition by the Organisation of Eastern Caribbean States (OECS). This is because it became obvious after some time, that persons who would have deposited significant sums could not have received their deposits with interest as contracted.

I had one such client, a good friend and fellow parishioner who was a medical doctor. He invested approximately five million (5M) dollars with British American Insurance Company Limited (BAICO). Certain inquiries were made regarding a withdrawal; however there was no guarantee at what point they would be able to disburse. This was an immediate red flag. A decision was made to file a civil suit so as to secure a judgment. Thereafter to proceed against the company for enforcement. A civil suit was filed and served on the company. There was no defence filed in the matter. An application for default judgment was applied for and obtained through the Supreme Court.

Upon the receipt of the judgment, there was an application by the State for a stay of all proceedings in relation to every matter involving BAICO. The stay was granted by the Supreme Court. This order seriously hampered our chances of financial recovery from the company. Despite our many efforts to circumvent the order for the stay, through court applications, all proved futile.

Hundreds of Grenadians lost money in this financial fiasco, professionals, lay persons and companies alike. The culture of saving money in banks and other financial institutions as a means of securing

## JUDICIAL MANAGER APPOINTED FOR BRITISH AMERICAN

*St. George's, August 6, 2009 — After several months of collaboration, the insurance regulators in the OECS have intervened in British American in an effort to safeguard the interest of policyholders and investors.*

*On Tuesday, August 04, 2009, the Grenada High Court ordered the appointment of Reuben M. John of KPMG Eastern Caribbean as Judicial Manager of the branch of British American Insurance Company in Grenada.*

*The Order followed a Petition to the Court by the Grenada Authority for the Regulation of Financial Institutions (GARFIN).*

*The Petition was brought to the Court in Grenada as part of a concerted Action Plan being undertaken by all OECS member states to protect the interests of OECS investors and policy holders in this troubled financial institution.*

*As part of that plan, Judicial Managers have also been appointed in St. Lucia, Antigua & Barbuda, St. Vincent and the Grenadines, St. Kitts & Nevis, Montserrat and Anguilla.*

*In developing their approach to this very delicate problem, the OECS Ministers of Finance adopted four guiding principles in respect of the British American and CLICO issue.*

*These principles, which were endorsed by the Monetary Council at its meeting in Dominica on July 10, 2009, are as follows:*

(i) To keep British American as a going concern in a form to be determined;

(ii) To craft a solution which is regional in nature ;

(iii) To protect, as far as practicable, the interests of depositors and investors; and

(iv) To ensure that British American does not become a systemic risk to the ECCU financial system.

The Plan also made provisions for the appointment of a Ministerial Sub-Committee on Insurance to provide oversight on this important matter.

The Sub-Committee comprises: Prime Minister Ralph Gonsalves of St. Vincent and the Grenadines (Chairman), Prime Minister Roosevelt Skerrit of Dominica, Minister Nazim Burke of Grenada and Minister Timothy Harris of St. Kitts and Nevis.

This Committee is working closely with the Regulators in each Country.

The Petition to the Court was heard by Honourable Mr. Justice Mario Michel. GARFIN was represented by Mr. Rohan Phillip, Acting Attorney General and Mr. Angus Smith, Executive Director.

This intervention by GARFIN is fully supported by the Government of Grenada and is fully consistent with the recent decisions of OECS Ministers of Finance.

The Judicial Manager is under the direction of the Court and has now taken control of all operations of the Company.

The Court has directed that an initial report be submitted within fourteen (14) days and a detailed report within sixty (60) days with specific recommendations for the way forward.

The key task of the Judicial Manager is to take all actions necessary to safeguard the interest of all policyholders and investors in British American.

In submitting his report to the Court, it is envisaged that the Judicial Manger will make recommendations as to whether a new company should be established to take over the operations of British American in the OECS.

The Governments of the OECS and Barbados are in an ongoing dialogue on the issue of CLICO. It is understood that discussions are ongoing with prospective purchasers of CLICO International Life Insurance.

The ultimate aim is to protect all investors and policyholders of CLICO in Grenada and other OECS member States.

Given the efforts undertaken so far to resolve this difficult issue the further patience of policyholders is needed in order to allow the Judicial Manager to take control of the company and to allow the Governments and the Regulators time to craft a regional solution to ultimately ensure the safety of all policyholders and investors funds.

***(The above was submitted by the Ministry of Finance headed by Finance Minister, Nazim Burke and GARFIN)***

*Grenada Today, 21 August 2009*

interest as a form of investment has brought tremendous heartache to persons who invested their life savings. I had an occasion to speak to the media who requested the status of the BAICO judgment as persons soon came to realise there was a judgment against the company.

The fact that my client had not the slightest clue as to when or how he would receive his hard earned cash, this led to tremendous frustration. He shared that frustration along with all the persons involved in the process of recovery. It was easy to understand that his pain was real. As a medical doctor who had spent numerous years in the United States of America, looking forward to returning to the land of his birth to build a state of the art oncology clinic to provide first class heathcare to the people of the country and also to the region through medical tourism, this dream was thwarted if not obliterated, by the collapse of BAICO. His lifelong dream was destroyed.

My client was a well decorated Grenadian oncologist, who had served well, not only in Grenada, but also in the United States of America. He was named in the publication, 'The Leading Physicians of the World' because of his impeccable work ethic, passion and quality patient care.

On every occasion when I spoke to him about the dream he had for his country, and how it was destroyed, I saw a Doctor's love for humanity; it really bothered him. He was very concerned about the quantity of cancer patients in Grenada; the lack of proper health care; also the high cost to get that care overseas and the absence of medical insurance. He felt it was his means of giving back to the country that allowed him to have the quality of life he has today. The judgment remains unsatisfied. The financial catastrophe rages on.

## Good news for Dr. Layne

A leading Grenadian Physician in the United States now has his name inducted into the renowned Publication, "The Leading Physicians of the World".

The New Jersey-based Dr. Trevor Layne was contracted by the former National Democratic Congress (NDC) government of former Prime Minister, Tillman Thomas to preside over the island's Oncology services.

A release put out by the publication said that, "as a result of impeccable passion and quality patient care, Trevor Joseph Layne, MD, has been selected to receive publication in "The Leading Physicians of the World".

The International Association of

Dr. Trevor Joseph Layne – recognized by US-based publication

Healthcare Professionals is proud to welcome Dr. Layne into a prestigious, supportive community for top physicians", it added.

Dr. Layne maintains a position at Lincoln Oncology, LLC located in West Orange, New Jersey.

A well experienced oncologist of over 20 years, Dr. Layne is responsible for the palliative care of patients with terminal malignancies and diagnosing cancer within his patients.

He is certified by the American Board of Internal Medicine in medical oncology and remains an active member of the International Oncology Network: a network that provides access for healthcare providers and industry companies to improve the efficiency, effectiveness, and quality of healthcare they can deliver to their patients.

When not serving his patients at Lincoln, Dr. Layne offers his experience to other facilities such as Newark Beth Israel Medical Center, East Orange General Hospital, and St. Michael's Medical Center.

He graduated in 1989 from St. George's University (SGU) with his medical degree. Upon completion, Dr. Layne attended Jamaica Hospital for his internship and residency; then the State University of New York Downstate for his fellowship training

*The New Today, 10 May 2013*

Local attorney-at-law, Derick Sylvester is experiencing difficulties in recovering a large sum of money invested in the financially-troubled British American Insurance Company (BAICO) on behalf of one of his clients.

According to Sylvester, the client was able to obtain a default judgement against the insurance company earlier this year.

He told reporters last week Thursday that his client who is a medical doctor by profession had invested more than five million dollars in the British American Annuity Plan.

He said that from all indications they are being shunned by the insurance company.

"To date not a single cent has been paid, neither no correspondece has been received from the other side as it relates to if this money could be repaid," he remarked.

However, the lawyer said despite the scant courtesy being shown to them they remain hopeful that with time British American could be resuscitated by the intervention of the regional governments.

Just last week it was reported that in a move designed to safeguard the interests of BAICO policyholders across the Eastern Caribbean, governments of the sub-region have agreed to create a new entity to take over the operations of the multi-national firm.

Under the plan, the new company would handle the traditional life insurance, medical insurance and annuity business of British American branches and would be headquartered in the Eastern Caribbean.

That plan ensures that British American does not become a systemic risk to the financial system of the sub-region, and is also designed to "protect, as far as practicable, the interests of depositors and investors, (and) to keep British American as a "going concern" in a form to be determined and to craft a solution that is regional in nature."

Sylvester expressed regrets that the Government of Trinidad and Tobago has pumped the bulk of bail-out money into Colonial Life Insurance Company, Trinidad and not the others run by the beleaguered CL Financial group.

This, he said is rather unfortunate since "the monies that hard-working Grenadians would have saved and invested, just passed through a company (British American), moved to another country (Trinidad) and you have Grenadians who are suffering".

Earlier this year, the Trinidad & Tobago government was forced to pump billions of dollars in a rescue package for British American's parent company, CL Financial, and particularly its flag ship company, CLICO.

The financial problems at the Port-of-Spain-based conglomerate have had a rippling effect on several Caribbean countries where the company had operations.

*Derek Sylvester – wants to get money for his client*

*The New Today, 10 May 2013*

## POLICE SHOOT RETIREE

The practice of law has taught me so many lessons; brought a series of joys, pain, anxiety and enthusiasm. Every day brought on new challenges. Being young and energetic was a blessing. On some occasions it would be magistrate courts which would cause me to travel around the country or being able to marshal numerous chambers or master's court on the same day. I loved what I did, so the physical exertion at the end of the day was minuscule in relation to the joy of practising.

Every student, if not all, would like to make their teachers proud, as it sends a resounding message that you did not waste their time and that their efforts were well appreciated. To be called upon as a professional to work for your teacher creates a measure of anxiety, as you do not want to fail them. This was what occurred in the year 2009. I received a phone call from my teacher Deloris James, who taught me at Wesley College Secondary School; she was rather distraught when she relayed the message to me. Her father Augustine 'Lahay' Antoine, who was 73 years of age, was allegedly shot by bandits when he was in his shop at Hope Vale, St. George. I immediately made the necessary phone calls to the police station to confirm the accuracy of the information received.

However to my consternation, I was informed that the police had shot the senior citizen in his back while in his shop, while they were proceeding to execute a search warrant. This was difficult news to be relayed but it was done. I proceeded to the General Hospital as I was notified that Antoine was housed there. I was unable to see him. My concern at the time was that he may have succumbed to his injuries.

Sometime after I visited Antoine after receiving instructions, I was convinced that a civil suit needed to be filed. It was subsequently filed.

Police Shoot [illegible]3 year old in Back

Augustine Lahay Antoine - Shot in the back

*Front Page, Spice Isle Review, week ending 19 March 2009*

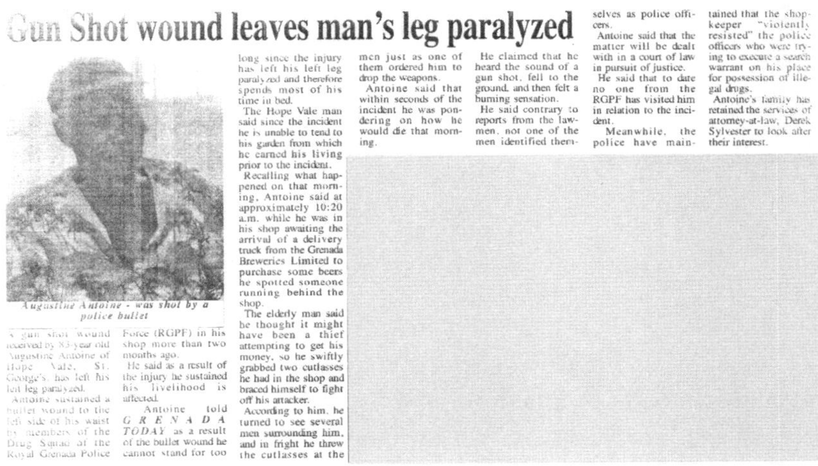

Gun Shot wound leaves man's leg paralyzed

Augustine Antoine - was shot by a police bullet

A gun shot wound received by 83-year old Augustine Antoine of Hope Vale, St. George's, has left his left leg paralyzed.

Antoine sustained a bullet wound to the left side of his waist by members of the Drug Squad of the Royal Grenada Police Force (RGPF) in his shop more than two months ago.

He said as a result of the injury he sustained his livelihood is affected.

Antoine told GRENADA TODAY as a result of the bullet wound he cannot stand for too long since the injury has left his left leg paralyzed and therefore spends most of his time in bed.

The Hope Vale man said since the incident he is unable to tend to his garden from which he earned his living prior to the incident.

Recalling what happened on that morning, Antoine said at approximately 10:20 a.m. while he was in his shop awaiting the arrival of a delivery truck from the Grenada Breweries Limited to purchase some beers he spotted someone running behind the shop.

The elderly man said he thought it might have been a thief attempting to get his money, so he swiftly grabbed two cutlasses he had in the shop and braced himself to fight off his attacker.

According to him, he turned to see several men surrounding him, and in fright he threw the cutlasses at the men just as one of them ordered him to drop the weapons.

Antoine said that within seconds of the incident he was pondering on how he would die that morning.

He claimed that he heard the sound of a gun shot, fell to the ground, and then felt a burning sensation.

He said contrary to reports from the lawmen, not one of the men identified themselves as police officers.

Antoine said that the matter will be dealt with in a court of law in pursuit of justice.

He said that to date no one from the RGPF has visited him in relation to the incident.

Meanwhile, the police have maintained that the shopkeeper "violently resisted" the police officers who were trying to execute a search warrant on his place for possession of illegal drugs.

Antoine's family has retained the services of attorney-at-law, Derek Sylvester to look after their interest.

*Grenada Today, 29 May 2009*

The injury to Antoine's back was serious, he had to undergo surgery, but he survived. He was indeed a strong man for his age. He was under the impression that he was about to be robbed by men who were in plain clothes, bearing guns and who crept up on him. It was alleged then that it was the incorrect location where the warrant had to be executed. The civil suit resulted in judgment against the State, a financial sum was awarded. It brought that aspect of the matter to an end. However, the psychological trauma, pain and immobility caused to a man who was otherwise very mobile and agile was dreadful.

The conclusion of the matter brought a sense of relief as I had not failed my teacher at a time when she needed me most.

## MURDER IN SOUBISE

Too many times, lives are lost. For all that is left are the memories of the deceased. Irrespective of their earthly behaviour, they are missed by the ones who love them most.

A mother's love has no boundary for her child. It is limitless. Even in the face of a son of hers allegedly committing serious offences, a mother would tell you how wonderful her son is. This may be correctly so, having never seen the other side of their child. I have learnt that sometimes

21-year-old Lindon Mason who was charged in connection with the murder of Shevon Augustine

**Mason Charged for Murder**

— Page 3 —

**Mason charged for Murder**

Six young men were arrested within hours after the body of 18 year-old Stevon Augustine, a resident of Mt. Fan, St. Andrew's was recently discovered around 5:45 am on the beach at Soubise.

However, hours later five were released as another former SAASS student was formally charged for the murder of Augustine.

21-year-old mechanic, Lindon Mason, a resident of Tuilleries appeared before Magistrate Paryag to answer the charge for murder at the Grenville Magistrate Court last week Thursday. Mason's legal representative, Derek Sylvester, one of Grenada's leading criminal attorneys wass disappointed as three state witnesses failed to appear as his client was remanded to Her Majesty's Prison.

Augustine died as result of a single stab wound close to his heart around 2:00 am while walking through the community of Soubise with a male friend on his way home from St Andrews carnival launch at the Grenville Car Park. It is said that the male friend who escaped unhurt and one of the five released from police custody revealed pertinent information that led to the arrest Mason.

***SIR*** confirmed that both Mason and Augustine were involved in a court matter that resulted in cross charges of wounding and causing harm from a previous incident that took place after an evening academic class. It is alleged that Augustine attacked Mason beating him with a piece of wood and the young man who escaped was also part of or witnessed the attack.

A reliable source alleged that Augustine made a report to the Grenville Police Station the day before he was murdered

The curious crowd who gathered at the front of the Grenville Magistrate Court expressed their dissatisfaction openly when they learnt that one person was charged in the attack in which Augustine lost his life.

*Spice Isle Review, week ending 23 July 2009*

even the best of us do err on the other side of the law. It may be a traffic offence of speeding, or a more serious offence. However on most occasions some thing or things would have motivated it. Even the most heinous murders may be motivated by revenge, greed or jealousy; the list is not exhaustive.

When a twenty one (21) year old mechanic inflicted a fatal wound to a young man of similar age, little did he know that this was the beginning of a nightmare. He must have thought that the injured man would recover maybe with medical attention. The accused went home and slept. However he was awakened the next morning by police officers seeking his assistance in solving a murder which occurred the night before. That young man had to face the reality and consequences of his action. He was detained and subsequently charged for murder.

The accused's parents were distraught. They were both teachers, but they were also in pain for the loss of life of the deceased allegedly at the hands of their son. I saw the parents' pain. It was a constant reminder how in the heat of one moment of attack or anger, one's action could lead to damaging consequences. The thought of incarceration was traumatic especially for young persons who are accustomed to enjoying their youthful life. So many times I heard the words, "if" or "if only". We must suffer the earthly consequences of our actions.

The preliminary inquiry was conducted at the Magistrate's Court. The court found that a sufficient case was made out on the evidence. The accused was indicted to stand trial in the High Court for murder.

The parents, family and friends of the accused were very uneasy at the prospect of the likely penalty which could have been imposed on the young man. However, they never forgot the pain and grief of the deceased's parents. That to me was commendable; one cannot be so consumed with one's own sorrow that one fails to recognise that the accused's action also caused unimaginable horror to the deceased's family.

The trial was heard before Justice St. Paul sitting with a jury. The days rolled by slowly. I always dreaded the moment of truth, the jury's verdict. The accused, family and friends waited in anticipation. I was hopeful that if self defence did not succeed, at least a compromise verdict of manslaughter would suffice, that would be appeasing to all.

The foreman announced that they were not unanimous in their verdict. I immediately felt there would be a retrial. This I always dreaded, as it

# Lindon Mason walks free

*Lindon Mason – set free by Court of Appeal*

After being incarcerated for just over two years at Her Majesty's Prison at Richmond Hill, St. George's, a Munich man, Lindon Mason is now a free man.

Mason was set free by the Eastern Caribbean Court of Appeal on Monday after the Justices squashed the conviction and sentence of manslaughter at the high court.

The Three Justices of Appeal did not order a retrial of Mason who was accused of causing the death of Stefan Augustine on July 13 2009 at Soubise, St. Andrew's

Defense counsel, Derick Sylvester argued that there were certain mis-directions given by the presiding judge Justice Lyle St. Paul to the jurors.

According to Sylvester, the Director of Public Prosecutions (DPP), Christopher Nelson was forced to acknowledge before the Court of Appeal that he was faced with an insurmountable hurdle to respond to his submission.

He said with his submission having been accepted, the court was left with the choice of whether or not to order a retrial.

Mason was sentenced to five years and has already served more than three quarter of the sentence, with nine more months remaining. He was due to be released this year.

The sentence was to run from the time the prisoner was placed on remand, in July 2009.

Mason who is a TAMCC graduate intends to pursue studies in the field of Mechanical Engineering.

*Defense Attorney Derick Sylvester – successfully appealed the conviction and sentence of his client*

*The New Today, 3 February 2012*

was like walking the same road twice to achieve the same objective. The question was then put: "In what proportion are you divided?" The foreman said 10:2. This was welcoming. I was just hoping the 10 was in the accused's favour. The time soon came as I was directly in front of the accused in the court room. They normally sit directly behind their attorney in the court. When the foreman said, "Not guilty of murder," I heard an immediate exhalation from the accused, then the foreman said, "but guilty of manslaughter." It was a relief albeit not an absolute one. The accused was sentenced to five (5) years imprisonment. However, an appeal was filed in the Court of Appeal with numeorus legal grounds. The three member panel of the court accepted the submission that was presented by me. He was acquitted.

## RAPE ACCUSED FREED

Sexual offence cases raise so many nuances; one such example is when there is a relationship between the parties and a child is involved. In the matter of COP v. Keron Brown, at the magisterial level, the issue was one of jurisdiction; whether the case was in the proper district, since a magistrate was a creature of statute, she was duty bound to have the case heard and determined in the district where the offence occurred or else she would be acting outside of her jurisdiction.

I was not involved with the matter at the magisterial level. However, when it got to the High Court, I was asked by the court to provide assistance pro bono to the accused, as the nature of the case was such that if the accused was convicted, this could have resulted in serious consequences.

The accused was a veterinarian. He denied the allegation in its entirety. I was determined to assist the court whenever called upon to do so. I was taught that my first duty was to the court and should not fail in that duty especially when called upon to assist an unrepresented accused. I accepted the responsibility that was placed on my shoulders. I took the file from the accused and had a long night researching every aspect of the law imaginable, including: corroboration, recent complaint, consent, voluntariness of statement, hearsay and prejudicial versus probative statements.

The next day after the jury was empanelled; I embarked on the trial journey. The accused was very calm, unlike most persons who would be in the position of a possible lengthy custodial sentence. The trial

Error in Court handling Guyanese rape suspect ?

"I want my cell phone back"

Page 2

21 year old Antonio Lewis in stripe jersey - - Story on page 3

32 year old Guyanese Kerron Brown

*Front page, Spice Isle Review, 14 May 2009*

proceeded with cross examination on every facet of the relevant facts. The addresses to the jury were to the point. I also bore in mind that the nine member jury panel in rape matters were adults and wise in the ways of the world. When the accused gave his evidence, he appeared very comfortable and caring. He not only cared for animals, but he came across as very loving to his girlfriend who was also the mother of his child. I was of the view that this matter would be an easy one and a unanimous not guilty verdict would be released very soon. Oh I was so wrong! The time rolled by when the jury exhausted their time for deliberation. They came out of the jury room all looking a bit perturbed. That was disconcerting for me.

However, they were not unanimous. The foreman indicated unanimity among them would not be possible. They were divided 7:2. I tried to read their faces, but they were emotionless. I was left to wonder. However, when the foreman was asked what was the verdict he paused, then said, seven (7) not guilty two (2) guilty. I breathed a sigh of relief, not as a result of the verdict but because the accused if found guilty would not have been able to care for his child, which was his desire. The Judge then asked the accused to stand. He was discharged. The accused disappeared from sight not even looking in my direction; I excused him because I felt then, that he was too excited to remain to express his gratitude.

**Errors in the handling of Guyanese rape suspect ?**

A citizen of Guyana employed with the Grenada Project was charged for the offence of rape. However, there has been a breakdown of the correct process at the Grenville Magistrate Court that may extend to other courtrooms in the country.

Kerron Brown, a 32 year old Guyanese citizen appeared before Magistrate Henry Paryag at the Grenville Magistrate Court last week Wednesday. He was granted bail in the sum of $10,000.00 dollars, two sureties and was required to surrender his travel documents.

Brown who resided at Belmont Estate at the time of the incident was an employee at the Goat Dairy located on the compound, the first of its kind in Grenada. It was planned, developed and implemented by the Grenada Project.

The decision of Magistrate Paryag to grant bail to Brown has not gone down well with some of the St. Andrew's residents present at the court. It has displayed levels of incompetence within the Royal Grenada Police Force. A dissatisfied female commented that the courtroom was now the playground for criminals on learning that Brown was granted bail. Another resident was of the notion that persons who commit or are charged for suspected crimes that are recipients of work permits should remain in the care of the state. However, unknown to both individuals the case itself was decided in the wrong jurisdiction.

The 19 year old female victim who reported the matter to the Grenville Police Station would have given a signed statement of where the alleged rape occurred. *SIR* has confirmed that Brown's case must now be moved to the Sauteurs Magistrate Court because the alleged rape incident took place within that jurisdiction.

According to an attorney-at-law "sometimes believe it or not," police officers do not know where one parish starts and the other ends. He noted that the "Jurisdiction always lie with the sitting Magistrate."

Many Grenadians are of the view that Grenada's Judicial System has collapsed and is laced with biases since the transfer of particular magistrates to specific jurisdictions.

To date there has been no explanation to the public on the decision of Brown's rape charge which should not have been decided at the Grenville Magistrate Court. This has prompted several questions; Did Magistrate Henry Paryag notify the magistrate in St. Patrick's or was the magistrate in St. Patrick's sitting or not give instructions on the matter involving Brown? Did this judicial mistake release Brown from police custody?

Recently, court decisions at the Grenville Magistrate Court have been the subject of discussion by many persons in the parish since the transfer of Magistrate Jerry Seales. Only months ago, an incident involving the alleged rape of a 12-year-old schoolgirl who attends a prominent secondary school in the parish was considered by some persons as another failure of the government to properly protect the youths of this nation.

*Spice Isle Review, 14 May 2009*

The days rolled by. I never saw the accused. I felt he would come by to express his thanks, but that did not happen. Subsequently we met on a few occasions, when he was summoned to the magistrate's court for maintenance of the said child. On no occasion did he ever express his gratitude. I have learnt that my duty is always to the court. Any benefit thereafter is collateral to the true cause of justice.

## CALYPSONIAN CHARGED

When an accused, a public figure is charged criminally, there is immense pressure as society holds that person out as an exemplar or role model. A famous calypsonian was charged with defilement of a female, it sparked tremendous debate in all media houses. It created a discussion ranging from the age of consent to penalty and punishment.

I completed the preliminary inquiry at the Sauteurs Magistrate Court. It was an interesting case for many reasons. There was the evidence of a 'peeping tom' who allegedly saw the encounter in the bushes. It was a defence at that time to a charge of defilement, that the accused honestly believed the complainant was 16 years or older. This was a very viable defence in this case. I have seen instances where the complainant is much bigger in size and stature than the male accused. In those cases, there is a viable explanation why a young person can be easily misled, eventually becoming a victim of crime.

The matter was later transferred to another lawyer, who represented the accused at the High Court.

# Calypsonian "Biko" charged with rape

Grenada's [illegible] Calypso Monarch [illegible] Biko Lewis has been slapped with a charged of rape, which has the potential of landing him behind bars for fifteen years.

Biko appeared before Magistrate Nevelyn John at the St Patrick's Magistrate Court last Wednesday to have the indictable charge of rape read out to him.

Being an indictable charge, the Calypsonian was not allowed to plead since his case, with sufficient evidence advanced by the prosecution, can be determine by a High Court Judge.

The twenty-four year old resident from the village of Chantimelle in St Patrick, who quickly rose to prominence after winning the National Calypso Monarch in 2008 with his selections "Ah cant Understand" and " I done with that", was accused of sexually molesting a fifteen-year-old child some three weeks ago.

Sources told the Informer that the alleged victim in this matter was on her way to Church when she was offered a ride by the Calypsion who lives in the same village.

It was then reported that the accused drove off to some nearby bushes where the incident allegedly happened.

During Wednesday's Court appearance, Biko was assisted by Lawyer - Mrs. Annette Henry, who acted on behalf of Attorney-at-law Derrick Sylvester.

In making a case for bail, Henry told the Court that Biko was no flight risk and no treat to society, and she assured the Court that he would show up for his trial when required to do so.

Additionally, the lawyer told the Court that the matter is a bailable one and therefore Biko, as a matter of right, is entitled.

Nevertheless, despite the case made by the Lawyer, the prosecution team hinted that it has no intention to oppose the request; however, he hinted that certain conditions should be in place if the Court is so minded.

Bail was granted in the sum of twenty thousand dollars ($20,000.00) with two sureties. In addition, Biko was asked to surrender all travel documents including ID, and seek permission from the police if he intends to leave the country.

Added to that, Biko was barred from going within 20 feet of the victim, plus he must report to the St Patrick's police Station once a week between the hours of 9 a.m. and 6 p.m.

Meanwhile, not many persons in the Chantimelle area, including the alleged victim in this matter, are buying the story as presented by the prosecution.

One individual told the Informer that the move is designed to tarnish the name of the upcoming artiste, and the young lady in this matter is just one of the many players in the game.

Despite the many claims, a Calypsonian's future is on the line and so too is the reputation of a young lady.

*Grenada Informer, 8 May 2009*

**$20,000 Bail Granted**

*Front page, Grenada Informer, week ending 8 May 2009*

## POLICE OFFICERS RUN AFOUL OF THE LAW

Policemen ought to be held to the highest professional standard in a democratic society. When they are charged with criminal offences it brings the police force into some form of public odium, in that members of the public immediately come to a conclusion as to the guilt or innocence of the policemen charged. The presumption of innocence is fully enshrined in the Constitution; but public sentiments sometimes ignore that presumption. On many occasions I have dealt with matters involving police officers. It distresses their colleagues to detain, arrest, proffer charges leading to arraignment and subsequently bail.

During the year 2009, I represented two police officers. One was for the indictable offence of indecent assault. The other for causing harm, assault on a police officer, obscene language and threat of unlawful harm. The offence of indecent assault was slapped on Officer No. 1 who was interdicted from duty with half month's pay pending the outcome of the matter. It was customary that police officers were prosecutors at the Magistrate's Court, therefore the police would be prosecuting one of its very own.

After the accused was charged, bail was granted to him. The preliminary inquiry commenced. Through cross examination the foundation was laid for the trial of the matter before a judge and jury. It was really a question of fact as to who the jury believed, since the evidence was diametrically opposed. The police officer had a lot at stake. Since, if he was convicted, apart from facing the likelihood of imprisonment, he also faced the possibility of losing his family, together with retirement benefits he would have gained from numerous years of service.

The trial was adrenalin infested as so much was at stake. The jury was empanelled. I maximised the jury challenges, to ensure there was a good mix of male, female, young and old, so as to ensure mature, measured discourse would take place in the jury room. The trial progressed. After completion of the evidence, both the Prosecutor and I addressed the jury. The Judge summed up the case to the jury, on the law and facts. It was at this stage that I drafted the possible grounds of appeal. This was just a precaution should my client be convicted. The issues were fresher in my mind at that time. I listened intently, but I got no substantial grounds should I have to file an appeal.

The fate of the accused was now in the hands of the jury. We braced ourselves for the likely verdict but at the same time we were hopeful. I had occasion to question the jury's verdict in the past, but I had faith in the jury system. I left the court room to return to my office which was just a stone's throw away. The criminal court at that time was in a building owned by the Anglican Church on Lucas Street. I could have seen the court from my office. I gave instructions to telephone me when the jury was ready. The accused at that time could not have departed the precincts of the court, but had to remain until the verdict was read, to know his fate.

Approximately two hours later, I received the phone call. Then made my way to the court. I sat quietly as the jury was escorted to their seats, to the usual scenario I have grown so accustomed to. The accused was on edge. But I encouraged him that the jurors were members of the community who were wise in the ways of the world. The foreman did not look our way but focused on the judge as he was asked the usual question, "Are you unanimous?" He answered in the positive. "Is the accused guilty or not guilty?" He lifted his head and answered in the negative.

It was a joyous moment when the accused was dispatched by the trial judge. Life's lessons are sometimes learned the hard way, but along life's road challenges and trials are sure.

# POLICEMEN RUN AFOUL OF THE LAW

*Commissioner Clarkson - planning to crack down on police officers operating buses in the Terminus*

Two local lawmen have found themselves on the wrong side of the law and are facing possible dismissal from the Royal Grenada Police Force (RGPF) pending the outcome of their court matters.

Police have confirmed that Wilfred Buckmire, a 39 year old officer, residing at Perdmontemps, St. David's, has been charged with the criminal offence of Indecent Assault.

Buckmire has been granted bail in the sum of $10,000.00 with two sureties.

According to a report from the Public Relations Department of the Force, the incident allegedly occurred on May 9.

Buckmire who is attached to the Police Fire Department at Point Salines will make his first court appearance on June 23 at the St. David's Magistrate's Court.

Meanwhile, Jason James, son of former Police Commissioner Winston James has been placed on bail in the sum of $4,000 with one surety for an offence that took place at the Bus Terminus on Melville Street last week Wednesday.

James, a policeman himself, was off duty driving a bus when he got into an altercation with Sgt. Reginald Sylvester who is attached to the Criminal Investigation Department (CID).

Four charges were laid against 28 year old James - use of obscene language, causing harm, assault on a Police Officer and threats of unlawful harm.

James who resides at Mt. Granby, St. John's, is scheduled to appear before the St. George' Magistrate Court on June 23 to answer the charges.

Officers of the Criminal Investigations Department (CID) have indicated that additional charges could be laid against James and he has been advised accordingly.

In response to the incident, Commissioner of Police, James Clarkson who was out of State attending the Annual Conference of Commissioners of Police of the region in Guyana, indicated that he intends to address the matter of Police Officers operating buses and other forms of public transportation without the proper authorisation and permission of the Office of the Commissioner of Police.

Clarkson gave the nation the assurance that the actions and conduct of the two Officers in question are not a reflection of the general membership of the Force, and both matters would be expeditiously dealt with.

"Unfortunately in every institution there would be these isolated occurrences, but within the ranks of the Royal Grenada Police Force we have zero tolerance for such behavior, and the consequences are clearly spelled out", he said.

Both James and Buckmire have been suspended from duties effective May 14, in accordance with Chapter 244 Section 39 (1) of the Police Act.

In unrelated news, police are also said to be carrying out investigations into an alleged beating of a police officer by two females.

Reports indicate that the officer who is attached to the SSU outfit at Point Salines received a severe beating including a busted head from the females in an incident which took place last week.

Information regarding this incident remains very sketchy.

However GRENADA TODAY understand that the officer who was allegedly under the influence of alcohol reportedly made some remarks to one of the ladies which led to the incident.

The beaten officer was once attached to the Police Musical Band before he was transferred to SSU.

*Front page, Grenada Today, 22 May 2009*

The police officer No. 2 was allegedly involved in an altercation with other police officers, wherein he sustained a laceration to his head. It was alleged that a fight ensued between them. It was highly irregular for police officers to fight with each other in public. The accused was off duty, driving a motor omnibus for hire at the time.

He was charged. I made numerous enquiries from the prosecution as to whether cross criminal charges would be filed against the other police officers. It was evident, though it was under consideration, nothing was likely to happen. There was a statutory period of ninety (90) days for filing summary complaints.

I then proceeded to file numerous private criminal complaints against the other police officers who were not charged. The same was filed and served on them. I was concerned then, that I had not spoken to or engaged the Director of Public Prosecutions on the matter. I knew he would allow the law to take its course and not intervene to interrupt the prosecution. As time passed I was right in my assessment of him. He did not intervene to terminate the matters pursuant to his powers to *nolle prosequi*.

The cross charges caused some stir since the other police officers now had to secure the services of attorneys to represent them. An attorney from the Attorney General's Chambers intervened to provide representation for them. The manoeuvre of the cross criminal complainant was effective as it was tactical. The end result of the matter was such that the officers returned to work. There was ultimately no resort to trial. The ends of justice were well served.

## BRITISH DRUG MULE

Drugs are a scourge on any society, and its mules are known to transit the Caribbean with drugs *en* route to England, North America and other Caribbean islands. Many times, unsuspecting persons are charged with these crimes. Young persons are normally sent on missions, to deliver packages and sometimes not even being aware as to the contents of them. On other occasions, when persons are aware that they are embarking on an illegal enterprise, uneasiness and nervousness consume them to the point that it becomes obvious to the trained police investigating eye that something is amiss.

On one occasion a female accused was nabbed at the airport with cocaine as she was about to board a flight *en route* to England. The drugs were placed inside souvenir craft. It was not easily noticeable, but it was discovered by the police. The accused being a British citizen, she had the option if convicted to apply to return to England to complete her sentence, if it was one of imprisonment. This was the arrangement, between Grenada and the United Kingdom. It was an option that the accused could have exercised.

The accused was sentenced to Her Majesty's Prison (HMP). I made periodic visits to see her. The detention and arrest of non-nationals always caused anxiety for the families in distant lands. Pre-trial remand was almost always the case, as the possibility of flight risk was so great that bail was almost always denied.

## British drug suspect caught again

One week after a Canadian woman fell victim to law enforcement officers in Grenada on suspicion of Possession and Trafficking the illegal drug – Cocaine, another young lady, this time a British national, has suffered the same fate.

Helen Theresa Hosang

According to information reaching the Grenada Informer, Helen Theresa Hosang was nabbed by members of the drug squad moments before she was due to board an aircraft en route back to England.

A source told the Informer the young lady showed clear signs of uneasiness, which led members of the Drugs Squad to carry out a search, finding what appeared to be hidden in some art and craft that the young lady was carrying.

Informer was told the crafts were specially made for the purpose for which the young lady was using it since on the outside everything seems ok but special carving on the inside made an easy carrier for additional luggage.

Sources told the Informer a number of packages were found in the crafts, samples of which have been sent for further testing by the chemist.

During her first Court appearance on Monday, Hosang appeared to be jovial, posing for the media as she made her way the Court.

The matter however did not get off to a start neither were the charges read, as the defense lawyer Derrick Sylvester hinted to the Court that he needed more time to converse with his client, in addition to full disclosure from the Prosecution team.

Drug-related offences in Grenada carry heavy penalties: prison term can exceed twenty years, fine in excess of two hundred and fifty thousand dollars and

*Grenada Informer weekly newspaper*

## CRUISE SHIP THEFT

There was an alleged stealing in excess of one million dollars on the high seas, when an employee of a cruise ship together with two other accomplices were detained in Grenadian waters, after the ship docked. I represented two of the three suspects. The challenging issue was where the crime occurred. Was it within our jurisdiction? However, the preliminary inquiry started. It was evident that the money was taken while the ship was docked at the port. The next question was whether some or all of the money was stolen at the port. The evidence soon came to light and the purported jurisdictional challenge was rendered nugatory.

In any event, the preliminary inquiry was exhaustive. There was tremendous anxiety on the part of the accused to complete the trial. On every occasion I had to urge the court to expedite the matter. Since most of the witnesses were employed on the tourist ship, the schedule for the hearing had to be prearranged for the occasions when the ship was in port. The court was a stone's throw away from the port. At the hearing you could look from the window of the court and see the ship docked at the Melville Street port. The preliminary Inquiry was of some duration, as numerous witnesses were called. However, both the defence and prosecution worked assiduously to complete the inquiry. One of the accused men had a medical condition. The other accused had injuries,

### P. I. starts into theft on Cruise Ship

*Two of the nationals of Honduras Marlon Roderiquez and Marcio Davila and the female suspect from Colombia, Claudia Vanegas as they made an appearance in the Magistrate's Court*

Efforts are being made to have a speedy trial in the case involving a Colombian woman and two men from Honduras who are accused of stealing just over one million dollars from a cruise ship that makes weekly calls to Grenada.

Marlon Geovanni Conelas Rodriquez, 3[illegible], 34-year old Marcio Gabriel Aguilar Davila, an international marketing officer, and 38-year old Claudia Graciela Otero Vanegas were arrested in Grenville, St. Andrew's late last month as they attempted to board the boat, Clarion J 3 to Trinidad which was being captained by Davis David.

The three non-nationals are accused of stealing cash from the MV Ocean Dream which was docked at the Cruise Ship Terminal on Melville Street, St. George's on January 27 cash amounting to EC $1,375,123.80 which Vanegas had access to by reason of her employment on the cruise ship.

The three suspects are also facing a charge of being in possession of EC $1,375,123.80 knowing the same to be proceeds of the cruise ship which visits Grenada during the winter months. .

The Preliminary Inquiry (P. I.) into the matter began on February 24 at the St. George's Number One Magistrate's Court with the Chief Accountant , Alba Nancy Penia who is employed with the ship's parent company, Pullmantur Cruises, giving evidence.

Penia who works on Ocean Dream is the senior accountant to Vanegas who served as an assistant accountant with responsibility for preparing the payroll and distribution of monthly salaries to workers.

The Colombian also had responsibility for receiving payments on board the ship, in addition to managing a float of 5,000 Euros that was assigned to her.

The P. I. continued resumed last Tuesday with evidence being provided by two other employees of Pullmantur Cruises who work on MV Ocean Dream - the Chief Purser, Adriana Reyes, and Miguel Martinez who is the chief of security.

Local police were forced to issue a bulletin asking Grenadians to be on the looking for Vanegas who was reported as missing after the boat had departed Port St. George without her.

The two Honduran men are being represented by attorney-at-law, Derick Sylvester, while Vanegas is being represented by his colleague, Francis Williams.

Director of Public Prosecution (DPP) Christopher Nelson who is leading the evidence on behalf of the State gave his commitment to the court to work along with the defense team to have the matter concluded expeditiously.

Both the Prosecution and Defense are looking to have the P. I. concluded quickly with the hope of having the case dealt with during the current sitting of the criminal assizes.

Just before the P. I. began last week Sylvester brought to the court's attention the medical condition of Davila who has had triple bypass surgery in the past.

The suspect claimed that he was having tremendous pain in his stomach, waist, forearm and head as a result of beating inflicted on him by the police in the course of their investigation.

A police source close to the investigation told ***GRENADA TODAY*** that at no time was Davila beaten by the lawmen.

According to the source, the Honduran tried to evade police custody after he was arrested, and could have damaged himself in the failed attempt to escape lawful police custody.

Sylvester again on Tuesday voiced concern about the medical condition of his clients.

He told the court that is being presided over by Magistrate Tamara Gill that both Davila and Rodriquez were passing blood in their faeces and sought the DPP's intervention to secure urgent medical attention for them at the St. George's General Hospital.

During Tuesday's court sitting, Davila who complained of stomach pain, was granted permission to use the bathroom.

The P. I. is due to resume on March 18.

*Grenada Today, 13 March 2009*

which were explained or justified by different versions depending on who you asked. The police had one version. The accused men had another.

It was interesting as there was an interpreter who was present during the investigation. He was able to shed some light on the differing versions; the interpreter supported one version. However, he was reluctant to provide a written statement. I was able to make several inroads in cross examination, but even if the statements were excluded, the video footage and other evidence were overwhelming. The preliminary inquiry was completed, with numerous objections and submissions on the law. The High Court trial was conducted by another attorney.

## UNSUSPECTING ACCUSED

When accused are charged with criminal offences, sometimes the circumstances surrounding the charge could be aggravating; for instance, when an employee placed in a position of trust, breaches that trust. An employee in a postal corporation, whose duty involved packaging, bore a serious responsibility. However, in a small society such as Grenada, persons tend to repose trust and confidence in others with whom they

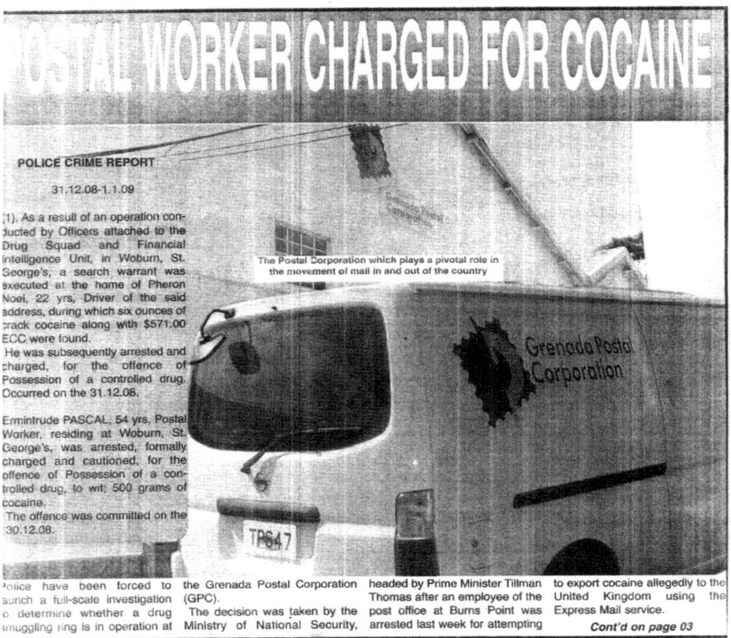

OSTAL WORKER CHARGED FOR COCAINE

POLICE CRIME REPORT

31.12.08-1.1.09

(1). As a result of an operation conducted by Officers attached to the Drug Squad and Financial Intelligence Unit, in Woburn, St. George's, a search warrant was executed at the home of Pheron Noel, 22 yrs, Driver of the said address, during which six ounces of crack cocaine along with $571.00 ECC were found.

He was subsequently arrested and charged, for the offence of Possession of a controlled drug. Occurred on the 31.12.08.

Ermintrude PASCAL, 54 yrs, Postal Worker, residing at Woburn, St. George's, was arrested, formally charged and cautioned, for the offence of Possession of a controlled drug, to wit; 500 grams of cocaine.

The offence was committed on the 30.12.08.

The Postal Corporation which plays a pivotal role in the movement of mail in and out of the country

Police have been forced to launch a full-scale investigation to determine whether a drug smuggling ring is in operation at the Grenada Postal Corporation (GPC).

The decision was taken by the Ministry of National Security, headed by Prime Minister Tillman Thomas after an employee of the post office at Burns Point was arrested last week for attempting to export cocaine allegedly to the United Kingdom using the Express Mail service.

Cont'd on page 03

*Front page, Grenada Today, week ending 9 January 2009*

are acquainted. On one occasion, a postal employee accepted a package for shipping. It was later discovered that there were illegal substances in that package. This placed the employee in a precarious situation.

The package was not opened or packed by her. A person's desire to help or assist another can be a catalyst for arrest even though that person may not have the knowledge of the illegality. Hence, the need for well researched and in-depth trials. If that is not done the unsuspecting innocent person may very well be convicted. The lesson in that trial was that you take nothing for granted.

## DEATH OF FLOWER LADY

When well-known persons in the society are killed under sudden tragic circumstances, it leaves a depth of deep seething grief. Particularly, in road traffic accidents. This was the occasion when Shirma Williams, a well-known florist and entrepreneur whose business was located in the city of St. George's, met her demise. On one fateful night on the western side of Grenada in the village of Palmiste in the parish of Saint John, the victim came from the gym. It was alleged she was wearing dark clothing. The time was approximately 7 pm. The road in the vicinity was not well

FLOWER LADY KILLED ON THE ROAD

The mini bus that brought a horrible end to the life of the small businesswoman

Grenada has recorded its second road fatality for the year.

Dead is 54-year Shirma Williams who operates Shirma's Floral - a small floral arrangement business on Gore Street in St. George's.

She was struck by a commuter bus, registration number HU 234 in Palmiste, St. John, just after 7:00 p.m. last week Wednesday night.

been dropped off from a c[illegible] when the accident occurred.

Reports say the Waterloo, S[illegible] John's resident attempted [illegible] stop the bus to take her [illegible] Gouyave when she came in[illegible] contact with the vehicle.

The white Toyota bus which [illegible] assigned to Zone 5 route trave[illegible] between Sauteurs and S[illegible] George's.

Cont'd on page 03

Shirma Williams - knocked to death on the Palmiste stretch in St. John's

*Front page, Grenada Today, week ending 20 March 2009*

# FLOWER LADY KILLED ON THE ROAD

[illegible] from front page

[illegible] the time of the acci- [illegible] the bus was being [illegible] by Andy James [illegible] is popularly called [illegible] Spider" from Mt. Rose, [illegible] Patrick's.

Police investigators [illegible] that Spider [illegible] he did not see [illegible] but only [illegible] the impact.

[illegible] the govern- [illegible] National [illegible] Congress [illegible] of Prime [illegible] Tillman Thomas has expresses condolences to the family of Williams on her untimely passing.

A statement issued by the ruling party said Congress is saddened and shocked at the recent vehicular accident that claimed the life of the business-woman.

"Words cannot begin to convey the extreme sadness we feel at the death of Shirma," said NDC General Secretary Peter David who is also the island's Minister of Foreign Affairs.

"It's a deep loss to her family, first and foremost. It is also a loss to all her friends, including Party Leader Tillman Thomas and the rest of the executive and members of the National Democratic Congress", he added.

One NDC supporter described Shirma who attended the NDC Convention on March 1 at the GBSS auditorium as a "loyal member and supporter of the National Democratic Congress."

"Our thoughts and prayers go out to Shirma's family and friends during this time of sorrow," the party supporter said.

The first road fatality took place on February 21.

The victim was 49-year old Donnet George from Hermitage, St. Patrick's.

Police are still continuing their investigations into the fatal accident.

*Grenada Today, 20 March 2009*

lit. As she alighted a vehicle, and in attempting to cross the street, she was struck by a passenger bus and killed instantly.

The driver whom I represented was distraught, since the victim would regularly commute on his bus. The lighting and other circumstances at the time created a hazardous situation coupled with the accident occurring at a bend in the road. The accused's licence was suspended. The rigors of the trial ensued. Despite his success at trial, it was a loss. He was a driver with numerous years of experience. Taking the life of another human being, even without a sentence of incarceration left him with a bitter pill to swallow.

## SCABBY KILLS MERCILESS

In the north eastern constituency of New Hampshire in the parish of Saint George, news broke that there was a murder. The deceased, aka Merciless, a relatively young man had received an injury inflicted by a fellow villager, aka Scabby, who was the owner of a shop. The village was shaken to the core, as it was commonly said that everyone in that village was related in one way or another. Therefore, when such tragedy strikes it causes division and unrest.

There was a 'blocko' or a street party when the altercation ensued. The fatal injury was inflicted sending the village of New Hampshire into mourning. The accused was charged with the murder of a young man and subsequently remanded to Her Majesty's Prison. The days rolled by, the preliminary inquiry was completed with numerous witnesses. I made a calculated decision not to apply for bail in this instance. I considered the difficulty the accused would have had, should he return to the village where the incident occurred. Having to face the deceased's family daily would be difficult while the matter was pending. In any event it was agreed that should there be a conviction at least the time spent on remand would be discounted or at least taken into consideration when sentenced.

The daughter of the accused was particularly concerned. Her numerous inquiries about the criminal process was explained. There were occasions when I had to explain the law to the accused or his family members. This reminded me of the occasions when my university lecturer Dana Seetahal would painstakingly explain legal concepts, then drill us by country of origin, to ensure each person understood the laws and its applicability. The trial ensued in the High Court before a twelve member jury panel. Mr Justice Francis Cumberbatch presided. The trial process was explored with submissions, and other legal challenges. The jury deliberated. A verdict of guilty to manslaughter was returned.

# SCABBY TASTES FREEDOM

*Eugene Bartholomew - a free man after three years of incaceration*

New Hampshire resident, Eugene Bartholomew, alias Scabby is once again a free man.

Bartholomew who was facing a charge of murder, was convicted on a lesser offense of manslaughter by a 12-member jury on July 19.

The farmer/security officer/shop keeper was charged with causing the death of Ian Whiteman, also known as Merciless from the same village on February 7, 2008.

High Court Judge, Justice Francis Cumberbatch who handed down a three-year sentence on Bartholomew on Monday at High Court Number Two credited the convicted man with time served.

Bartholomew was informed by his counsel Derick Sylvester that he will now be going home since he has been on remand for just over three years.

The 49-year old father of seven was at the time hosting a blocko at his shop in New Hampshire when the incident occurred in 2008.

The court was told that during the event, Whiteman's older brother, Neilon came into the shop in a disorderly manner using obscene language and giving trouble.

Bartholomew reportedly asked Neilon to get out of the shop, but he refused.

The convicted man then turned to the younger brother and told him to get his brother out of the shop, but he said he was not taking part in the encounter.

As a result Bartholomew forced the older Whiteman out of the shop and a confrontation developed with Whiteman who started pelting bottles into the shop which damaged some of the goods on the shelves.

A struggle developed between both men and in the process Bartholomew was stabbed on the left side of the chest with a bottle.

The injury on Bartholomew's chest measures 19 centimeters in length. He also received a curve eight centimeters laceration on the right forearm.

In handing down sentence, Justice Cumberbatch said he considered three factors - retribution, defense and prevention.

The High Court Judge believed Bartholomew did not intend to kill anyone, that he had a clean record, and is known to be a law-abiding person who maintains and upkeeps the law.

Prior to the incident, Bartholomew worked as a Security Officer with the Department of Forestry of the Ministry of Agriculture.

Justice Cumberbatch felt that it was a most unfortunate case as there was no premeditation, and there was no sign of extensive force used for the single stab wound that Whiteman received.

The autopsy concluded that Whiteman died as a result of severe loss of blood.

Justice Cumberbatch also commended Bartholomew for not testifying against the other brother for the injuries he inflicted on him.

*Front page, The New Today, week ending 24 September 2010*

The accused could not understand how he could have found himself in a situation of that gravity at that stage in his life. I reminded him as I did to many others, that no one was perfect. The accused was released on the said date of sentencing. Character witnesses were called and social inquiry reports were presented to the court. The assessment that was made, to not apply for bail, was a correct one, in that the three (3) years the accused spent on remand was treated as time spent. The accused did not return to the village to reside. He relocated. This was necessary, not that he had to, but the wounds were still fresh. The village was still going through a period of mourning.

## HOLDING MOTHERS RESPONSIBLE

To curb an increase in crime society has to take responsibility and desist from attributing blame to the judiciary and other arms of the justice system. For example; sexual crimes have been on the increase for years. On many occasions one of Grenada's most seasoned and experienced Judges Lyle St. Paul, made a clarion call to hold the mothers responsible for minor children being out at parties and other events late at nights. He emphasised that parenting is a serious calling; the decisions made by young persons can influence the rest of their lives. It was a call that should have been heeded. Only time will determine if it resonated where the message was sent.

### St. Paul: Hold the mothers responsible

Retired High Court Judge, Justice Lyle St. Paul wants to see a change in the laws of the land so that mothers can be held responsible for their girl children who fall victim to sexual offences.

Justice St. Paul who came out of retirement to assist with the October Assizes told the closing ceremony that mothers have a big part to play in protecting their girl children by taking up their responsibility towards them.

The High Court Judge said he cannot understand how a young lady, around 12 to 14 years of age, can leave the home in the night and return the next morning in time to go to school.

During the just-ended Assizes, the cause list comprised of 93 cases with 30 of them being sexual matters.

Former President of the Grenada Bar Association (GBA), Ashley Bernardine who also addressed the court revealed that he did over ten cases of sexual offenses involving young offenders.

The attorney-at-law spoke of being concerned about the crime situation in the country and pointed to the level of disrespect that is shown to women.

He believes the issue of socialisation can be a factor for the levels of rape and unlawful carnal knowledge that are taking place.

Bernardine also spoke about the issues of wounding and maiming with offensive weapons.

He said he cannot understand why a cutlass or knife can be so readily available in the country to commit crimes.

Officers of the court have expressed satisfaction over the just concluded October sitting of the criminal assizes.

The assizes began on October 5 with 93 cases on the list, and at the close on December 17, 61 cases were completed.

Senior resident High Court Judge, Madam Justice Clare Henry who addressed the court during the closing ceremony said this is the largest number of cases to have been complete since she has been on the Bench in Grenada in the past three years.

The Antiguan-born Judge referred to the assizes as being highly successful and said that she believes the collective responsibility of everyone can be credited for the success achieved.

The High Court Judge was particularly pleased with the level of commitment by the jurors who exercised their civic responsibility and demonstrated their faithfulness in serving the court.

Justice Henry noted that the jurors by showing their willingness to serve, have reaffirmed the rights of a person to have a free and fair trial as guaranteed in the Constitution.

However, she expressed the hope that they were able to learn something about the criminal justice system from the experience of serving as jurors.

Senior Crown Counsel, Harold Pinnock who spoke on behalf of the Office of the Director of Public Prosecutions said although there is a sense of satisfaction over the success of the assizes, there is always need for improvement.

Pinnock said there are seven murder cases still left on the list of traversed cases for the next sitting of the assizes that commences on January 11, 2011.

He said the number of murder cases is a cause for concern since homicide matters consume a lot of time during any sitting of the assizes.

Pinnock acknowledged the presence of the media who found time to attend court on a regular basis to carry reports on matters of public interest during the assizes.

*Justice Lyle St. Paul – concerned about the security of young girls*

*Justice Clare Henry – satisfied with the outcome of the October Assizes*

*The New Today, 30 December 2010*

## JIGGER WALKS FREE

Freedom from incarceration is only one facet of freedom, for when someone has committed a crime the guilt remains with them. Such a person is imprisoned for life.

In another matter an accused was charged for murder. He was accused of pushing the deceased, who was intoxicated, unto oncoming traffic. However, the accused version was that he was trying to escort him to safety when he pulled away and drifted into the road. There were eye witnesses to the incident who indicated there was neither altercation between the parties nor any apparent motive. The murder charge was substituted with manslaughter by negligence. The accused was freed on the day of sentencing.

### Jigger walks free

Carenage resident Damian "Jigger" Depradine is once again a free man in the society.

Depradine was originally charged with murder, but it was reduced to manslaughter by negligence.

The Carenage resident who pleaded guilty to the charge of manslaughter was released from prison last week Wednesday when the court ruled that he had spent time in prison for the crime that was committed.

However, Madam Justice Clare Henry placed him on a $3,000 bond for two years. In default he would be imprisoned for two years.

The charge of murder was laid on Depradine in connection with the death of Christopher Williams of Lagoon Road, St. George's.

The accused who had just returned home from the Canada Farm Workers Programme was charged by police for pushing 23-year old Williams into the road at Grand Anse which resulted in a vehicle running into him.

*Damian 'Jigger' Depradine – a free man*

Williams succumbed to his injuries at the St. George's General Hospital two weeks after colliding with the vehicle on December 5, 2009.

The court was told that at the time of the incident both men were among a group of persons who were out on the streets drinking alcoholic beverages.

Unfortunately, Williams apparently became intoxicated, and at various intervals Depradine had to come to his assistance.

At one point, Depradine took away a beer from him and emptied it onto the ground.

Following the accident Depradine carried Williams to the hospital and then proceeded to report the matter to the police, and the victim's mother, Valerie Williams.

*The New Today, 23 December 2010*

## ANGEL DUO

In or about the year 1993, I had the benefit of meeting a gracious couple, Mr. and Mrs. Osbert and Latisha James, an angel duo who not only gave me great advice on life, but also charted my course, and supported me along the way. I am forever indebted to Mr. and Mrs. Osbert and Letisha James. Mrs. James was caring, loving and gentle. She was short in stature. Mr. James on the other hand, was in excess of six feet, a gentleman, quiet in demeanour and wise.

They both lived at Mama Cannes in the parish of Saint Andrew on the eastern side of the island. When I was asked to deliver the eulogy at her funeral I immediately accepted without reservation. It was a small token in comparison to what I had received from her.

Mr. James, on the other hand, was the Commissioner of Police in Grenada from 1975 to March 13th 1979, the day of the Grenada Revolution. He was incarcerated and spent years in prison until he was released in November 1982. He always spoke of the years he spent in prison without charge or trial. He was so experienced in the ways of the world, he had a quiet and well composed demeanour whenever he spoke on any subject. It was only age and experience that could have allowed him to be so graceful.

He encouraged me during my years of study, as did his wife. They both looked forward to me completing my studies and contributing to

*Delivering the eulogy at Mrs. Letisha James's funeral*

# Former COP given official send-off

[illegible]

as honoured as former COP Osbert James. He died just about twelve days short of his eightieth birthday.

**Eulogy**

Osbert Emmanuel James, popularly known as "OJ" and to a lesser extent "Teacher Osbert", was born on 7th April 1929. He was the only child of his mother Meltisha Lett, and the only son of his father Alexis James. Osbert attended the Pomme Rose RC School and later taught at the same school for two years. During that time Letisha George was one of his students and later she became his wife. They were married on 7th November 1964. In November 1949 OJ was enlisted in the Royal Grenada Police Force. Sixteen years later he attained his first promotion to Corporal. After one year and four months he wrote the promotional examination; he passed with flying colours and was promoted to the next rank – that of Sergeant-of-Police. He was promoted to Inspector in 1967. In 1969 he was sent to Trinidad to assist the Regiment there dealing with the Black Power Movement. He returned to Grenada in 1970 and was put in charge of the Eastern Division. In 1972 he was promoted to Superintendent-of-Police and he became Commissioner-of-Police in 1975, a position he held until 13th March 1979, when the Government of the day was overthrown. He was taken from his home on 15th March to the Richmond Hill Prison where he was held until November 1982.

Teacher Osbert was a loving father and grandfather, a devoted husband, a policeman committed to duty and a friend to all. He can aptly be described as an excellent organizer and very supportive both at home and on the job. He was a brave man who acted with astuteness, always encouraging, very respectful and thoughtful in whatever he said and did. OJ was a man of action. He was fond of saying "don't tell me that you love me; show me that you love me". He was a devoted member and leader of the St. Vincent de Paul Society (SVP), an active member of the Cursillo Movement as well as the Pensioners Association. He was a very popular person and enjoyed fishing and playing dominos. He will be greatly missed. May his soul Rest In Peace. Amen

*Grenada Informer, 10 April 2009*

the society. One day we had a conversation on the revolution and he was sympathetic to the men who arrested and imprisoned him. He even championed for their release. I realised he had grown so much in wisdom that he could have seen both sides of the revolution. He never attributed blame to any one side. He forgave all involved. His ability to forgive and embrace all was commendable. When he succumbed to his illness he received a grand send off, and although he predeceased his wife, they were buried next to each other at the yard of the Crochu Catholic Church. The church where they both worshipped.

May their souls rest in peace!

## CHAPTER SEVEN

# IN FLIGHT: THE MISSION UNFOLDS

*"Few things are brought to a successful issue by impetuous desire, but most by calm and prudent forethought."*
THUCYDIDES

The West Indies Act 1967 was passed by the UK Parliament, which provided for a new status of association for several countries of the Eastern Caribbean States which comprise; Antigua, Dominica, Grenada, St. Vincent, St. Kitts & Nevis, Anguilla and St. Lucia. This resulted in a new status of association with the United Kingdom. The Act provided for Her Majesty by Order in Council to establish common courts for the Associated States with such jurisdiction and powers as may be so specified or determined.

It allowed for provisions to be made for the establishment of a commission to appoint judges and officers of the court including, pension, emoluments and payment package.

The making of the West Indies Associated States Supreme Court Order allowed for the establishment of common courts referred to as, 'The West Indies Associated States Supreme Court' and was given constitutional recognition in the 1973 Grenada Constitution Order. That Supreme Court comprised a High Court and a Court of Appeal. With countries participating in the Court attaining independence, the Court became the Eastern Caribbean Supreme Court (ECSC).

The West Indies Associated States Supreme Court's first Chief Justice was Sir Allen Montgomery Lewis who served from 1967 to 1972, followed by Justice P. Cecil Lewis 1972-75; Sir Maurice Davis 1975-80; Sir Neville Peterkin 1981-83; Justice Neville Berridge (Ag) 1983-83; Sir Lascelles Robotham 1984-91; Sir Vincent Floissac QC, OBE, CMG 1991-96; Sir Dennis Byron 1996-2004; Justice Adrian Saunders (Ag) 2004-05; Sir Brian George Keith Alleyne SC, KCN (Ag) 2005-08 and Sir Hugh Rawlins 2008-2012.

In the year 2012, the ECSC saw the appointment of its first female Chief Justice: Dame Janice M. Pereira DBE, a legal luminary with years of experience, having served as Magistrate, Registrar, Chief Registrar of the Supreme Court. Her Ladyship was appointed High Court Judge of the ECSC States and later served as a Justice of Appeal of the Court of Appeal prior to being elevated to the chair of Chief Justice.

The advent of our first female Chief Justice was a monumental achievement for the Eastern Caribbean. I had the opportunity to appear before her in the Court of Appeal. Her professional eloquence and incisiveness in the manner in which she dissected the legal issues were impressive. When the announcement was made that Justice of Appeal Pereira would be the next Chief Justice, it was the dawn of a new day. Not only was legal history in the making but by someone well known in the region for her professional legal composure and ethics.

That said year saw the appointment of another female to the Court of Appeal, Justice of Appeal Louise Esther Blenman, a legal luminary whose wealth of experience included serving as Magistrate, Law Lecturer, Deputy Solicitor General (Guyana), Solicitor General (St. Lucia) and High Court Judge of the ECSC. I had the opportunity of appearing before Justice of Appeal Blenman; she is well learnt in the law. Having a Court of Appeal bench now with two females was welcoming. The Grenada Bar Association left no stone unturned welcoming the Chief Justice Dame Janice Pereira and Justice of Appeal Louise Blenman. There was a special sitting of the court wherein the Chief Justice pledged that the hallmarks of the court would be that of fairness, accountability and equal access to justice, a cause she continuously champions.

The task of being a leader is never an easy one. The continuous quest for justice calls for wisdom. The leadership of the Chief Justice can be aptly summarised by a quote from John C. Maxwell when he inscribed, "A leader is one who knows the way, goes the way and shows the way". The business of the court is always challenging, for its administration, human resource, judgment writing and continuous travel to eight different islands on an itinerant basis is gruelling. I have pondered about the judges having to live out of their suit cases, having to travel to all the OECS territories and the impact that would have on their family life. This to me is one of the greatest services to humanity in the realm of dispensing justice; not just giving of your time but literally your life.

# Special Sitting for Chief Justice

## Hon. Janice Pereira

Six months after becoming the first woman to be elevated to the position of Chief Justice of the Eastern Caribbean Supreme Court, Honourable Janice Pereira gets an official welcome from the legal fraternity in Grenada.

Moments before taking the Bench on Monday in her first sitting of the Grenada Appeal Court as Chief Justice, Hon. Pereira was greeted with a special sitting of the Court to formally mark ascension to her new position.

Among those present to welcome Chief Justice Pereira was the Hon. Attorney General Rohan Phillip who complimented the University of the West Indies' Graduate on her new position and her taking the lead among women in that field.

Phillip said given the trend that is now set, he has no doubt that in years to come the region will see a lot more women elevating themselves to Justices of the Appeal Court in the region and to this the Government of Grenada pledged its full support going forward.

Director of Public Prosecution Christopher Nelson lauded the new Chief Justice whom he said has now joined that elite group of female Chief Justices around the world and is therefore worthy of the commendation bestowed on her, having made history by becoming the first female in the Eastern Caribbean Supreme Court to have joined that rank.

Nelson said the Prosecution Department is convinced that given the wealth of experience possessed by the new Chief Justice, she is well qualified for the position and possesses the courage and quality that the office requires.

Nelson also took the opportunity to congratulate Justice Marion Michel and Justice Jusha Louise Blanman on their new elevation as Justices of the Court of Appeal.

Special commendations also came from Queens Council Celia Edwards, who deemed it an honour to be addressing the Court wherein a female has risen to the position of Chief Justice.

Edwards said special praise must go to the UWI for the impact they continue to have on the legal fraternity in the region, and helping women in more ways than one to take their rightful place in society.

President of the OECS Bar Association Ruggles Ferguson, who spoke on behalf of the Grenada Bar Association, said the decision to appoint Hon. Pereira was indeed an obvious one and the region should be justly proud.

Ferguson said the New CJ possesses several exceptional qualities but key among them is that she is an excellent listener and therefore brings to the Bench a new sense of calm.

Special commendation also came from the two new Appeal Court Judges Michel and Blanman both of whom pledged their full support to the new C J.

In her maiden speech in Grenada as CJ having replaced the Hon. Chief Justice Hugh Rollins in September 2012, CJ Hon. Pereira commended her predecessors for ensuring that the Court maintains its independence in the face of the many challenges as the bastion of the rule of law in the region.

Now that the baton has been passed, Pereira said, she could only pledge to do her best in continuing to build capacity, and strengthen the processes of the Court so as to ensure that the Hallmark of the system continues to be those of fairness, accountability and equal access to justice for all.

*Grenada Informer, 1 February 2013*

## JAMAICAN ENTERTAINER CHARGED

When famous Jamaican entertainer Leroy Russel aka Tommy Lee, came to Grenada to perform at a concert, he wooed the fans with his lyrics; it was a carnival like atmosphere. He was scheduled to depart the airport back to his homeland. However, during a security check, when he emptied the contents of his pocket, a hand rolled marijuana cigarette was found. The entertainer was detained, arrested and later charged for the offence of possession of marijuana. I represented the accused. His level of remorse was commendable. When a client shows deep contrition it always gives me added impetus to fortify the sentencing hearing, with a mitigation detailing the accused acceptance of responsibility and regret for running afoul of the law.

The hearing was expedited. At the hearing the Magistrate accepted the mitigating factors as overwhelming. The accused was otherwise a law abiding citizen, except for that singular infraction. His apology to the court was real, coupled with a commitment to not reoffend, which was accepted as genuine remorse. A small fine was ordered to be paid. An order for no record of conviction was made. This was an ideal situation for the court to ensure that a singular infraction did not criminalise an accused, since at that time a criminal conviction remained on an accused police record for the rest of his life.

JAMAICAN ENTERTAINER CAUGHT WITH GANJA

LOCAL NEWS — NEW TODAY Fri., April 27, 2012 — Page 03

Jamaican Entertainer Caught with Ganja

*The New Today, 27 April 2012*

Derek Sylvester

## Young lawyer Sylvester considered for AG

ONE OF THE COUNTRY'S most successful lawyers, Derek Sylvester turned down an invitation to become the island's Attorney General, opting instead to remain in private practice.

This is according to government sources.

Legal Affairs Minister Elvin Nimrod confirmed that Sylvester was one of three persons considered for the post that was eventually given to Cajeton Hood.

"Mr Sylvester made it clear he was willing to help in any other capacity, but at this time he had to decline because he had other pressing matters that he has to complete that will take some time," Nimrod said.

*Carib Update, 27 March 2013*

## PUBLIC SERVICE COMMISSION APPOINTMENT

The appointment to constitutional posts is normally subject to the sanction of the Prime Minister, who would advise the Governor General. The Governor General then issues the instrument of appointment after the requisite oath is administered. When I was asked by the Prime Minister of Grenada, to serve either as Attorney General or Chairman of the Public Service Commission, it soon became obvious to me that the latter was the clearer choice.

In November 2013, I accepted the constitutional appointment of Chairman of the Public Service Commission. The wealth of experience it brought me was immense. I had many occasions in my practice either to file civil suits against the Public Service Commission or to file appeals to the Public Service Board of Appeal. It was a revelation to be sitting in that chair.

My passion and love for the law grew with each passing day. I hated injustice as I did unfairness; those qualities were fortified by my personal experiences.

## WHITE AND WHITE CARNIVAL FIASCO

Grenada is known for its carnival celebrations, which occur once every year with a weekend of activities culminating with carnival Monday and Tuesday festivities. These activities previously occurred in February, but it has now been moved to August. It is an exposition of music, calypso competition, carnival shows, steel band music, Kings and Queens of the bands, costume competition and Carnival Queen Show. The winner of the Carnival Queen show would reign for the ensuing year. There is usually an influx of visitors during that season; a blend of family, friends and well-wishers. Calypso normally takes centre stage. The competition to crown the Calypso King is held on the Sunday prior to the dual days of carnival.

As part of these celebrations, there is the popular 'white in the moon light' show, where patrons dress in all white and party from midnight to dawn. There were two competing shows carded for the 9th August. They were styled, 'Digicel White in the Moon Light' and 'Pure White in the Moonlight'. The organisers of the former, through their attorneys filed an injunction against the latter, to not only discontinue the use of the word white, but also to prevent both shows from occurring on the same day, as the advertisements were confusing to patrons. The applicant would suffer tremendous losses.

I was retained to represent 'Pure White in the Moonlight'. It was alleged that the public would be misled even though there were two

THE DUST HAS SETTLED

The Judge rules both of Saturday's shows can go ahead See Page 20

(Right) Diego Peters and other defendants in discussion with attorneys after court ruling in their favour

*Weekly newspaper, 8 August 2014*

## THE DUST HAS SETTLED- The Judge rules both of Saturday's shows can go ahead

High Court Judge Madam Justice Margaret Mohammed on Tuesday delivered her judgment in a heated legal battle involving promoters of this Saturday night's shows and the rights to use certain names to promote the different shows namely, Digicel White in the Moonlight and Pure White in the Moonlight.

Both shows are carded to be held on this Saturday August 9th however promoters of Digicel White in the Moonlight last week filed an injunction asking the court to intervene on the grounds that their competitors are involved in what is called 'passing off,' tricking patrons into believing that both shows are the same by the use of the word 'white' in their promotion.

Based on their argument, the promoter of White in the Moonlight Nimrod Ollivierre wanted the court to get the promoters of Pure White, to remove the word White from the title of their Show. However in court on Tuesday the Judge agreed that the two shows are different and the issue is of no moment.

*Promoter of White In The Moonlight Nimrod Ollivierre outside High Court after judges ruling against them*

Moments after the decision was handed down in Chambers at the Number 3 Court in St. George's one member of the defense team Derrick Sylvester told the media that having heard the evidence the judge concluded that some of the defendants among them Dwain Lewis, Angus Steele, Curt Ross and Daniel Diego Peters were not proper parties to the suit or matter before the court and therefore the charge against them was struck out.

In so doing Sylvester said the issue of cost was then looked at and all named defendants to the suit were awarded costs in the sum of two thousand dollars.

Lawyers for the Claimant Digicel 4g White in the Moonlight Francis Paul told the media that the injunction put forward by his client was not granted and both shows would now go ahead. It is now left for all parties to go and promote their shows.

Paul said it must be made known that there was no intention on the part of his client to stop any competing show from being held. The issue the lawyer said was to get the competitor to stop using promotional material similar to or to confuse the public over which show is being held where.

One member of the Pure White in the Moonlight team told the media he is disappointed that the matter reached the court, however he said this is business and all that is left for both parties now is to do the best they can in the little time left to promote their shows to get maximum results.

*Weekly newspaper, 8 August 2014*

different venues for the two activities albeit on the same day. The island of Grenada by itself is 121 Square miles. The possibility of being misled as to which show was being held where may not have been an issue. The central issue was whether one side was attempting to eliminate the competition. In any event the legal arguments unfolded. The judge delivered her ruling that both shows should be proceeded with.

The interesting issue which unfolded was that promoters were now aware that the court would not use its coercive powers to thwart competition. Unless the court is of the view that one party is trying to 'pass off' their product as that of another, it may not intervene.

## CALYPSONIAN'S REMORSE

In my practice I have had to represent a client who participated in Grenada's Independence Calypso completion held in the United States of America. He was a popular calypsonian. He was disheartened with having placed, sixth (6th) three times in a row. This caused him to be very angry because he was of the view that three sixes were equivalent to the mark of the beast. It was his protest that the competitors who placed before him performed badly; in one instance his competitor 'burst' three times while signing.

His expression of anger went viral. It created headline news. This caused a stir among his supporters, fans and would be supporters. Recognising the error of his ways he was apologetic and had to find a

### Randy Isaac Apologizes

One week after being laced with "disgracing himself and Grenada during Grenada's Independence Calypso Monarch Competition in New York recently" as reported in a front page story in last week's issue of the Grenada Informer Newspaper , Randy Isaac one of the island's celebrated Calypso artistes has issued a public apology. Speaking in the presence of his Legal Council Derrick Sylvester via Skype on Tuesday, Isaac said he wanted the nation and the Diaspora to know that this is not the Randy that they've grown to know over the years, and he assured them that a situation like this would never happen again. The article in the newspaper stated that "on learning that he did not win the competition, Mr. Isaac decided he was not satisfied with the judges' decision and showed his blatant dissatisfaction by ripping up the citation in front of everyone, damaging the participation trophy and kicked them both to the floor." Isaac said the entire incident stemmed over the outcome of the show where he felt that he did not deserve the position that was given to him, considering that one of the persons who defeated him burst on three occasions in the same song, and for the third consecutive time he was placed sixth in that competition.

Isaac said he was not expecting to win, however he felt he did far better that he was placed, and therefore he was upset. Having captured almost all major titles in the Calypso art-form in Grenada, Isaac said if he were able to rewind the hands of time he would behave differently and he wants the Grenadian public to continue supporting him. Be that as it may, Isaac said upon somber and Solomonic reflection he has taken the decision to apologize to the judges, lovers of the calypso art-form, people in the Diaspora and all those who were affected by his actions; he is deeply sorry.

By the same token Randy said that some of the information that appeared on the Informer was inaccurate in that there was no outburst on stage, no kicking, and no cursing of judges. He stated that whatever took place that night all happened back stage. Randy said, "Everyone is entitled to make a mistake and he felt that he made a big mistake. "I'm here to apologize to you Grenada and the Diaspora; love you always and I will always be a patriot".

*Grenada Informer, 7 February 2014*

way of expressing this to the fans and all who were offended or hurt by his outburst. It was agreed that we would conduct a Skype interview with the media including; radio, television and print. In that case, the widest cross section of the country. The Diaspora would be covered. The interview was held at my law office. It was well received by the public. A sincere apology serves the purpose of an expression of remorse; it mitigates human frailty and imperfection.

The household name of this calypsonian continues to blaze the air waves with his sweet sounding renditions and melody. The public once again embraced him with love.

## AN ICON DEPARTS

There are many personalities who influence my life in one way or another; some by way of continuous encouragement. One such person was Anthony 'Jericho' Greenidge an Icon. When I was hired at Cable and Wireless as an international telephone operator, Anthony Greenidge had just resigned from that position. It was evident to me then that his resignation may have created a position for me. Later, I met him on a professional and social level. His constant encouragement and motivation remains forever with me.

### Tributes for Jericho

One of Grenada's better known radio announcers and cultural artiste has passed on.

Anthony "Jericho" Greenidge, whom many often called "De Duke", passed away in New York last Thursday morning after travelling to the U.S for medical treatment.

Greenidge, a past student of the Grenada Boys Secondary School is a former national track and field athlete, and keen basketball player in his younger years.

He was also the Vice-President of the Media Workers Association of Grenada (MWAG).

Jericho's passing spread throughout the country within minutes of his death.

It only became official when his employers, Wee FM issued a statement confirming that the popular radio talk show host had succumbed to his illness in the United States.

The statement read: "WeeFm Radio regrets to inform our valued listeners that announcer "Anthony Jericho Greenidge" passed away today (Thursday) in the United States.

"Our prayers go out to his family especially his kids and his loved ones. Our prayers also go out to his fans who showed unwavering support towards him and his popular morning programme.

"We encourage all to be strong as we mourn this great loss.

As a result of his passing our programming will be adjusted for the next few days".

Many local groups and personalities followed with similar statements, expressing grief at the loss of this household name with many years of service in the media.

In its message, the Grenada Carnival Committee (GCC) expressed its deepest

*Anthony "Jericho" Greenidge - "De Duke"*

sympathy to the family, friends and colleagues of Anthony Jericho Greenidge.

"The news of the passing of this great Grenadian was received with a profound sense of sadness. His contributions to carnival and culture are very well documented and his leadership in embracing our unique traditions will never be forgotten.

"This calysonian, parang master, poet, pan lover extraordinaire and guardian of things Grenadian has left an indelible mark on our hearts.

"Sing on Jericho. Play on our brother. May burn brightly.

The operators of the website, PartyGrenada.com also issued a statement on the death of "Jericho".

The statement said: "The Partygrenada.com team wishes to express its condolencences to the family, friends, members of the media, Men from the Mainland and co-workers on the passing of Anthony "Jericho" Greenidge aka "De Duke".

"Jericho's contribution to both Carriacou and Grenada's Carnival, the media, partygrenada.com, culture and entertainment always be remembered as a Radio personality, Calypsonian, master of ceremony, parang master, poet, sportsman and for both his early morning 'informal news' on Weefm and his yearly hilarious 'mele parang' renditions.

"Jericho touched the lives of many and he will be surely missed by all. May his soul rest in peace.

The group known as Citizens in Defence of Grenada's Lands and Heritage also joined in extending condolences to the family, friends, colleagues and fans of "Jericho".

It described him as "a talented and creative individual" who carved a niche for himself in broadcasting with the "Jericho brand".

"His morning programme entertained, motivated, informed and educated the nation", said the statement.

It went on: "Citizens recalls with deep appreciation the support he lent to our cause, No Buildings on the Lagoon Park, when he and his band performed at our concert in the car park on World Environment Day, June 5th, 2008 to bring attention to the issue.

"The audience was treated to entertaining, witty pieces with very pointed messages. Jericho has passed on but he has left a legacy to be celebrated. May he rest in peace".

*The New Today, 11 November 2011*

# Tributes for Jericho

*FROM PAGE 11

Representative for the Town of St. George, Tourism Minister Peter David also joined in extending condolences on the passing of Jericho who lived on Upper Grenville Street, one of the few remaining residential areas in the heart of the city.

David remembered "Jericho" as one who was at the heart of the community where he lived, as well as an individual who had left a legacy of community and professional success.

Minister David described the late radio personality as a "dear friend" who loved his community and country".

He said: "Jericho, as a huge radio personality, belonged to the nation; but he also never lost touch with his immediate community in Four Roads. When anything was to be done in Four Roads - whether sporting or cultural - I know I could call on Jericho to assist. He was a dedicated and conscientious person, a hard worker and a dear friend of the nation and the Town of St. George."

The senior government minister who visited Greenidge's sister last week Thursday evening to convey his sympathies, recalled his last conversation with the late WEE FM announcer.

"That conversation was about two months ago when Jericho was invited to be a representative of the Town of St. George on a delegation I was leading on a visit to China.

"Everything was arranged but he withdrew from the trip hours before we left because he said he wasn't feeling well. But he was in good spirits and we had promised to reconnect on my return. However, by the time I returned from China, he had left for medical treatment in the United States."

"His death is sad and heart wrenching. We all grieve for Jericho and sympathise with his family and friends. But Jericho has left a legacy in media and culture that we ought to recognise, cherish and embrace."

Minister of State with responsibility for Culture, Senator Arley Gill also joined in expressing his deep sense of sadness at the passing of "De Duke", saying that the former broadcaster, calypsonian, athlete and Master of Ceremony had left an "indelible mark" on the Grenadian cultural and media landscape.

"It is not a cliché to say that there will never be another Jericho," said Sen. Gill.

"In the pantheon of Grenadian culture," Sen. Gill said, "Jericho has left an indelible mark. He was calypsonian and extempore artiste; calypso commentator and critic; Master of Ceremony; and a Parrandero who entertained us as a member of Men from the Mainland."

According to Sen. Gill, "the nation's media and cultural communities have lost a giant. May Jericho rest in peace. I'm sure I speak on behalf of many in saying that he will be surely missed, and in expressing heartfelt condolences to all his family members, including his children."

Another who paid tribute to Jericho's contribution was the island's Ambassador to Brussels, Stephen Fletcher.

His statement said: "It is with deep shock and sadness that the Grenada Embassy in Brussels learnt about the untimely passing of Anthony "Jericho", "the Duke" Greenidge, on Thursday 3rd November, 2011.

"Jericho" was a true voice for all of our people, a genuine son of the soil and the main bridge with the Grenadian Diaspora. Through "Jericho's" morning programs we were kept in touch with the happenings on the island and our communities.

"At a personal level his programs provided me with the daily source of inspiration needed to persevere in the interest of the people of Grenada, Carriacou and Petit Martinique.

"I'm personally indebted to "Jericho, the Duke" for his voluntary actions in keeping the "WEE FM" audience informed and up to date with the work of the Brussels Mission.

"The Grenadian Community in Europe and Zurich (Switzerland) in particular, joins with the Embassy of Grenada in Brussels in extending our deepest heartfelt condolences to the family and friends of Anthony, "Jericho, The Duke" Greenidge.

The Funeral Service for Jericho will be held on Monday at the National Stadium at Queen's Park.

Viewing of the body will begin at 9:00 a.m. and Tributes and Cultural Presentations to celebrate his life will start at Noon.

The Funeral Service will start at 2:00 p.m. No other details are immediately available for the burial of the radio announcer with a huge following both at home and abroad.

*The New Today, 11 November 2011*

I recall occasions when he would visit me at my office when it was located at Church Street in the city. We would sit to enjoy a good evening of chatting with Johnson Richardson, another member from the print media. His conversations were always thought provoking, with a sense of humour, but within the humour always rested serious life messages and lessons. He was a radio announcer, Master of Ceremony, parang artist, entertainer and much more. He would always speak to me about my cases while encouraging me to do my best; always admonishing that the improvement of humanity should be one of life's goals. Even on his radio programmes, he would mention me, even if it was to just to say, "Good morning," or words of encouragement to me, members of the judiciary, legal profession, police service and other State agents.

After he fell ill, he remained strong in spirit. His encouraging words would forever live on. In life, the simplest of things said could have a lifelong impact. He disliked injustice. He said it as he saw it. He grew to be the person to look forward to listening every morning on the radio. His famous phrases were "Table knock" and "donkey bray". His parang music continued to charm the listening public even after his death.

Life is fleeting. Jericho left a positive impact on my life and on the people of Grenada, Carriacou and Petit Martinique, by his music, poetry, satire, calypso, forthrightness – calling a spade a spade – and his genuine love for humanity.

CHAPTER EIGHT

# THE MISSION CONTINUES

*"In order to find the edge, you must risk going over the edge."*
DENNIS DUGAN

In most situations, when an accused person who has been charged with a criminal offence is a non-national, bail is almost always denied. Some of the considerations are; that the accused may abscond the jurisdiction, not having sureties to sign the bail bond; interference with witnesses and numerous other factors.

When a Guyanese national was charged the issue as to his bail arose. The accused was a journalist who formed a company that was allegedly competing with his employer's business. The issue was whether it was fair competition or was it an issue of stealing his employer's money, through the company he owned, despite the work being done by him in an unrelated manner.

The prosecution vehemently opposed the accused's application for bail, as the major concern was flight risk and the likely consequences if convicted. Submissions, as well as oral arguments, were delivered on both sides. Further, the accused had to seek constant medical attention, since if he failed to do so he could possibly suffer the loss of his leg. The accused was able to secure sureties from within the jurisdiction. After much deliberation bail was granted in the sum of one hundred thousand dollars ($100,000.00) with two sureties and other attendant conditions.

The accused was relieved, as the possibility of entering prison was a frightening thought. He was a stranger to that institution with no family within the jurisdiction.

Despite his joy at being granted bail, the psychological, emotional and financial saga was just beginning. The accused was dismissed from his place of employment. Certain conditions in his employment contract were not fulfilled. The issue was whether he was precluded from operating

# Rawle Nelson seeks medical relief from bail conditions

The Police Prosecution in the matter involving Guyanese Journalist Rawle Nelson - who was charged with two counts of stealing EC$15,394.28, by reason of employment, forgery and uttering a forged document on April 20th 2014 has until Monday 23rd to respond to a request made to the St. George's Magistrate Court for the accused to be granted permission to travel abroad for medical reasons.

Following his arrest, Nelson retained Attorney-at-Law Derek Sylvester to represent him.

Sylvester was successful in securing bail for Nelson in the sum of $100,000 with two sureties on the grounds that he is Claustrophobic and suffers from chronic diabetes.

The journalist was also required to surrender all travel documents, national and otherwise and told that he should not leave the jurisdiction without the permission of the court.

One of the Police Prosecutors in the matter was unavoidably absent during Tuesday's sitting of the court and the other requested that the matter be adjourned to a later date.

However, in light of the urgency of his client's medical dilemma, Sylvester argued that the matter against Nelson has been adjourned on one too many occasions and called for it to be struck off the Court's list or that his client be granted permission to travel abroad for medical reasons" and that "his passport be returned to him forthwith."

Sylvester told the siting Magistrate that the court should also "take into consideration that the accused is not a Grenadian national and is suffering."

"An adjournment would be more strenuous at this time", he added, noting that Nelson is currently in and out of the hospital as a result of his illnesses and that the situation is so severe that his client's foot could be amputated if not given the appropriate medical attention.

He also said that Nelson, who has been "unemployed for over a year" currently "has no source of income and is living practically at the generosity of the Grenadian public."

Nelson used Tuesday's Court sitting to express his frustration and pointed out that he is very sick and needs to seek medical attention overseas as soon as possible.

The Prosecutor did not budge on the handing over of the passport and instead requested time to respond to the lawyer's submission.

Magistrate Tahira Gellineau obliged.

Nelson began working as a consultant and managing editor with Moving Target Ltd., the Company that owns Meaningful Television and is also the publisher of the weekly Grenada Informer newspaper, in July 2013.

The Guyanese national who allegedly worked in St Kitts and Antigua is also the owner of a marketing company in Grenada called Optimum Solutions.

It is alleged that the case brought against him relates to dealings involving Optimum Solutions and Moving Target.

Information on whether the company is still functioning has not been forthcoming.

*Guyanese journalist Rawle Nelson wants to travel abroad*

*The New Today, 20 March 2015*

a similar business as his employer. Was it criminal, unethical, fair trade or contractually prohibited?

It was agreed between the accused and myself that a civil suit would be filed against the employer. It was subsequently filed. The employer then had to defend in the civil court its alleged breach of an employment contract. There were therefore parallel proceedings in the civil and criminal courts concerning similar subject matters albeit not the same.

The accused's family was extremely anxious, as there were possible criminal sanctions that could be imposed, which may have resulted in imprisonment. The accused maintained his innocence, as he was extremely concerned about the future of his professional life, career and family. The perception of committing a crime, even if found not guilty at the end of the trial, is as damaging as the allegation itself.

The civil matter proceeded. The accused being in this position of an accused for the first time, was now living the stories he wrote on over the many years as a journalist. In the end, both matters were resolved to the satisfaction of all parties. The criminal matter was discontinued. Notwithstanding the completion of the matters, this traumatic experience of being arrested, being brought to court, having to sit and listen to the arguments to determine his fate as to whether he would be remanded or released on bail, was as much a punishment as incarceration. The accused returned to his homeland thereafter.

## FOUR SECONDARY SCHOOL MURDERS OVER TWO DECADES

I have had to deal with numerous tragedies in secondary schools where death was the end result. On each occasion the trauma was bone chilling to staff, students and parents.

Teachers have a special role in the life of their students. At school they are mothers, fathers, guardians, nurses, counsellors, spiritual advisers, caregivers, mentors, social workers and this list is not exhaustive. Incidents of feud among students in school are normal. This continues to the present day, but the use of weapons was rare in Grenada. There were four instances, over approximately the last two decades, where charges of murder or manslaughter were instituted against young persons, while attending school.

At the Happy Hill Secondary School, a report was made of a female student allegedly inflicting a fatal wound on a male student. The school was immediately thrown into mourning. Tears rained down the faces of

*Front page, Grenada Informer, week ending 25 November 2016*

students; emotions were raw for the teachers, principal and family members; as a young life was lost under circumstances that could have been avoided. The young accused, in all instances I have dealt with, never intended to kill, they would say, but used the weapon thinking that death would not ensue. The female accused was visibly shaking when I visited her at the police station. Her mother was in no better condition.

It would have been difficult to sit in the same class where the deceased once sat, looking at the empty chair that only yesterday was filled. The students at that school had to undergo a period of counselling.

On one occasion while I was a student at Wesley College Secondary School, one of the students inflicted a fatal stab wound on another at a field event. This was an incident which did not even occur on the school compound but was still very traumatising. The accused used a 'ratchet'. I recalled the deceased's family was left in a state of perpetual loss.

After I secured bail for the young accused, there was no victory in sight, for society was permanently scarred. In this type of scenario, there are only losers. The accused, in the Happy Hill Secondary School fatality after her release on bail, was convicted of manslaughter and placed on a bond with numerous other conditions. The deceased's life was terminated at a young age. The stigma remains with the school.

Within one decade of the first incident, at the same school during the school's recess, there was an altercation between two young men that was not contained. The accused inflicted a fatal wound in the presence of numerous children on the school compound. The accused was otherwise a well behaved student from all accounts. The deceased was recently transferred from another school. Irrespective of the circumstances, nothing could possibly justify the presence of weapons on a school compound.

The parents of both children descended into anguish. I can recall when I visited the accused at the Criminal Investigation Department he cried, even the investigators appeared sorrowful. The young offender was crying hysterically as he begged for forgiveness. He even begged to rewind the time so he could have undone the wrong committed. His tears were not about him being detained but the life he had taken. He

# Another Fatal Stabbing at a Secondary School

Four years after a stabbing incident at the Happy Hill Secondary School ended the life of 15-year-old fifth form student Alex Gabriel, another of its students has perished in similar fashion.

According to information reaching the Grenada Informer, dead is i6-year-old form three student Zibon Jeffery from the village of Mardigras in St. George's.

Sources told this paper that Jeffery died just after midday on Wednesday moments after receiving a stab wound to the chest. Sources said he was pronounced dead at the General Hospital. Informer was told that the incident stemmed from an altercation between Jeffery and another young man believed to be a student from form four.

Although information surrounding the cause of the incident remained sketchy, Informer learned that both young men who appeared to have been good friends prior to the fateful day, started and argument over a bag of juice belonging to one of them that had accidently fallen to the ground. Sources said a scuffled ensued between the two ending in another tragedy for the Happy Hill Secondary School.

Informer was told that Jeffery, the victim in this case had recently transferred from the Grenada Boys Secondary School.

The Happy Hill Secondary School in recent times has been one of the many schools in Grenada to insist on increased police presence at the compound. Students we are told are made to subject themselves to a search on entry through the school gates on a daily basis. It is therefore not clear how the weapon allegedly used in this incident found its way onto the school compound.

While this incident is the latest, it must noted that the accused in first stabbing incident, at the time a thirteen year-old female student, is presently at Her Majesty's Prison having broken a bond imposed on her by the court.

The accused in this matter was up to press time, in police custody and was expected to make his first court appearance today (Friday). Defense lawyers Catisha Williams and Hazel Hopkin of the law firm of Derick Sylvester and Associates would have carriage of the matter.

*Grenada Informer, 25 November 2016*

begged to see the deceased's mother to plead for forgiveness and mercy. The state of the accused was disconcerting. When I held his hands it was cold as winter. I urged him to calm himself. I asked him about his faith and encouraged him to hold on to that. I promised to visit him periodically which I did. I would never forget the image of the accused. He was small and frail. He appeared almost lost, as his eyes wondered all over the room as if he was looking for a source of strength.

I recalled the police investigators, in an effort to put him at ease, striking up a conversation with him about whether he liked fishing. Then a book on fishing was provided to him as they sat to discuss the topic. The investigators had a job to do. Difficult as it was, they tried to put the accused at some measure of internal peace. They all had children I am sure, of similar age, but the grace and professionalism used in handling that delicate situation was admirable.

The accused was remanded to a juvenile facility. At such tender teenage years, to commit an act as heinous as murder, the effect on a young person is normally disastrous. This is especially so if a strong family support and mechanism for continued academic development is not put in place for him. The accused spent some time at the juvenile centre. After entering a plea of guilty to manslaughter, was placed on a bond with a series of conditions and other strict monitoring programmes.

In another secondary school in the city of St. George's, a female student was charged for the murder of her three (3) year old sister while at her home. The school was thrown into a state of disbelief. The situation was horrible as social media erupted with the news. Notwithstanding the legal restriction on reporting the names of young offenders, this did not thwart the bloggers or some of the news media, including radio and talk show programmes in reporting the incident.

Young children require continuous monitoring and mentoring. Sometimes their cries go unheard. The young offender had much to deal with. Her father was allegedly murdered. No arrest had been made to date. Consequently, there was insufficient monitoring or mentoring for her. This in no way explains or justifies her alleged wrong. However, timely intervention could have played a part in discovering a potentially dangerous situation thereby preventing it before it occurred.

The precarious position the mother was placed in, in these circumstances, became patently obvious. One of her children was now dead at the hands of another. She was entitled to love both of them. However, now she was mourning for the deceased while being worried about the accused.

The accused was remanded and later sentenced to eight and a half years in prison. The court ordered her to visit forms 4 and 5 students of various secondary schools to speak to them about issues concerning violence so that these students could benefit from her experience. The accused visited the various secondary schools while an inmate at prison to speak to students who now sat in the classroom as she once did.

Upon the release of the accused subsequent to serving her sentence, she visited me at my office to express her appreciation. She had matured so much that she was much more conversant, articulate and eloquent. The programmes at the prison coupled with additional classes did her well.

The fourth case dealt with a young offender in another secondary school where there was an altercation which went on for a prolonged

ANEKA GETS EIGHT-AND-A HALF YEARS IN PRISON

A prison sentence of eight and a half years was handed down on 20 year old Aneka Charles who appeared in court on Wednesday morning to know her fate in connection with the death of her younger sister in 2011.

The ruling was handed down by Madam Justice Margaret Price-Findlay at High Court No. 1 in the presence of her Legal Representative, Derek Sylvester and family members.

Charles had earlier spent time on remand at the Richmond Hill Prison for the death of the youngster and twelve months will be deducted from the eight and a half year sentence.

Also, as part of the sentence, Charles will have to do some Community Service specifically speak to students of the Programme for Adolescent Mothers (PAM) and Forms 4 and 5 students at a selected secondary school.

The ruling from Justice Price-Findlay would see the 20-year old serve an additional two years in prison if she fails to comply with the court order.

Upon release, Charles, now mother of a toddler will be place a Bond of $20, 000.00 with sureties to keep the peace for t years.

She was found guilty in Febr 2015 for the 2011 murder of her year old sister, Sharian Charles.

The three-year old child was re ed missing and a search of the discovered her body in some bu close to their home.

The toddler was found with clothes wet and froth coming fror nostrils and mouth.

She was pronounced dead b Gail Friday and a post-mortem cluded that she died from asph tion.

Police reports suggested tha elder sister was the victim of a within the family home and too her rage on the younger sister was fathered by another man.

Charles was 17 at the time c murder and a student of St Jos Convent, St George's.

d to prison for the death of her sister

*Front page, Grenada Today, week ending 17 April 2015*

## Annica Charles Sentenced To 8 ½ Years

More than three years after being charged with the November 6, 2011 drowning of her three year old baby sister, sentence has been handed down to Annica Charles by Justice Paula Gilford at the Number One High Court in St. George's.

The case that has gathered much media and public attention over the years due to its unusual nature and the age of the perpetrator who was 17 years old at the time, finally came to an end on Wednesday April 15.

Charles, now 21 has been sentenced to eight and a half years in prison but not much of that time will actually be spent behind bars. Time spent on remand will be subtracted and three years will be suspended; the remainder will be actual prison time.

In addition Charles has been placed on $20,000.00 bond with three sureties; violating that bond will earn her another two years in prison.

Charles' repayment of her debt to society does not end there but she has been mandated by the Court to spent time speaking to fourth and fifth form students to help them avoid the inclination to commit similar offences. She will also perform 200 hours of community service, attend personal development classes and anger management and alcohol abuse classes.

The then teenage student was arrested when the body of her baby sister was discovered in bushes just meters from their home, some three hours after she was reported missing. Medical examination had revealed that the infant died of asphyxiation.

The young offender had alleged abuse by her stepfather, the child's father, as part of the reason for her actions. Charles was represented in Court by Attorney-at-Law Derek Sylvester.

*Grenada Informer, 17 April 2015*

period. It drew a large crowd of students. The security, though present, was unable to stop the fight. The crowd grew as the fight continued. The fight was transferred from the outside of the school to the bathroom; it ended in one of the classrooms. After the fatal injury was inflicted, the crowd disbursed almost in an instant. The stigma of murder was transferred yet to another secondary school.

Two young lives were again destroyed, due to the lack of discipline, the inability to terminate a prolonged altercation and a youthful crowd that was more interested in cheering on the saga than discontinuing it. Every matter that I have handled with young offenders resulting in murder on a school compound could have been avoided. The devastating effect this has had on the teachers and principal is exponential as there is a symbiotic relationship between teachers and their students; even the ones who are prone to breaking school rules and deviating from the accepted mode of behaviour.

The accused in this case was bonded, with numerous conditions attached; however the mere fact that he had to withdraw from the formal institution resulted in him losing out on his childhood years. These years could never be replaced; the memories the accused could have cherished would be smeared with the incident which enveloped him.

## GRENVILLE MURDER TRIAL

In the eastern parish of Saint Andrew, at Grenville, a young man aged twenty one (21) was charged with the offence of murder. He was attacked by the deceased who inflicted numerous injuries to his head and other parts of his body. The accused then left the scene. He went to the Mirabeau Hospital to seek medical attention. The hospital was about twenty minutes (20) drive from the site of the altercation. Upon receipt of medical attention, it was alleged, the accused returned to the scene of the incident to retrieve a bag he had left. A second confrontation ensued. The accused's account was that he had a second altercation and was forced to defend himself. The prosecution's case was that the accused returned to the scene for the purpose of retaliation. Further, the fact that the police station was a street parallel to where the altercation occurred meant that the accused could have reported the matter to the police prior to going to the hospital.

Of course, the defence's retort was that medical attention was immediately required and reporting the matter to the police may have

(Continues on page 3)

APRIL 14 IS D-DAY FOR MURDER CONVICT

Ricardo Edgar – awaiting sentencing for murder

A St. Andrewês farmer has to wait until April 14 before he knows his faith in connection with a stabbing incident that led to the death of another St. Andrewês young man.

A 12-member jury last week Thursday returned a guilty verdict of murder on Ricardo Edgar for the fatal stab wounds inflicted on Enoch Noel

(Continues on page 13

*The New Today, 18 March 2011*

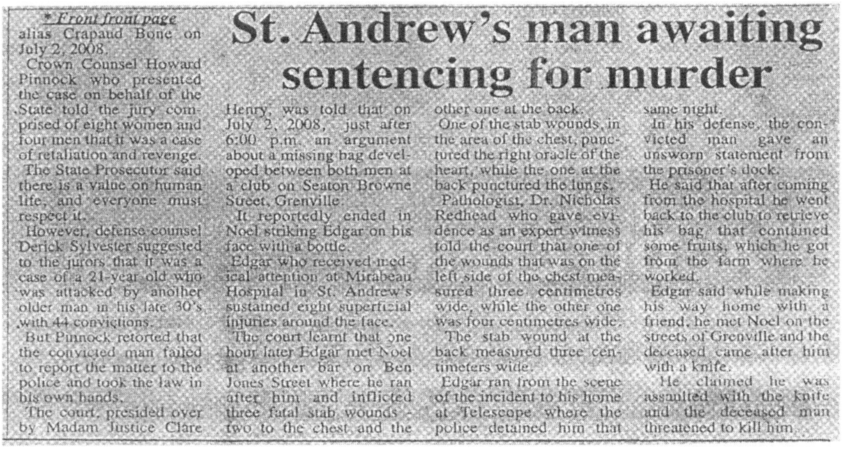

** Front front page*

alias Crapaud Bone on July 2, 2008.

Crown Counsel Howard Pinnock who presented the case on behalf of the State told the jury comprised of eight women and four men that it was a case of retaliation and revenge.

The State Prosecutor said there is a value on human life, and everyone must respect it.

However, defense counsel Derick Sylvester suggested to the jurors that it was a case of a 21-year old who was attacked by another older man in his late 30's with 44 convictions.

But Pinnock retorted that the convicted man failed to report the matter to the police and took the law in his own hands.

The court, presided over by Madam Justice Clare

## St. Andrew's man awaiting sentencing for murder

Henry, was told that on July 2, 2008, just after 6:00 p.m. an argument about a missing bag developed between both men at a club on Seaton Browne Street, Grenville.

It reportedly ended in Noel striking Edgar on his face with a bottle.

Edgar who received medical attention at Mirabeau Hospital in St. Andrew's sustained eight superficial injuries around the face.

The court learnt that one hour later Edgar met Noel at another bar on Ben Jones Street where he ran after him and inflicted three fatal stab wounds - two to the chest and the other one at the back.

One of the stab wounds, in the area of the chest, punctured the right oracle of the heart, while the one at the back punctured the lungs.

Pathologist, Dr. Nicholas Redhead who gave evidence as an expert witness told the court that one of the wounds that was on the left side of the chest measured three centimetres wide, while the other one was four centimetres wide.

The stab wound at the back measured three centimeters wide.

Edgar ran from the scene of the incident to his home at Telescope where the police detained him that same night.

In his defense, the convicted man gave an unsworn statement from the prisoner's dock.

He said that after coming from the hospital he went back to the club to retrieve his bag that contained some fruits, which he got from the farm where he worked.

Edgar said while making his way home with a friend, he met Noel on the streets of Grenville and the deceased came after him with a knife.

He claimed he was assaulted with the knife and the deceased man threatened to kill him.

*The New Today, 18 March 2011*

resulted in the accused bleeding to death. Additionally, his return to the scene of the incident was to secure his bag, then to make the report to the police station. Furthermore, the accused could not have reasonably foreseen that the deceased would have remained in the same location where the first altercation occurred.

Notwithstanding the fact that the deceased had forty four (44) prior convictions, with the accused having none, the jury accepted the version of the prosecution and convicted the accused for murder. This was a verdict that surprised me, even though on many occasions I would have said no verdict can. The accused was 'tongue tied' as the jury convicted for murder and not even manslaughter. During the trial an application was made to visit the murder scene. A twenty seven (27) seater bus was provided to carry the court as empanelled to the site. The evidence unfolded with the witnesses detailing the points where they would have witnessed their varying accounts of the events. We were of the view that such site visit could only benefit the accused, but we were wrong. The jury accepted the prosecution's version; hook, line and sinker; in other words, in totality.

The jury sometimes sees through differing factual lenses. Many times I wonder whether they really understood the complicated explanation of the law on intention, provocation, self-defence, accident, diminished responsibility (if applicable) and insanity. If they did not understand it, an unexpected verdict could result.

Upon receipt of the verdict the accused's mother seemed to have lost all hope. To appease my apparent failure to secure a different verdict, I reminded her that the parents of the deceased were now grieving. But at least her son was alive albeit in prison. That was not much consolation to her. But she seemed to have understood what I wanted to convey. She looked at me in dismay when I mentioned those words to her. I wish I could have read her mind. I assured both the accused and his mother that I would examine the record to see whether there were any possible grounds of appeal. Normally, I would draft the grounds of appeal during the summation by the trial judge to the jury. However, that trial was so demanding, after the site visit to the north eastern part of the island where the incident occurred, I was drained. I had decided to examine the record upon receipt of it.

My visits to the accused in prison were a painstaking venture as his sole question was always how long would he remain in prison, as his sentence was an extended one. I encouraged him to have faith. We were hoping that a review of the record would reveal that there were substantial grounds of appeal to aid in either the quashing of the conviction or at a minimum a retrial wherein I would apply for bail, so as to enable him to experience freedom once again.

Upon receipt of the record of proceedings, I had a restful day as I would always do prior to spending the night reading the numerous pages repeatedly. Upon first reading, I would determine whether a mistake was made on the law. On the second and third readings, whether somewhere in the record the error of law may have been corrected by the trial judge. While perusing the record I saw minor misdirection but not fatal enough to presumably quash the conviction. I examined each defence individually and was hopeful there would be misdirection on self-defence, as it relates to the onus and burden of proof being on the prosecution to negative self-defence. Such misdirection would render the conviction fatal, since the plea of self-defence is a complete defence the accused would most likely walk away a free man. But the direction was perfect in every material particular. The defence of provocation was then examined in detail and when I saw there was no direction on the onus and standard of proof in relation to the prosecution negating the defence I screamed, "Yes! I found a great legal point, I found it". After finding the misdirection I counted every page of the record to ensure none was missing. I did so twice, then I read the proceedings again to ensure the error was not corrected anywhere in the record. It was not.

The drafting of the submission, accumulation of authorities were paramount on my mind and I focused on it until I completed. I was ready for the hearing. The appellant wanted to know what his chances were; my standard response usually was, "I cannot tell the future". I was not cynical, it was just my means of ensuring I never gave a client false hope, having always reminded them that the outcome of a matter was always in the hands of the judge and jury. But this was no excuse for not being thoroughly prepared.

The accused was in his early twenties then, as the years flew by since his incarceration and hearings at the Magistrate's Court, to the High Court and Court of Appeal. He had grown much bigger than when I first saw him; years in prison had matured him, for he had spent about eight years there. The appeal was heard. The court accepted the submission on the misdirection of the law on provocation which had the legal effect of reducing the offence of murder to manslaughter. The court accepted that submission. It was not the end of the matter as I was of the view that it may very well be a retrial, however after eight years, it was highly unlikely. The court then unanimously agreed to quash the murder conviction, substituting the offence of manslaughter. The accused was then released immediately, on time served. This was a joyous day for the appellant to have regained his freedom. His mother who walked into my office and the prison more times than I could count was overjoyed. But after the dust had settled the appellant returned to a state of normalcy.

## SPANISH BOYS CHARGED WITH MURDER

The plight of non-nationals, when they are accused of crimes, becomes evident when bail is applied for. The court is always mindful of preserving its integrity and ensuring its orders are not breached. If such breach occurs, this brings the system of justice into disrepute.

When a Cuban and a Venezuelan citizen were charged with the offence of non-capital murder, in circumstances where the deceased was also a citizen of Venezuela, the issue as to their bail arose. Two young men in the prime of their lives were detained by the criminal investigation department. They were remanded to the Richmond Hill prison. After a protracted preliminary inquiry, with numerous witnesses, bail was applied for in the high court.

Despite the fact that both accused men had, within the jurisdiction, a parent each and either a business or a stable job, the arguments did not persuade the court to grant bail. Arguments were levelled as it related to

*Front page, Grenada Informer, week ending 3 June 2016*

posting cash bail, surrendering travel documents, having computerised notices at every exit port, reporting to the police station daily and being confined to a curfew. Notwithstanding all of this, the court refused bail. Instead, there was a solemn undertaking by the prosecution that the conduct of the proceedings would be expedited.

The probability of granting bail in the above circumstances would have been greater, if the accused men were citizens of Grenada. Although there is no guarantee that they would show up for their trial, the probability of absconding in the court's view was less. The system of justice and its administration is not perfect. Sometimes decisions are based on probabilities and possibilities. However, justice must not only be done but must be seen to be done. It is often said, perception is reality.

I represented the Cuban national throughout the preliminary hearing, High Court and Court of Appeal. Prior, to the commencement of the trial, the prosecution offered a reduction of the murder charge to that of manslaughter. After consultation with my client he readily accepted the plea. The same was entered on the day of the trial.

The accused was sentenced to sixteen years imprisonment. On appeal, the sentence was reduced to eight years and six months.

## One Venezuelan National dead, Cuban and Venezuelan charged with Non-Capital Murder

A twenty-one year old Cuban national, together with a Venezuelan national aged 22 have een slapped with a charge ·ith non capital murder following a weekend incident that left another Venezuelan national dead after sustaining serious head injuries.

The two men Arturo Plutin Rodriquez from Cuba and Gabriel Pestana from Venezuela, appeared before Chief Magistrate Tamara Gill on Tuesday, accompanied by legal counsels Derrick Sylvester in the case of the Cuban national and Anselm Clouden in the case of the Venezuelan national, where the charge was read to them making them the main suspects in the death of Jinardo Martinez Rojas.

According to information reaching the Grenada Informer, Rojas' lifeless body was found wrapped in a sheet close to a dwelling house on Lowther's Lane in St. George's in the early hours of Saturday morning. According to a police report, a postmortem conducted hours after the death revealed that the cause of death was extensive skull fracture.

At the time of writing, no one had come forward as an eyewitness to the killing, however, sources told the Informer that Rojas was one of three men who rented a house one day earlier, close to where his body was found. Our source also hinted that the police retrieved pieces of baluster from the crime scene bespattered with blood, blood was also seen on the floor and sidewall of the rented house.

The motive for the killing remains a mystery, although there are widespread speculations that it had to do with arguments over some financial proceeds that would have been derived from illegal deals.

Sources told the Informer that the police was alerted by a neighbor who happened to open his door just in time to see what appeared at the time to be a body being pulled into the street by two men, who later fled the scene. The neighbour, we were told was awakened by strange noises and loud barking of dogs in the area for a lengthy period.

During Tuesday's short sitting, both defense counsels chose not to apply for bail given the nature of the matter, however they requested full disclosure in the matter before the next hearing date on June 16th. The prosecution indicated that a total of six witnesses would be called to prove their case.

Meanwhile in a brief interview with members of the media on Tuesday, defense counsel Anselm Clouden said he is confident that his client Pestana would be vindicated given the strength of his case and he would be going all out to prove his client's innocence in the matter. Clouden also noted that his client has been living in Grenada for some time together with his parents, went to school in Grenada and therefore is no stranger to this country.

Defense lawyer Sylvester on the other hand said his client Rodriquez had been living in Grenada permanently for just over one year. As it relates to the strength of his case Sylvester said he is not prepared to speak on that as yet but promise to do his best under the prevailing circumstances.

If convicted, both men face life in prison.

*Grenada Informer, 3 June 2016*

The anxiety, the stress, associated with the incarceration of non-nationals is indescribable. Firstly, they are in a strange land, away from their family and friends. There are occasions when they are of a different race, culture and have to assimilate to the prison life. For instance, the type of food may not be that to which they are accustomed, and the lockdown normally at sunset to sunrise could be a chilling experience.

The lesson to be learnt is, crime has 'no winners only losers'.

CHAPTER NINE

# MARAN IN MOURNING

*"Dear God," she prayed from the very depth of her soul, "help me not to grieve-to willingly let him return to You and the Heaven he so well deserves."*
THYRA FERRÉ BJÖRN, PAPA'S DAUGHTER

In a small fishing village on the western side of Grenada, nestled a close knit community called Maran. This community has a large population of East Indian descendants; they had settled there eons ago and had grown vastly in numbers. There were other areas where Indians settled as well, including; Clozier, Florida, Grenville, parts of St. David, Sauteurs and parts of St. George.

On Christmas day in 2007, the village of Maran was torn apart by the murder of a young man known as Cosley Beharry. He was in the prime of his life and was shot in very close proximity to his house. The deceased was an ice cream vendor, well-loved in the community and throughout the island of Grenada, as he would drive his musical ice cream truck around the island to sell ice cream in cones to children and adults alike.

When I received the phone call from a family member indicating that they needed my representation in the matter involving an accused who had allegedly shot and killed someone, I immediately sprung to action. Despite, being Christmas day, the time when family and friends gather, the nature of the job demanded my attention. Numerous phone calls were made to the police station to confirm the accuracy of the report I got; it was confirmed that the accused was a suspect. I notified the family member that I would visit the police station in an effort to speak to the detainee.

It was brought to my attention then, that the murder occurred in very close proximity to the house of the deceased and the road, as the house was a step or two from the road where the incident actually occurred. It was alleged then that the accused was armed with a gun and the deceased a cutlass. The police investigation was thorough. ASP Trevor Modeste

# MURDER ON CHRISTMAS DAY

The ice-cream van that was often used by Beharry to conduct his business throughout the island

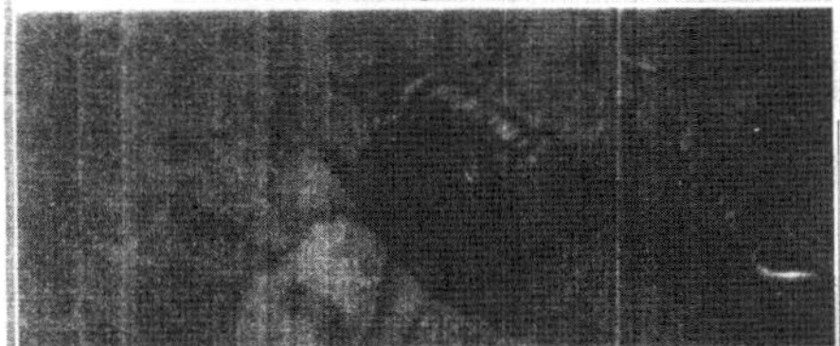

Picture taken with camera from a cell phone by a villager minutes after Beharry fell to the ground

Family portrait of Costley Beharry and his daughter, Ally.

Villagers in Maran are mourning the senseless loss and killing popular ice cream vendor, Costley Beharry who was gunned down on Christmas Day.

Beharry, originally from the small village of Clozier, had just started up his own business after working for many years with Bernie's Ice-cream in St. John's.

The dead man had parted ways with his previous employer in order to develop his own ice-cream business.

See full story on Page 3

*Front page, Grenada Today, week ending 28 December 2007*

# Murder On Christmas Day

...ly get-together in ...tion of Christmas ...n December 25, ...in tragedy in the ...ful village of ... St. John's.

...e cream salesman, ...y Beharry lost his ...a result of a bullet ...he received out- ...f his partially-built ...at around 7:00 p.

...e at the Gouyave ...n have detained a ...s plant owner of ... Bay, St. John's, ...n also known as ...to assist them with ...vestigation.

...y is accused of ...g Beharry at close ...with a licensed ...in the area of his

Cosmus Noel - father of the deceased

...ered at his house.

An eyewitness spoke of Beharry pushing the young lady outside of his house because of the embarrassment he faced.

The young lady reported the incident to her father. Pussy who later showed up at the dead man's house in Maran.

According to the eyewitness, there were heated exchanges between the two men before Pussy left the scene.

He spoke of seeing the girl's father returning a short while later with three other persons and once again confronting Beharry.

The villager said he decided to close up his house and ignore the quarrelling party since on the first occasion he had advised Pussy to forget the incident and go back to his home.

He spoke of hearing a gun shot and concluded that the weapon might have been fired into the air.

He said it was only when he heard someone in the road shouting out that the man was shot that he looked outside to see what was happening.

It was then that Pussy called on him for assistance in getting the shot man into a vehicle to seek medical attention.

The villager said he took a look at the man on the ground and concluded that he was dead and deciced not to get involved in the affair.

Father of the dead man, Cosmus Noel who lives in Diego Piece, St. Mark's described his son as a genuine and loving person.

Noel said that Beharry along with his family, girlfriend and daughter, were first scheduled to have dinner with him in Diego Piece.

"Next thing, his girlfriend called and say he (Beharry) is beating her daughter and they would not leave it so," he said.

Noel said his wife still called on Beharry to come for dinner and he promised to do so. He said that around 7:00 p. m. he received the news that his son was shot dead.

"When I came... I saw the police and them cover him, (and) he well dead," he said.

The dead man is a close cousin of Grenadian-born, Private Johnson Beharry, the world famed and highly decorated British solider as a result of his heroics in the War against Terror in Iraq.

Attorney-at-law, Derek Sylvester has been retained by Pussy's family to look after his interest.

Beharry's death brought the number of murders for the year 2007 to ten.

*Grenada Today, 28 December 2007*

went into work mode with his forensic skills together with police photographers. The Criminal Investigation Department officers all went into high gear.

The incident was tragic and the memory of a death on a day as solemn as Christmas, when the deceased's family would have been at home, was a painstaking hurdle for them to surmount.

The father of the accused stated publicly that he lived in Diego Piece, a village away from his son. He was waiting to have dinner with him when he got the news. A family altercation went totally awry when the deceased had an altercation with the accused daughter. The accused visited the location of the deceased's residence and it was there on that fateful day that violence escalated and resulted in the death of one man, by a single bullet.

The accused was detained in police custody, and the normal process of the investigation ensued. The professional manner in which the police conducted their investigation was commendable. They were very careful in their dealings with the accused in relation to the taking of statements from him, visiting the *locus in quo* (where the incident occurred) taking photographs and agreeing on the location where the incident occurred. The police ensured that the normal challenges I had raised in the past with the numerous matters I had dealt with, and succeeded on, would not occur on this occasion. The public's outcry was deafening. The whole community and the nation, for the greater part, were unhappy with the state of affairs; that a murder should occur in these circumstances, especially the day we were celebrating the Birth of Christ.

The forty eight (48) hours statutory limitation period prior to arrest and charge of an accused soon expired. However, the police did not have sufficient evidence to charge the accused, as it was alleged then that the accused was confronted by the deceased who was brandishing a cutlass or machete, and the accused used his gun. The police photographs confirmed the cutlass on the scene of the incident. The photographs were provided as a means of disclosure which is mandatory in criminal proceedings.

The Director of Public Prosecutions took on his lead constitutional role and the investigation intensified. The issue as to where the incident actually occurred became the focus of the investigation. I was notified that the government's Land and Survey Department was involved. There were conflicting versions as to whether the accused went into the deceased's property and inflicted the fatal wound; or whether the deceased armed with the cutlass came into the road to meet the accused, causing the accused to use the firearm. The measurements were taken and the results remained with the investigators. The issue was not probed further by the police or the prosecution department.

The accused was released two days after without being charged as the investigation was continuing. This was mandatory, as it would have been a violation of the accused's constitutional right, to keep him in custody beyond that period without being charged, and if he was charged he had to be brought to court within the shortest possible time. The liberty of the subject is sacrosanct. Upon the accused being released from custody, there was a huge outcry from the public. Call-in programmes, articles and other forms of social media communication went viral as to

## ›PP: The Investigation is continuing

*ristopher Nelson - requested additional information from the police*

rector of Public osecution (DPP), ristopher Nelson has egorically stated that re is no sinister mo- e in the release from stody of Black Bay ident, Kelvin Antoine o known as Pussy.

e 47-year old Antoine alleged to have been olved in an altercation th a resident of Maran, John's, Cosley harry which ended adly.

eharry, 42, lost his life a result of a bullet wound he received outside of his partially-built house on Christmas Day at around 7:00 p.m.

Pussy was immediately detained by police officers attached to the Gouyave Police Station to assist with the investigation, but was released from custody two days later without being charged.

There has been a public outcry over the release of Pussy, especially with him not having been charged.

However, Nelson told reporters that in keeping within the confines of the law, no one should be kept in police custody beyond 48 hours once he is not charged.

The DPP gave the assurance that no final decision was made on the shooting incident.

He said the police have commenced investigations into the alleged murder of Beharry under his direction and there are some outstanding matters which he declined to revealed, that the police are currently working on.

"As soon as those outstanding matters are completed, then a decision will be made. In the meantime, the suspect is presumed innocent and is entitled to be at liberty. He cannot be held beyond 48 hours without being charged," he added.

"The (investigation) process is on course in this matter as with all matters. There are many a crimes where police conduct investigations and we, having reviewed the file, see areas that we think should be explored.

"And in this case as in other cases, we are directing them in relation to that and I hope they would conclude whatever they are doing pretty speedily, and we decide from there.

According to Nelson, this is a pending investigation into a possible murder and he is not at liberty to discuss the details of evidential matters.

"The police commenced investigation, a file was referred to me with certain statements. There are other matters that I would like them (the police) to address, and they are addressing that. That is as much I can say, it is still a pending matter," he said.

The DPP made it clear that it is his constitutional role to make a judicial determination if there is sufficient evidence to warrant charges in criminal offences on the island.

He said this can only be done based on an assessment of the entire case relating to all of the evidence.

Nelson is warning the media and the general public to not prejudge the issue since there is still an ongoing investigation by the police.

He said he is getting the impression that people seem to be making assumptions when at this moment the investigation is continuing.

*Grenada Today, 4 January 2008*

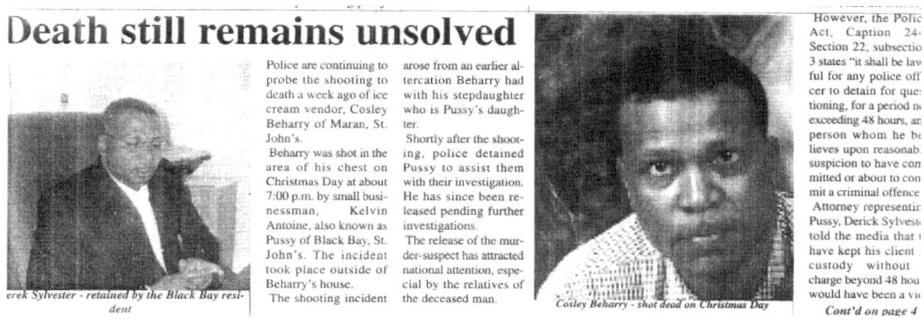

## Death still remains unsolved

Police are continuing to probe the shooting to death a week ago of ice cream vendor, Cosley Beharry of Maran, St. John's.

Beharry was shot in the area of his chest on Christmas Day at about 7:00 p.m. by small businessman, Kelvin Antoine, also known as Pussy of Black Bay, St. John's. The incident took place outside of Beharry's house.

The shooting incident arose from an earlier altercation Beharry had with his stepdaughter who is Pussy's daughter.

Shortly after the shooting, police detained Pussy to assist them with their investigation. He has since been released pending further investigations.

The release of the murder-suspect has attracted national attention, especial by the relatives of the deceased man.

However, the Polic Act, Caption 24 Section 22, subsectio 3 states "it shall be law ful for any police off cer to detain for que tioning, for a period n exceeding 48 hours, an person whom he be lieves upon reasonab suspicion to have com mitted or about to com mit a criminal offence

Attorney representir Pussy, Derick Sylvest told the media that have kept his client custody without charge beyond 48 hou would have been a vi

Cont'd on page 4

erek Sylvester - retained by the Black Bay resident

Cosley Beharry - shot dead on Christmas Day

*Grenada Today, 4 January 2008*

the legality or the lack thereof, of the accused being kept in custody and released without charge. The Director of Public Prosecutions had the arduous task of explaining to the public the reason for the release and the continuation of the investigation. Further, there was the possibility of charges being filed upon completion of the investigation.

The nation was spewing venom on the justice system, police, lawyers, politicians and the accused. I had the further task of having a television interview where I explained to the public that the law had to be obeyed and the release of the accused was in keeping with section 22 of the Police Act Cap 244. A detainee could not be held in custody beyond 48 hours without charge. The prosecution department must have sufficient evidence, if any charge was to be laid, it had to be proffered during the statutory period.

Public pressure increased. The family of the deceased printed jerseys and placards with the deceased's face and demonstrated in the streets of Gouyave close to the police station and court.

The Director of Public Prosecutions came under tremendous public scrutiny. I admired his candour, professionalism and composure under the pressure. He was well respected; he was a man of his word and performed his duty with utmost integrity. I had to defend him when there were attacks over the delay in charging and we were repeatedly questioned about political interference with the process. A member of the public said, "If it was marijuana that a poor man was selling to maintain his children, they would have locked him up and throw away the key". I thought about what he said for a while and realised society was indeed scrutinising the judicial system.

The DPP was asked whether or not there was political interference with the process of investigation and he retorted, in his usual professional manner:

> "I haven't a clue what you are speaking about. I have always worked independently. I will continue to work independently and it is my constitutional and professional duty to work independently I am surprised at the question!"

I had no option but to immediately clear the air of suspicion circling the Director of Public Prosecutions and the administration of justice, by stating to the reporter as follows:

> "To say so would impute the police operates on the basis of political considerations, or for that matter the Director of Public Prosecutions. To say so would be malicious and improper."

The newspaper documented certain portions of the interview verbatim, and published these for the public consumption.

It was publicly stated that the accused may be charged for manslaughter, which did not go down well with the public. I understood

"PUSSY" COULD BE CHARGED WITH MANSLAUGHTER

Cosley Beharry - shot dead on Christmas Day

A charge of manslaughter could be slapped on 47-year old Black Bay resident, Kelvin "Pussy" Antoine in connection with the shooting to death of Cosley Beharry on Christmas Day in the village of Maran in St. John's.

Informed sources told **GRENADA TODAY** that Antoine was taken into custody early Wednesday morning for the second time to the Gouyave Police station for questioning by the lawmen.

Director of Public Prosecutions (DPP), Christopher Nelson confirmed to this newspaper that the murder suspect was re-arrested as part of the "continuing investigation" into the slaying of Beharry.

According to Nelson, the probe is now at "a very critical stage" and that "we have had additional information" to assist the State in taking a decisive decision on whether to charge or eventually release Antoine.

He did not give details but sources said that the DPP had requested advise from both local and foreign ballistics and forensic experts on the shooting incident.

Nelson is also known to have visited the crime scene and interviewed several "critical witnesses" to the shooting to help him arrive at a decision.

Cont'd on page 03

DPP Christopher Nelson - when he arrived in the yards of the Supreme Court Registry on Wednesday, minutes before giving additional instructions to the police

*Front page, Grenada Today, week ending 11 January 2008*

## "PUSSY" COULD BE CHARGED WITH MANSLAUGHTER

Inspector of Police, Earl Dunbar was spotted by this newspaper on Wednesday morning outside the DPP's office awaiting the arrival of Nelson to get further instructions on the shooting incident.

Insp. Dunbar who is based at the main office of the Criminal Investigation Department (CID) in St. George's is believed to be playing a key role in helping Gouyave Police Station in the Maran shooting incident.

According to Nelson, the Maran killing of Beharry is not " a straight forward case" *as some persons in the public* are trying to make it out to be.

47-Year old Antoine is accused of shooting Beharry to death on the night of December 25 outside the home of the deceased at Maran, St. John's with a licensed firearm.

The suspect was detained by police on the night of the shooting but was released 48 hours later pending further investigations by the police.

His release without charges being laid against him sparked public outcry, particularly from residents of St. John's.

This prompted DPP Nelson to address reporters at a press conference and giving assurances to the public that investigations into the shooting incident are continuing given the circumstances under which Beharry was shot.

He said there are some outstanding matters which he had directed the police to work on as part of the probe.

According to Nelson, he was getting the impression that people seem to be making assumptions about the failure of the police to lay charges while the investigation is still continuing.

Speculation is rife that political involvement in the matter is staggering the process of the investigations.

Pussy is believed to be a major financier of the New National Party Constituency Group in St. John's.

When asked by a ***GRENADA TODAY*** reporter if there was political interference in the investigations, Nelson said, "I haven't a clue what you are speaking about."

When pressed on whether he was working independently of the politicians, the DPP said, "I have always worked independently. I will continue to work independently and it is my constitutional and professional duty to work independently. I am surprised at the question."

Antoine's attorney, Derek Sylvester also denied that there was political interference in the case.

"No, no, no, no! I would say no, and I would say so categorically. As far as I am aware when the incident allegedly occurred, the family (of Antoine) contacted me, and that is the only person that contacted me", he said.

"I immediately returned the call and on Boxing Day (December 26). I went to the (Gouyave) Police Station and I had discussions with the accused. I asked him to co-operate with the police, he gave the police a full statement while I was there," he added.

Sylvester charged that it would be malicious and improper for anyone to say that there is political interference in the case.

"To say so would be to impute that the police operates on the basis of political considerations, or for that matter, the Director of Public Prosecutions," he remarked.

The defence attorney described the DPP as one who was very professional in the execution of his duties.

Opposition Leader, Tillman Thomas and leading criminal defense attorney, Anselm Clouden have made public statements suggesting that the police should get on with the job on hand.

Sources close to the police investigation indicated to ***GRENADA TODAY*** that the lawmen collected five witness statements which point to the 47-year old accused man acting in self defence when he fired the shotgun at close range at Beharry.

Sylvester was adamant that in order for his client to be picked up again by the police "there must be an intervening cause," something that has happened and nobody was aware of it.

"But from my lens, from what I am seeing I do not see it as being probable, but it is practical," he added.

In the absence of Antoine being charged for Beharry's death, there would be a coro-

*Grenada Today, 11 January 2008*

the legal difficulty that the DPP had to proffer a charge as the evidence was weighted so heavily in favour of self-defence. However, later additional forensic and other evidence came to light and it was decision making time. The accused was released for about two weeks awaiting the DPP's decision, while the deceased's mother, father, relatives and friends mourned the loss of their loved one.

The DPP visited the crime scene and sought to dot the 'I's' and cross the 'T's' thereby completing the legal tittle. The public pressure mounted to volcanic level, but the calm collected nature of the professional who was well schooled did not crumble under public pressure but conformed to the legal principles.

The accused was rearrested, and it became obvious to me then that he would be charged. A second detention must result is some form of criminal charge. The accused was instructed to cooperate fully with the investigation and this he did. Full statements were provided and his witnesses were named. The accused was expecting at its highest a charge of manslaughter where bail could be granted at the Magistrate's Court. I kept all options open because I knew not what smoking gun the prosecution had and at that stage I did not want to know. I would be made aware in due course. The accused wanted every possibility explained to him. The charge of murder, and having to be incarcerated, was a hard pill for him to swallow. I quickly requested that he awaken himself to that reality, as in fact that was an option.

Finally, the charge of murder was laid on the accused. The family of the deceased was pleased but saw it as a first step on the road to justice. The accused upon receipt of the charge was in utter bewilderment. I reminded him that the trial was a process. The DPP spoke to the media and called for calm as he attempted to fulfil his constitutional duty. The family of the deceased planned on staging demonstrations throughout the streets of Gouyave and other areas. This was discouraged but the demonstration culminated later in the proceedings.

The pain of the mother of the deceased was evident throughout every part of the proceedings. I recalled on every occasion when she spoke about the issue, the intensity of her pain grew stronger, calling for justice and in some instances vengeance. On the day when the accused was brought to the Gouyave Magistrate's Court, I was notified that there was a mob-like crowd outside. I had represented so many persons in that parish that I knew most of them, but their familiarity with me did not minimise their hurt, pain and anger.

On the day of the hearing, on approaching the courtyard, I got more than I bargained for. I was of the impression there would be a few angry persons, but I was wrong. There were scores of people in the courtyard and the main road, shouting, screaming and demanding justice. They were all wearing jerseys with the deceased face printed on them. I entered the yard and parked my vehicle. As I was about to alight, the shouts and screams erupted in unison. I saw so many people there that I knew, even persons whom I had represented before. The police was in close proximity so that was comforting. I was concerned about missiles of any kind being thrown from the crowd. I saw the mother, and siblings of the deceased in the courtyard.

## Pussy Charged For Murder

The first chapter in the Christmas Day fatal shooting of Rickey Cosley Beharry of Maran, St. John's has now come to a close.

After 16 days, Police have finally charged 47-year-old Kelvin Antoine also known as Pussy from Black Bay, St. John's with murder for the offence of shooting to death the 42 year old Beharry, an ice cream sales man.

Beharry was shot in the area of his chest outside of his partially built house and subsequently died on the spot from a single bullet discharged by Pussy's licensed gun.

The murder suspect was immediately arrested by police officers attached to the Gouyave Police Station but was subsequently released 48 hours later pending further investigations.

Pussy's release from custody without charge became a national issue.

However, two weeks following the shooting incident he was again detained by police, and the charge of murder was laid against him early last week Friday.

Pussy made his first court appearance at the Gouyave Magistrate's Court that same morning and was remanded in custody by female magistrate, Tamara Gill-Ferguson.

He is due to re-appear in court on February 1 for the start of the Preliminary Inquiry into the charge.

During his court appearance, the two police Constables who escorted Pussy into and out of the courtroom was seen jogging with him in an effort to get away from the lens of the media.

This annoyed the people who were gathered outside of the court house saying that there was politics involved in the matter.

Pussy is believed to be a major financier of the St. John's Constituency Branch of the ruling New National Party of Prime Minister, Dr. Keith Mitchell.

A number of Beharry's relatives including his parents who were present at the court house broke down in tears.

Iris Beharry, the mother, openly wept inside of the courtroom when Pussy made his entrance before the Magistrate.

Before fainting, Beharry cried out for her son saying that he was an innocent man who got killed.

"I want my child! I want my son! He (is) innocent. My son (is) innocent," she declared.

Before the charge of murder was finally laid on Pussy by the police, Beharry's family was said to be planning a public demonstration to get justice for their loved one.

A younger brother, Dave Beharry, said that the police did not even have the decency to inform them that Pussy was charged with the murder.

He indicated that one of their cousins called early Friday morning while they were still in bed to inform them that the charge of murder was laid on Pussy and that he will be making his court appearance that morning.

According to the younger Beharry, they are not satisfied with the manner in which the initial investigation was conducted by the police into the incident.

He claimed that the lawmen failed to cordon off the crime scene, that his brother's home was left open and that his girlfriend who occupied the place was no where to be found on that fateful Christmas night.

He said that people could have tampered with things inside and outside of the house.

Pussy was released on December 27, a mere 48 hours after he was arrested, pending further investigations.

Following Pussy's release, Director of Public Prosecutions, Christopher Nelson told the media that after reviewing the file that was brought to him by the police he noticed that there were some outstanding matters that they (the police) needed to address.

He gave the assurance that as soon as those outstanding matters are completed a decision would be made about whether to charge or release the suspect in the shooting incident.

The initial police probe concluded that Pussy shot Beharry in self-defence.

*Grenada Today, 18 January 2008*

## DPPspeaks out: Murder charge slapped on Pussy Antoine

One day after addressing member of the media on what he dubbed disquieting information reaching the public surrounding the Christmas night fatal shooting in Maran, St. John, a charge of murder was leveled on key suspect Kelvin "Pussy" Antoine.

Antoine made his first court appearance at the Gouyave Magistrate's Court last Friday amidst a heavy police presence and in the company of his lawyer Derrick Sylvester.

Antoine was not required to plea since his matter would be heard indictably. He was, however, remanded at the Richmond Hill Prison until his second court appearance on February 1st.

It is hoped that the commencement of a preliminary hearing to determine whether a strong enough case is made out to have Antione stand trial at the High Court would also get going on that day.

Meanwhile, defense lawyer Sylvester is not ruling out the question of bail for his client; however he said he would be making an application, when the time is right, before the Judge.

Antoine's murder charge early Friday morning came on the heals of growing public concern particularly from the family of the deceased Cosley Rickey Beharry who felt that sixteen days were way too many to have the man tagged with the murder of their family member, roaming the streets untouched.

In fact, members of the Beharry family were on the verge of taking matters into their own hands by staging a public demonstration but, in his address to the media on Thursday, DPP Christopher Nelson told the media that he had to discourage that practice since it would not have been in the best interest of both parties.

Nelson said then that murder is a serious offence for both the victim and the suspect and it has not been the practice in Grenada that an arrest and prosecution follows immediately after a crime.

The DPP went further to say that in order to lay a criminal charge his department must be satisfied that there is admissible evidence and reliable witnesses who can be taken to Court so that a jury, if properly directed in law, would be more likely than not convict.

It was also stated that investigators in the matter are in no rush to come to any conclusion but they were giving this case, as with any other case, the kind of attention it deserves, irrespective of the victim or the accused.

While Nelson was addressing the media, Antoine was already in police custody for a second time since the fatal Christmas night shooting, and although the DPP said is was all part of the ongoing investigation process, the forty- eight hours expiration time for which a suspect case can be held without charge was fast approaching.

That charge did come and did so, we were told, in the final hour much to the satisfaction of many who were looking forward to some form of action from the authority.

Scores of family members lined the streets outside the Gouyave Police Station to get at least a glimpse of the man who is alleged to be responsible for the death of their family member.

During those very touching moments several comments were made, many pointing to what they consider as flaws in the system and the need to get justice in the matter.

One man was heard to say "God is not dead and when the nation free them, Mammy, God will deal with them".

Beharry 42, father of three, meet his death on Christmas day, gunned down in front of his home in Maran, St John.

Key suspect in the matter, Kelvin "Pussy" Antoine, now remanded in connection with the murder, told police he acted purely on self-defense, and had no other option but to

circumstances.

*Grenada Informer, 18 January 2008*

While I was walking to enter the court which was located upstairs the post office, the onlookers hurled abuses in my direction. I waved them good morning and proceeded upstairs. I fully understood their reaction but I had a job to do, as a professional.

As I went upstairs, there was additional commotion downstairs, loud shrieking and screaming. The accused was being escorted to the court. The noise was minuscule in relation to the words I got on the way up. The tears and curses from the crowd were loud, harsh and brutal. The mother of the deceased fainted outside the court house.

After the first court hearing, the accused was rushed from the court with full police protection. The crowd was enraged; slurs were thrown at the accused regarding his political affiliation, wealth and apparent connections. Claims both the DPP and I had to debunk. The public's perception of the facts was devoid of the true state of the law surrounding the case. The law of self-defence, provocation and intention to kill.

The remand to prison of the accused had calmed the society as the accused was charged with murder. I explained to the accused, that his

PUSSY CHARGED FOR MURDER

Family members attend to Iris Beharry, the mother of the deceased, Cosley Beharry after she fainted outside the court house

" makes his way from police station to the court house to answer the charge of murdering Cosley Beharry

Members of the Beharry family address the press outside the court house

*Front page, Grenada Today, week ending 18 January 2008*

## People are angry in Gouyave

A mob-like commotion developed last week Friday following the first court appearance of murder suspect, Kelvin Antoine who is also known as Pussy as he was taken from the police station to the nearby Gouyave Court House.

Pussy has been finally charged with murder following the shooting to death on Christmas Day of ice cream salesman, Rickey Cosley Beharry of Maran, St. John's.

He was first detained by the police immediately following the shooting, but was released two days later pending further investigations.

The Block plant owner was again arrested last week Wednesday, and the murder charge finally laid on him early Friday morning.

The two uniformed police officers who escorted the 47-year old Pussy in and out of the court room ran with him through the yard where both the police station and the Magistrate's Court are located.

This angered the crowd that gathered on the street outside of the court house.

One female person shouted out that because Pussy has money he is not allowed to face the media.

She went on to say that had it been a poor person who was less influential he would not have received that preferential treatment.

"He has the money so he can't face the media. I hope all you write up on this. I want to see this on T. V. I hope the camera pick up how the police pulling him and only running with him," said the angry woman to the group of media personnel covering Pussy's court appearance.

Another woman was heard saying: "The police and them wicked. Ah doh fraid all you (the police). He (Pussy) don't even show no remorse. He came out laughing".

Some of the onlookers proclaimed that politics was involved in the police investigation of the alleged murder.

However, a few known political activists of the ruling New National Party (NNP) who also assembled outside the court retorted by saying that there was no politics in the affair.

"It have politics in that, yes it have politics. So who stupid in Grenada? He (Pussy) is the first one that ever kill and they don't arrest him and put him in jail," one male person responded.

"All you lie! So is the government that put him there, to tell him kill? It don't have no damn politics in it. Hush all you a..," the NNP activists replied.

There are reports that Pussy is a major financier of the NNP Constituency Branch in St. John's.

*Grenada Today, 18 January 2008*

remand was for his own personal safety. The days and months went by as the preliminary inquiry dragged on and the evidence unfolded day by day. The unfortunate circumstances surrounding the incident became obvious. There was no material variation of the evidence between the witnesses. The inquiry was completed with expedition. The accused's thirst for freedom from incarceration grew daily. While at prison and speaking to other inmates, it led him to question the possibility of the death penalty or even life imprisonment. That was staring the accused in his face.

The preliminary inquiry was completed and the matter was committed to the High Court for trial before a judge and jury. An application for bail and no case submission were unsuccessful, but it was for good reason, which unfolded with the passage of time. The law and its intricacies can sometimes be very difficult to reconcile. In this case the pain of the mother of the deceased was enormous and it was difficult for her to reconcile the length of time the matter was taking.

There was the possibility of a trial in the matter, where the fate of the accused would be in the hands of the jury. The accused had an option to accept a plea of guilty to manslaughter, where the maximum penalty then was fifteen (15) years. Such a plea would result in the attendant discounts, where the court would examine the aggravating and mitigating factors. The public sentiment was nearing boiling point and the radio programmes continued unabated. Every time the matter was called before the court, the resurgence of 'The Christmas Day Murder' rang throughout the tri-island state.

The accused elected to accept the plea of guilty to manslaughter as offered by the prosecution department. However, not until we had lengthy discussions on the law, explanation of the facts, applying the law to the facts and any and every possible outcome regarding the verdict. The moment of truth which was the day of sentencing had arrived. The accused was well attired. The court room and yard was filled with family members, onlookers and media personnel. Everyone was looking forward to the verdict and sentencing of the accused.

The High Court was housed in a two story building on the upstairs at the top of Market Hill; there was one entrance to and from the court. For the purpose of police security and escort it was easy for the police to 'manoeuvre' the ingress and egress of the accused. When the charge was read to the accused you could have heard a pin drop in the court. The court clerk then asked, "How say you, are you guilty or not guilty?" The accused responded, "Guilty sir." There was some rumbling in the court that was quickly quieted as the judge lifted his head in the direction of the sounds. The *allocutus* was read and the accused was now ready for sentencing. Character witnesses, social inquiry report and a report from the prison authority on the accused's behaviour were all accumulated

*Front page, Grenada Informer, week ending 3 April 2009*

# Pussy sentenced to 8 years in jail

Beharry's Mother & Father

As the curtains came down on Monday on the much talked-about 2007 Christmas night killing of forty-two year old businessman Cosley Beharry in the village of Maran in St. Mark, family members are outraged over the sentence meted out to their son's killer - Kelvin Pussy Antoine.

Antoine, himself a businessman from the village of Black Bay in St John, was sentenced to eight years in prison after pleading guilty to a lesser count of manslaughter.

Sentencing in the matter was handed down Tuesday afternoon by High Court Judge [illegible] St. Paul presiding at the number two High Court in St George's.

Beharry was gunned down within touching distance from his home in Maran moment after he entered into a heated argument with Pussy over treatment meted out to his lover, one Margaret Preudhomme, who incidentally is the former lover of the gunman - Pussy.

Information reaching the Grenada Informer at the time revealed that Pussy, on a liming spree being the usual Christmas holiday, was called in to put peace between the two lovers - Beharry and Margaret by his former brother-in-law one Roger Preudhomme.

The information at the time hinted that as Pussy approached the Beharry's home, they called out to Margaret who was still hiding in the bushes allegedly from her lover Beharry. He (Beharry) came out, only to confront his former rival - Pussy.

Sources said within minutes of an argument between both men, a gun shot was heard, and Beharry fell to the ground.

*During* the sentencing hearing on Monday, mainly dominated by defense council Derrick Sylvester, he sought to bring to the Court's attention, that his client, Pussy, was merely acting in self-defense as he was attacked with a cutlass by the deceased and had to use his gun.

Sylvester went on to tell the Court that despite what had happened on that night his client is a model citizen, a good father, a businessman with exceptional qualities, and more recently a model prisoner.

"It was regrettable what had happened on that night", Sylvester told the Court and his client is extremely remorseful. In fact he went on to say that Pussy had since written a latter to Beharry's mom apologizing for his role in her son's death.

Paraphrasing portions of the letter to the Court Pussy was quoted as telling Baharry that he feels her pain, having lost a son but urge to fine it within her heart to forgive him for what had happen.

Sylvester's time on his feet in the Court was spent trying to impress upon the Court that his client - a first time offender, in not entirely a bad person.

This was done by soliciting views from various members of the public, most of whom a respectable persons, caring, hard-working and one who would go out of his way to ensure that others are happy.

Prior to handing down sentencing on Pussy Judge St Paul commended Sylvester for a job well done. However, he reminded him that, despite all that he had said, a life was lost.

The Judge told Pussy that he faces a maximum sentence of fifteen years in prison, however in handing down his reduced sentence, St Paul said consideration was given to the fact that he pleaded guilty to the charge, had already some time in prison among others.

The Judge's sentence however did not go down well with the Beharry family who felt their son did not get justice.

Speaking to members of the media moments after Monday's verdict, Iris Beharry, mother of the deceased man said she was upset and thought the entire exercise was to show up Pussy as this good man when her son was the person who died.

"There is no justice in Grenada", she told members of the media.

*Grenada Informer, 3 April 2009*

into a sentencing bundle, together with a number of cases both locally, regionally and from other Commonwealth countries on sentencing for manslaughter in similar circumstances.

I presented a historical analysis of the accused life from birth to the present day as well as his contribution to society. His witnesses did the same and the hearing culminated with the reports from the prison authority and the social services department.

The accused spent almost two years in prison, as the homicide occurred in December 2007. The sentence was handed down swiftly, but not before the Judge embarked on a lengthy discourse on the use of firearms, dispute resolutions, societal breakdown of law and order and

# Pussy Walks Free

After two years in prison from the date of sentencing, lack Bay businessman - elvin "Pussy" Antoine, alked from prison a free ian.

ussy was sentenced to eight years in prison in March of 2008 on a lesser charge of manslaughter, after accepting responsibility for the death of St. Mark's businessmen - Cosley Beharry.

Beharry was gunned down in front of his home in the village of Ma-an on Christmas night of 2007, following a heated argument between himself and Pussy over treatment meted out to Pussy's ex-lover, who incidentally was Beharry's lover.

**Kelvin *"Pussy"* Antoine** on his way to Court

High Court Judge - Lyle St. Paul in 2008, handed down the sentence of eight years.

The decision to free Pussy was handed down by Judges in the Court of Appeal - namely Hugh Rollins, Michael Gordon and Bruce Lyle, who were in agreement with some six grounds of Appeal raised by defense, Derrick Sylvester, challenging the sentencing meted out to his client by the High Court Judge, after his client pleaded guilty to manslaughter.

The Judges upheld the agreement of Sylvester, despite opposition from Director of Public Prosecution - Christopher Nelson and sentenced Pussy to time spent as time served.

The freed man left the compound of the Court ir all smiles.

Meanwhile murder accused - Nigel Abraham who also challenged the sentence meted out t him, was not so lucky anc would be made to serve hi full time in prison as handed down by the High Cour Judge.

PUSSY WALKS FREE

*Front page, Grenada Informer, week ending 26 November 2010*

the fateful day ( Christmas day) of the incident, the day that the birth of Jesus Christ was celebrated. The accused was sentenced to eight years, and the sound of the gavel was loud as the Judge stood and the court was adjourned for the day. The accused was quickly escorted out.

The family of the deceased was irate as they immediately felt justice was not done; the continued outcry and plea resulted in immense emotions outside the court. At that time I was faced with an accused who was hopeful that the time he had spent on remand was a sufficient penalty, based on the factual circumstances. The option then, as I indicated to him, was solely that of an appeal, and he welcomed the idea. I promised to examine the factual matrix and get back to him before the fourteen (14) days, the period within which to appeal. The accused was convinced that an appeal was necessary. The appeal was filed and the date for the hearing was scheduled for approximately one year later.

The appeal submission, involved the filing of six grounds of appeal, attacking various aspects of the sentencing hearing and what factors were

# PUSSY IS FREE

Three years after serving time in prison for the death of Rickey Cosley Beharry, Maran resident Kelvin "Pussy" Antoine has been released back into society.

The Eastern Caribbean Supreme Court on Tuesday handed down judgement in favour of "Pussy" rendering him a free man.

"Pussy's" freedom follows three years of imprisonment at the Richmond Hill Prison after he was charged and subsequently pleaded guilty for the offence of manslaughter.

The Maran resident was originally charged with murder for the 2007 Christmas Day shooting to death of Rickey Cosley Beharry of Maran, St. John's.

However, the 49-year old block plant operator pleaded guilty to the lesser offence of manslaughter when the matter came up before the #2 High Court on March 12, 2009 and was sentenced to eight years imprisonment by retired High Court Judge, Justice Lyle St. Paul last year.

Beharry, a 42-year-old ice cream salesman, was shot in the area of his chest outside of his partially built house and subsequently died on the spot from a single bullet discharged by Antoine's licensed gun.

Director of Public Prosecutions (DPP), Christopher Nelson, represented the Crown in the appeal while Antoine retained defense Attorney-at-Law, Derick Sylvester.

Both put forward their arguments to the Appeal Court however the Court ruled that the mitigating factors in the incident outweighed the aggravating factors and therefore ruled that the time served behind bars should be taken as time spent.

The maximum sentence for manslaughter in Grenada is 15 years.

*Kelvin "Pussy" Antoine*

*Weekly newspaper, week ending 26 November 2010*

not taken into consideration. The Court of Appeal heard the submissions and the response from the prosecution. The court deliberated and returned the judgment. The accused sat directly behind me, as was the practice then both in the High Court and Court of Appeal.

The Court of Appeal upheld the appellate grounds; the accused was released forthwith. The accused was discharged, yet he remained in the 'prisoners dock' not comprehending the court's ruling. After I explained to him, that he was free to go and not having to return to Her Majesty's Prison, he left the court at an alarming speed. It was a day of freedom for the accused from the walls of the prison. Never to return.

CHAPTER TEN

# SPREADING MY LEGAL WINGS

*"Progress lies not in enhancing what is, but in advancing toward what will be."*
KAHLIL GIBRAN

Since 19th October 2001, when I was admitted to practise as a Barrister in the Supreme Court of Grenada, it was my desire then to practise in other Commonwealth jurisdictions. For the breadth and scope of practising in numerous countries would serve to widen my experience while creating a legal network that is ever so important in a globally changing legal landscape.

However, being inundated with legal cases, the years flew by as a passing cloud on a sunny day. On the 30th day of October 2015, there was an appeal due to be heard in the appeal court, in the matter of Technical and Allied Workers Union (TAWU) V. St. George's University (SGU) (GDAHCVAP214/0008), which emanated from an arbitration hearing. The issue to be determined was whether all maintenance workers were entitled to receive overtime pay, pursuant to an interpretation of the labour agreement which was signed by the parties. Each side had a different interpretation of the said clause, which was skewed to their benefit.

I was instructing a Senior Counsel from the Republic of Trinidad and Tobago in the matter. The workers at the SGU were anxious to have the matter resolved. The hearing was due to be heard in the island of St. Lucia on the 18th day of February 2016. As I was not admitted to practise in St. Lucia then, it became obvious to me that I should embark on the journey of being admitted to practise in a few of the jurisdictions, including, St. Lucia, Guyana and Trinidad and Tobago.

It was in the year 2016, that I contacted a distinguished colleague in the island of St. Lucia. She made contact with a local attorney there, who graciously agreed to move my admission to the Bar. After I forwarded

IN THE HIGH COURT OF JUSTICE

STATE OF SAINT LUCIA

**Practising Certificate**

(Section 23 (3))

*Pursuant to the Legal Profession Act, 2000 it is hereby certified that*

DERICK SYLVESTER

*whose name is registered on the*
*Roll of Attorneys-at-Law is entitled to practise as an Attorney-at-Law*

*Dated this* 19th *day of* February, 2016.

THIS CERTIFICATE IS
31 DEC 2016
VALID UNTIL

*Registrar of the High Court*

CERTIFIED TRUE COPY
OF ORIGINAL DOCUMENTS

11th April 2016

*Admission to practice in St. Lucia*

all the documentation, and ensured the procedural requirements were adhered to, a date was set by the court for the hearing. I was pleasantly surprised to learn on the date of the hearing that my admission to the Bar of St. Lucia would be heard by Justice Francis Belle, whom I knew as a Judge in Grenada. I had the opportunity of appearing before him on numerous occasions.

The hearing was formal. After the presentation was made by the local Attorney, I thanked the court expressing my commitment and dedication to the noble profession. Subsequently, the oath was taken. I was admitted to practise in the beautiful island of St. Lucia.

Approximately one year thereafter, I decided it was time to embark on my mission to be admitted to practise in the Republic of Guyana. The legal jurisprudence in Guyana is rich. I appreciated reading the detailed and scholastic judgments of the judges. Grenada benefitted from many jurists and teachers from the Republic of Guyana. It is a country where academic acumen was never wanting. I had the good fortune of meeting Dr. Nigel Gravesande who taught me in my formative years and

*Dr. Nigel Gravesande (Registrar of the University of Guyana)*

*The Registrar of the Supreme Court*
*Tel.: No. (592) 226-8487*

***Victoria Law Courts***
***Avenue of the Republic***
***Georgetown, Guyana***
***South America.***

31st August, 2016

**CERTIFICATE**

**I, SUEANNA LOVELL,** Registrar of the High Court of the Supreme Court of Judicature, in whose custody the Roll of Attorneys-at-law of the said Court is kept, DO HEREBY CERTIFY that **MR. DERICK FIELDS SYLVESTER** was admitted to practice as an Attorney-at-law on 26th day of February, 2016 by the Supreme Court of Judicature of Guyana.

AND THAT his name is still on the Roll of Attorneys and has never been removed therefrom.

AND THAT no order has ever been made directing him to be suspended from practicing his profession.

AND THAT no charge is pending against him for professional misconduct.

THEREFORE he is in good professional standing.

GEORGETOWN DEMERARA

Dated this 31st day of August, 2016.

IN THE TESTIMONY WHERE OF
I HAVE HERETO SET MY HAND

SUEANNA LOVELL (Mrs.)
Registrar
of the Supreme Court of Judicature

DEPUTY REGISTRAR

*Admission to practice in the Republic of Guyana*

encouraged me to visit Guyana to be admitted to practise there. His initial conversation with me was a mere passing comment. However, as time went by, his request persisted every time we met. I agreed to take on the challenge.

On the 25th day of February 2016, I travelled to Guyana, at his behest, to be admitted to practise in the Republic. The admission was heard before the Chief Justice of Guyana.

It was my first visit to Guyana, a country rich in architecture, resilient people, respect for authority and great food. There were many firsts for me. I experienced pepper pot with a colleague of mine from the Hugh Wooding Law School, who was then a sitting judge. While enjoying the food, with great company, I was reminded how time flies. Every now and again we should stop and find time to smell the roses.

Dr. Gravesande ensured I experienced Guyanese cuisine, culture, craft and hospitality during my short sojourn. I had the opportunity of visiting the Public Service Commission in Guyana, meeting its Chairperson and staff. It was a welcoming experience as I was Chairman of the Public Service Commission in Grenada, so the exchange of information as it relates to our respective functioning was necessary. I had a tour of the University of Guyana where Dr. Gravesande was Registrar. He had recently taken up assignment in Guyana; he was the former Registrar at the T.A. Marryshow Community College in Grenada. I wanted to have as much experience with the practice of law as possible and wherever it took me I was willing to travel.

Dr. Gravesande's hospitality was not complete without ensuring a full press coverage at the University of Guyana, where we both addressed the media. My experience in Guyana has shown me that the South American country is steeped in protocol and correctly so. Everyone I met was punctual, respectful and courteous.

My colleagues in the Republic of Trinidad and Tobago, Elvis O'Connor and Asaf Hosein, whom I had the pleasure of meeting at the Hugh Wooding Law School, shared a close bond of friendship. I then invited them to come to Grenada in 2005 to file a petition for their admission to the Bar. Their applications to be admitted as Barristers in the State of Grenada were heard before a Trinidadian Judge. It was an auspicious occasion, as they were pleased to be admitted before a judge from their jurisdiction. They both had the pleasure of completing matters before our courts and in the case of Asaf Hosein to the level of the Court of Appeal and Privy Council.

# Derick Sylvester set to broaden his scope regionally

Chairman of Grenada Public Service Commission and the one of island's most aspiring legal luminaries Derick Sylvester, has taken the decision after fifteen years in the profession to extend his legal services beyond the boundaries of Grenada.

Less than one year after he was given the green light to practice his profession in the island of St Lucia, Sylvester is again breaking new grounds, this time in the Republic of Guyana where he was admitted to the bar during a brief visit to that country last month.

Speaking to reporters shortly after he returned to Grenada on his decision to go regional with his practice, Sylvester described himself as a regionalist who is not prepared to be deterred by legal short sightedness but is willing to embrace every opportunity that will bring on board experience and exposure in his profession.

Sylvester said given the present conditions where admission to the bar in one jurisdiction does not give one access to practice in another jurisdiction, the process that he has now embarked on is just the prudent thing to do. Additionally, it would be an asset down the road, as the region moves towards the Caribbean Court of Justice. He said now that St Lucia and Guyana are on board, he would soon be looking at other jurisdictions, among them the Republic of Trinidad and Tobago, Tortola and St. Vincent and the Grenadines.

Asked whether his new vision would not interfere with the level of efficiency with which matters are dealt with in Grenada, Sylvester said its all about time management, opening up to new challenges and not restricting one's self solely to what exists in any single space.

With fifteen years of legal practice beneath his belt Sylvester has argued cases before some of the most renowned judges across the region, representing clients in different areas of the law.

When asked what he hopes to leave as his legacy he replied, "If the good Lord gives me life, I want to be able to look back, as someone that has served the people of the Caribbean with distinction, professionalism, honesty and integrity."

The energetic Sylvester said he does not want leave a legacy of being rich, or having to say that he has been to all of these islands and made lots of money; this to him isn't important. Instead he noted, what is important is his reputation, what legal footprint he would have left in the sands of time and what impact his life would have had on young people. " If therefore in my sojourn I find just one young person who said that he/she went to study law because of me, then I would feel satisfied because it would mean that I would have done something right."

When asked about some of the challenges faced during his fifteen year sojourn as a practicing attorney, Sylvester responded by saying life's road is never smooth and therefore there would be obstacles, however he noted that the only challenge he faces daily is to be a better lawyer than he was yesterday, being better at what he does.

Sylvester, whose areas of practice embraces administrative, criminal, civil litigation, commercial, constitutional, conveyance, family law, human rights, insurance, labour, public law, mediation and non-contentious matters, took the opportunity to thank a number of individuals who would have assisted him along the way in the profession. Among those he mentioned were Anslem Clouden under whom he did his legal training and internship, Leslie Ann Seon and Associates and the law firm of Ciboney Chambers.

*Grenada Informer, 11 March 2016*

# Local attorney looking to boost his regional image

"If the good lord gives me life, I want to be able to look back and say that I would've served the people of the Caribbean and I would've done so with distinction, professionalism, honesty, and integrity; that is the legacy I want to leave."

Those were the words of Attorney-at-Law, Derick Sylvester who is also Chairman of the Grenada Public Service Commission (PSC).

The barrister was speaking to reporters on Monday at his office shortly after returning home from Guyana where he was called to the bar in Georgetown on February 26.

During his trip to the South American mainland, Sylvester held meetings with members of Guyana media at the University of Guyana, Turkeyan Campus in the presence of Registrar, Dr. Nigel Gravesande and paid a courtesy call on Chancellor of the Judiciary and President of the Guyana bar.

Guyana is the third Caribbean country in which Sylvester has been admitted to practice law.

With over 15 years experience, the local attorney who has his eyes also set on sitting as a judge in the future, was admitted to practice in St Lucia in 2015.

According to Sylvester the time has come for him to experience other jurisdictions as, "I believe we should not think myopically, lest we suffer from short sightedness."

"I'm a regionalist and believe that if we're heading to the Caribbean Court of Justice (CCJ) that is only the proper thing to do because we do not have any law in place wherein if you're accepted in one OECS country or any island in the Caribbean, you automatically (are) accepted to the bar in the other country", he said.

*Attorney at Law – Derick Sylvester is making strides in the Caribbean in his law profession*

"...Guyana has acceded to the CCJ and we're heading in that direction, so what better place to be admitted other than Guyana", he added.

Sylvester believes that he is ready to "explore other jurisdictions" due to his 15 years experience in practicing administrative, criminal, civil litigation, constitutional, commercial, constitutional, conveyance, family law, human rights, insurance, labour, public law, mediation and non-contentious matters in the local courts.

He went on to say: "... Guyana is in the process of acceding to the new Civil Procedure Rules 2000 and since Grenada has been using the said rules since 2001 and having practiced with those rules, it would be an added benefit.

"...Once you are a lawyer who loves the law, reading, analysing, interpreting an indepth analysis is a matter of advantage. You must be able to read not only what is on the line but what is within the line." he remarked.

Sylvester told reporters that his decision to practice law in other jurisdictions would not disrupt the flow of business here in Grenada, as it is all about time management.

*Weekly newspaper, 2016*

# Distinguished Grenadian admitted to local Bar

**GRENADA Public Service Commission Chairman, Attorney-at-Law Derick Fields Sylvester, has been admitted to the Bar in Guyana.**

Hours prior to his admission on Friday, the Attorney-at-Law met with the local media at the University of Guyana, Turkeyen Campus in the presence of the University's Registrar Dr Nigel Gravesande.

Sylvester, who has been an attorney for the past 15 years, said the time has come for him to experience other jurisdictions given the limitations in Grenada.

Grenada has a population of approximately 100,000 and according to him, this presents a limitation with regard to the quantity of cases.

He practises in the areas of administrative, criminal, civil litigation, commercial, constitutional, conveyancing, family law, human rights, insurance, labour, public law, mediation and non-contentious matters.

In a quest to broaden his horizon, the Attorney-at-Law after being admitted to local bar in Grenada in October 2001, moved to be admitted in St Lucia in 2015.

"It is a means of embracing other jurisdictions and not restricting yourself to your country of birth.... and I believe that is what the Caribbean is all about and that is what Caribbean integration is all about," the Chairman of the Grenada Public Service Commission said, describing himself as a champion of Caribbean integration.

He was encouraged to practise law in Guyana by Dr Gravesande, who taught him history back in Grenada. For him, Dr Gravesande has provided yeoman service to the people of Grenada, having served as the Registrar of the T.A. Marryshow Community College; Director of Trade, Tourism, and International Economic Cooperation in Grenada; in addition to being the Director of Planning and Projects at the Ministry of Education.

"Dr Gravesande contributed to our country for the last 28 years, and he has done so with pride, grace, elegance and intelligence," Sylvester posited.

Like Dr Gravesande, Attorney-at-Law Sylvester continues to serve his country with pride.

In addition to being the Chairman of the Grenada Public Service Commission, he serves as the Chairman of the Grenada Football Association Appeal Tribunal Disciplinary Committee.

Between February 2013 and October 2013, he served as the Director of the Board of Directors of the Grenada Housing Authority; and from January 2009 to November 2013 as Chairman of the Allied Health Professional Council.

Sylvester was also appointed by the Ministry of Foreign Affairs as a diplomat for the tri-island State of Grenada, Carriacou and Petite Martinique in October 2014.

In December, 2011, he was declared 'Personality of the Year' by the Grenada Informer, one of the leading local newspapers; and also declared one of the 'Top 3 Male Personalities' in the State of Grenada for the year 2013 by the said newspaper.

He was also a part of the legal team at the High Court, Court of Appeal, Privy Council and Re-Sentencing in Grenada's most historic case which arose out of the fall of the Grenada Revolution in 1983- Case No. 19 of 1984, The Queen vs Callistus Bernard, Lester Redhead, Christopher Stroude, Hudson Austin, Bernard Coard, Liam James, Leon Cornwall, John Anthony Ventour, Dave Bartholomew, Ewart Layne, Colville McBarnette, Selwyn Strachan and Cecil Prime.

**Sylvester has done over 30 homicide cases in the Supreme Court of Grenada, with over 20 murder trials included, and has successfully represented clients in all areas of the law throughout the various courts in the legal system.**

**Attorney-at-Law Derick Fields Sylvester and University of Guyana Registrar, Dr Nigel Gravesande**

*Guyana Chronicle, 27 February 2016*

REPUBLIC OF TRINIDAD AND TOBAGO

SUPREME COURT OF JUDICATURE

IN THE HIGH COURT OF JUSTICE
(Legal Profession Act, 1986)

*Certificate of Enrolment*

ATTORNEY-AT-LAW

*It is hereby Certified that* **DERICK FIELDS SYLVESTER**

*is registered on the Roll of Attorneys-at-law under section 14 of the Legal Profession Act, 1986 his/her name having been included in the Roll*

*Dated this* **11TH** *day of* **NOVEMBER, 2016**

*Registrar of the Supreme Court*

*Certificate of Enrolment as an Attorney in the Republic of Trinidad & Tobago*

Thereafter, they were instrumental in ensuring I was admitted to practise in the twin island Republic of Trinidad and Tobago.

The admission to the bar of Trinidad and Tobago and the legal networking created, had propelled me to the Privy Council; a debt of gratitude is owed to my Trinidadian brothers who embraced me as part of their legal team and the experience gained at that hearing was memorable.

CHAPTER ELEVEN

# PUBLIC APPOINTMENTS

*"You cannot acquire experience by making experiments. You cannot create experience. You must undergo it."*
ALBERT CAMUS

It has become the annual practice that at the end of the year the print media houses in Grenada will name someone personality of the year. I have read the articles annually and was told the nomenclature was determined by a poll that was conducted via phone calls, surveys and nominations from the public. On or about the 17th December 2011, I received a phone call from the editor of the *Grenada Informer* newspaper, Mike Noel, informing me that among other candidates I was chosen as 'Personality of the Year'; he requested an interview. It was in recognition of my contribution as a lawyer coupled with the assistance I gave to persons who otherwise would not have had legal representation in court. It became my practice that once there were unrepresented clients in court, to assist. My practice then caused me to travel throughout the tri-island State of Grenada, Carriacou and Petite Martinique, and more persons became aware of my contribution.

My desire and appetite for the law was solely to ensure I did my best in my chosen calling. I enjoyed the practice; I was merely a servant. It was my desire since I left law school that the practice of law for me should be characterised by decency, humility and honesty. Again, in the year 2014, I was surprised when I purchased the weekly newspaper as I normally do and saw that I was listed as the 3rd personality of the year, in the male category, with Joseph Ross and Sir Royston Hopkin in first and second positions. This was society's annual accreditation of the persons who would have contributed to it in meaningful ways.

During the year 2008, there were two major political parties in Grenada: the New National Party (NNP) headed by Dr. Keith Mitchell, and the National Democratic Congress led by its Political Leader, Tillman

# Personality of the Year - *Derick Sylvester*

On Saturday 17th December Informer spoke with Attorney-at-Law - Derick Sylvester. Mr. Sylvester has been practicing Law for the last ten years and has been instrumental in helping many people in the Court System who do not have any legal representation.

However, the most inspiring aspect of the young Attorney's story are his struggles to achieve clearly defined goals. He was clear in his mind as to what he wanted in life. Some of his ambitions were not as easily achievable as he initially thought; but once he put his hands on the plough he never turned back. He appears to love challenges particularly at a time when so many young people prefer to shy away.

Derick Sylvester

Informer: Good Morning Mr. Sylvester, congratulations on being chosen as Grenada Informer's Personality of the Year.

Derick: First of all, I want to say Thank You for the interview and I am humbled by the accolade. I am very humbled for being chosen by Informer as Personality of the Year.

Informer: Derick, can you enlighten us a-bit on your background? Where were you born etc?

Derick: I was born in a small village called Corinth, St. David, on the 3rd of February 1972. I was born to Ms. Maria Sylvester and Mr. Lashy Salfarlie, who later came into my life in my teenage years. My father is a lawyer and has been for a long time. I was raised by my grandparents Ms. Norma Sylvester and Mr. Ashley Morrain who had eleven children. I lived with them until I was around four or five. My mother had seven children, I am the first. For the first six years of my life I attended the St. Peter's RC School which is now known as the Corinth RC School. The principal of the school at the time was Mr. Victor Ashby. Thereafter my family moved to Morne Jaloux, where I attended and passed Common Entrance from the Morne Jaloux RC School. After passing the Common Entrance my family moved back to Corinth, St. David.

Informer: What Secondary school did you attend?

Derick: I attended the Wesley College Secondary School from 1982 to 1988. There I sat 7 O'levels but passed 5.

Informer: What did you do after completing Secondary school?

Derick: After completing my studies at Wesley College I went to work with my uncle who was an electrician from July 1988. My first formal job was with the Ministry of Construction as a Road Supervisor, where I remained employed until May 16th, 1989. After that I was employed with Cable and Wireless for the following eight years. I left in August 1997 to study Law. During my eight years at Cable and Wireless I completed my GCE A'Levels privately along with my first year of Law at Maryshow House, since I did not attend the Institute for Further Education (IFE). Shortly thereafter, I continued my studies at the University of the West Indies (UWI) to complete my Law degree. I graduated from UWI, Cave Hill in 1999, and in 2001 I graduated from Law School.

Informer: What attracted you to the Legal profession? Was it because of your dad being a Lawyer? What influenced you?

Derick: Initially, I always had a love for the Justice System, be it policing or law. I remember when I just completed secondary school, I inquired about the procedures to get into the service. There was a height requirement, which I did not fulfill so I decided to go into the field of Aviation. In the 90's, we formed a group called the Grenada Light Airplane Club. We would contract a plane from Barbados to come Grenada through which we would complete our classes during the week. There were other persons who started with me, and now they were pilots with LIAT. But my real passion has always been the Justice System. When the opportunity arose where I could complete my first year of Law in Grenada, I immediately accepted it. Thus, I only had to complete two years in Barbados then another two in Trinidad. When I returned to Grenada, I worked for one year with Leslie-Ann Seon and Associates, whose practice was mainly in Civil Law. I then became employed with Cibony Chambers for the following three years. It was there, I can say, I got most of my experience, working with Mr. Anslem Clouden.

Informer: What were some of the struggles you endured on the road to success?

Derick: From 1989 to 1996, every year I applied for a scholarship and was never successful. I applied through the Department of Personal and Management Services. I applied for Dentistry, Medicine, Computer Information Systems and Law. I applied for everything conceivable. I decided if I would not get any assistance from anyone I will have to finance myself, so I applied for a loan to buy a bus, while working in Cable and Wireless. During the day, my brother would drive and on weekends I would assist him. I used the revenue from the bus to study for two years in Barbados and one year in Trinidad. In my last year in Trinidad my funds were depleted so I applied to the Grenada Development Bank for a loan. Mrs. Lewis and Ms. Grant ensured I got the loan for my final year. In 2001 I invited them to my graduation ceremony and specifically mentioned them. I had numerous financial struggles.

Informer: Are there any lawyers you look up to, or who have influenced your career?

Derick: No, I mean, I will be honest with you, I like good advocacy. There is a lawyer I had the benefit of accompanying at trials, Carl Hudson Phillips. He taught me about preparing submissions, etc. There are also other persons who I respect as lawyers; for instance, when I began studying law, Mr. Anslem Clouden was instrumental in teaching and molding me, and I always say Thank You to him. His was the first Firm which opened its doors to me, and gave the opportunity, as I had applied to numerous Firms at that time. This is because during the 90's the practice of Law was like a closed shop. People, during that time, were crying out for justice, so I felt that one of the things I would do is to be the best for my client, and practice as professionally as possible. So I respect other Attorneys. The reason I do not hold any Attorney as a mentor is because men are fallible. What I have done is benchmark myself in-so-far as saying that I will do my best always in every circumstance. I will do my best professionally, ethically, and academically.

Informer: What form of Law do you practice?

Derick: I practice in all fields from civil matters, to criminal matters, and divorces. I recall, I had a civil matter that changed the Law in regards to persons who are convicted and incarcerated, losing their pension. This Act was passed during the Revolution. There was a gentleman called Eric Williams who worked for years at the Grenada Electricity Services (Grenlec) who was convicted of a matter. He was a senior citizen and no longer incarcerated. NIS wanted to terminate his pension so I filed a Constitutional Motion against the Attorney General stating that it is unconstitutional to deprive a man of what he has worked for. The matter went to Court and that Law has been repealed.

Informer: What is one of the major cases on which you have worked?

Derick: One of the major cases we worked on has been, the "Bernard Coard and Others" trial. That case took us all the way to the Privy Council. This was my first appearance in the Privy Council. We started off with Constitutional Motions; we failed in some, and we succeeded in some. We went to the High Court, then to the Court of Appeal, and then we went to the Privy Council. So that was one of the matters that has really taken me to the highest Appellate Court. We went to England in 2006, and the Court ordered re-sentencing of all of the accused. I then represented Selwyn Prime in the re-sentencing and he was released by Justice Francis Bell. I have represented numerous persons over the years and it is fair to say that I have no favorite case.

Informer: What's next for Derick Sylvester?

Derick: I don't mind remaining in the field of Law, but I've always been a dynamic person in terms of my thinking and way of life. I will not like to practice Law for the rest of my life; I want to do something else. I would like to do something else maybe be on the Judiciary or work in another country, but I am almost sure that I will not restrict myself to Grenada.

Informer: Do you have any words of motivation for the youth who may be experiencing the same setbacks you did when you decided to go study?

Derick: I have two pieces of philosophy in life by which I live: "Never be contented with failure because success is all to which you should aspire", and "Quitters never win, and winners never quit", so my position is, never give up. Once you set your mind to achieve something you should expect hurdles; no road is always smooth. Where I am today - it wasn't easy, because even to go and study has been years of struggle. I worked two jobs, working with Cable and Wireless and driving a bus on weekends, to accomplish my goals. I knew that nothing was going to stop me.

Informer: Congratulations to you, Mr. Sylvester, on your achievements so far, and thank you for allowing the discussion.

*Grenada Informer, 30 December 2011*

*Grenada Informer, 3 January 2014*

Thomas later V. Nazim Burke. The national elections in the said year resulted in the NDC winning 11 of the 15 seats, thereby forming the new government. Peter David an attorney at law and I were practising in the firm of Ciboney Chambers at the time, together with the Deputy Political Leader of the NDC, V. Nazim Burke. There was therefore an exodus of lawyers from chambers by virtue of the election victory.

Peter David was installed Minister of Tourism; he nominated me as one of the Directors of the Grenada Airports Authority (GAA), as he was statutorily authorised to do pursuant to the GAA Act. This was a nine (9) member committee including the General Manager and the Commissioner of Police, the latter as an *ex officio* member.

It was there that I started to experience the workings and decision making process of statutory bodies. The procedural and ethical requirements necessary to ensure the mandate of the statute was properly adhered to with accountability and responsibility indicative of a responsible team. One bad financial decision could result in an economic fiasco. This could have serious political and social consequences.

The monthly meetings were to ensure the mandate was carefully followed, minimising financial wastage, in addition to managing human resources as the need arose. There was the requirement of fulfilling the government policy mandate in an efficient, effective and productive manner. The decision making process had to be well informed and intentioned. It should be devoid of considerations that were not in the

*GAA Performance Review 2011*

**Board of Directors**

Mr. A. L. Andall (General Manager), Mr. D. Sylvester, Mr. B. Romain, Ms. Y. James, Mr. R. Evans (Dep. Chairman), Mrs. A. Buckmire-Outram, Mr. G. George, Mr. C. Felix, Mr. Rodney. George (Chairman)

**Management Team**

General Manager: Mr. Lester Andall
Divisional Director of Operations: Mr. Sydney Charles
Manager Air Traffic Services: Mrs. Roselyn Charles
Manager of Security: Mr. Eric Peters
Marketing & Properties Manager: Mrs. Cristina Joseph
Accountant: Mrs. Ria Daniel-Smith
Manager Maintenance (Ag.): Mr. Glen Forsyth
Manager of Meteorology: Mr. John Peters
Duty Manager: Mrs. Myrna Charles
Duty Manager: Mrs. Wendy Austin-Honoré

**Mailing Address**:
Grenada Airports Authority
P.O. Box 385 Maurice Bishop International Airport, St. George's, Grenada W.I.
Telex: 3480 PSIA.GA
Fax: (473) 444-4838
Tel.: (473) 444-4555/4155/4101

E-mail: gaa@mbiagrenada.com. Website: www.mbiagrenada.com    Page 3 of 44

*Grenada Airport Authority (GAA) Performance Review 2011*

best interest of the statutory body and the State. It was quite an experience as it was then that I understood what the Directors did at Cable and Wireless when I was employed there, prior to my sojourn at University.

Subsequently, I demitted office as a Director on conclusion of two terms and was appointed Director of the National Housing Authority (NHA). The appointment to that post was of a different character as the mandate of the housing authority was to provide housing in a cost effective manner, to implement policies, plans and programmes for approval by government. This had to be in the best interest of the population. The meetings were frequent. As the need arose, meetings were called to ensure the management team was in sync with its mission. The Manager then had a clear mandate to minimise money owing to the Authority, manage with minimum wastage, maximise productivity and ensure full utilisation of its human resources.

The size of the staff at the NHA was smaller than the Airport Authority. It was much more intimate and I knew almost everyone by name. There were similarities between the Airports Authority and the NHA, in so far as it relates to their individual mandates. However, there was a much more direct line of communication with the NHA as everyone was housed in the same building on the same floor.

Subsequently, I had to resign from the NHA as additional responsibilities were placed on my shoulders. I then assumed a position at the Ministry of Health. The Ministry of Health in conjunction with its functional responsibility of providing adequate health care to the citizens of Grenada was required to ensure persons who were required to provide any form of medical professional services were qualified and registered. As a result, all non-medical personnel had to be registered and licenced pursuant to the requirements of the Allied Health Professionals Council.

I was a member of the said Council, and subsequently appointed Chairman. Our mandate was to ensure the proper qualifications were met for persons applying and the requisite licences issued. In other words it was a means of ensuring the State received properly trained professionals whose names were recorded in a database for ease of reference together with the payment of the appropriate registration and licensing fee.

The Council was recently appointed by an Act of Parliament. Many teething problems had to be ironed out in the interest of its smooth functioning. The qualification for each type of service to be provided had to be itemised and approved by the Council, also ensuring the certifications are from qualified and certified institutions. Overall, the experience gained at that august body, showed me a deeper working of the public service and how ultimately decisions were made.

Later, I had to tender my resignation as Chairman of Allied Health Professional Council. This was necessary since I had to assume a new assignment that consumed most of my time outside of my legal practice.

I did a stint with the Grenada Football Association (GFA). I was first appointed a Director of the Grenada Football Association's Disciplinary Committee and thereafter Chairman of the said Committee. It was a three member committee.

The many decisions we adjudicated were guided by the rules of the GFA. It was a continuation of the legal procedures I was accustomed to following in relation to all the other committees. The underlying philosophy was to ensure the principles of natural justice were followed, *audi alteram partem* in that each side was given an opportunity to be heard, to present their cases fairly and thereafter ensure the correct procedure was followed prior to making a decision in accordance with the rules of the Association.

Later, I held the constitutionally appointed position of Chairman of the Public Service Commission (PSC) which is dealt with in the following chapter.

A weekly contributor to the newspaper, Dr. Terrence Marryshow wrote in his article 'Food for Thought' that a fresh face heads the Public Service Commission. He highlighted the Commission's mandate.

The pressure was on to be fair, impartial and non-partisan.

Another prominent newspaper, headed 'Sylvester assumes the chair of Grenada's PSC' levelled additional expectation as to the impartiality of the Commission and its independence. This responsibility I was ready to shoulder. I was prepared to fulfil my constitutional mandate without fear or favour.

Another newspaper was keen to write that there was a tossup for the position of Attorney General and Chairman of PSC, including my possible involvement with the Citizenship by Investment Programme. The inaccuracy of these statements was later revealed.

By virtue of my position then as Chairman of the Public Service Commission, I was ex officio member of the National Awards Committee pursuant to the National Honours and Awards Act CAP 204A, which was responsible for the recommendation of awardees for national awards to the Cabinet for their approval. This was normally done on Independence Day 7th February each year, under the auspices of the Governor General.

The procedure was that recommendations would be received from the public at large. The Committee then embarked upon a process of investigation to determine whether the persons fit the requirements necessary to be awarded. If the committee was of that view, then a submission would be sent to the Cabinet for its approval. Once the Cabinet approved, the Governor General would then give assent. The awardees would be notified and presented with the award at the Independence celebration.

## Fresh new face heads Pubic Service Commission

Just over a week ago the Public Service Commission saw the appointment of a fresh new face to head its operations. He is none other than Derrick Sylvester, prominent local attorney who in the last couple of years has become a household name as far as the legal profession is concerned. Among the many graduates of this profession in recent years, one name has emerged time and time again who can be considered as a trailblazer with a no-nonsense approach and he is Derrick Sylvester. Until I met him and became aquainted with him, his reputation as an efficient, fearless attorney preceded him and as he began to chalk up victory after victory on be-

out a name and a reputation that was the envy of many. Say or think what you want to about him, you cannot say that he does not enjoy his job and you cannot help but be impressed with the methodical, painstaking way he approaches the majority of his cases. He leaves no stone unturned in his quest to give the best representation to his clients.

As the new head of the public service commission, his ap-

tion that has been held by people who have given many years of public service and have retired. He is the youngest person to be appointed to this position and also the first time that a practicing attorney has received such a distinction. Obviously, to place such a young person to preside over a group of several older people bespeaks the confidence that the Prime Minister has in him when he decided to nominate him to the position.

The job of the commission is not one to be taken lightly, it

by Dr. Terrence Marryshow

overseas the hiring and firing, promotions and demotions of those persons who are employed in the government service. Once appointed by the commission, the position with government remains permanent until and unless that individual falls foul of the standing orders or regulations that guide the conduct of workers of the government. Sometimes a worker may feel that he/she has been unjustly dismissed by the Commission but this worker has the right to appeal this decision before an appeals board which at the end of the day will either uphold or overturn the decisions of the commission. For this and many more reasons, it is important to have at the helm someone who is level headed, with a certain level of experience in dealing with people and someone who can be trusted to make decisions that are impartial, balanced and well thought out. As a trained legal mind, he will be able to advise the commission on these cases that appear before the Appeals board, which has some prominent attorneys associated with it.

This is why the Government must be applauded for their bold choice in appointing Mr. Sylvester to that position. He himself has promised one thing as he takes up his new role and that is that he will be fair and impartial. He will not allow politics to influence his decisions and that persons can be assured that he will also be guided by the opinions of those that surround him on the commission. He brings his wealth of experience as a practicing attorney and as a defense lawyer to bear on his position and this makes him more sensitive to the plight of the ordinary man.

While in many cases the appointment of some people can be considered as the proverbial putting a round peg in a square hole, this is one case where the complete opposite is the truth. He is in fact the right man for the job and given his youth the commission can be assured of many years of competent, serious leadership. I would personally like to take the opportunity to wish him every success in this lofty and important position confident that he will approach this new position with

thriving legal practice. On a personal level, he is only writing another brilliant chapter in what has been an illustrious career thus far........ ***Just Food For thought!***

*Grenada Informer, 6 December 2013*

## Sylvester assumes the Chair of Grenada's PSC

One of Grenada's leading criminal lawyers Derrick Sylvester was sworn in as Chairman of the Grenada Public Service Commissioner last Friday.

According to Information reaching the Grenada Informer Sylvester who have being practicing law in Grenada for almost thirteen years, received his instrument of appointment after he was sworn in just after midday on Friday before Governor General Dame Cecile La Grenade.

Sylvester, who is expected to serve for the next three years, replaces outgoing chairperson Gloria Payne Banfield. Also appointed to the Public Service commission last Friday was former school principal Hudson Mc Phail, Prescott Swan, Trade Unionist Madonna Harford and Delano Viechweg.

Although new to the PSC chair, Sylvester who has acted in similar capacity on several boards on the island among them, former Chairman of the Allied Health Professional Council, President Chairperson of the Grenada Football Association (GFA) disciplinary committee, former Director on the Airport Board of directors, and Director on the Board of Directors of the National Housing Authority.

As a practicing Attorney, Sylvester served at the Law Firm on Leslie Seon and Associate Ciboney Chambers and presently heads the firm of Sylvester Derick F. and Associates.

Meanwhile according to section 83 of the Grenada constitution; The PSC shall consist of a Chairman and four other members- The Chairman and two members shall be appointed by the Governor-General, acting in accordance with the advise of the Prime Minister;

The Governor-General shall appoint two members, after the Prime Minister has consulted the appropriate representative bodies;

The Commission shall, in the exercise of its functions under this Constitution, not be subject to the direction or control of any other person or authority.

The Commission may by regulation or otherwise regulate its own procedure and, with the consent of the Prime Minister, may confer powers or impose duties on any public officer or on any authority of the Government of Grenada for the purpose of the exercise of its functions.

The Commission may, subject to its rules of procedure, act notwithstanding any vacancy in its membership or the absence of any member and its proceedings shall not be invalidated by the presence or participation of any person not entitled to be present or to participate in the proceedings.

Derick Sylvester

*Grenada Informer, 29 November 2013*

# Sylvester heads PSC

Local Attorney-at-law, Derick Sylvester has been appointed to head the Public Service Commission (PSC) in Grenada.

Sylvester who is the main Attorney of the Law Firm of Derick Sylvester and Associates on Lucas Street, St. George's replaces Gloria Payne-Banfield whose term in the chair has come to an end.

The barrister will be in charge of a five-member Commission whose members received their instruments of appointment last week Friday from Governor General, Dr. Cecile La Grenade, a former PSC Head herself.

The recommendation of Sylvester to the top position did not come as a surprise.

Prime Minister Dr. Keith Mitchell had identified the lawyer as one of two persons who were short listed by the New National Party (NNP) to be considered for the post of Attorney General following its 15-0 victory at the polls in February.

The job was eventually given to another attorney-at-law, Cajeton Hood allegedly on account of his working knowledge of the civil service given his background as a Permanent Secretary as a civil servant.

According to NNP insiders, Sylvester is also being considered by the Mitchell-led government as one of the attorneys to be involved as an agent in the sale of passports scheme known as the Citizenship By Investment (CBI) programme.

Apart from Sylvester, the other persons who will sit on the PSC are former school principal Prescott Swan, a political activist of the NNP, as well as Trade Unionist Madonna Harford, Delano Viechweg, and former Educator, Hudson McPhail.

One of the main responsibilities of the PSC is to approve the appointments of persons to be hired in the public sector.

Sylvester who has been an Attorney for the past 12 years made several appearances over the years before the Appeal's Board of the PSC to challenge the dismissal of workers.

He was called to the bar on October 19, 2001.

*Derick Sylvester – to oversee the functioning of the Public Service*

*The New Today, 29 November 2013*

The experience gained from these appointments could not have been attained by any other means, other than by being a direct part of the decision making process.

The most memorable are the decisions of the Public Service Commission, with the many nuances associated with the process, including the rendering of legal advice in each case by the Ministry of Legal Affairs, Attorney General's and Solicitor General's Chambers. The PSC has not always agreed with the legal advice emanating from the Attorney General's and Solicitor General's Chambers. There were occasions when the PSC acceded to the advice of the said chambers since the Attorney General is the principal legal adviser to Government. I had to constantly remind myself, despite being a practising lawyer, my role was not to render legal advice. There were occasions, however, where I had to refute it.

**GRENADA**

By: Her Excellency **DAME CÉCILE LA GRENADE,** Dame Grand Cross of the Most Distinguished Order of St. Michael and St. George, Officer of the Most Excellent Order of the British Empire, Governor-General of Grenada.

..................................................

**GOVERNOR-GENERAL**

**INSTRUMENT OF APPOINTMENT**

**TO: MR. DERICK SYLVESTER**

In exercise of the powers vested in me by subsection (1) (a) of Section 83 of the Constitution of Grenada and acting in accordance with the advice of the Prime Minister, I hereby appoint you **DERICK SYLVESTER,** to be a member of the Public Service Commission and to be chairman of the same and to have and to exercise all the functions and authority appertaining to that office, for a period of three (3) years with effect from $22^{nd}$ November 2013.

GIVEN under my hand and the Public Seal of Grenada at the Governor-General's Office in Grenada this day of November, two thousand and thirteen and in the Sixty-first year of the Reign of Her Majesty Queen Elizabeth the Second.

**GOD SAVE THE QUEEN**

*Instrument of Appointment as Chairman of the Public Service Commission (2013)*

CHAPTER TWELVE

# AT THE PUBLIC SERVICE COMMISSION

*"A good decision is based on knowledge and not on numbers."* PLATO

*"It is in your moments of decision that your destiny is shaped."* TONY ROBBINS

The Constitution of Grenada is schedule 1 to the Grenada Constitution Order 1973. Section 83 of the Constitution mandates there shall be a Public Service Commission for Grenada. This comprises five members. The Chairman, and two members are appointed by the Governor General, acting in accordance with the advice of the Prime Minister. Two members are appointed by the Governor General, after he would have consulted with two representative bodies, namely, Grenada Union of Teachers and Grenada Civil Service Association.

The Commission has delegatory powers, however, its function is subsumed in section 84 of the Constitution which states:

"… the power to appoint persons to hold or act in offices in the public service (including the power to confirm appointments), the power to exercise disciplinary control over persons holding or acting in such offices and the power to remove such persons from office, and the power to grant leave, shall vest in the Public Service Commission."

In or about the month of October 2013, I had a meeting with the Prime Minister of Grenada, Dr. Keith Mitchell at which discussions were had in relation to possibly accepting the position of Chairman of the Public Service Commission (PSC). I gave my commitment to serve in the position if selected. It was a surprise request to me then, as I had matters against the PSC both at the appellate level of the Public Service Commission Appeal Board and at the level of the High Court. I was now asked to perform the role that I had occasion to challenge previously. I recall I had filed judicial review proceedings in relation to the procedure leading to the promotion of a senior police officer. I was successful at the hearing at the Supreme Court, since the State consented at one of the hearings. So it was indeed a feeling of mixed emotions to now have to assume such a role.

On the 22nd day of November 2013, I took the Oath of Office and Secrecy administered by the Governor General of Grenada, Dame Cecile La Grenade. I was installed as Chairman for a period of three years as constitutionally mandated. Further, on the 23rd November 2016, for another term of three years, together with Prescott Swan and Hudson Mc Phail appointed by the Governor General acting on the advice of the Prime Minister. Madonna Harford and Delano Viechweg were appointed by the Governor General, they represented the representative bodies on the Commission.

The four (4) members brought a wealth of experience to the Commission as the other members held numerous positions in the civil service prior to being sworn in as members of the Commission. The members held a compilation of Public Service positions including, Principals, Teachers, Police Officers, Permanent Secretaries, Chief Education Officers and numerous other portfolios.

## Derick Sylvester Re-Appointed Chairman of PSC

**Derick Sylvester**

Attorney at law Derick Sylvester who was appointed Chairman of the Grenada Public Service Commission has been given another stint.

According to information reaching the Grenada Informer, Sylvester whose three-year term ended earlier this month was re-appointed to the post of Chairman on Monday having taken the Oath of Office before Her Excellency Governor General, Dame Cecil La Grenade acting on the advice of the Prime Minister Dr. Hon. Keith Mitchell.

Other members of the commission also took the Oath of Office and the Oath of Secrecy on Monday. They included Delano Viechweg representing teachers, Madonna Swan representing the Public Workers' Union, Hudson Mc Phail and Prescott Swan.

The present commission would serve for another three years.

During his first stint as chairman Sylvester was called upon by members of the media on numerous occasions to make public pronouncements on matters deemed to be of public interest. However Informer learned that having taken the Oath of Secrecy, persons holding such offices are prohibited from such practice, even if it is in defense of their own personal interest.

*Grenada Informer, 25 November 2016*

*Members of the Public Service Commission in November 2013. (Left to Right) Delano Viechweg, Madonna Harford, Derick Sylvester, Prescott Swan and Hudson Mc Phail*

The Chief Personnel Officer was the secretary to the Commission. During my time there I worked with three; Jacinta Joseph, Barbara Charles and Desiree Stephen. They shouldered the gargantuan task commendably. In Grenada the Public Service Commission, is responsible for all public officers; nurses, police, teachers, doctors, prison officers and other officers. Unlike, other Commonwealth countries where there are Police Service Commissions and Public Service Commissions. The work load therefore was bountiful. The weekly meetings commenced every Monday at 9 or 10 am until completion. The dedication of the staff at that office was admirable. I owe them a debt of gratitude for making our task at the Commission a smoother one, since a chain is as strong as its weakest link.

Our mandate in the Commission was to be fair to all concerned. Our mission was to ensure that procedural fairness and other principles of natural justice were adhered to as the foundation pillars of the decision making process. Of course our mandate, though independent, ensured we had to seek legal advice from varying legal quarters. There were occasions when some of these decisions were challenged in the Supreme Court. Some were successful others were not. Despite this, we have never wavered in our position that our goal was to obey the law and its principles; if we did err, as is human, we would correct it.

One of the first major decisions the Commission had to revisit, in November 2013, when I just assumed the chair of the Commission was to deal with the issue as to whether two senior ranked officers could be retired in the 'public interest'. They were Assistant Commissioners of Police Smith Roberts and Dowlyn Bartholomew. They were away from duty, either placed on administrative leave or off the job pending the resolution of that issue.

It was the intention of the legal department then to so retire them. The Commission having no legal advisers except the legal department, I therefore had to assume that responsibility with the concurrence of the other members and conducted the research as to its legality. I extended my research to Senior Counsels and Queen's Counsels in the region and returned to the Commission armed with a bundle of cases in support of the argument against such retirement. The opinions were at variance with the legal department. We were adamant that the first decision of the Commission while I was Chair should not be wrong, it would be starting off on a bad footing.

The Commission sought audience with both ACPs. We held extensive discussions with them. In the interim the law in relation to their purported retirement was being examined. We listened intently to their respective positions. However, the time soon came for a decision to be made. After many meetings it was agreed that there could not be retirement in the public interest. Consequently, the Attorney General's advice was deviated from. The officers were recalled. However, they were reassigned to Government Ministries where they were in receipt of their allowances and benefits as police officers.

The baptism in the Public Service Commission had only just started as tough decisions had to be made.

In the year 2013, when the New National Party won the National Election, Wilan Thompson was the Commissioner of Police. There

*Front page, Grenada Informer, week ending 13 December 2013*

# PM To Recall Top Brass Of RGPF

Two senior ranked officers of the Royal Grenada Police who were retired by the Grenada Public Service Commission (PSC) earlier this year could be back in the service.

Informer has being reliably informed that the PSC under its new chairman Derick Sylvester was called upon to revisit the decision taken by the Commissioner Acting on the advice of the Governor General, in October to retire Assistant Commissioners of Police Smith Roberts and Dowlin Bartholomew and from all indications, a number of new developments have emerged.

Sources told the Grenada Informer that Police Commissioner Winston James together with Governor General Dame Cecil La Grenade, newly appointed Chairman and Lawyers for the retired men during a lengthy meeting earlier this week, were asked to reinstate the retired men, given the fact that the approach taken initially to have them sent home, was incorrect.

Informer learnt that the two senior ranked officers who were accused of being aligned to the former National Democratic Congress (NDC) ran into problems shortly after the Police Commissioner Winston returned to the chair as head of the Royal Grenada Police Force.

Shortly after his return to the Force, sources said the Commissioner complained that he had difficulties working along with a number of key figures within the RGPF, a comment that would have result in rapid changes within the force.

Meanwhile, in his first official press briefing with members of the media at the Ministerial Complex Prime Minister and Minister of National Security admitted that he was aware of the changes among the top brass of the RGPF and whatever was done had his blessing.

Now almost two months off the job, awaiting a final decision, on the matter, sources told the informer that it is possible, both men could be back on the job in a matter of days, however informer also learnt that there is even a strong possibility that both Roberts and Bartholomew could be placed within an undisclosed Government ministry.

Both men we were told are yet to reach retirement age and therefore the decision to have retired them at an earlier age Informer was told, is based on negotiations rather than dictation.

This ruling by the commission depending on its outcome would be significant in that it would be the first major ruling under the newly appointed Chairman, who took over the chair just over one week ago, and according to sources, it would speak volumes as to the level of impartiality on the part of the new chairman, who vowed to uphold the law and let the chips fall where they may.

*Grenada Informer, 13 December 2013*

was then a request for his transfer from that position to one of an equivalent grade with like emoluments, however in a different area of the Public Service. The application was for a transfer to the position of Clerk of Parliament.

The issues were; whether in these circumstances there was a violation of the Public Service Commission Regulation or the Constitution. Whether the Police Service was a closed unit wherein transfer outside of that unit was not permitted. The procedure was followed in relation to the transfer of the officer. He assumed his position as Clerk of Parliament.

A legal action was mounted in the Supreme Court of Grenada, challenging the constitutionality of the transfer and whether the decision was correct in law. The challenge was a novel one as officers were transferred in the past but these were not challenged. Officers were transferred to the National Disaster Management Agency (NADMA) and other areas of the service. This ruling would therefore be instructive to the decision making process of the Commission.

ANOTHER COURT CASE INVOLVING PM MITCHELL...

as COP Thompson Takes Legal Action Against The State

Flashback to September 30, 2011 at Fort George when there was a changing of the guard within the Royal Grenada Police Force (RGPF) as Willan Thompson (r) took over from James Clarkson (l) as the island's Chief of Police

Commissioner of Police Willan Thompson - was not favoured by PM Mitchell to remain in charge of the nation's Security

Embattled Commissioner of Police Willan Thompson could square off in the high court with Prime Minister Dr. Keith Mitchell in a legal battle over the manner in which he was removed as head of the Royal Grenada Police Force (RGPF).

Court documents contained by **THE NEW TODAY** newspaper indicate that the Supreme Court Registry has set December 4 as the date for hearing a case brought by COP Thompson who is now serving as Clerk of Parliament.

The case was brought by the law firm of Lex Fidelis Chambers against the Attorney-General of Grenada, Cajeton Hood and the Public Service Commission (PSC), headed by barrister-at-law Derek Sylvester.

COP Thompson is asking the court to rule that the circumstances in which he was removed from the post after the February 2013 victory at the polls by Dr Mitchell and his New National Party (NNP) was "in reality a termination" of his appointment as the island's Police Chief to facilitate the re-organisaton of the police force.

He also wants the court to declare that the Office of Clerk of Parliament is not an office or post in the Public Service of Grenada of an equivalent status to that of the Commissioner of Police within RGPF.

The legal action is seeking to get the court to make a declaration to the effect that COP Thompson was forced by the Mitchell government into retirement and that he "is entitled to be paid his salary, allowances and benefits as if he had attained the compulsory retirement age, as guaranteed by section 84 (8) of the Constitution of Grenada".

Former Accountant-General in the Ministry of Finance, Richard Duncan who is now the Manager of the Grenada Co-operative Bank Limited had won a similar case against the 1995-99 Mitchell-led NNP government and is now receiving a monthly pen-

(Continues on pg 22)

*Front page, The New Today, week ending 22 August 2014*

The simple issue despite being laced with numerous legal submissions was whether the officer could be transferred outside of the police service without the consent of the said officer. Whether the Constitution and every other enabling law thereto was violated to the extent that he was terminated thereby entitling him to be paid his salary and other emoluments up to retirement.

I always reminded the members of the Commission, to which they agreed, that the legacy we should leave was that our decisions should be legally sound and we should treat persons in the manner we would have wanted to be treated, if we were in their position. The other members supported this purposeful mantra. Their support in the Commission was unwavering. The discussions were healthy although each member had their own individual perspective on issues.

While we awaited the Thompson decision the members and I debated the matter in relation to transfers and re-examined the issues we would be plagued with should the court rule against transfer outside of the police service.

The decision was delivered by Justice Gerhard Wallbank, in favour of the decision to transfer. A contrary decision would have affected even the persons who were transferred to the security department at the International Airport and other areas. It was not the end of the matter, as the decision was appealed to the Court of Appeal, with the continued challenge likened to that at the High Court. The Court of Appeal being led by its Chief Justice Dame Janice Pereira, Justice Mario Michel and Paul Webster QC, upheld the decision that the officer could be transferred outside of the police service, in effect agreeing that the police service was not a closed unit.

This matter brought an end to the litigation regarding this issue, under my Chairmanship at the Public Service Commission. The business of the Commission continued.

## Thompson loses court battle against government

Embattled former Commissioner of Police, Willan Thompson has lost his court battle against the Keith Mitchell-led government in relation to his transfer from the post of Chief of Police to Clerk of Parliament.

The Court of Appeal, which sat in the country last week, has ruled in favour of the State on Thompson's transfer, which was done without his consent shortly after the New National Party (NNP) won the 2013 general elections.

The ruling was handed down last week Monday at High Court No. 1 in St. George's by the Justice of Appeal of the Eastern Caribbean Supreme Court, Chief Justice Janice Pereira, Justice Michel Mario and Paul Webster QC.

Following the 2013 general elections, Thompson, along with Assistant Commissioners of Police, Smith Roberts and Dowlin Bartholomew were transferred from the Police Force by Governor General, Dame Cecile La Grenade and the Public Service Commission (PSC).

The incoming Prime Minister had indicated that he had no confidence in Thompson as the island's chief security officer in the public service.

The Police commissioner retained the services of former Attorney General, Rohan Phillip to challenge the decision.

Thompson was contending that pursuant to Section 89 of the Constitution, as a senior police officer, he could not be transferred either by the Governor General or by the PSC to a post outside RGPF without his consent or the permission of the Public Service.

However, the State took the position that commissioned officers above the rank of Sergeant are liable to be transferred.

High Court judge, Justice Gerhard Wallbank ruled in favour of the State in January 2015 and Thompson appealed the decision.

*Willan Thompson – lost the appeal*

In commenting on the ruling to ***THE NEW TODAY*** newspaper, Solicitor General, Dwight Horsford, noted that "it was his (Thompson's) case in the High Court that the Royal Grenada Police Force is a closed department of the Public Service and (that) Gazetted or Commissioned officers of the RGPF can't be transferred to other parts of the wider civil service.

"We argued in the High Court, the High Court agreed with us, the government's arguments (and) Justice Wallbank ruled that yes, they can be transferred to any other position in the wider civil service once they don't lose their grade or emolument.

"He (Thompson) took this matter on appeal because he was not satisfied. We argued again as respondents in the Court of Appeal that the trial judge was right to agree with us and happily the Court of Appeal agrees with us that Commissioned or Gazetted officers in the RGPF are liable to be transferred by the Public Service Commission and in the case of the Commissioner of Police by the Governor General acting on the advice of the Public Service Commission to any office of equivalent grade or lateral rank in the public.

Horsford expressed satisfaction that the matter has finally been legally resolved.

Thompson still has an option of seeking judicial review before the Law Lord at the Privy Council in London.

The Court of Appeal usually sits in Grenada for one week three times per year.

*The New Today, 1 July 2016*

The experience I had while practising allowed me to ensure that fairness and equity prevailed on all sides. I did not want to leave a legacy of legal impropriety or procedural irregularity, for then the Commission would have failed in the execution of its constitutional mandate.

There was a senior police officer who was charged with 'fraud' and granted bail. As a result, upon receipt of correspondence from the Ministry of National Security and the Commissioner of Police, a decision had to be taken, regarding the continuation of his work as a police officer while the case was ongoing. The Commission interdicted the officer on half month's pay, pending the outcome of the court's decision.

Some political pundits followed the story relating what they understood it to be. The officer was nearing his retirement age of sixty (60) years and therefore the issue as to his retirement would soon be brought to the fore, if the criminal matter had not been completed. Some persons used the media to politicise the nature of the true facts leading to the decision of the Commission.

"I am ashamed of my government," says Jones



PSC Chairman Derick Sylvester

*Grenada Informer, 22 July 2016*

*Protestors in front of the Public Service Commission Building at Belmont, St. George, protesting the reinstatement of ASP Coutain*

On one occasion, the Commission was publicly accused of unlawfully reinstating the officer. There was a three man protest, with placards calling for my resignation. This was due to the inability to understand there was a constitutionally guaranteed right to the presumption of innocence.

I was off island at the time and was notified of the development in Grenada as it related to the inaccurate interpretation of the Commission's decision. It was alleged that the officer was reinstated so as to enable him to receive his benefits and pension. It was further alleged that he was a known supporter of the ruling political party, hence the reason for 'special treatment'.

There was no effort to clarify and verify the truth or falsity of the allegation of the 'officer's reinstatement into the service'.

The story ran for two weeks consecutively in the weekly issues of the newspaper, without any legal or analytical intervention. I returned to the State of Grenada and immediately checked in with the Commission to determine whether any 'decision' was made in my absence regarding the matter. I was relieved to learn there was not any, so the story was indeed misleading. The government was blamed. I was asked to step down.

The decision was inaccurately reported. Despite having taken the oath of secrecy, we issued a press release on the inaccuracy of the public

## Call for Derick Sylvester to step down

*ASP Coutain – the public not happy with decision to reinstate him by PSC*

Talk show host, Kem Jones has called on attorney-at-law, Derick Sylvester to step down as head of the Public Service Commission (PSC) in the wake of public outcry in the Claudius Coutain matter.

Coutain, an Assistant Superintendent of Police (ASP) in the Royal Grenada Police Force (RGPF), was reinstated into the post in the wake of an ongoing court case into criminal charges brought against him connected with an alleged driver's license scam.

Jones took to the streets Wednesday to stage as one-man protest outside the Office of the PSC located in the junction between Belmont and Butler House Gap.

The talk show figure who is associated with the main opposition National Democratic Congress (NDC) called for the immediate resignation of Sylvester who flew out of the island two days earlier for the United States alongside his female companion who was seeking medical attention.

ASP Coutain was reinstated to RGPF on June 13 by the PSC to the annoyance of several persons in many quarters including some police officers who regard the action as unfair since the suspended senior police officer will be re-instated with full pay despite the fact that the court action is still pending against him.

Jones called on patriotic Grenadians to join him outside the PSC building to send a strong message to the PSC, as well as Governor General, Dame Cecile La Grenade, and Prime Minister and Minister for National Security, Dr. Keith Mitchell, that the move involving Coutain will not be accepted because it was an attempt to undermine the credibility of the force.

"I am standing up today as a citizen of Grenada and saying to Derick Sylvester that you should resign forthwith because this is a serious blunder. I don't know who influenced you, I thought you were a brilliant chap and you would be able to do the right thing but in this instance you did the wrong thing by allowing ASP Coutain to be reinstated in the RGPF", he told reporters.

Describing the PSC decision as "a travesty", Jones accused Sylvester of taking part in a decision that diminishes his integrity and credibility.

He said: "As a citizen of Grenada I am saddened. I couldn't have contemplated that a brilliant chap as Derick Sylvester (would) compromise his integrity. He is a lawyer, he should have known better - the matter is before the court of law, the gentleman has been charged, seven charges, investigations were carried (out), and he was been suspended from the Force.

"I cannot fathom how Derick Sylvester could reinstate this guy into the system. What kind of example is this," he questioned.

According to Jones, his biggest concern in the issue is the precedence being set for the junior officers of RGPF.

"Are you saying to the younger officers and public servants generally (that) you are free to break the law (and) once you are a supporter of any political organisation, you would be reinstated because you are close to retirement so that you can get your gratuity and pension? I mean it is a serious concern that I think all citizens should have (as) it is tantamount to corruption".

Jones alluded to several instances in which other police officers found themselves in trouble with the law but were not afforded the same privilege of reinstatement as ASP Coutain.

The senior police officer was slapped with seven fraudulent criminal charges in 2015 in relation to an alleged driver's license scam.

Sources close to Coutain told this newspaper that the embattled officer is confident of winning his case in court.

According to Jones, the reinstatement of ASP Coutain in the force should not come before the court makes a ruling on the criminal matter and that the laws of the country should be carried out without interference.

(Continues on pg 15)

*Derick Sylvester - called to step down by Kem Jones*

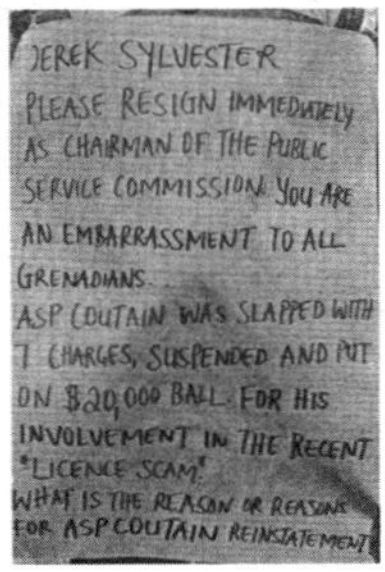


*The New Today, 22 July 2016*

utterances culminating in the 'three-man demonstration', outside of the Public Service Commission's office.

The officer was approaching the age of sixty years (60) which was his compulsory retirement age. He had vacation days pending. This would have exceeded the date for his retirement therefore the Commission had to act swiftly. There was an attrition policy wherein civil servants could not be employed and paid beyond their retirement age. The officer was therefore granted his vacation leave and subsequently retirement on his 60th birthday as was the normal practice. Procedurally, he was reinstated for the purpose of taking his accrued vacation leave, as he could not have been granted vacation while on suspension. He was not yet convicted as the criminal charges were still pending. Therefore the Commission could not pre-empt the court's ruling and had to await the determination of his trial.

## PSC release on ASP Claudius David

Retirement from the Service – Mr. Claudius David (a.k.a.) Claudius Coutain – Assistant, Superintendent of Police – Royal Grenada Police Force – Ministry of National Security, Disaster Management, Home Affairs, Public Administration, Information and Implementation

On 21st September, 2015, the Commission interdicted Mr. Claudius David (a.k.a. Claudius Coutain), Assistant Superintendent of Police from the performance of his duties with effect from 1st September, 2015, pending the outcome of a court matter.

Mr. David (a.k.a. Coutain) was informed of his imminent retirement from the Public Service, given that he would attain the compulsory retirement age of sixty years on 30th November, 2016, which was verified by a copy of his birth certificate.

Mr. David (a.k.a. Coutain) would have accumulated one hundred seventy calendar days vacation leave prior to his interdiction and was due to proceed on the said leave which covers the period 13th June to 29th November, 2016, to be immediately followed by his retirement.

The Commission therefore:

- terminated the interdiction of Mr. David (a.k.a. Coutain) with effect from 12th June, 2016;
- granted Mr. David (a.k.a. Coutain) one hundred and seventy calendar days vacation leave from 13th June to 29thNovember, 2016 to be immediately followed by his retirement from the Service with effect from 30th November, 2016, on the Ground of Age.

Mr. Claudius David (a.k.a.) Claudius Coutain

It must be noted, that Mr. David (a.k.a. Coutain) has been re-instated into the Public Service solely for the Public Service Commission to execute the normal procedures for his retirement, pending the decision of the Court. This does not mean that he has resumed duties and therefore he is not physically present within the Royal Grenada Police Force. The Commission is not at liberty to judge the outcome of the court matter at this time and as such, cannot take its own decision. Mr. David (Coutain) is being assumed innocent in the meantime and has to be treated in that way until proven guilty by the Court. If guilty then the Commission will have to act in accordance with the judgment of the Court and if innocent the normal procedures continue.

*Grenada Informer, 22 July 2016*

The Commission therefore was at pains to explain its actions that the officer was not reinstated in the service, as was popularly advertised. Despite the clarification, there was a deafening silence from the perpetrators of the falsehood. The decision of the Commission was made independently, since there was no direct or indirect political or other interference in its process. Only the departments that were directly involved with the matter would have been made aware of the decision of the Commission.

The presumption of innocence is enshrined in the Constitution, it being the supreme law, every other law is subordinate. Therefore, any decision must be subject to the supreme law or run the risk of being struck down as null, void and of no effect. The promotion of police

## PSC speaks on ASP Coutain issue

On 21st September, 2015, the Commission interdicted Mr. Claudius David (a.k.a. Claudius Coutain), Assistant Superintendent of Police from the performance of his duties with effect from 1st September, 2015, pending the outcome of a court matter.

Mr. David (a.k.a. Coutain) was informed of his imminent retirement from the Public Service, given that he would attain the compulsory retirement age of sixty years on 30th November, 2016, which was verified by a copy of his birth certificate.

Derick Sylvester - Chairman of PSC

Mr. David (a.k.a. Coutain) would have accumulated one hundred and seventy calendar days vacation leave prior to his interdiction and was due to proceed on the said leave which covers the period 13th June to 29th November, 2016, to be immediately followed by his retirement.

The Commission therefore:-

*terminated the interdiction of Mr. David (a.k.a. Coutain) with effect from 12th June, 2016;

*granted Mr. David (a.k.a. Coutain) one hundred and seventy calendar days vacation leave from 13th June to 29th November, 2016 to be immediately followed by his retirement from the Service with effect from 30th November, 2016, on the Ground of Age.

It must be noted, that Mr. David (a.k.a. Coutain) has been reinstated into the Public Service solely for the Public Service Commission to execute the normal procedures for his retirement, pending the decision of the Court. This does not mean that he has resumed duties and therefore he is not physically present within the Royal Grenada Police Force.

The Commission is not at liberty to judge the outcome of the court matter at this time and as such, cannot take it's own decision.

Mr. David (Coutain) is being assumed innocent in the meantime and has to be treated in that way until proven guilty by the Court.

If guilty then the Commission will have to act in accordance with the judgement of the Court and if innocent the normal procedures continue.

In the face of the PSC move, Prime Minister Dr. Keith Mitchell has sought to distance himself from the decision taken by the Sylvester-led body.

A statement from the Botanical Gardens said: "Government has been made aware of a decision by the Public Service Commission to reinstate suspended Assistant Superintendent of Police, Claudius David (a.k.a. Claudius Coutain), to the Public Service, on vacation leave ahead of retirement.

Prime Minister and Minister of National Security, Dr. the Right Honourable Keith Mitchell, and the Government of Grenada categorically deny any previous knowledge of this decision, and are as surprised as the rest of the Nation to learn of this from various Media outlets.

Like the rest of the Nation, Government is awaiting the facts of this matter from the relevant authorities".

Speculation is rife that the day before the story was broken in the local media, a top official of the PSC was seen in the vicinity of the Top Floor of the Ministerial Complex.

*The New Today, 22 July 2016*

officers above the rank of Sergeant is the function of the Public Service Commission. The hierarchy of the police force in descending order are as itemised hereunder:

1. Commissioner of Police
2. Deputy Commissioner of Police
3. Assistant Commissioner of Police
4. Superintendent of Police
5. Assistant Superintendent of Police
6. Inspector of Police
7. Cadet Officer
8. Sergeant of Police
9. Corporal of Police
10. Constable
11. Rural Constable

The Commission is mandated by the Constitution to conduct its business fairly, independently and impartially. This dictates transparency, procedural fairness and being devoid of bias. The issue of promotion always raises anxiety among police officers, since there are normally limited spaces yet numerous police officers in line to fill the available positions. There is no dispute that our police officers work diligently and under trying circumstances. Having to deal with the public at that level, officers encounter numerous dangers and among them the possibility of their demise while on duty.

During my practice I had represented police officers by filing judicial review proceedings, challenging the operation of the promotion process. These suits were filed against the Public Service Commission and the Attorney General. I recall during the hearing of the application the emphasis was on the review of the process and procedure employed by the Public Service Commission. It brought an end to the matter. Numerous civil suits were filed by other attorneys.

The issue of police promotions is mandated by the Public Service Commission Regulations.

However, Sergeants and lower ranks were the responsibility of the Commissioner of Police, as stated both in the Constitution and the Police Promotions Regulations Cap 244. There was a panel that ought to be constituted comprising, the Commissioner of Police, a Deputy Commissioner of Police and an Acting Commissioner of Police.

The Commission's responsibility was an arduous one in relation to police promotions. Since I had practiced for many years I knew most if not all the police officers. There was a total of approximately nine hundred men and women inclusive. I had on occasions the opportunity to cross examine some of these officers in court. The Commission, therefore had to eliminate personalities. A committee was appointed to examine and make recommendations for the promotion of officers, giving reasons therefor. The recommendation therefore had to accord with seniority, merit, ability, dedication, promotional examination and other criteria. The candidates would normally be graded. The commission therefore delegated its responsibility to the committee setup for the purpose of making recommendations.

The promotion of police officers was one of the most tedious and trying issues the Commission had to deal with. The procedure had to be correct and the recommendations of the committee would, in proper cases, be adopted by the Commission. The members therefore had to be devoid of bias and partisan interest. The criteria laid down for promotion must be in accordance with the prescribed law. One of the goals of the Commission was to avoid legal challenges and therefore be on the correct path of legal history. The Commission promoted thirty six (36) officers. A ceremony was held wherein each received their individual appointments. A charge to continue to protect and serve the public was given going forward.

The policy of the Commission was to ensure we heard all sides of any complaint prior to making a decision which would affect the life of

# 36 Senior Police Officers Move Up The Ranks

Inspector Linford Cummings

ASP Simon Dickson

**The Grenada Public Service Commission (PSC), chaired by attorney-at-law Derick Sylvester, during a special sitting on Monday confirmed the appointment of thirty-six senior police officers within the Royal Grenada Police Force to higher ranks; among them head of the Drug Squad who has now moved to the rank of Inspector.**

Linford Cummings who has led the RGPF in several successful drug raids in the last year resulting in the confiscation of large quantities of drugs, thousands of dollars into the treasury and putting a number of known drug dealers behinds bars has been operating as a Sergeant for the past eight years. His promotion therefore came as no surprise to many; infact there are those who feel that it is long overdue.

According to information reaching the Grenada Informer a total of sixteen sergeants including Cummings were promoted to the rank of Inspector, the others, Michael Pursue, Raymond Lockiby, Garson Gill, Errolyn Garraway, David Nelson, Trevor Rodney, Kenny Stanislaus, Andy Lewis, Wilbur Francis, Glen Charles, Gillian Thomas, Terrine Mason, Reginald Sylvester, Adrine Lewis and Rondel Baptiste.

Ten officers were promoted to the rank of Assistant Superintendent of Police (ASP), Anthony George, Simon Dickson, Bernard Nelson, Paul Christopher, Watson Edwards, Terrence Julien, Richard Langdon, Wayne Wilson, Nola Lewis and head of the Traffic Department of the RGPF Linford Kingston.

Seven officers were promoted to the rank of Superintendent; they were Solomon Stafford, Earl Dunber, Gregory Mathurine, Leroy Langaigne, Glen Paul, musician Brian Hurst and Sylvan Mcintyre.

There were two promotions to the rank of Assistant Commissioner of Police (ACP) given to Jesmon Prince and Trevor Modeste and one elevation to the rank of Deputy Commissioner of Police (DCP) in Edvin Martin.

Meanwhile sources told the Grenada Informer that Monday's promotion, the first of what is tipped to be a series of promotions in 2017 became necessary to restore a level of equilibrium at the upper echelon of the RGPF that has realized a vast number of vacancies in recent time due largely to officers attaining retirement age, ailments, among other variables. The move we were told also creates the opportunity for junior officers to elevate themselves to fill the positions that have now become vacant.

However, the position of Commissioner of Police remains vacant as the veteran Winston James continues to lead the men and women in Uniform as Acting Commissioner, a position we were told would remain as it has for some time, although word on the ground suggests that Deputy Commissioner Frank Redhead might be thrown in the hot seat.

Word is also that certain officers, who believe they were eligible for promotion but were overlooked, are considering legal action.

At least one officer has delivered and received a response to a letter of complaint on the matter of him not being promoted. Information reaching our news desk is that on Tuesday another two officers were set to deliver their letters. The officers who feel they have been unfairly left out of the promotions have retained legal counsel.

Such an action has been taken in the past and upon hearing the cases of a number of officers the court decided that there was merit in their claims and higher ranks had to be awarded to them.

Meanwhile another set of promotions are expected shortly. These are the promotions for police officers not yet at the rank of Inspector and are handled by the Commissioner of Police.

Sergeant Rondel Baptiste and Inspector Linford Kingston

Superintendent Sylvan Mcintyre

Chairman of PSC Derick Sylvester

*Grenada Informer, 13 January 2017*

an officer in the service. The fair hearing principle *audi alteram partem* was the pillar of the Commission.

I became more aware of the importance of listening to all sides before making a decision. It is often said that each story has three sides, the Plaintiff, the Defendant and the truth. The Commission was always destined to find wherein the truth lay.

Police promotion has been a newspaper headline, many times accusing the political directorate of interference with the process. Despite this, the Commission tried its utmost to not allow extraneous consideration to influence its decision making.

# MAJOR PROMOTIONS IN RGPF

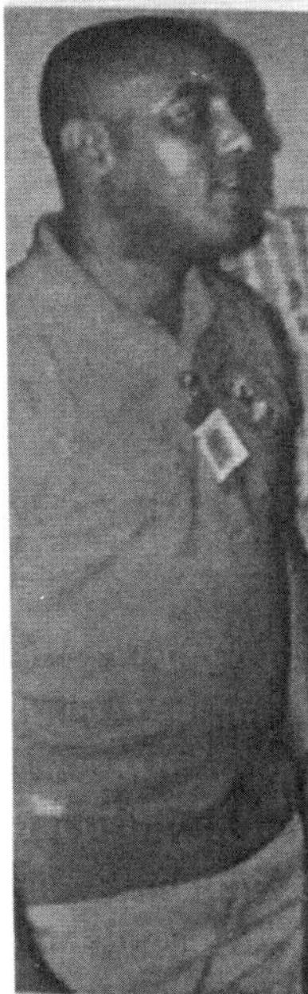

dy Connaught also promoted to ASP

Earl Dunbar - promoted to ASP

Police Commissioner Winston James

Derek Sylvester head of the PSC

**THE NEW TODAY** understands that a number of major promotions took place within the Royal Grenada Police Force (RGPF) with effect from July 1.

A reliable source told this newspaper that the officers who were promoted were asked to make appearances in person at Monday's weekly meeting of the Public Service Commission (PSC), headed by attorney-at-law Derek Sylvester.

According to the source, the PSC members were reluctant to grant the promotions without seeing first hand the persons whose names were submitted to the body for promotion by the Office of the Prime Minister.

When contacted to obtain the names of the promoted police officers, the Community Relations Department of the force was not forthcoming.

The female officer in charge of the department, ASP Rebecca Jones said she is not in a position to disclose this kind of information since it should come from the PSC itself.

Keisha Grant-Alexander, the Press Secretary in the Office of the Prime Minister was said to be out of the country and Senator Winston Garraway, the Parliamentary Secretary for Information was reportedly attending a meeting and could not be reached for comment.

The Secretary to Cabinet Secretary Lana Mc Phail took our call and indicated that her boss informed her that she would return a call but up to the time of going to press, no call reached our News Desk.

**THE NEW TODAY** understands that four persons were appointed as full-fledged

*(Continues on pg 3)*

*Front page, The New Today, week ending 4 July 2014*

# MAJOR PROMOTIONS IN RGPF

** From page 1*

Superintends of Police such as Assistant Superintend of Police and Second in Command of the Drug Squad, Esau Pierre, as well ASP Osmand Griffith of the Coast Guard, and ASP Terrence Noel of the Special Services Unit (SSU) at Point Salines.

Two officers were promoted from the rank of Inspector to Assistant Superintendent of Police - Earl Dunbar of the Criminal Investigation Department (CID), and Randy Connaught, a former Immigration Officer who is now serving as the Aide to Governor-General, Dame Cecile La Grenade.

*Sergeant Maureen Stanisclaus was promoted to Inspector*

There were also a few promotions from Sergeants to the rank of Inspector – Ryan Hall of CID and Hudson Buckmire, an officer attached to the Radio Room at Police Headquarters at Fort George which during the days of the 1979-83 Grenada Revolution was renamed as Fort Rupert, after the father of slain Marxist leader, Maurice Bishop.

*THE NEW TODAY* was also informed that three Sergeants of Police who are attached to the Police Prosecution Department in the Eastern Division including Quintell Charles and Simon Douglas were promoted to Inspector of Police.

One member of the Finlancial Intelligence Unit (FIU), Sheldon Thomas is said to have been promoted from Sergeant to Inspector.

The lone female in the midst is Sergeant Maureen Stanisclaus who was promoted to Inspector – the same rank held by her husband, Doyle Stanisclaus.

The promotions come against the backdrop of calls made this week by the Washington-based International Monetary Fund (IMF) on the 16-month old Keith Mitchell-led administration in St. George's to address the nation's already massive wage bill.

No figures are immediately available on how much the monthly wage bill of the civil service will now increase by as a result of these latest promotions within the police force.

Speculation is rife that the Mitchell government might have been hard-pressed to avoid the promotions out of fear that some of the officers might have taken them to court to grant the promotions since most of them were successful in the last known exams held for promotion.

The exams were reportedly held during the reign of embattled Commissioner of Police, Willan Thompson

During the February 2013 general elections, it is believed that the vast majority of police officers voted in favour of the then opposition New National Party (NNP) of Dr. Mitchell to help dethrone the National Democratic Congress of Tillman Thomas.

*The New Today, 4 July 2014*

There were occasions when I questioned my role as Chairman of PSC. Should I approach my constitutional responsibility as a lawyer sitting as Chairman of the PSC or as Chairman of the Public Service Commission, irrespective as to my legal training and therefore blindly relying on the legal advice of the state lawyers? Whether the former or latter approach was taken, there were occasions when decisions had to be made that could have resulted in serious legal consequences. On these occasions my legal training kicked in automatically and sometimes in high gear.

I had the fullest support of the other members of the Commission. We had mutual respect and admiration for each other. This made the task of managing the public service simpler. Discussions and disagreements were had but never was there an outburst or an impolite word.

The members of the Commission were a blessing to work with. The good faith of all the members was altogether unquestionable. No matter by whom they were selected, they all put Grenada first, with an effervescent passionate love of country, which made itself felt strongly. So, whatever differing points of view surfaced, we had full respect for each other's contributions. There were no hidden agendas, only a genuine commitment to honour the oaths we took. Going to meetings of the Commission was an event to look forward to.

There was a past secondary school Principal and Pastor, Hudson McPhail. Sometimes before meetings of the PSC begun, McPhail constantly reminded us of the deity and our mission on earth, which was a temporary one, thereafter judgment; constantly reminding us never to deviate from our sacred constitutional oath and hold fast to the biblical principles. He would say, "We must be our brother's keeper," and, "Do unto others as you would have them do unto you."

Delano Viechweg was calm. He was a well learned student of the English language, and always spoke of it. He was the Teachers' representative on the Commission.

Prescott Swan was very experienced, having served on the Commission for many years. He had a great sense of humour. He challenged McPhail on issues concerning his faith; their discussions always ended with smiles and gestures of cordial disagreements. I admired and revered the comradery and respect they had for each other.

Madonna Harford was the lone female on the Commission; she represented the Public Workers Union on the Commission. We referred to her as, "The rose among the thorns." On other occasions we jokingly said she was, "The thorn among the roses." Whatever was our final conclusion, she was the female stalwart on the Commission.

As Chairman, I ensured the level of cohesion existed in a manner wherein healthy and high spirited discussion could be had in an environment of cordiality and mutual respect. With that, the stage was set for the continued work of the Commission, enabling the fulfilment of its constitutional mandate.

The Commission was tasked with the unenviable task of interdicting senior police officers whenever charged with criminal offences. During my tenure there were two (2) decorated officers who the Commission had to interdict on half months pay. Other than the public scrutiny they had to face, they were confronted with decrease in their salaries wherein financial problems ensued. When they were interdicted their salaries were cut in half pending the outcome of the criminal matter.

While an officer was interdicted on half month's pay, he can file an application to the Commission detailing financial hardship which could result in an increase in pay above 50%.

As Chairman of the Public Service Commission I was *ex officio* member of the National Awards Committee pursuant to Act No. 32 of 2007. The committee consisted of seven (7) members. I was conferred with the instrument of appointment by the Governor General.

As a natural corollary to the above appointment I had occasion at the Independence Day celebration to present awards to numerous persons, including Commissioner of Police, Winston James.

I saw the machinery of the state in motion first hand as persons who made yeoman's contribution to the island received their awards with pride.

As Chairman of the PSC I was able to participate in numerous state activities and the stage seemed to have been set to enable other public appearances.

I was asked to deliver the address at the passing out parade of the 42nd division of the Royal Grenada Police Force in my capacity as Chairman of the Public Service Commission. That was on the 6th October 2016. It was a hot sunny day, down at the Special Services Unit (SSU), on their playing field, at Camp Salines, around the corner from the Maurice Bishop International Airport. I charged the officers to go forth with dignity and professionalism. It was a memorable experience to witness the highlight of the parade and the perfect execution of the drills of the recruits.

**GRENADA**

**NATIONAL AWARDS AND HONOURS ADVISORY COMMITTEE APPOINTMENT**

By: Her Excellency **DAME CÉCILE LA GRENADE**, Dame Grand Cross of the Most Distinguished Order of St. Michael and St. George, Officer of the Most Excellent Order of the British Empire, Governor-General of Grenada.

In exercise of the powers vested in me under the provisions of the National Honours and Awards Act No. 32 of 2007, I hereby appoint you, **DERICK SYLVESTER**, as a Member of the National Awards and Advisory Committee.

The Chairperson of the Committee is Mrs. Meryl Forsyth.

The other Members of the Committee are as follows:

Mr. Winston James
Ms. Ruth Elizabeth Rouse
Mrs. Madonna Harford
Dr. Rev. Osbert James
Mrs. Gloria Payne-Banfield

Dated this 12th of January 2016.

**GOVERNOR-GENERAL**

*Certificate of Appointment as Member of the National Awards Advisory Committee*

*Presenting the Independence Award to Commissioner of Police, Winston James in 2016*

I examined the recruits. The officers who performed excellently in specific areas of training were awarded. Their faces radiated with vigour and enthusiasm for the task ahead.

I admired the well adorned officers, their white tunics sparkling in the evening sun. It was evident that great effort and pride went into their preparation. I congratulated a few of them and inspected each individually.

Thereafter, I delivered the speech to the forty eight (48) recruits. I exhorted them to abide by the law, be respectful, honest and decent. I forewarned the officers that life and death lay in their hands. Therefore their responsibilities were onerous. I also reminded them that Commissioner Cosmos Raymond was shot and killed in the line of duty

# Grenada honours its people

As part of the country's 42nd anniversary of Political Independence, a number of Grenadians were recognised for the outstanding contributions to society, and for their personal achievement.

Governor General, Dame Cecile La Grenade consented to present most of the 2016 national awards at celebrations held at the national sporting stadium at Queen's Park.

The Companion of the Order of Grenada went to former Governor General, Sir Daniel Williams who is the country's fourth Head of State.

Sir Daniel was the sitting Governor General when, on December 31st 2007, the National Honours and Awards Act number 32 of 2007 came into effect.

*Governor-General Dame Cecile was called up to do the honours to one of her predecessors in office, Sir Daniel Williams*

Also receiving the Companion of the Order of Grenada Award is Baroness Rosalind Howells of St. David's, now a Member of the House of Lords in the United Kingdom.

Grenada's lone Olympic Gold Medalist, Kirani James has also received the Companion of the Order of Grenada Award.

Former President of the Senate, Dr. Lawrence Joseph received the Knight Commander of the Most Distinguished Order of the Nation for his service to Grenada.

Also receiving the Knight Commander of the Most Distinguished Order of the Nation were former Editor of the Grenadian Voice newspaper, Leslie Pierre (deceased) for his contribution to press freedom and investigative journalism, former diplomat, Dr. Lamuel Stanisclaus of Petit Martinique for his long standing service to Grenada and the region, Chancellor and Chairman of the Board of Trustees of St. George's University, Dr. Charles Modica for his service to education and the economic development of Grenada, as well as late Broadcaster, Leslie Seon for his services to broadcasting and journalism.

The Order of Grenada Gold Award for Excellence was presented to Founder of the St. John's Christian Secondary School, Melvin Schaper (deceased), for his contribution to education, former Team Leader of Grenada's exhibits at Chelsea Flower Show in London, Suzanne Gaywood, Vice-Chancellor of the Cave Hill Campus, Barbados of the University of the West Indies, Professor Eudine Bariteau from Chantimelle, St. Patrick's for contribution to education, and Governor of the Eastern Caribbean Central Bank, Timothy Antoine.

Receiving the Camerhogne Award were Grenadian Yachtsman, Joel "Jex" Mark, Nurse Veronica Alexis, Formula One Champion in Car Racing, Lewis Hamilton, former Educator and Principal of St. Andrew's Anglican Secondary School, Creswell Julien who also wrote the National Pledge, and Irva Baptiste-Blackette who wrote the National Anthem.

*Attorney Sylvester was at centre stage as he presented the award to the Acting Commissioner of Police, Winston James*

The Spice Isle Award went to Sportsman Alleyne Francique, Joachim Mark for his contribution to the Grenadian Diaspora in New York, former Teacher at St. Joseph's Convent, St. George's, Eleanor Pilgrim, and Music Director Lauren Ramdhanny.

The Medal of Honour went to Acting Commissioner of Police, Winston James for his service to law enforcement in Grenada, Cultural Artist Evelyn Mark, former Educator and Principal of St. George's Anglican Senior School, Ursulla Antoine, Dr. Lawrence Gibbs for his dedicated contribution to the local health sector, and Police Sergeant Frankie Roberts who recently saved the life of a three-year old child by performing CPR after the infant was pulled from a swimming pool.

Simone LaQua who designed the logo and theme for the 42nd independence celebration was also presented with her prize by Minister of Tourism, [illegible]

As a build up to Independence Day, a number of activities were staged, and the various winners were also presented with their awards.

In the sporting discipline awards went to MacDonald College for winning the under-15 Secondary Schools Cricket Competition, St. Paul's Government School for the male category in the swimming competition, while Happy Hill Roman Catholic Primary School and St. George's Anglican Primary School were joint winners of the female category.

The Parish of St. George received the award for being the winner of the inter-parish independence volleyball tournament.

[illegible] Rootsman Kelly who won the 2016 Independence Calypso Competition along with [illegible] Douglas and Allan G received their prizes.

The Ministry of Labour was judged as the winner of the inter-ministerial independence competition.

*Dame Cecile did the honours of presenting the award to SGU's Dr. Charles Modica*

*Prime Minister Dr. Keith Mitchell hands over the award to Dr. Eudine Barriteau*

*Chairman of the Public Service Commission, attorney-at-law Derick Sylvester was called upon to present outstanding award to Ursula Antoine*

*(Newspaper) The New Today, 12 February 2016. (Inset) Pictured at the 2016 Independence Day celebrations.*

*Pictured with the Commissioner of Police and other high ranking members of the police force, flanked by the new recruits*

*Highlights of the police passing out parade of the 42nd division. Grenada Informer, 14 October 2016.*

*As Chairman of the Public Service Commission, awarding one of the top recruits*

# Female Officer takes top award at police training course #42

**The Royal Grenada Police Force (RGPF) Passing Out Parade for training course number 42 was held at the Police Training Camp in Point Salines last Thursday, and for the first time a female has walked away with the Baton of Honor, the course's highest award.**

Meritorious, her performance, highest aggregate, academically inclined, best at physical training, exemplary demeanor and exceptional leadership qualities were some of the phrases used to describe Woman Police Constable # 3 Anika Charles, as she approached the podium with confident strides, as the first Woman Police Officer to be awarded, the Baton of Honor Award. Presenting [illegible] of Honor at the ceremony and Chairman of the Grenada Public Service Commission Derick Sylvester.

In a brief citation preceding the presentation of the award, Officer Charles was described as one who showed consistency in the realization of the objective of the training, a role model to her colleagues who performed with distinction thus winning the most sought after award for anyone entering the Police Training School.

Other officers awarded during last Thursday's graduation ceremony were Officer #290 Wesley Williams for best drill, Officer # 201, Odison Fraser, Best at Physical Training and Self Defense, Officer # 569 Asran Williams for Best at Pistol Shot, Officer # 273 Leron Andrew for best Turned out, WPC #106 Judy Moses, Best in Self Defense among the females, and WPC # 13 Chris Anne James for Best at First Aid.

A total of forty-eight officers, among them twenty females, the highest number of female officers ever graduated from any one training class, were graduated last Thursday bringing an end to course number 42 after six months of intense training.

Commandant of the Police Training School Assistant Superintendent of Police Gregory Mathurine, in addressing the gathering that included senior members of the RGPF among them; Acting Commissioner of Police Winston James, Government officials, diplomats and relatives of the grandaunts, described the course as a resounding success.

The senior ranked police officer said apart from its success, the course, was his- [illegible] Course 42 had the longest period of vetting prior to the intake of trainees, the highest percentage of women in any course and additionally it the first time the Regional Police Training Manual was used at the training school.

Mathurine said the new recruits were given basic theoretical and practical police training, that included among other things administrative training, personal development, legal training, defense, pistol training, operational skills, traffic and road safety, crime and criminal activities among others.

Acting Police Commissioner Winston James also addressed the gathering and complimented all who played a role in the success of Course 42. He welcomed the latest group of recruits to the GRPF and challenged them to go out and make Grenada proud while keeping the image of the force in esteem.

The highlight of the evening's function was however a rousing address by Derick Sylvester, wherein he called upon the recruits to be mindful of the role and responsibility that is now entrusted on them as members of the RGPF. He reminded them that the entire nation depends on them and therefore they should do all in their powers to avoid falling short of their expectations.

Attorney-at-Law by profession, Sylvester reminded the recruits that having been selected as the best of the best, let it be said at the end of their service with the RGPF, it was one of high repute, having left behind positive marks in the sands of time and on the hearts and minds of fellow officers, the society and the state. "As of today," he told them "it cannot be business as usual." Demeanor, attitude, manner of dress, de- [illegible] duct he said, must be commensurate of an upholder of law, order and discipline.

Sylvester reminded the graduates that others would look them upon for guidance and therefore they should live up to that expectation, and act within the ambit of the law, failing which there would be consequences. The new recruits were told that their role is to ensure the maintenance of law and order, to act with in the confines of the law and make sure they are acquainted with those laws.

"To whom much is given," he said, "much more is expected." "Avoid the abuse and misuse of power, be fair but fearless, exercise your power with restraints, and use force only when necessary with perfect command of temper."

The officers were warned to avoid falling victims to the law, since no one is above the law, but to be valiant even in the face of adversity.

Police Constable # 3 Anika Charles

Officer #290 Wesley Williams

*Grenada Informer, 14 October 2016*

*Inspecting the new recruits*

# As police officers, do not be victims of the criminal justice system

Chairman of the Grenada Public Service Commission and one of Grenada's leading practicing attorneys' Derick Sylvester, has issued a stern warning to the newly recruited officers to avoid becoming victims of the Criminal Justice System.

Sylvester who was at the time addressing police graduates, as the guest of honor at the recently held police passing out parade, for course 42 at the police training camp in Point Salines, told the new recruits to strive to remain victors rather than finding themselves as victims of the system.

The Royal Grenada Police Force he said, like other organizationsis comprised of people from different backgrounds, different upbringing and therefore it is necessary he said for young officers to guard against becoming crooked or corrupt. Society he said would never forgive an officer who has betrayed the trust and confidence placed in him or her.

Sylvester noted that internal police corruption is a challenge to public trust, cohesion of departmental policies, human rights and legal violation involving serious consequences. Corruption he said could take many forms, among them he said, flouting the code of conduct to gain unfair advantage over civilian and suspects, deliberate participation in organized crime among others. He urged the young officers to be aware of the rotten egg theory that says one bad apple can spoil the entire crop.

Derick Sylvester

It must be noted Sylvester said, that one bad officer could bring what is construed to be a good police department to its knees within a short space of time. It is for this reason he called on the young men and women who had just taken on the responsibility of policing to be ever vigilant, speak out against wrong doing and injustices, and ensure that when the journey of serving is over, they leave behind a rich legacy.

The chairman also took the opportunity to remind the recruits of the seriousness of the task at hand, one in which a number of other officers he said have lost their own lives in attempting to serve. Among the names mentioned were former Commissioner of Police Cosmos Raymond, Constable 656 Bernard "Brenty" Thomas and more recently Corporal 414 Daniel Edgar. The contribution made by these fallen soldiers Sylvester said, should never go unnoticed, they having paid the ultimate price in the line of duty.

Sylvester charged the young men and women to allow their legacy in the RGPF to be rich ones, allow themselves to blossom in the garden of humanity, serving their fellow men with unparalleled distinction.

The highly regarded attorney-at-law told the officers to let this be said at the end of their stint with the RGPF, that they left an indelible mark in the sands of time, hearts and minds of their colleagues and the society in which they served.

Becoming a police officer, Sylvester noted would bring with it a number of changes. He cited demeanor, attitude, behavior, manner of dress, deportment and general conduct must be commensurate with that of an upholder of law and order and discipline.

"I admonish you to act within the ambit of the law", Sylvester told the officers, "Since there are consequences for failing to do so. You are the guardians of our independent constitution, and on most occasions, the first to be met with complaints from the citizen. It therefore means that to properly enforce the law, you must first have a thorough understanding of the working of the law." This he said could only be achieved by becoming acquainted with the law.

*Grenada Informer, 21 October 2016*

by another officer while sitting in his office chair. That Corporal Bernard 'Brenty' Thomas was stabbed and succumbed to the injury he received from a civilian. More recently CPL Daniel Edgar who was killed in the line of duty by an armed assailant. These three officers perished in the line of duty, I wanted to bring home to the recruits the serious nature of their job. That it was not business as usual. They are no longer civilians, but now enlisted in the Royal Grenada Police Force (RGPF) to protect and serve.

I trust they accepted the charge, since history would judge whether they did or did not. Time alone will tell. Their gleaming faces, mature poise and attention during my delivery was a ray of hope.

The time soon came when I had to retire as Chairman of the Public Service Commission as the demand of my law practice grew. I was therefore duty bound to channel my energies in that direction. It was widely felt that my resignation was part of a strategic plan to either be appointed Attorney General or enter the political arena.

# Is Derrick Sylvester's move part of a strategic plan?

*The Grenadian Voice* has been tipped that a prominent local lawyer is making preparations to become the main legal advisor to the Government.

This newspaper has received information that Derrick Sylvester, who recently resigned as Chairman of the Public Service Commission (PSC) may be making preparations to take up the post of Attorney General (AG) of Grenada soon.

News of Sylvester's resignation from the commission broke last week after a five year stint. He received his instruments of appointment to that position in November 2013.

As head of the PSC, Sylvester, along with the other four members were responsible for giving advice and recommendations to the Prime Minister on:

The making of appointments to the Public Service

The removal of persons from the Public Service

The exercise of disciplinary control of public officers

The PSC also ensures that all appointments, promotions and recruitment within the Service are made in an equitable, fair and impartial manner; free from favoritism, patronage and discrimination and is based on the principle of merit.

Story continues on Page 06

*Front page, The Grenadian Voice, week ending 8 June 2018*

CHAPTER THIRTEEN

# A MOTHER'S TEARS: THE OSCAR BARTHOLOMEW CASE

*"There is nothing worse than the grief of a parent for a child who dies."*

UNCLE ANTHONY

The practice of law has been a meandering journey of concealed emotions for me, having to deal with parents who lost children either through murder, vehicular accidents or self-inflicted actions resulting in suicide; even children who lost their parents in like situations.

On 26th December, 2011, I received communication from frantic family members requesting legal assistance as one of their relatives, Oscar Bartholomew, was detained in police custody. It was usual to receive calls of that nature, so there was nothing alarming at that time about such a call. It was revealed to me that he was detained at the St. David police station.

Upon receipt of the phone call I immediately contacted the police via telephone, and was met with scant information from the person who answered. I enquired as to the whereabouts of Oscar Bartholomew and was told the detainee Bartholomew was taken to the hospital. A light bulb immediately went off in my head as I was informed then, that it may have been an alleged traffic violation. The officer in charge of the St. David police station at the time was not available to speak with me. Later, on the said day, news started circulating that the detainee succumbed to his injuries. This immediately sent me on a legal tail spin. I spun into immediate action, as I arranged to meet with the family members the following day.

The death was confirmed. I immediately called for an investigation as it was alleged then that Oscar Bartholomew died in police custody. More information came to light, as it was brought to my attention that he was a Grenadian who was married to a Canadian citizen, both of whom were visiting for the Christmas holidays; he was also a 'resident' of Canada, not having yet obtained his citizenship.

The information reaching me, at the time was that Oscar Bartholomew was driving through St. David with his wife when he stopped by the Police Station to enable her to use the bathroom facility. He allegedly approached a female police officer with a hug, someone whom he thought he knew, but turned out to be someone else. He was immediately detained by numerous officers and taken inside the station. The police station was located about fifteen feet (15 ft.) from the main road, mere steps to enter. However, it was inside the station that he succumbed to his injuries, in circumstances left to be explained.

I made numerous calls to the police station seeking information and was met with a brick wall. Legally I intervened as the family instructed me to ensure a full investigation was launched.

The mother, wife of the deceased, brothers, sisters and extended family were in a state of immense emotional pain, the indescribable pain of human suffering where a loved one had departed this life in circumstances such as these. Also, the deceased and wife were due to depart the State of Grenada on 3rd January 2012. They had purchased a brand new car in Canada. He had decided to drive it upon his return to Canada. Little did he know that this would be his last trip.

In my practice, I have dealt with numerous cases where substantial force was warranted and some occasions less force. The trained policeman must therefore ensure the proper balance is struck and that he remains within the confines of the law.

Police officers have a heavy mandate; the power to kill is in their hands but must be used with restraint and only in the most extreme of circumstances. A life is irreplaceable and the extraction of a loved one from their family can have lifelong disastrous and catastrophic psychological consequences. The same applied if a police officer is killed in the line of duty. Upon calling for an independent investigation, the family of Oscar Bartholomew demanded answers. There was deafening silence from where the request was sent. I wrote letters to the Director of Public Prosecution, Commissioner of Police and the Canadian Consulate in Barbados. I sought answers as to what actually transpired at the station. I had numerous witnesses who were present and willing to give statements.

There was a local pathologist who conducted the autopsy. I was in receipt of the report. On the instructions of the family of the deceased

## Canadian/Grenadian Man Dies in

# POLICE BRUTALITY

Bartholomew in Canada recently

The battered head of the deceased

*Front page, Grenada Informer, week ending 30 December 2011*

# The Oscar Bartholomew death

Dear Editor,

This is Huan Golsorkhi from Toronto Canada. You were very kind before to me and it is a pity that I could not extend our cooperation between The New Today and The Association of North American Journalists (Canada).

We are recently NORTHAM JOURNALISTS also.

As you may know I have been closely involved with Grenada since 1976, to the point that mention and my picture is given spot in Carriacou Museum (a great honour for me). I love Grenada to an extent that it may be hard to believe for her natives.

I am greatly saddened by the murder of Oscar Bartholomew not only for himself and his large numbered family here, but also for The Lost Innocence and tarnish of, unique clean reputation of our beloved land as a whole.

Grenada is on the first page of the largest North American Press, so far every day. This is the most serious test of a most civilized people in the eyes of others. This is the most serious allegation, police force which is to protect citizens, is accused of assaulting a Human Being (who also is a Canadian), was a prisoner in custody so ruthlessly that, he dies 24 hours later.

What security does the tourist have in Grenada if for any reason they end up in the Police station?

If the Government of Grenada thinks this will be swept under the rug may be as the Chief Editor of the most popular Grenadian Press you should let them know, that unfortunately it would not go in that direction.

The murder of a Canadian Woman ZAHRA KAZEMI in Iran custody after seven years is still as fresh. Mexico has been wiped off the tourism map of Canadians and many Americans because of a few similar situations.

The economy of Grenada and tourism was doing bad enough already. You recall your previous Prime minister gave a figure of 48% unemployment.

You are a professional journalist, you know what to do with this letter, which you have received from a good friend of Grenada who is also the PRESIDENT OF THE ASSOCIATION of NORTH AMERICAN JOURNALISTS (Canada)

***Hutan Golsorkhi***
***Northam Journalist***

*The New Today, 6 January 2012*

we contacted a well-known Caribbean Pathologist Dr. Hubert Daisley, who resided in the Republic of Trinidad and Tobago. I requested his immediate intervention for the purpose of a comprehensive pathology report, including the cause of death.

After the body of the deceased was handed over to the family and placed at the La Qua Brother's Crematorium, we requested it remained for the second Pathologist examination prior to interment. The Pathologist flew into Grenada and was greeted by the family members all too distraught to hold themselves up. He penned a twenty five page report, with numerous photos that would later form the basis of the civil trial in this matter. Later, it was alleged that numerous police officers were involved in causing the death, but no names were forthcoming.

By that time the Canadian press was alerted. Numerous reporters flooded the island; my office was inundated with calls, emails and television interviews. The Canadian authorities needed answers and seemingly were very concerned about the state of affairs of our justice system. I assured them that this was an unfortunate incident that will be investigated thoroughly. The perpetrators would be brought to justice.

The Canadian press was relentless and could not understand how an offence of such nature could happen. A demand for answers increased with each passing day. Letters were written from different organisations with citizens demanding answers. The police had to investigate the police. It was causing a lot of concern among the family members of the deceased.

I reassured the family members that the Director of Public Prosecutions was a professional who historically executed his duty with professionalism. Further should there be a case against the officers he would undoubtedly pursue it. I implored them to trust his judgment, but the days rolled by. They got more anxious. During that time every aspect of the news media, both locally, regionally and internationally were seeking answers. They keenly followed the story of the death of Oscar Bartholomew. The Royal Grenada Police Force was placed in the spotlight and the hierarchy of the force had no easy task to answer for the actions of a few.

By that time I received some requests from police officers to represent them in the said matter, but it was too late, since I had already committed to the family of the deceased. It was a matter of who contacted me first for legal representation. On this occasion it was the family of the deceased. The officer in charge of the St. David Police station was transferred to another location. The demand for answers and action continued.

najor shakeup has en place at the St. id's Police Station at te Esperance.
:s was announced by nmissioner of Police, lan Thompson at a :s conference held at ice Headquarters on t George last week rsday.
major casualty of the ceup is the removal of d of the Station, istant Superintendent 'olice (ASP) Anthony es.
hough Commissioner mpson was reluctant lisclosing the new ation of Jones who ed as a bodyguard to ner Prime Minister Keith Mitchell up il the July 8, 2008 eral Elections, The Today Newspaper been reliably ormed that the senior iceman is now based he Victoria Police ion.
ASP who operated at Grenville Police

## ASP Jones removed from St. David's Police Station

*Commissioner Willan Thompson – no cover up in the investigation*

Station has been sent to take charge of the St. David's Police Station.

Accompanied at the press conference by the top echelon of the Royal Grenada Police Force (RGPF) that includes Deputy Commissioner Franklyn Redhead, Assistant Commissioners Dowlin Bartholomew and Smith Roberts, and Superintendents Edvin Martin and Dunbar Belfon who moderated the press conference, Commissioner Thompson said that an undisclosed number of police officers will be transferred from the station.

The shakeup at the St. David's Police Station is

*Superintendent Dunbar Belfon and ACP Dowlin Bartholomew listening intently to a conversation with Superintendent Edvin Martin*

largely due to the alleged beating of Grenadian-born resident Oscar Peter Bartholomew at the hands of some police officers on Boxing Day.

Bartholomew who sustained injuries to the head subsequently died the following day at the St. George's General Hospital.

The Canadian resident was taken into custody by police officers at the St. David's Police Station after he allegedly assaulted a female police officer who, he said, was dressed in uniform and was on duty.

There are reports that Bartholomew mistakenly took the female officer for an old friend.

The Chief Cop was adamant that an assault on a police officer did ... incident inside the station.

Commissioner Thompson sought to justify his assertion by stating that assault is defined as getting close to an individual with an intention to touch or putting that person in fear of being harmed.

"Any advancement that was made on the (female) officer by Bartholomew was unwanted, was unwelcome and was not instigated by herself," he said.

Sources told ***THE NEW TODAY*** that the severe beatings started after an officer was allegedly kicked inside the station by Bartholomew.

Commissioner Thompson said the reassignment of the police officers to other areas of RGPF is to allow a police investigation into what lead to the incident at the St. David's Police Station to allow the investigation to proceed quickly and unimpeded.

ASP Ignatius Mason of the Criminal Investigation Department has been assigned as the officer with responsibility for investigating the matter which he said is of a criminal nature.

"Anyone found to be culpable will find that justice will take its course," Commissioner Thompson said.

The top COP spoke of having a discussion with Head of CID, Superintendent Anthony Joseph after learning of the death of Bartholomew.

"I advised him (Supt. Joseph) of the need for a thorough and proper investigation into the matter. I also spoke with the Head of Operations, Supt. Edvin Martin," he told reporters.

The Police Commissioner said he commanded Supt. Joseph to proceed quickly with the investigation.

Commissioner Thompson described the incident as being an isolated one which, he said, does not reflect the wider RGPF.

However, he said anything that is done wrong will definitely have some negative impact.

"However, we do hope that negative impact will be short-lived," he said.

*The New Today, 6 January 2012*

I had daily meetings, phone calls and interviews with the deceased's family. His mother's pain was just indescribable. Her son was the source of her joy, he was all she had she would repeat daily, "I looked forward to my son's phone calls, his care, and the barrels at Christmas, he was my bread winner, my all." The pain reflected in her eyes when she spoke. On the many occasions when she visited my office and said nothing, but listened to me explaining the legal processes. It was obvious she had no care for such explanation except justice for her son. I urged her repeatedly to have patience and reminded her that it was a virtue.

There was a public announcement that five (5) police officers would be charged as a result of the death of Oscar Bartholomew. It was a sigh of relief for the family. I had to explain the law to them that since murder then was a crime of specific intent, it had to be shown beyond a reasonable doubt that the intention was to kill solely, and not cause grievous bodily harm. If it was the intention to cause grievous bodily harm and death resulted, then the charge was manslaughter. However, the law has since been amended, and now in Grenada, murder is no longer a crime of specific intent, an intention to cause grievous bodily harm would also suffice for a charge of murder.

The five officers were brought to court at the St. David's Magistrate Court. There was a massive crowd awaiting their entrance who chanted slogans and held banners seeking justice for Oscar Bartholomew. It was a carnival-like crowd, screaming and demanding swift and expeditious justice.

The five police officers were remanded, since they were brought to court in St. George's. The issue of bail was best dealt with in St. David, the parish where the incident occurred. This was a dreadfully terrible

The crowd cry out for justic

*(This page and facing page) The New Today, 6 January 2012*

thought for policemen to be at Her Majesty's Prison together with convicted men they may have been responsible for putting behind bars. They now had to face them head on. It was reported that they would be kept in safe custody. It was no easy day for the RGPF who had to deal with this mammoth criminal spectacle hovering over it.

The police officers all retained attorneys as their criminal matter was due to commence. In the meantime, I wrote the then Minister of Tourism, who was also a Lawyer who had practiced with me at Ciboney Chambers. I knew the empathy he had for like circumstances and his desire to ensure justice was done. I arranged a meeting at my office with the deceased's mother, wife, brothers and other relatives so as to enable an open

# Police Officers Charged With Manslaughter

A mob-like crowd converged in the precincts of the Number One Magistrate's Court on Tuesday as five police officers were brought to court in connection with the death of Grenadian-born Canadian resident Peter Oscar Bartholomew.

The officers are Police Constables 649 Edward Gibson, 675 Shaun Ganness, 237 Ruddy Felix, 748 Kenton Hazzard, and Rural Constable Wendell Sylvester.

They are each charged with manslaughter in the death of the 39-year old Bartholomew.

The police officers are accused of beating Bartholomew while he was in police custody at the St. David's Police Station on Boxing Day, December 26.

The naturalised Canadian citizen subsequently died at the St. George's General Hospital the following morning as a result of the injuries he sus- [illegible]

local attorneys - former Attorney General, Dr. Francis Alexis, Anselm Clouden and Cajeton Hood, is representing the accused policemen.

The lawyers sought to present Chief Magistrate Tamara Gill with a bail application on behalf of their clients but it was rejected.

Gibson is being represented by Constitutional Lawyer, Dr. Alexis, QC, Attorney Clouden is representing Felix and Sylvester, while attorney Cajeton Hood is representing Hazzard and Ganness.

Chief Magistrate Gill indicated that the matter having taken place in the Eastern District has to be heard at the St. David's Magistrate's Court and it is her intention to have the resident magistrate there, Nevlyn John deal with the bail application on Friday (January 6) when the Preliminary Inquiry is expected to start.

She noted that there is a constitutional requirement that after someone brought to court at the first available opportunity, hence the reason why the police officers have been brought before her.

The five police officers were remanded in custody at the Richmond Hill prison until their next court date.

Tight security measures were put in place protection for the accused police officers.

A police operation headed by Assistant Superintendent of Police, Sylvan McIntyre managed to slip the policemen in and out of the court and away from the large crowd who became vocal and were heard shouting: "Police

Attorney-at-law, Derick Sylvester who is representing the Bartholomew family's interest met with the media after the police officers' appearance in court and called on the nation to observe a sober reflection over the situation.

According to Sylvester, [illegible]

mourning and make an impassionate plea for members of the public including Bartholomew's family to be temperate by respecting police officers, and do not lose sight that there is still a country to build.

He urged persons not to interfere with the investigation, police officers, or witnesses in the case.

"I would ask everyone to let us continue to respect our police officers, and we expect the same in return... Let the administration of justice take its course," he said.

Sylvester believes that the Boxing Day incident should serve as a wake-up call for everyone involved and that now is the time for an introspective look to be taken as to how "we behave and how we treat other persons."

The city attorney felt that if mutual respect had existed Bartholomew would have been alive today.

Bartholomew was in Grenada with his … Christmas Holiday.

The alleged beating occurred while the wife went to use the bathroom facilities at the St. David's Police Station.

Bartholomew is said to have mistakenly took a young female police officer as an old friend and proceeded to embrace her and uttered the following words: "Ah get you now, ah going with you, ah don't care what happen".

The female officer then called out to some of her colleagues for help and Bartholomew was then taken into custody and brought inside the police station.

The family used the services last Saturday of Professor Dr. Hubert Daisley who conducted a second autopsy to determine the cause of death.

A first autopsy was conducted by the State, which concluded that Bartholomew died from trauma to the head with multiple skull fractures, sub dual hemorrhage.

Daisley's five-page autopsy report is much more thorough and descriptive about the injuries on Bartholomew.

In a brief statement, Bartholomew's wife said it is unfortunate what occurred at the St. David's Police Station.

Although she misses her husband, she too is urging the nation to begin the healing process and not engage in fighting.

The Canadian/Grenadian spoke of Grenada being a beautiful country, and promised to speak of the beauty of the country to other Canadians although "one bad thing happened."

*The New Today, 6 January 2012*

discussion on the matter. As Minister of Tourism, he was destined to show the world that the incident was an isolated occurrence and Grenada was still a safe place to vacation, as well as to sympathise with the family members in his capacity as Minister of Tourism.

The mother of Oscar Bartholomew, who was present at the meeting, had few words to say, but the few she spoke expressed her grief and loss. I looked at her and I was reminded of the words of Henry Wadsworth Longfellow when he penned: "There is no grief like the grief that does not speak."

And the old Jewish saying, "The deeper the sorrow, the less voice it has."

I have learnt from my life experiences in practice that when sorrow is not expressed, its wounds are devoid of healing. I later came to understand what led to the demise of Oscar Bartholomew's mother.

## David expects no tourism fall-out from killing

*Tourism Minister Peter David extends government's condolences to Dollette Cyra Bartholomew on the death of her husband Peter Oscar Bartholomew at the hands of local police officers*

Tourism Minister Peter David has said that Grenada remains an "extremely safe destination" for visitors, adding that government intends to keep it that way.

He made the comment in response to questions about the potential impact on tourism of the death of Oscar Bartholomew.

The 39-year-old Grenadian, who resided in Canada and was visiting his homeland with his Canadian-born wife, died at the St. George's General Hospital where he was taken following an altercation with officers at the St. David's Police Station.

Officers of the Criminal Investigations Department of the Royal Grenada Police Force, who are conducting a probe into the Boxing Day incident in St. David, have charged five policemen with manslaughter in connection with Bartholomew's death.

"This is a tragedy on all counts, especially for the Bartholomew family," said Minister David, who also hold

Culture portfolios in the Tillman Thomas-led National Democratic Congress (NDC) government.

"Like all Grenadians, including all my colleagues in government, we would have preferred this not to have happened to anyone, particularly to a national who was visiting with his wife," the minister added.

"But from the perspective of visitor safety, and in comparison to other tourist-dependent nations of the world, Grenada still is - and will continue to be - an extremely safe destination for travelers from around the world."

The Bartholomews' legal representative in Grenada is lawyer Derick Sylvester. He said Bartholomew's mother and his wife, Dolette, had expressed interest in meeting with government representatives.

Prime Minister Thomas had earlier visited the grieving mother to express government's condolences on the death.

According to Sylvester who was a former legal partner with David at Caboney Chambers, he was successful on Friday in setting up a meeting with the senior government minister who talked with Bartholomew's mother and wife.

Minister David conveyed his sympathies to the couple and their families, and again extended government's condolences that were first expressed earlier in the week by Prime Minister Thomas.

For Sylvester, having Minister David meet with the two grieving Bartholomew family members was "a step in the right direction."

Meanwhile, the main opposition New National Party (NNP) has issued a statement expressing its sadness with the alleged beating of Bartholomew, a Grenadian-born Canadian Citizen while in Police custody over the Christmas Holidays.

NNP's political activist, Devon Rachae, a former Candidate for the St. David Constituency, was seen Tuesday morning leading a group of protestors from the court house on Upper St. John's Street to the front of the CID head office on Hillsborough Street in the city calling for justice in the Bartholomew killing.

Bartholomew who later succumbed to his injuries hours after at the General Hospital, generated a series of protest actions by residents in the St David's area.

*Former Opposition Senator Devon Rache addressing the crowd outside CID on Tuesday*

The NNP statement said "Given the present state of the economy and the negative publicity the country has been receiving both locally and regionally in the past few months, this incident could further damage its image as a tourist destination creating road blocks and unnecessary challenges for the already difficult task of removing the economy from its present state of malaise.

"In light of the above and having regards to the value of tourism to Grenada, we call on Prime Minister Tillman Thomas to immediately launch a full investigation to ascertain the facts surrounding this case, and in so doing, ensure that justice is not only done but seen to have been done.

"To the beloved family and friends of Mr. Bartholomew both here at home and abroad, our hearts go out to you in this time of great loss. We are aware of the tremendous pain death brings, more so in this tragic circumstance. We want to assure you the entire party mourns with you; also, our prayers are with you.

"To the Grenadian population, we could only take courage from the knowledge that as Grenadians we have the capacity, as demonstrated many times in the past; to transcend every challenge which confront us.

"Let's continue to join hearts and hands in the true spirit of brotherhood to help ease the obvious pain that the family is enduring at this time. May the Peace of God continue to be with us all during this very difficult period".

*The New Today, 6 January 2012*

*Meeting held at the conference room of the law office of Derick F. Sylvester & Associates, with Minister of Tourism Peter David (top right), together with the wife (top left), mother (middle) and family of Oscar Bartholomew*

## PART II

On the instruction of the family of the deceased, I filed a civil suit claiming compensation, damages for wrongful death and numerous other remedies against the five (5) police officers and the Attorney General. The lawyers all applied for a stay of the proceedings, as it was alleged that the filing of defences would affect the fairness of the trial in the criminal proceedings. There were submissions filed and arguments made. The court agreed that a stay should be ordered in relation to the civil matter, until the criminal matter was finally heard and determined. The civil matter was therefore stayed.

### Legal appeals holding up trial in Oscar Bartholomew's death

by Lincoln Depradine
STAFF EDITOR

FLASHBACK: Protestors demonstrate after the five police officers charged with beating Oscar Bartholemew to death were granted bail on Friday, Jan. 6, 2012. (COLIN PERKEL / AP)

Lawyer Derek Sylvester

A year after Grenada grabbed international headlines for the beating death of Oscar Bartholomew, no one is closer to knowing why he was allegedly pummeled inside the St. David's Police Station.

Five police officers – Kenton Hazzard, Wendell Sylvester, Edward Gibson, Shaun Ganness and Ruddy Felix – were charged with manslaughter in Bartholomew's death.

They were released on bail on January 6 and there are two cases pending against them: one is civil in nature and the other is criminal. Both are tied up in legal appeals.

The incident leading to Bartholomew's death was a "tragedy" for him and also for the police officers facing criminal and civil charges, lawyer Derick Sylvester toldCaribupdate Weekly.

"They all have families and they would want the matter to proceed as quickly as possible so that they would want to know what their fate is, both in the civil matter and in the criminal matter," he said.

Sylvester is representing the Bartholomew family in the civil case. The criminal proceedings are being handled

Continued on pg 21

*Weekly newspaper, 2013*

...by the Director of Public Prosecutions, Christopher Nelson.

Grenada-born Bartholomew was visiting Grenada last year with his Canadian wife, Dolette, when he stopped at the St. David's Police Station on December 26, reportedly to use restroom.

He was unconscious when taken from the station to the St. George's General Hospital, where the 39-year-old died shortly after arriving.

Bartholomew's family claims that police beat him into a coma and has instructed Sylvester to file a civil suit against the cops.

"We're asking for general damages for wrongful death; and for compensation for the beneficiaries of the deceased that, obviously, include his wife and children," said Sylvester, whose civil suit has been filed with the Attorney General's Chambers.

Two autopsies were conducted on Bartholomew's body. They discovered trauma to the skull and multiple injuries to the body.

"The autopsies were both compatible in some ways," Sylvester said. "It's just that one is more detailed; it's about 35 pages while the other is just two pages. I would be relying on both autopsies in the civil proceedings."

The "ball is in the court" of the attorney general in determining the start of the civil case and its resolution, said Sylvester.

"The attorney general sought to, and was successful, in applying to the court for an application to stay the civil proceedings, pending the outcome of the criminal matter," the lawyer explained.

"the state has taken the position that it intends to defend both matters to the hilt"

"The crux of their argument is that if they were to tender a defense (in the civil matter) it would prejudice the criminal case. Of course, we disagreed with that. So, we're going for leave to appeal the decision of the learned judge who would have granted a stay of the civil proceedings, because that was the same judge who would have granted the stay in the criminal matter."

Each of the five officers has retained legal counsel and has filed defense in the civil case, Sylvester said.

He wants the civil case started, saying it is "totally different" to the pending criminal trial.

"I am saying that the civil matter is independent of the criminal matter," Sylvester argued. "There are different burdens and standards of proof; and there is no significant prejudice that the Attorney General's Chambers would ensue by virtue of defending the action because the individual police officers have entered defenses already."

Bartholomew's wife and family, Sylvester said, would like both cases "completed as expeditiously as possible."

He said he was "under the impression that the state would have taken a particular course on the civil matter; and, if they were to take a particular course on the civil matter, then that would no doubt have alleviated the concern of the complainant in so far as it relates to the criminal proceedings".

But, as Sylvester put it, "the state has taken the position that it intends to defend both matters to the hilt".

In the criminal case, lawyers for the officers have filed judicial review proceedings, challenging certain sections of the Coroner's Inquiry Act.

"Basically, they a dicating that th should first e upon a coroner quiry because it death that occur a public place. I been notified tha are awaiting a jud in that matter," Sylvester.

The cops, if found on the criminal ch facepossible pe ranging from a fi maximum of 15 y prison.

"My position," S ter said, "has a been that, even defendants were pated in the cri proceedings, the is whether or n civil proceedings still remain alive. my position is it sl The burdens are ent."

*Weekly newspaper, 2013*

# Officers dismissed of manslaughter charges yet to be reinstated

**Winston James**

Five police officers who were previously charged with manslaughter are yet to return to work. During a media conference last week Wednesday, acting Commissioner of Police, Winston James made the confirmation. The five officers Edward Gibson, Shann Ganness, Kenton Hazzard, Ruddy Felix, and Wendell Sylvester was charged in connection with the death of Grenadian/Canadian citizen, Oscar Bartholomew.

Bartholomew, who was on vacation from Canada, was killed while in the custody of the police at the St David's Police Station on December 26th, 2011 – Boxing Day. The charges were dismissed against the lawmen. A Court ruled that the charges be dropped and a Coroner's inquest be held. It also ruled that the men be reinstated and compensated.

Acting Commissioner Winston James said that the DPP is handling search matters; however he said that the Court made a ruling and as Commissioner of Police he has a responsibility to obey the ruling of the Court. "I will do nothing less or more than obey the ruling of the Court." He added that a man or a woman is presumed to be innocent until he or she is found guilty or pleads guilty.

"So whatever allegations that are made outside there we have to understand that the men have a right according to law - not according to me." "I can tell you as of this time the men have not been reinstated on the Force," he added.

During the inquest the Coroner will sit, hear the evidence and decide from the evidence whether or not anyone of the five policemen who were charged are responsible for the death of the deceased. If in the case that they are found responsible then charges will have to be laid against them again.

*Grenada Informer, 29 March 2013*

The defence lawyers again mounted a legal challenge on the criminal proceedings and filed by way of judicial review, an attack on the criminal charges as filed, alleging a Coroner's inquest pursuant to the Coroners Act was mandatory when death occurred under such circumstances, prior to the proferring of criminal charges. The matter was argued at the High Court level where the defence succeeded, in that the court held that the criminal charges should be dismissed and a Coroner's inquest be held. The police officers therefore had to be reinstated in the service with pay. It was a hard pill for the family and public to swallow.

The Director of Public Prosecutions abided by the court's ruling and expressed his intention to appeal the ruling to the Court of Appeal, which he did.

## PART III

This was a welcomed relief, as the criminal matter was now brought to an end, and the civil matter could now continue. I immediately wrote the Registrar requesting the matter be replaced on the list for case management. The defendants in the civil matters therefore had twenty eight (28) days to file their respective defences. The appeal court was an itinerant court which visited Grenada tri-annually, so it was my desire that much could be done with the civil case before the appeal was heard. The stay was now lifted on the civil proceedings.

## PART IV

The defence was filed on behalf of the State. The scope and tenor of it was that the officers were acting outside of the ambit of their duties. Their actions therefore could not result in the State's liability. The other defences were each a blanket denial of inflicting injuries on the deceased. The civil matter was therefore on the trial route, pleadings were closed and the pre-trial review date was set. The hearing was conducted and dates were given to file our respective bundles for trial.

## PART V

In the interim, the Director of Public Prosecution called for the repealing of the Coroners Act, in that if such a decision be upheld it would impinge

**DPP calls for Coroner's Act to be repealed**

Director of Public Prosecution (DPP) Christopher Nelson is calling for the Coroner's Act of 1896 to be repealed from the law books of Grenada.

Nelson's call came in light of a decision handed down by High Court Judge, Justice Septimus Rudd to squash a criminal charge of manslaughter against five Police Officers who are accused of causing the death of Grenadian Oscar Bartholomew.

The St David's resident who obtained Canadian Citizenship was visiting Grenada with his French-speaking Canadian wife, Dollette Cyr Bartholomew when he was allegedly beaten at the St. David's Police Station on December 26, 2011.

He suffered severe head injuries allegedly at the hands of Police Constables, 649 Edward [illegible], 675 Shaun [illegible], 237 Ruddy Felix, 748 Kenton Hazzard and Rural Constable Wendell Sylvester before succumbing at the St. George's General Hospital.

Justice Rudd ordered that a Coroner Inquest be held to inquire into the circumstances that lead to Bartholomew's death.

At a Press Conference held at his office last week Tuesday, DPP Nelson declared that the Coroner's Act is outdated, and that his recommendation to the government is to have it repealed.

He said Justice Rudd's judgement has definitely brought out the need to recommend that the Act be repealed.

"It (the Coroner's Act) is useless, there is no need to maintain that," he argued.

DPP Nelson indicated that in countries such as England, Canada and some other territories in the Western Hemisphere, the criminal jurisdiction of the Coroner has been repealed.

The State Prosecutor described the Coroner's Inquest as being an old institution which he said rose to prominence in the thirteenth and fourteenth century.

According to him, there have been instances where there have been deaths at institutions and the matter was prosecuted directly without any issue.

*DPP Christopher Nelson - in favour of repeal of Coroner's Act*

The DPP told the media that an inquest is one avenue through which criminal charges can eventually be laid against persons.

However, he said in these modern times, the desired route for a prosecution is not a Coroner's Inquest.

DPP Nelson indicated that the Constitution of Grenada created the Department of the Director of Public Prosecution to lay criminal charges against anyone for any offense.

"The specifically designed agencies of the State, namely the Police Force and the Director of Public Prosecution Office are the key and the main players in the determination of laying a charge and carrying on a prosecution, not the Coroner's Inquest," he said.

He added that a Coroner's Inquest may be required when the death of someone is accidental, and there is no question of foul play or criminal liability arising.

"The Coroner's Court is formulated to satisfy the General Public that any death is properly accounted for," he told reporters.

In a Coroner's Inquest there is no accused person, no Prosecutor or defense, but a Magistrate who conducts a fact-finding mission to determine the identity of the dead person, and how and by what means the individual met his death.

The Coroner's Inquest into Bartholomew's death is scheduled to commence on April 5 at the St. David's Magistrate's Court.

Following police investigations into Bartholomew's death, the DPP directed that criminal charges be laid on the five Police Officers.

A Preliminary Inquiry was already in progress when Lawyers for the accused persons filed for a stay of proceedings to allow for judicial review on the issue of the Coroner's Inquiry.

The police officers were placed on bail in the sum of $100,000 with two sureties to be secured by the deposit of original land title deeds, and were suspended from the RGPF and placed on half month's salary.

*The New Today, 28 March 2013*

on the future conduct of criminal matters. The Coroners Act was indeed a fact finding mission and criminal charges could be laid thereafter in any event.

## PART VI

The burden seemed too heavy for the mother of Oscar Bartholomew, Adrianna Bartholomew, to carry. I would speak to her about the legal process but that was not much of her concern except the thought of the release of the accused men and their reintegration into the police force was a hard pill to swallow.

It was a difficult process to explain to the mother of a victim the legal nuances associated with various legal challenges. I fully understood her grief. She reminded me that the most difficult time of the year for her was now at Christmas because this was when her son came to visit her and met his death. She claimed if it was not for that visit he would have been alive today. The Christmas season was laced with too much pain.

However, in January 2016, soon after the Christmas vacation, she committed suicide; her body was found hanging from a cocoa tree in the village where she lived. When the news broke, it struck me like a jolt of lightning. All her conversations immediately came flooding back.

It was later that said year that the court office gave the date for the civil trial as November 2016; unfortunately the mother of the deceased was not around to witness or receive the judgment.

## Mother of Oscar Bartholomew found hanging

January 14, 2016 | LOCAL NEWS

12

Adrianna Bartholomew – was allegedly distraught over the death of her son

Five years after losing her son in controversial circumstances following a brawl with the police, 76-year old Andrianna Bartholomew of La Tante, St. David apparently took her own life.

The elderly lady was the mother of the late Oscar Bartholomew, a naturalised Canadian citizen who died on December 29, 2011 after being embroiled in a struggle with police officers inside the St. David Police Station.

The mother of the slain man was found Tuesday morning hanging from a cocoa tree.

***THE NEW TODAY*** understands that the senior citizen was found by family members around 7.00 a.m. in her hometown village of La Tante.

A release from the Community Relations Department of the Royal Grenada Police Force (RGPF) confirmed the incident and indicated that an autopsy is to be

Residents in the area told this newspaper that the elderly lady was never the same after her son's death and became distraught over the failure of the State to bring closure to its investigations into the death.

A male resident who knew the Bartholomew family stated that the woman was almost senile as her health rapidly deteriorated in recent years.

Oscar Bartholomew attracted international attention, especially in Canada when he was deemed to have died at the hands of police officers five years ago.

He was allegedly beaten into a coma by five police officers after he allegedly hugged a female officer that he had mistaken for a friend.

The incident happened on December 26, 2011, while Oscar was in the country visiting his family for the Christmas holiday.

Since then, charges against the five officers have been dropped and they were reinstated. In 2013 a Coroner's Inquest was ordered to be conducted to show if the accused persons were culpable for the death of Bartholomew.

***THE NEW TODAY*** understands the inquest is ongoing with no signs of an early end.

Family members continue to accuse the State of dragging its feet on the matter and not showing interest in justice for the Bartholomew family.

*New Today Online, 14 January 2016*

## Oscar Bartholomew inquest to commence next week

By Linda Straker

**DIRECTOR of Public Prosecution (DPP), Christopher Nelson, has announced that preparations are being made to have the Coroner's Inquest into the death of Oscar Bartholomew commence on April 5, 2013.**

Recently, the High Court ruled that the five Police Officers charged for causing the death of Oscar Bartholomew be reinstated to the Police Force and that an inquest be held to determine who is or are culpable for his death.

Bartholomew was a Grenadian/Canadian citizen who, on December 26, 2011, was allegedly beaten by police officers at the St. David's Police Station while on an island tour with his wife, Dolette. They had stopped to use the washroom at the station. While awaiting his wife, he mistook a plain-clothes female officer for a long lost friend and hugged her. Her screams reportedly resulted in other officers running to her rescue and beating him. He died hours after getting admitted to hospital. A pathology report said he died from blunt force trauma to his skull and body.

The Coroner's Inquest will involve a Magistrate questioning a number of persons and his findings will determine if anyone should be criminally prosecuted. However, Nelson has expressed his concern over the High Court ruling, which ordered that the coroner's inquest be conducted before any criminal proceedings.

"The Constitution provides the DPP with power to order criminal proceedings and in my view there is something fundamentally wrong with this ruling ... my hands, the Office of the DPP and the Commissioner of Police are practically tied," said Nelson, who is yet to receive the written judgement which was read out by Madam Justice Margaret Price-Findlay. The matter was heard by Justice Septimus Rhudd.

Nelson argues that the Coroner's Act, which dates back to 1896, lost relevance when Grenada established a Police Force to deal with criminal matters in the 1960s and with the island becoming an independent nation in 1974.

"The Coroner's Act is not an act for prosecutorial prosecution. The criminal aspect of the Coroner's Act was repealed when we adopted our Constitution; the Coroner's Act is outdated! How the Judge used an archaic legislation to make that judgement, it beats me," Nelson said, who explained that the order from the court is not an acquittal of the charges on the accused officers.

"It's not an acquittal, it means we have to wait until the Inquest is heard."

The Coroner's Act provides for an inquest to be undertaken whenever someone dies while in confinement in a public place of unknown cause. Nelson said that the inquest is really a fact-finding inquiry and it's not the appropriate vehicle for criminal prosecution.

"The Coroner can only determine if any person is to be charged for murder or manslaughter, but I as DPP will determine the final charge," he said.

**Director of Public Prosecution, Christopher Nelson.**

*The Grenada Advocate, 29 March 2013*

## PART VII

The Coroner's inquest started. Evidence was taken from numerous witnesses before a five (5) member jury panel, whose duty it was to determine and give answers into the circumstances surrounding the death of Oscar Bartholomew.

## PART VIII

The civil matter was listed for hearing in November of 2016; it was a welcomed relief for the family, as a trial date was set. The wife of the deceased returned from Canada to give evidence. The statement of the mother of the deceased was tendered in evidence as that of a dead witness, since she had already signed the witness statement. An application was made in writing to the court for that purpose. The civil matter was now completed.

The judgment was subsequently delivered in favour of Oscar Bartholomew the matter was forwarded to the master's court for assessment of damages.

# The Oscar Bartholomew Civil Matter is Complete

Oscar Bartholomew

Civil proceedings aimed at holding the state responsible for the December 2011 death of a Grenadian born Canadian Citizen while in police custody at the St David's Magistrate Court has been completed.

According to information reaching the Grenada Informer Newspaper, three of the five police officers who were initially charged in connection with the death of the thirty-nine year-old Oscar Bartholomew, were present to give evidence at the Number Three Supreme Court last Thursday bringing closure to the six year-old matter.

Sources told our news desk that apart from the main witnesses, evidence was taken from the wife of the deceased, Delette Cyr Bartholomew, pathologist Dr. Hubert Daisley as well as Shane Pierre and Samora Bishop. Superintendent Ignatius Mason gave evidence on behalf of the Attorney General's Chambers, which was represented in court by Solicitor General Dwight Horsford and Marisa Johnson. Lawyers Dr. Francis Alexis, Anselm Clouden and Olay BC Clouden looked after the interest of the police officers.

The Bartholomew family through their lawyer Derick Sylvester is seeking compensation from the state for what they claim is the wrongful death of Bartholomew while in police custody. The family has also brought a Dependency Action against the state seeking compensation for Bartholomew's dependents. In addition, they are seeking special damages for funeral expenses, cost of the pathologist's report, aggravating damages and cost with interest.

Informer learned that since the death of Bartholomew, the family has been advocating settlement of the civil aspect of the proceeding, jointly and severally between the state and the police officers but that, it was said, was not forthcoming until recently a move was made to have one aspect of the claim settled. That we were told, was not accepted by lawyers for the family who held the view that the police officers were at the time acting as servants of the state.

Sources told the Grenada Informer that based on the present position, all that is left before judgment is delivered is for the various lawyers to hand in legal submissions to the court and the deadline given is December 30th 2016. It is believed that a written judgment in the matter could be handed down in the first quarter of 2017.

It is not clear, the amount that is being sought by members of the family but sources hinted that it could run into the millions.

Meanwhile the coronas inquest ordered by the court to determine who should be held responsible for Bartholomew's death is also nearing completion with December 16 set as the date for the final sitting at the St David's Magistrate Court

to be followed by a decision in January of 2017.

*Grenada Informer, 25 November 2016*

# All evidence taken in Oscar Bartholomew Coroner

Lawyers involved in the Oscar Bartholomew Coroner have been urged to have their final statements, if any, on the behalf of their clients, ready to be made before the 6-member jury at the next sitting of the court, which is scheduled for September 22.

District Coroner, Magistrate Teddy St. Louis, who is hoping to complete the matter before the end of the year, made the request when the inquiry into Bartholomew's death continued last week Friday at the St. David's Magistrate's Court.

The sitting saw the last of the five police officers, Rural Constable (RC) Wendell Sylvester, presenting his side of what transpired on that

*Oscar Bartholomew – beaten inside a police station*

dreadful day in December 2011.

RC Sylvester was previously represented by Attorney-at-law, Peter David who was also retained by fellow police officers and co-accused – Police Constables 675 Shaun Garness and 748 Kenton Hazzard.

However, due to what was described as a conflict of interest, Attorney David withdrew his services and the Marlmount, St. David resident, was advised to seek another counsel.

He retained attorney Nigel Stewart from the sister isle of Carriacou to assist him in the matter.

During last week's sitting of the Coroner's

*Shaun Garness – was at the station on the day of the Bartholomew beating*

*Police Officer 327 Rudy Felix – one of the policemen implicated in the beating*

Inquest, Sylvester was accompanied by his attorney, who requested that the court grant him enough time to review the documents, given that he was recently instructed by his client in the matter.

The State prosecution, which is being led by

*Rural Constable (RC) Wendell Sylvester – among the five officers named in the St. David policer station incident*

Director of Public Prosecution (DPP) Christopher Nelson also brought back one of its witnesses, Tevin Thomas, for the purpose of clearing up some misunderstandings in the evidence that he had already provided to the court.

sion to reserve time on the next occasion for cross examination of 675 Garness, by attorney Stewart, who was not on the case when his evidence was taken.

Back in 2012, RC Sylvester along with Police Constables 748 Kenton Hazzard, 675 Garness, 327 Rudy Felix and 649 Edward Gibson were charged with Manslaughter after they were suspected of beating the 49-year-old Grenadian-born Canadian citizen into a fatal coma at the St. David's Police Station.

The altercation occurred on December 26, 2011, (Boxing Day), after Bartholomew bear-hugged a plainclothes police woman, whom he allegedly mistook for a long-time friend.

Bartholomew was vacationing on island with his Canadian wife who reportedly went into the police station to use the washroom facilities.

He was taken into custody and ended up in hospital after the alleged beating inside the station.

A Coroner's Inquiry was ordered based on a March 2013 order from High Court Judge, Justice Septimus Rudd, who squashed the laid against the officers and opted for a Coroner's Inquest to take place in keeping with Section (9) of the pre-Constitutional Coroner's Act.

DPP Nelson, QC filed an appeal with the Eastern Caribbean Court of Appeal into Justice Rudd's judgment.

The Court of Appeal has since ruled in favour of the DPP, who recently informed the Coroner of his decision to continue the Inquest despite the ruling in his favour.

The Coroner's Inquest, which commenced in April 2013, is expected to determine the circumstances under which Bartholomew died, where he died, whether it was by accident or an act of violence.

The officers who were originally suspended from active duties were reinstated into the police force based on the ruling of Justice Rudd.

*Kenton Hazzard and Edward Gibson were also charged for the offence*

*The New Today, 25 August 2017*

## PART IX

The Court of Appeal in the meanwhile, heard arguments for and against the ruling of the court quashing the criminal charges and ordering a Coroner's inquest. The decision was returned in favour of the State in that the ruling of the High Court was reversed. The Coroner's inquest was therefore not necessary prior to filing the criminal charges. However, since the inquest was almost concluded it was allowed to run its course.

At the end of the inquest one officer was exonerated and the other four (4) were indicted by the Director of Public Prosecutions. There was the possibility of murder charges being filed against the accused men as it was within the purview of the said Director.

He was constitutionally responsible for instituting, filing, undertaking, overtaking, continuing or discontinuing any criminal charge (Section 71 of the Grenada Constitution).

The four police officers were therefore charged for manslaughter. Bail was granted to them, pending the start of the criminal trial.

# DPP NELSON NOT RULING OUT MURDER CHARGE AGAINST FOUR COPS

*Oscar Bartholomew – the manner of his death left a bad taste in the mouths of many*

Director of Public Prosecution (DPP) Christopher Nelson, QC has dropped strong hints that a charge of murder could be slapped against the four police officers implicated in the December 2012 death of 49-year-old Oscar Bartholomew.

Nelson told ***THE NEW TODAY*** newspaper that new evidence in the possession of the Prosecution could see the charge upgraded from Manslaughter to Murder.

He said that based on the availability of certain evidence, which the prosecution was not privy to at the initial stage of the case, there is a possibility that the charge could be upgraded from Manslaughter to Murder.

According to the DPP, he is anticipating a speedy trial in the case against the four officers who last week Friday were committed to stand trial for Manslaughter for the death of Bartholomew.

He said that he will be pushing for a "speedy trial" because of the already long delay in the legal proceedings which commenced in January 2013.

"The delay has been so long...it has been a long time and I think it's in the public interest that there is no further delay in the matter", he told our News

*(Continue on pg 15*

*Officer Rudy Felix – a case was made out against him*

*Edward Gibson – is now a retired police officer.*

*Rural Constable Sylvester – will have to stand trial for the killing*

*Shaun Garness – one of the four to face high court trial*

*Front page, The New Today, week ending 24 Month 2017*

## DPP Nelson Not Ruling Out Murder Charge Against Four Cops

*From front pg*

News Desk.

"Based on the amount of time that has already passed we will certainly press for a speedy trial", he added.

DPP Nelson expressed optimism that the matter would be put before the High Court in the January 2018 criminal assizes.

The delay in the Oscar Bartholomew matter was due to a high court ruling in 2013 for a Coroner's Inquest to be held at the St. David's Magistrate Court before District Coroner Magistrate Teddy St. Louis to determine who should be held culpable for the death of the naturalised Canadian citizen.

The Inquest ended just after 5:30 p.m. last week Friday when the Coroner's Jury returned a verdict that found four of the five officers in question liable to be charged with Manslaughter for Bartholomew's death.

The 6-member jury panel exonerated 32-year old Police Constable 748 Kenton Hazzard from the charge.

The officers who will go before the high court on trial are Rural Constable Wendell Sylvester, 36, Police Constables 237 Rudy Felix, 29, 675 Shaun Garness, 41, and retired Police Constable 649 Edward Gibson, 63.

The officers listened quietly as the verdict was handed down and shortly afterwards were taken into custody at the St. David's Police Station.

There was a flurry of activities to make arrangement for bail which was granted to them in the sum of $20,000 each, with one surety.

Police sources told *THE NEW TODAY* that the officers will once more be suspended from active duties and put on half month's pay.

DPP Nelson had initially charged the officers with Manslaughter for Bartholomew's death but a high court judge overturned the ruling and ordered that a Coroner's inquest should have been commissioned before the Manslaughter charge was laid.

According to the DPP, who had appealed the decision, which the Eastern Caribbean Court of Appeal reversed and ruled in his favour for the charges to be reinstated against the five officers, this process would have largely contributed to the six-year delay in having the matter dealt with in the high court.

Nelson expressed the view that while lawyers are entitled to take whatever steps deemed appropriate to defend their client(s), in his view "the outcome (of the Coroner's inquest) is a foregone conclusion."

He said, "it was most unfortunate that the judge who heard the police officers judicial review application agreed with them when it was my view that the state, notwithstanding the Coroner's law, had the power to proceed with the preliminary inquiry".

He added that "the legal maneuvering consumed a lot of time and resulted in the delay".

The DPP, who is not constrained to maintain the Manslaughter verdict against the officers, is now waiting on the written dispositions, which are expected to be filed by the Coroner with the Registrar of the Supreme Court and copied to his office, before proceeding with the indictment against the officers.

The law does not provide for a Coroner's verdict to be appealed.

However, the defense attorneys for the four officers have the option to apply for another judicial review.

At the time of his death, Bartholomew, who grew up in the small village of La Tante in St. David's and later became a naturalised Canadian citizen, was on island vacationing with his wife.

He was arrested and taken into police custody on December 26, 2011 (Boxing Day), after bear hugging a plain clothes female police officer who he allegedly mistook for a longtime friend.

He died in hospital days after receiving a fatal beating by police officers inside the St. David's Police Station.

The autopsy report showed that he had sustained more than 40 injuries, including multiple skull fractures and had choked on his vomit after receiving blunt force trauma to the skull.

The report also spoke of blunt force trauma to Bartholomew's chest and hemorrhaging in both lungs, especially on his right side.

*The New Today, 24 Month 2017*

*A meeting with Oscar Bartholomew's widow and the then Prime Minister, Tillman Thomas*

CHAPTER FOURTEEN

# TEARS OF A NATION: MAURICE BISHOP MURDER TRIAL PART 1 (High Court Motion)

*"When elephants fight, it is the grass that suffers."*
AFRICAN PROVERB

*"All men have an instinct for conflict: at least, all healthy men."* HILAIRE BELLOC

On the 13th day of March 1979, the Government of Grenada headed by Sir Eric Matthew Gairy, the political leader of the Grenada United Labour Party (GULP), was overthrown by a military coup d'état undertaken by the opposition party under the leadership of Maurice Bishop, New Jewel Movement (NJM). The NJM set up the People's Revolutionary Government (PRG), with Maurice Bishop being the Prime Minister. The PRG assumed full legislative and executive authority.

As a little boy then, nestled in my grandmother's arms, the transistor radio which was being played by her, periodically brought the news, as there was no internet in those days. I recall the radio personality announcing the overthrow of the Eric Gairy Government . Panic and hysteria reigned at my grandmother's house, as she was an avid supporter of Uncle Gairy, as Sir Eric was referred to by his supporters. My grandmother would sing the political song while she was working or maybe just at home relaxing. Some of the words went like this:

> *We would never let our leader fall; for we love him the best of all; we don't want to fight to show our might, but when we fight, we will fight, fight, fight ... I will fight, fight, fight with all my might ...*

I recalled more of the song but with the passage of time it was erased. The new slogans and chants of the revolution which energised the youths and the whole nation took over. Slogans like, "Forward ever! Backward never!" "Down with imperialism"; "Eat what we grow and grow what we eat"; "Education is liberation"; "It takes a revolution to make a solution!"

In an effort to eradicate illiteracy, the island wide programme, Centre for Popular Education (CPE), was formed. The mission then was to educate the populace both old and young. There was a thirst for learning from all. Elderly persons who were illiterate learned to read, write and on some occasions writing their names for the first time. These were some of the early memories I had of the revolution as a child. Then there came the CPE slogans: "Adult education is a must"; "CPE takes you from where you are to where you want to go"; "CPE is a freedom school"; "With adult education the working people cannot be beaten"; "You and me in CPE learning free"; "CPE says knowledge is power"; "Study and learning are regular habits of a conscious people"; "Every worker a learner"; "CPE for all ah we"; "Never too old to learn, work, study earn"; "Adult education to liberate the nation"; "CPE is good for you"; and many more slogans geared towards awakening the consciousness of the populace.

The numerous military parades, uniforms, inspiring speeches and huge rallies were some of the things I remember about the revolution. The free powdered milk, (called Revo Milk), that was served at the community centres; and yellow butter was a welcome treat. In the parish of Saint David and other parishes, banners, slogans, paintings, white flags with red circles in the middle were all over the island. Women's groups, CPE groups, young militia groups sprung up in every parish. However, I was warned by my grandmother do not join any group, focus on my education and be home as soon as school was finished. The latter advice was later proven to be one of the best bits of advice ever given to me by her, among the many others which were imbedded in me.

During three and a half years of the Revolution, Grenada experienced tremendous development in education, manufacturing, economy and other growth.

The morning of October 19th 1983, I was a student at the Wesley College Secondary School situated at River Road, St. George's. There was a militant, eerie feeling that morning; there was the buzz of students all around the school, speaking about freeing Maurice Bishop who was under 'house arrest'. My grandmother consistently urged me to be home early. She had a famous saying, "As bird wife say 'shreee' get home".

Whatever that meant to her I did not know, but to me it meant be home as soon as school ended. There was the urging from teachers to have students in class, but the idea of freeing Maurice Bishop kept all in a militant mode. We had a male teacher from Russia who was urging students to calm down, but his singular voice was no match for the crowd of students, who were about to embark on a journey to free their leader. The whole nation it seemed had descended onto the capital city. I left school early that morning, walked from River Road to the town of St. George's. It was about a ten (10) minutes' walk. When I got to the town, numerous persons were assembling to demonstrate. The youthful urgings and the force of the crowd were tempting, but I decided to head homeward, I heard my grandmother's voice in my head.

I immediately boarded a bus *en route* to Corinth, St. David, destined to be nestled in the comfort of my grandmother's house and company. As I disembarked the bus I went home and was greeted with joy by my grandmother. She was delighted. I told her what was happening in the city and she said, "Son, you did the right thing, if anything has to happen to you, let it happen where I could see you." The love and tender care emanating from her words, the depth of her love for me was immeasurable. I grew to love and appreciate her more with each day.

Later on in the evening I learnt that Maurice Bishop and seven (7) other persons including members of his cabinet were killed at Fort Rupert, which was the headquarters of the military establishment, the People's Revolutionary Army (PRA). The demonstrators freed Maurice Bishop from house arrest and marched to Fort George; the result was catastrophic. That state of affairs brought tremendous panic, and fear among all in the village of Corinth and the wider country. Communication was limited, so the transistor radio was the main means of island wide communication. On the 19th day of October 1983 at about 9:00 pm, there was a radio announcement that a curfew was in force. Anyone violating the curfew would be shot on sight. All schools were closed. My grandmother ensured no member of her family violated that curfew, not only was she afraid of guns, but also, she was a law abiding citizen. Breaking the law was definitely not going to be entertained, she was a disciplinarian and ensured the radio had batteries; there was kerosene for the lamps and food to eat. My grandfather was an avid farmer so the presence of food was never a cause for concern.

Then on the 25th October 1983, there was an announcement that a United States of America led invasion supported by Caribbean troops descended on the island of Grenada. The mission was referred to as an invasion by some, but a rescue mission by others. At that time I was not concerned about the nomenclature. I just wanted to be free to go outside and play, go back to school to continue my childhood life. I was aware then that there were numerous fatalities and injuries as a result of the incident on October 19th 1983. Numerous persons were detained, arrested and charged for the offence of murder.

There was clamour from family members of deceased persons for the bodies of their deceased loved ones, as they wanted a Christian burial. It was a period of mourning, weeping and anger. Quickly the political tide changed. As a child, flags, slogans, chants, school programs, scholarships, education, local manufacturing industries, National Insurance Board, local banks, the airport construction were all part of the revolution. Grenada was then to my puerile eyes and mind, a beacon in the Caribbean. However, after the death of Maurice Bishop and his colleagues, the positives of the revolution were stifled by the voices of the unlawful arrest, property deprivation, detention without trial and other atrocities allegedly committed during the revolution. During the four and a half years of the revolution, I enjoyed the societal splendour and was oblivious or maybe too young then to understand the full import of the revolution, including its advantages and disadvantages. As I grew older, I was better able to understand and appreciate the 'Grenada revolution', from different lenses.

The Maurice Bishop Murder trial was dubbed, "The Trial of the Century". I was in form four at Wesley College Secondary School, when the trial was being conducted. The weekly newspaper brought a ball by ball commentary of what was happening. There was a strong, outside military presence at the time. I was eager to follow the trial, my love for the law, since then, tempted me to go to the court after school, but I was told children were not allowed.

The trial was conducted on the prison compound, in Richmond Hill. I recall hearing of the men chanting that they were not getting a fair trial. They were placed away from the court, and the mantra on the street then was that all the men should be 'hung'. I was trying to analyse then, in my childish mind, if it was a charge of murder, should not the ones who pulled the trigger solely be charged, and maybe the persons who gave the orders, charged for other offences. With nineteen persons being charged, should there not be separate trials? Would the jury remember all the evidence in relation to nineteen individual accused? I saw numerous 'Perry Mason' movies so I was merely analysing from that perspective. I was extremely quiet, so I never vocalised my thoughts, as it was a principle I learnt at home, that little children should be seen and not heard. I ensured I abided by that principle.

In the interim, the numerous deaths which occurred on Fort George, took a serious toll on Grenadian families and the psyche of its people. It was a sad day in our history.

On the 4th day of December 1986, thirteen of the fourteen persons charged were convicted on eleven counts of murder; and another one was convicted on nine counts of murder. The sentence of death was pronounced on them. There was one lone female in the midst of the accused persons named, Phyllis Coard, the wife of Bernard Coard, who was also sentenced; it was startling for me to hear that pronouncement.

**Mrs Coard being lead away at the time of her sentencing**

*Newspaper article depicting Mrs. Coard being escorted for sentencing*

The newspaper articles and radio programmes consistently spoke of the trial. Numerous persons expressed their views. The brutality of the slaying of Maurice Bishop, Jacqueline Creft, who was allegedly pregnant, and numerous others seemed to outweigh any public sympathy for the accused men.

My appetite for understanding the Maurice Bishop trial only grew, but I was not bold enough to seek answers then. But I knew studying law was my primary passion. I would embark on getting into the legal journey even if all those convicted of murder were to be executed. In or about the year 1997 to 1998, during my period of internship with the law firm of Anselm B. Clouden and Associates, I had numerous occasions to visit Her Majesty's Prison, to interview inmates and to take instructions for the purpose of applying for bail in the High Court. I developed then a great professional relationship with the Prison authorities. On one occasion while visiting, I met and spoke with Ewart Layne, one of the men who were sentenced to death in 1986. My first impression upon seeing him was how tall, calm and well composed he appeared. I was thinking then that so many years in prison would have taken its toll. I am sure it had, but a mechanism for survival there had developed, I was certain, however I never asked.

I was a final year student at the University of the West Indies, Cave Hill, Barbados then, I was of the opinion that Layne immediately saw through me, in that my interest in their case grew as I asked him question after question about the trial process. We agreed to stay in touch. That was the first of many visits. This resulted in a legal relationship that led me on a great legal journey.

On another prison visit, I was introduced to Bernard Coard. I was at the reception area. I saw him walking through the remand yard. He was wearing short pants, a jersey, and had glasses perched on his nose. He was calm, professional, well-spoken and polite. Not the kind of demeanour you expect from a convicted murderer. Despite the fact that I was young enough to be his grandson. His demeanour and respect for me was commendable. I was a bit taken aback. I later learned that he had grown in wisdom, humility, patience and prayer while incarcerated. My interest in their case caused me to develop a visiting prison relationship with them. Whenever I was sent to prison to visit inmates, one or more of the Grenada seventeen were added to the list.

Upon completing reading for the degree in law at Cave Hill campus, I was accepted to the Hugh Wooding Law School to complete the bar exam. My legal journey continued and I kept in contact with Ewart Layne and Bernard Coard. I would periodically send to them via post, 'Trinidad newspapers', or any material of interest. As part of the law school's curriculum a ten (10) week period of internship was mandatory. My period of internship was conducted at the firm of Anselm B. Clouden and Associates. Again, the firm's practice was criminal as well as civil, but my usual errand was the prison and court visits.

During one of my prison visits, Ewart Layne requested that on my return trip to Trinidad, I seek audience with a Trinidadian Lawyer Keith Scotland, who came highly recommended, about the possibility of reviewing their case in an effort to have it reopened either by filing judicial review or constitutional motion application. I had the address and phone number of the attorney, it was memorised: St. Vincent Street, Port of Spain, Trinidad. I was once a telephone operator, so numbers I never forgot. I looked forward to meeting the Trinidadian lawyer.

I met the other inmates on my many visits at prison. On one occasion I met Cecil Prime, who was also convicted. We spoke for a while and he said to me, "If my matter is going to court I would like you to represent me." I was surprised because I was not even a lawyer then. He knew that, but he said, "I just looked at you, and you are the person I want to represent me, no one else." I had a first prospective client. His confidence in me was a bit startling but my desire to get into their case legally was growing with each passing day.

On my return trip to Trinidad to continue my academic studies, I visited the city of Port of Spain and sought the Law office on St. Vincent Street, where I was to meet Scotland. The Secretary whom I interfaced with requested that I wait as she informed him. I waited for what felt like eternity. Then I was summoned to his office. Of course I had no consultation fee but was on a mission to secure an attorney for inmates in another country. As I entered the room I was met with an air of legal confidence. I told him why I came. When I mentioned that I was sent to secure his services for the 'Grenada 17' as they were normally referred to, he immediately leaned forward in his chair, and verbally demonstrated his immediate interest. I got his commitment and contact information. He decided to visit Grenada to meet with the '17'. We developed a professional relationship which carried us on a journey that started in Grenada, continued in St. Lucia, the Privy Council in England and finally back to Grenada, where the case was concluded.

After I graduated from Law School, while I was employed with Ciboney Chambers, it was there that the local, regional and international team of lawyers was garnered for the launch of a new legal attack on the trial of the 'Grenada 17'. The Prison authorities denied lawyers having audience with the Grenada 17, as it was perceived by them, that they were condemned to die and later pardoned, therefore they had no right to counsel. However, after the intervention and legal challenge of such a decision, the authorities relented and allowed the accused men their right to counsel.

To fully appreciate the constitutional challenge mounted by the lawyers, a brief legal historical outline of the background in chronological order is necessary. It was succinctly put in the judgment (GDAHCV2002/443A) of Benjamin J. as he then was, and is reproduced for ease of reference:

## GENERAL UNDISPUTED BACKGROUND

3. On March 13, 1979 the elected Government under the Prime Ministership of Sir Eric Gairy was overthrown by a Revolution led by the New Jewel Movement, then the main opposition party under the leadership of Maurice Bishop. The Revolution set up the People's Revolutionary Government (the PRG) with Maurice Bishop as its Prime Minister and assumed full executive and legislative authority.

4. Shortly, after the date of the Revolution, the judges of the High Court of Grenada and the Associated States and the judges of the Court of Appeal then headquartered in Grenada left Grenada. As a consequence, the PRG proclaimed People's Law Nos. 4 and 14 establishing the Grenada Supreme Court to replace the void left in the court system. Judges were appointed to the said Court at both trial and appellate levels.

5. On October 19, 1983, Prime Minister Maurice Bishop and other persons including members of his Cabinet were shot and killed at Fort Rupert (now styled Fort George) in the town of St George's, the then headquarters of the Revolutionary Army.

6. On October 25, 1983, there was an armed intervention by a coalition of United States military personnel and forces of seven

Caribbean States. During the campaign, some of the Applicants were captured by or surrendered to the invading troops; others were subsequently detained.

7. On October 31, 1983, the Governor General assumed executive power under the Constitution and between that date and November 12, 1983 proclamations were issued preserving the existence of the Grenada Supreme Court established under the People's Laws No. 4 and 14 by the PRG.

8. On February 22, 1984, all the Applicants save for Cecil Prime and others were charged for various offences relating to the death of Maurice Bishop and the others who lost their lives on October 19, 1983. In or about March 1984 the charge of murder was laid against all the Applicants.

9. Following a preliminary inquiry into the charges held between April and August 1984, the Applicants were committed to stand trial on the charges laid and on September 28, 1984 an indictment was preferred in Case No. 19 of 1984 containing eleven counts of murder.

10. General Elections were held on December, 1984 and Parliament was convened for the first time, since the Revolution on December 29, 1984.

11. By an originating motion filed in or about October 1984, the Applicants challenged the validity of the High Court. The motion was dismissed and the Court held that the High Court had jurisdiction to hear the charges against the Applicants. An appeal against the dismissal was unfavourably disposed of by the Court of Appeal of Grenada on May 10, 1985.

12. The trial on the Indictment in No. 19 of 1984 commenced March, 3 1986, before Hon. Mr. Justice Dennis Byron (as he then was). The Prosecution alleged that a series of acts resulted in the deaths of the eleven persons named on the indictment.

13. On December 4, 1986, the Applicants were convicted of murder on all eleven counts of the indictment by the Jury. The sentence of death

was pronounced in respect of each Applicant as prescribed by the Criminal Code of Grenada.

14. During the course of the trial, the trial judge heard an interlocutory motion filed by the Applicants in November 1985. The motion was dismissed and an application for a stay of the trial pending an appeal against the said motion was refused. The appeal was heard and disposed of on May 17, 1986.

15. On June 3, 1986 the Applicants filed Civil Suit No. 191 of 1986 seeking constitutional redress arising from the ruling of the Court of Appeal on May 17, 1986. The said suit was dismissed and an appeal was made therefrom. That appeal (No. 5 of 1998) was heard by the Court of Appeal on July 23, 1986 and the decision was reversed. The Court of Appeal, however, refused to accede to the granting of a stay of the trial on Indictment.

16. On December 10, 1986 the Applicants lodged appeals against their convictions and sentences. On July 12, 1991 the Court of Appeal dismissed the Applicants' appeals and affirmed their convictions and sentences. It is common ground that although the judgments were read in court, the judgments in written form and copies of the proceedings have not been issued.

17. On July 19, 1991 the Governor General assented to the Constitutional Judicature (Restoration) Act No. 19 of 1991 and by Proclamation S.R.O 14 of even date, August 1, 1991 was appointed as the date for its coming into force. The Proclamation was revoked on July 30, 1991. The said Act was eventually brought into force by Proclamation with effect from August 15, 1991.

18. On July 29, 1991 the Applicants filed Motion No. 1 of 1991 in the Court of Appeal of Grenada. The Motion was heard by the said Court of Appeal, which court, after rejecting a preliminary objection to its jurisdiction, went on to dismiss the Motion, refusing to re-hear the appeals and to stay the execution of the death sentences.

19. On August 15, 1991 a warrant was read to and served on each Applicant. The document was signed by the Governor General and

is headed "Commutation of Death Sentence and Warrant for Imprisonment". His Excellency purported to exercise the powers vested in him by section 72 (1) of the Constitution. The said Warrant (the full text of which is set out in this judgment) purported to grant a pardon to the respective Applicant on condition that he be kept in custody to hard labour for the remainder of his natural life and confined at Richmond Hill Prisons. Each warrant is of the same wording.

20. The Applicants have since been kept in confinement at the said Prison and so remain.

21. On January 30, 1992 the Applicants brought a notice of motion to the Court of Appeal of the Eastern Caribbean Supreme Court as restored by Act No. 19 of 1991. The Court of Appeal heard the Motion and dismissed same on November 8, 1993.

The death penalty was mandatory for all persons convicted of the offence of murder, irrespective as to the nature and character of the offence. The Privy Council in 2001 in the case of Reyes v. R No. 64 of 2001, and Hughes v. R PCA No. 91 of 2001 and Fox v. R PCA no. 66 of 2000, ruled that the mandatory imposition of the sentence of death on persons convicted of murder was degrading, inhumane and therefore unconstitutional. There was therefore an apparent opening for the Grenada 17 to challenge their conviction and sentence. However, because they had so many challenges and in one instance to the Privy Council, the question arose as to whether they exhausted the appellate process? Or could they now benefit from the new change in the legal position which was not the case when they filed their numerous appeals.

The commutation of the death penalty by the Governor General to the rest of their natural lives was also challenged as unconstitutional null and void. The accused men never received their record of proceedings or transcripts from their trial or a written judgment in their cause and as a result, a constitutional challenge was launched in that regard. Also filed was a request for compensation, an order for the accused release forthwith, an order for the quashing of the sentence 'for the remainder of the accused natural lives' and costs.

There was a team of lawyers for the accused men namely; Keith Scotland, Ruggles Ferguson, Sola Coard, Cajeton Hood and myself.

The Attorney General was represented by Karl Hudson Phillips QC and Rohan Phillip. The arguments lasted a period of two days, the 14th and 15th July 2003, judgment was delivered on 16th March 2004. In sum, the court agreed with our arguments and concluded the following:

## CONCLUSION

In conclusion, the following are the declarations and orders of the Court:

1. It is declared that the sentence imposed upon the Applicants at their trial was unconstitutional and illegal.

2. It is further declared that the imposition of the term of imprisonment for the remainder of the applicants' natural lives by the Governor General pursuant to advice of the Chairman of the Advisory Committee on the Prerogative of Mercy is unconstitutional, illegal, null and void.

3. It is further declared that the failure by the Respondent to provide the Applicants with the written reasons, used to justify the dismissal of the Applicants' appeal against conviction is unconstitutional and illegal.

4. It is ordered that:

    a. The sentence of imprisonment for the remainder of the Applicants natural lives be quashed.

    b. The Applicants be remanded to custody and brought before a judge of the High Court within 42 days to be sentenced under the convictions dated December 4, 1986.

    c. The Applicants be paid monetary compensation to be assessed by a Judge in chambers and paid to the Applicants with the said written reasons.

5. The Respondents shall pay the costs of the Applicants in the sum of $15,000.00

This was the accused first sighting of the possibility of being released into society since their incarceration in 1983. It was in excess of twenty years after their initial arrest. One newspaper's headline read, "Bishop Killers smell freedom". It was a well-reasoned decision by Benjamin J. and despite the appellate process, his judgment was pivotal in the final determination of the matter.

Tactically, the accused men could not have been released until forty two (42) days since they had to be resentenced pursuant to the court's order. The Attorney General's Chambers, through the Court of Appeal, filed an application to stay the judgment pending the outcome of an appeal they had filed.

On the 26th day of April 2004, the Court of Appeal, delivered a written decision in Appeal No. 10 of 2004, by Justice of Appeal Michael Gordon QC, exercising the discretion of the court to stay the judgment of Benjamin J.

The legal journey continued with preparation for the hearing of the matter in the Court of Appeal, which included legal research from around the world and tapping into every legal resource available. Many of the

BISHOP KILLERS SMELL FREEDOM!!!

Leon Cornwall holds onto a little child

Comrades Selwyn Strachan and Chester Humphrey

Lieutnant-Colonel Ewart Layne walks out of the court in a jovial mood as she smiles at the decision in their favour

'Sello" Strachan takes a hug from a white female

*Front page, Grenada Today, week ending 19 March 2004*

# Bishop Killers Smell Freedom!!!

*Selwyn Strachan (r) talks to two of his supporters outside the court house*

After 23 years in solitary confinement at the Richmond Hill Prison a High Court Judge in Grenada on Tuesday morning quashed the existing death and life sentence imposed on thirteen revolutionary soldiers convicted of killing former Prime Minister Maurice Bishop.

The forty four page judgement which brought some measure of relief to members of the Bernard Coard gang described the death and life sentences as illegal and unconstitutional.

That Judgement was handed down during a sitting of the Court by resident High Court Judge Justice Kenneth Benjamin.

"In conclusion the following are the declaration and orders of the Court; 1: it is declared that the sentence of death imposed upon the applicants at their trial was unconstitutional and illegal"

2: "it is further declared that the imposition of the term of imprisonment for the remainder of the applicants natural life by the Governor General pursuant to the advice of the chairman of the advisory committee on the Prerogative of Mercy is unconstitutional, illegal, null and void"

3, "it is further declared that the failure by the respondents to provide the applicants with written reasons used to justify the dismissal of the applicants appeal against conviction is unconstitutional and illegal"

4; "It is ordered that, (a): the sentence of imprisonment of the applicants for their natural life be quashed, (b): the applicants be remanded to custody and brought before a judge of the High Court within 42 days to be sentence under the convictions dated December 4th 1986, (c) the applicants be paid monetary compensation to be assessed by a judge in chambers and paid to the applicants by the respondents as a result of their failure to provide the applicants with the said written reasons

5; "The respondents shall pay the cost of the proceedings in the sum of ECC $15,000.00".

Those were the orders of the Court as pronounced by Justice Benjamin in respect to the constitutional motion filed by former deputy Prime Minister Bernard Coard, ex-military commander General Hudson Austin, former Minister of Mobilization Selwyn Strachan, Major Leon Cornwall., ex-Lieutenant-Colonel. Ewart Layne and others convicted of killing marxist revolutionary Prime Minister Maurice Bishop along with 17

*'Comrade' Selwyn Strachan and fellow convict Leon "Bogo" Cornwall leaving the court after the landmark decision by Justice Benjamin*

*(Continues on pg 16)*

*Grenada Today, 19 March 2004*

accused were holders of law degrees and in some instances Master's Degrees in law which they had pursued while incarcerated. The accused men not only pursued studies to enhance themselves not knowing whether they would ever be released but also during their many years were instrumental in creating classes at the prisons for teaching inmates, thereby enabling them to reintegrate into society upon release. In some instances being self-sufficient.

The submission was filed by the Respondent and response filed on behalf of the accused men. The lawyers and accused men were patiently awaiting the hearing date for the appeal. It soon came. A notice was issued, that the matter would be heard in the Court of Appeal in the island of St. Lucia from the 22nd to the 24th of November 2004.

CHAPTER FIFTEEN

# TEARS OF A NATION: MAURICE BISHOP MURDER TRIAL

## PART 2 (Court of Appeal Hearing)

*"In extreme youth, in our most humiliating sorrow, we think we are alone. When we are older we find that others have suffered too."* SUZANNE MOARNY

*"When sorrows come, they come not single spies. But in battalions!"* WILLIAM SHAKESPEARE (HAMLET, ACT IV, SCENE V)

The flight arrangements were made to travel to St. Lucia for the appeal hearing. A total of four lawyers embarked on the journey on behalf of the accused men. Keith Scotland and Cajeton Hood were the lawyers for all the accused men except Bernard Coard and Ewart Layne. Ruggles Ferguson and I were the lawyers for Bernard Coard and Ewart Layne. We embarked on the Leeward Islands Air Transport (LIAT) flight destined for St. Lucia. We made preflight accommodation arrangements with the Bay Gardens Hotel at Gros Islet, in the said island. I had visited that hotel many times before, it was like home to me; the surrounding was all too familiar.

The evening we landed. Preparation was finally made for the court hearing as we continued the legal journey which started years ago. We awoke early in the morning of the hearing and decided to take a jog to the direction of Castries; Ruggles, Scotland and I. The adrenalin rush catapulted the run almost to Castries, as there was the need to clear our minds. We soon got back to the hotel, dressed in full legal regalia and departed for the Court of Appeal located in the city of Castries in St. Lucia.

The hearing lasted a total of three days, being the 22nd, 23rd and 24th November 2004. The court's quorum consisted of; Justices of Appeal Hon. Brian Alleyne SC, Hon. Michael Gordon QC and Hon. Suzie d'Auvergne. Upon the conclusion of the matter, we all speculated as to the likely outcome as there was no indication as to what direction the court would take, and even when there was the slightest of indication there was absolutely no guarantee until the judgment was delivered.

The court reserved its judgment. We all departed the island of St. Lucia returning to our respective places of abode. The wait for the judgment felt long and arduous for the accused men. However, they seemed calm, composed and peaceful. It occurred to me that maybe the years in prison had caused them to develop a deep sense of humility, patience and acceptance.

Within ninety (90) days after the arguments at the Court of Appeal in St. Lucia, the judgment was delivered, as promised. On the 14th day of February 2005, the court delivered its written judgment.

The decision of the Court of Appeal was indeed a disastrous blow as it in effect reversed the decision of the High Court and, effectively, allowed the appeal of the Attorney General's chambers. The court ruled that; there was no legal constitutional violation sufficient to quash the conviction or the sentence. The sentence for the remainder of the accused natural lives was not unlawful. The grant of a pardon on condition that the accused serve a sentence for the remainder of their natural lives was not unconstitutional or unlawful. The failure to provide written reasons cannot amount to an award of damages (money payment), since, an oral ruling was delivered. Finally, the issues before the court could have been or were raised before the former Court of Appeal prior to the restoration of the present Court of Appeal by the Constitutional Judicature (Restoration) Act No. 19 of 1991. The appeal therefore was dismissed in totality.

The resilience of the defence team would not allow a decision reversing the lower court to suffer a final blow; it was decided long before the decision was delivered, should the court disagree with the appeal in totality, an appeal to the Privy Council was mandatory. The case was indeed a politically charged one, it affected the lives and psyche of the whole island of Grenada, in that there were dates on the calendar which resurrected annual emotional significance for many persons for diverse reasons.

The newspaper gave the case national appeal. The headlines always portrayed every move that was being made legally on behalf of the accused men. The Court of Appeal defeat was extensively reported.

In the year 1991, it was widely circulated that five (5) of the accused men were due to be hung by the neck until dead, which was the means of

# DEFEAT AGAIN FOR COARD!!!!

*Keith Scotland - The Trinidad lawyer representing some of the Bishop killers*

*Bernard Coard- to remain in Prision*

The OECS Court of Appeal has turned down yet another move by the Bernard Coard Gang of Prisoners in Grenada to be released from the Richmond Hill prison.

In a decision handed down Monday in Castries, St. Lucia, the court brushed aside the latest court action by Coard and company as a "further collateral attack" on the former Court of Appeal which presided over their matter in the Maurice Bishop Murder trial in 1986.

One of the Court of Appeal Justices, Michael Gordon cited the arguments put forward on behalf of the imprisoned men as representing "a misuse of the court's constitutional jurisdiction".

According to Gordon, the OECS Court of Appeal has no jurisdiction to enquire into matters adjudicated upon by the former court.

"I am in full agreement.... that as these matters were canvassed before the former Court of Appeal, this precludes the applicants (Coard and Company) from seeking to have (new) Courts examine the issues afresh", he said.

The latest court case involves an appeal by the State of Grenada against a ruling in March 2004 by Guyanese high court judge, Kenneth Benjamin that the death sentence imposed on the prisoners was "unconstitutional and illegal".

Justice Benjamin also ruled that the prisoners should be brought before a judge of the high court for proper sentencing.

Coard, the former deputy Prime Minister of the ill-fated 1979-83 leftist People's Revolutionary Government (PRG) was sentenced along with fourteen other government and military officials for the murder of Prime Minister Maurice Bishop on October 19, 1983.

The trial was heard in a high court which Coard and Bishop created to replace the constitutionally-recognised court of Grenada which owed its existence on "the doctrine of necessity".

The Grenada Revolutionary leaders were forced to set up their own court system after the OECS court pulled out of the island in the wake of the suspension of the Grenada constitution by the PRG.

As part of his ruling, Gordon described as "another collateral attack" the arguments put forward by lawyers representing the Grenada prisoners that the Court of Appeal has the power to further enquire into whether the constitutional rights of the Coard Gang were breached on the important issue of jury selection.

The Court of Appeal judge also commented on the contention of the prisoners that the death sentence imposed upon them in the previous court was "unconstitutional and illegal".

He noted that the defendants had articulated that despite the conclusive nature of the proceedings and the dismissal of their appeal against conviction and sentence, they nonetheless had a right to rely on "subsequent judicial decisions" in their matter.

"By that language I understand them to be acknowledging that they have had the benefit of, and exhausted, all of the opportunities of appeal available to them in a criminal trial and that they are seeking to tread that very narrow path around issue estoppel amongst other things", he remarked.

Justice Gordon ruled that the conviction of the Coard Gang cannot be considered in terms of the ruling which the Privy Council in London handed down in the Pratt and Morgan case from Jamaica.

The Privy Council ruled that if a person was on death row for five years without the death sentence being carried out then the State is duty-bound to lesser the sen-

*(Continues on page 7)*

*Front page, Grenada Today, week ending 18 February 2005*

# *Coard stays behind bars*

***It is now public knowledge that the Bernard Coard Gang of Prisoners have lost another legal battle in their attempts to be released from the Richmond Hill prison.***

***Coard, the former deputy Prime Minister of Grenada from 1979-83, was convicted in 1986 for the murder three years earlier of marxist Prime Minister Maurice Bishop and half his Cabinet in a bloody coup at Fort Rupert (George).***

***The killings were sparked off by a bitter feud for leadership of the New Jewel Movement (NJM) which created the Grenada Revolution when the party seized power on March 13, 1979 in a coup d'etat against the elected Eric Gairy Government.***

***Just over a week ago, the OECS Court of Appeal after hearing arguments from lawyers representing Coard and twelve other former revolutionary figures delivered its judgement on the matter.***

***As a public service, GRENADA TODAY has decided to bring some of the high points in the judgement delivered by Court of Appeal judge, Justice Brian Alleyne of Dominica:***

*Jacqueline Creft - the executed Minister of Education of Bishop's PRG*

*Sir Frederick Smith - the Barbadian jurist who headed the Court of Appeal which dealt with the Maurice Bishop murder trial*

It is contended on behalf of the respondents, however, that life imprisonment as a common law punishment was abolished by the operation of sections 10 and 11 of the Criminal Code of Grenada. Even if that is so, section 11 (e) explicitly preserves, if that were necessary, the power of her Majesty, or of the Governor General as the representative of Her Majesty, to grant a pardon or to remit or commute in whole or in part, or to respite, the execution of any sentence passed or to be passed.

Learned counsel for the respondent (Coard and Company) submitted that the sentence of life imprisonment in Grenada as a statutory sentence is provided for in only a very few cases not including murder.

However, the Constitution, at section 72, empowers the Governor-General, among other things, to grant a pardon subject to lawful condition, or to substitute a less severe form of punishment for any punishment imposed on any person for any offence.

It cannot I think be questioned that life imprisonment, even 'for the rest of natural life', is a less severe form of punishment than the death penalty.

Learned counsel for the respondents (Coard) argued that the power to substitute a less serve form of punishment is limited to the power to determine the nature of the punishment, but does not extent to the power to decide the extent of the punishment.

To paraphrase counsel's words, the Governor-General could properly determine that the respondents should serve a term of imprisonment, but could not properly determine the extent of the term of imprisonment, a matter which could be determined by a court.

*(Continues on page 10)*

*Grenada Today, 25 February 2005*

# Coard and gang to stay in jail

for the brutal killing of Prime Minister, Maurice Bishop, and other cabinet colleagues during the 1983 coup d'etat.

Hon. Justice of Appeal, Bryan Alleyne on Monday handed down the judgement during a special sitting in St. Lucia, squashing the March 2004 judgement handed down by Grenada Supreme Court judge, Kenneth Benjamin.

In a lengthy judgement handed to the Court, the Appeal Court judge, which also included Justice Michael Gordon and Acting Justice of Appeal, Suzidid Auvergna ruled that the grounds under which the men were convicted were well within the constitution.

Lawyers for the fourteen, Trinidadian -born Keith Scotland, and Grenadian Cajeton Hood, Ruggles Ferguson and Dereck Sylvester, argued that the continued detention of the men was illegal. Additionally, it was illegal for the Governor General at the time to have pronounced a death sentence in law, and to date, no written judgement is being given in the matter.

Having heard the argument, the judge, Benjamin, handed down judgement favouring the lawyers argument.

However, before the men were released, the government led by Jamaican-born, Hugh Wildman, appealed the judge's ruling and asked for a stay of execution, which was subsequently granted.

One day after having his judgement overturned, leading defence lawyer, Scotland, told reporters he is disappointed, but not discouraged.

The Trinidadian lawyer said, his team would now be heading to the Privy Council, having satisfied themselves that they have a strong arguable case.

Scotland said, he is now hoping that his team would approach the matter with

the greatest level of urgency.

The application for leave he said, would be filed within a fortnight and he hopes thereafter to have the matter heard as quickly as possible.

The men were convicted on December 8th 1988 and sentenced to death. However, in 1991, the sentence was commuted to life in prison on recommendation of the Mercy Committee led by the Governor General.

*Grenada Informer, 18 February 2005*

carrying out the death penalty in Grenada. There was no option of firing squad or lethal injection. The Grenadian Voice Newspaper reported that the five men earmarked to be executed were; Bernard Coard, Ewart Layne, Lester Redhead, Callistus Bernard and Leon Cornwall.

The sentences were later commuted to life imprisonment and in some instances for the remainder of their natural lives.

Consequent upon the Court of Appeal ruling; proceedings to the Judicial Committee of the Privy Council, which is the final appellate court for the State of Grenada and its dependencies, was the final hope. The services of a London based attorney Edward Fitzgerald QC was sought and he was instrumental, together with regional and local attorneys, to finally bring an end to the matter.

Pursuant to notice of motion filed in the Court of Appeal, an application for conditional leave to appeal to Her Majesty in Council was heard before the Court of Appeal on the 27th and 29th June 2005,

## Appeal Court rejects freedom for the 13

fter keeping the appellants and he prisoners waiting for months or the result, the Eastern aribbean Court of Appeal finally ruled in favour of the Government of Grenada, approving their appeal to hold 13 of the "Grenada 17" in prison.

In a 43-page judgment, the three-member Eastern Caribbean sided with the government — represented by Mr Karl Hudson-Phillip — by ruling that the 13 prisoners' arguments had already been ruled on, effectively striking down a March ruling by Grenada's High Court that overturned their life sentences.

Monday's ruling also barred the prisoners from "re-litigating" their case, though it wasn't clear if this would block their representative, Keith Scotland, from appealing to the Privy Council, the highest court of appeal for most former British colonies in the Caribbean.

In a judgment written by Justice Brian Alleyne, SC; and endorsed by Justice Michael Gordon, QC; and Acting Justice of Appeal, Madam Suzie d'Auvergne, the Court ruled that the arguments presented had been heard and ruled on years ago.

· *Please turn to Page 03*

## The Hangers
## *Plan to hang five*

*By our Political Reporter*

**THE NATIONAL Democratic Congress government has elected to go down in history as "The Hangers" or, in local parlance, "The Hengmen".**

**Cabinet has decided to hang five of the fourteen persons whose death sentences were upheld by the Court of Appeal two weeks ago at the end of the legal processes in the Maurice Bishop Murder Trial.**

Before cabinet was the report of the Advisory Committee on the Prerogative of Mercy which, *The Grenadian Voice* understands decided not to recommend mercy for any of the convicts.

According to one report the government here was being pressured by regional governments to carry out the sentence of the court speedily. It is also known that there are several persons and groups which feel that the fourteen should be hanged as well as a large section of the community - including such groups as the Conference of Churches, a Group of Concerned Women and the local group of Amnesty International who feel that not only should they not be hanged but that the death penalty should be abolished as being cruel and inhumane punishment.

The five which the cabinet decided to hang are former Deputy Prime Minister, Bernard Coard; former PRA officers Lieut. Col. Ewart Layne; Captain Lester Redhead; and Lieut. Callistus Bernard, as well as former Ambassador to Cuba Leon Cornwall.

It is reported that the hangings are to take place as early as next week but head of the mercy committee Mrs. Joan Purcell would make no comment other than to confirm that the committee had met and considered the matter and had submitted its recommendations to Governor General, Sir Paul Scoon.

*Part of Front Page of*
**The Grenadian Voice**
*July 27, 1991*

*Front page, The Grenadian Voice, week ending 19 February 2005*

## Privy council to hear case of Grenada 17

**By Michael Bascombe**

LAWYERS representing the so-called Grenada 17 head to London this week to present their case to the Privy Council, to have the remaining prisoners released.

Their petition follows the weekend release of three of the 17, Andy Mitchell, Vincent Joseph and Cosmos Richardson, who spent the last 23 years behind bars for the killing of former Prime Minister Maurice Bishop and some of his cabinet colleagues in the 1983 coup.

The team of lawyers, led by Edward Fitzgerald QC, contends that the men did not get a fair trial following the coup and that the mandatory death sentence imposed at the time was illegal and unconstitutional.

The British Law Lords will hear arguments from December 11 to 13, during which the attorneys will make a case for the release of the remaining 14 men.

On their release, Mitchell, Joseph and Richardson refused to give comments to waiting journalists while some family members and friends greeted them, but their lawyer Keith Scotland said it was an historic moment in their lives.

"My clients Messrs Andy Mitchell, Vincent Joseph and Cosmos Richardson express their relief and happiness on being released from prison.

"They express their thanks to family friends and other well-wishers in and out of Grenada, who have supported them in many different ways over the years.

"They desire to put the terrible and traumatic past behind them and to re-unite with their families and loved ones and to re-build their lives in a peaceful, disciplined and productive manner," Scotland told reporters.

Under the law governing sentencing regulations, inmates' sentences are reduced by one-third if they have been deemed to be industrious and well-behaved.

However, the Ministry of National Security said that the release of these men was not based on any court action, but is instead as a direct result of the sentences being completed.

"It is government's hope that Mr. Joseph, Mr. Mitchell and Mr. Richardson will rejoin society as productive members of the community and will live a peaceful life, having learned from their experience," the ministry said in a statement.

**Savouring freedom after 23 years, the former revolutionaries pose with their lawyer Keith Scotland.**

*The Grenada Advocate, 8 December 2006*

before Hon. Brian Alleyne SC, Hon. Michael Gordon QC and Hon. Denys Barrow SC. A written decision was delivered. Despite opposition from the Attorney General, conditional leave was granted. Thereafter, final leave was filed as was the procedural requirement, prior to the Privy Council having legal authority to hear the appeal.

It was agreed that should the Court of Appeal refuse leave to appeal, the Privy Council would be petitioned directly for leave, as could also be done. However, that step was avoided as leave was granted. The date was set for the hearing of the appeal, December 2006. The third leg of the journey was in preparatory stages, as the lawyers prepared to travel to England to have the legal issues heard and determined by five (5) Law Lords of the Judicial Committee of the Privy Council.

CHAPTER SIXTEEN

# TEARS OF A NATION: MAURICE BISHOP MURDER TRIAL PART 3 (Privy Council Appeal)

*"Sorrow ends not when it seemeth done."*
WILLIAM SHAKESPEARE (RICHARD II, ACT I, SCENE II)

In December 2006, the legal journey in England was being led by Edward Fitzgerald QC. It was a rewarding and enriching legal experience at the highest appellate court. Since my admission to practise law, it was my desire to appear before the said court. I had the good fortune of having other visits to Her Majesty's Privy Council since then.

There was a team of lawyers from Grenada including Ruggles Ferguson, Cajeton Hood and myself; from Trinidad and Tobago Keith Scotland. We were greeted by a London based Lawyer from Grenada, Jacqueline Mc Kenzie, whose reception, hospitality and courtesy we were grateful for.

The Privy Council's office was then located at #9 Downing Street, in the city of London. We resided at Jury's Inn, West Croydon. On the day of the hearing we relocated to accommodation much closer to the court.

We were joined by Edward Fitzgerald QC, who presented the arguments before the court. The court was set up in a manner that the attorneys for the Appellant used a separate door to enter the court to that of the attorneys for the Respondents. It ensured there was no communication between respective parties during the conduct of the proceedings.

We all sat at the Bar Table, fully robed as each party had a microphone to address the Law Lords. The court reporter then announced court was in session; that all should rise. The five Law Lords emerged from behind the court and sat. Their tables were at the same level with ours, which was unusual for every other court that I have appeared. In the Magistrate's Court, High Court and Court of Appeal the Judges sit at an elevated position.

The Law Lords were; Lord Bingham of Cornhill, Lord Hoffman, Lord Carswell, Lord Phillips of Worth Matravers and Lord Brown of Eaton-under-Heywood. The arguments took the form of an intellectual legal discourse on the law. An in-depth analysis into the individual appeals was conducted in an atmosphere of utter humility, respect and dignity for all involved. Both sides presented their arguments. The matter was adjourned for decision.

It felt like a roller coaster ride, as there was no indication whether the court was leaning in any particular direction. I believed they had ensured that they would allow the proceedings to be fully ventilated, thereafter deliberate and produce their reasons. Within ninety days of the hearing, on the 7th February, 2007, which was the day celebrated as Grenada's Independence, the Privy Council delivered its written decision.

The judgment of the court was delivered by Lord Hoffman. It was a day of elation for the accused men since the Privy Council ruled that: "... The appeal should be allowed and that it be declared that the sentence of death imposed upon the appellants was invalid and that the case should be remitted to the Supreme Court of Grenada for the appellants to be resentenced in accordance with the construction of section 230 of the Criminal Code, taking into account the progress made by the appellants during their time in prison."

## CONVICTIONS PRESERVED

The convictions for murder in the Maurice Bishop murder trial were preserved by the Privy Council. Mr. Edward Fitzgerald QC asked the Privy Council for leave to challenge the constitutionality of the convictions; and for that purpose, sought leave to introduce affidavits concerning the facts of the case, the pre trial investigation and the conduct of the trial. The Privy Council refused the application, branding it as simply an attempt to use the procedure of a constitutional motion to obtain from the Privy Council a review of the 1991 decision of the Grenada Court of Appeal. The Privy Council pointed out that, as the law then stood, the decision of the Grenada Court of Appeal was final, and section 7 (4) of the 1991 Act made it clear that the said decision was not to be any less final because an appeal to the Privy Council had been restored. The Privy Council said that all the points raised by Mr. Fitzgerald in support of his application, supported by the new affidavits were or could have been taken at the Grenada Court of Appeal. The Privy Council, reiterating its earlier jurisprudence, emphasised that the use of a constitutional motion to avoid the finality of a decision dismissing a criminal appeal is ordinarily impermissible; because there may not be regarding every criminal case parallel remedies available: one by appeal, the other by originating constitutional application; lest the Constitution be given an interpretation quite irrational and subversive of the rule of law.

# Privy Council Appeal No. 10 of 2006

Appellants
**Bernard Coard**
**Callistus Bernard**
**Lester Redhead**
**Christopher Stroude**
**Hudson Austin**
**Liam James**
**Leon Cornwall**
**John Anthony Ventour**
**Dave Bartholomew**
**Ewart Layne**
**Colville McBarnett**
**Selwyn Strachan**
**Cecil Prime**

v.

**The Attorney General** - Respondent

From:
**The Court of Appeal of Grenada**

- - - - - - - - - - - - - - - - -

**Judgement of the Lords of the Judicial Committee of the Privy Council**

Delivered the 7th February 2007.

- - - - - - - - - - - - - - - - -

Present at the hearing:
**Lord Bingham of Cornhill**
**Lord Hoffmann**
**Lord Phillips of Worth Matravers**
**Lord Carswell**
**Lord Brown of Eaton-under-Heywood**

- - - - - - - - - - - - - - - - -

[Delivered by **Lord Hoffmann**.]

**1.** On 4 December, 1986, the 13 appellants were convicted by Byron J and a jury of the murders of Maurice Bishop and ten others and sentenced to death. Mr. Bishop was at the time Prime Minister of Grenada, having come to power as a result of a revolution which ousted the previous constitutional government in 1979. In 1983, the revolutionary party split into two factions led by Mr. Bishop and the appellant Mr. Coard respectively. On 19 October, 1983, there was a violent confrontation in which Mr. Bishop and the others were executed by Mr. Coard's supporters. A week later, Grenada was occupied by the armed forces of the United States and other Caribbean islands and constitutional government under the Governor-General restored. Elections for a new Parliament were held in December 1984.

**2.** Until the 1979 revolution, Grenada shared a Supreme Court with five other Associated States pursuant to the West Indies Associated States Supreme Court (Grenada) Act, which gave effect in Grenada to the West Indies Associated States Supreme Court Order SI 1967. The Act was repealed by People's Law No. 4 of 25 March 1979, which established instead a Supreme Court of Grenada, consisting of a High Court and Court of Appeal.

**3.** The West Indies Associated States (Appeals to the Privy Council)(Grenada) Order 1967 SI 1967 No. 224 contained machinery for an appeal to the Privy Council from the Court of Appeal established under the West Indies Associated States Supreme Court Order. Section 3 provides that:

"An appeal shall lie to Her Majesty in Council from decisions of the Court given in any proceedings originating in a State in such cases as may be prescribed by or in pursuance of the Constitution of that State."

**4.** Section 104 of the 1973 Constitution of Grenada conferred a right of appeal to the Privy Council, as of right in some cases and with special leave in any case. But People's Law No. 84 of 1979 abolished appeals to the Privy Council with effect from 13 March, 1979. The first Act of the restored Parliament (Act 1 of 1985) confirmed the validity of all laws made by the revolutionary government. Thus, at the time that the appellants were indicted on 28 September, 1984, the Grenada judicial system consisted of a High Court and Court of Appeal established under People's Law No. 4 of 1979. The appellants brought a constitutional motion challenging the validity and jurisdiction of the High Court, but this was dismissed. An appeal to the Court of Appeal was likewise dismissed. The appellants then petitioned the Privy Council for special leave to appeal, but leave was refused in July, 1985, on the ground that the right of appeal had been abolished by People's Law No. 84 of 1979: see Mitchell v Director of Public Prosecutions [1986] AC 73.

**5.** At the trial, the appellants withdrew instructions from their counsel and took no part. In fact, they behaved disruptively and from time to time, had to be removed from the court room. Although they gave no evidence, they made what they called "indicative statements" from the dock, saying what they would have said in their defence if they had been minded to do so. The jury convicted them. Section 230 of the Criminal Code, which has remained in force at all material times, provides that the mandatory sentence for murder is death. The appellants were sentenced accordingly.

**6.** After conviction and sentence, the appellants appealed to the Grenada Court of Appeal. The appeal was heard over a lengthy period during 1990 and the appellants raised such matters as the unfavourable publicity at the time of the trial, the selection and attitude of the jury, the circumstances in which confessions were obtained, non-disclosure of material in the hands of the prosecution and alleged defects in the summing up. The Court of Appeal dismissed the appeals in July, 1991. It appears that detailed oral judgements were given over a period of three days. No written judgement has been provided and it appears that no transcript or written note of the oral judgements was made.

**7.** Section 74(1) of the Constitution provides that where any person has been sentenced to death, the Minister designated for the purpose must refer the case to the Advisory Committee on the Prerogative of Mercy and, after obtaining its advice, "decide in his own deliberate judgement" whether to advise the Governor-General to exercise his powers under section 72(1), on behalf of Her Majesty, to (among other things) "grant a pardon, either free or subject to lawful conditions" or to "substitute a less severe form of punishment". By section 72(2), these powers must be exercised in accordance with the advice of the Minister.

**8.** On 15 August, 1991, the Governor-General signed warrants in respect of each of the appellants which recited that the Minister had decided to advise the Governor-General to commute the sentence of death to one of life imprisonment. The warrant then said that the Governor-General, in accordance with that advice, granted the appellant a pardon "on condition that [he] shall be kept in custody to hard labour for the remainder of his natural life".

**9.** Since then, the appellants have remained in custody. During that period, there have been developments in the law. On 2 April, 2001, the Eastern Caribbean Court of Appeal,

Lord Bingham of Cornhill.

presided over by Byron CJ (who had been the trial judge in this case), held in an appeal from St. Lucia that the mandatory death penalty was an "inhuman or degrading punishment" and unconstitutional. This decision was affirmed by the Privy Council on 11 March, 2002: see Regina v Hughes [2002] 2 AC 259. In consequence, the appellants filed a constitutional motion on 23 September, 2002, claiming that the sentences imposed upon them had been unlawful. It followed that the warrants of commutation under which they were held in custody had no legal basis and were likewise unlawful.

**10.** To this central submission, Mr. Fitzgerald QC, on behalf of the appellants, added further grounds of complaint. Their Lordships will briefly deal with these before returning to the substantial point in the appeal.

**11.** First, he submitted that, as much of the trial took place in the absence of the appellants (they having been removed because they were attempting to disrupt it), section 8(2) of the Constitution precluded the imposition of a sentence of death or imprisonment. The relevant part of this section reads:

"...except with his own consent, the trial shall not take place in his absence, unless he so conducts himself as to render the continuance of the proceedings in his presence impracticable and the court has ordered him to be removed and the trial to proceed in his absence:

Provided that, in such circumstances as may be prescribed by law, the trial may take place in the absence of the person charged, so long as no punishment of death or imprisonment (other than imprisonment in default of payment of a fine) is awarded in the event of his conviction."

**12.** Their Lordships do not think that there is anything in this point. The structure of the provision is that the first part lays down a rule (no trial in the absence of the accused) subject to two exceptions (consent and disruption). The whole of the first part is then subject to a proviso, allowing legislation under which people may be tried in their absence for minor offences. In this case, the trial did not infringe the rule because it fell within one of the exceptions. It follows that there was no need for it to come within the proviso. The appellants' construction would produce the absurd result that

**APPEAL on Page 6**

*The Grenada Advocate, 16 February 2007*

The newspapers each had an article on the ruling as it was a landmark decision. The complete judgment of the Privy Council was reported in the *Grenada Advocate* newspaper of 16th February, 2007.

It was not the final chapter in the trial process but it was indeed the culmination of hard work, deep legal introspection and collective legal research.

Upon our return to Grenada from England and the subsequent court's ruling, the media continued to follow every step of the journey. It was a sour pill in the mouth of some persons who would have lost loved ones; and understandably so. However, as professionals we had to do that which we were trained to do, professionally and dispassionately.

It was widely reported that Amnesty International welcomed the court's ruling. They issued a statement to that effect. The Privy Council recognised the political nature of the accused case and the inability of any Government to take an objective view of the matter. Therefore the issue of resentencing should take the form of an independent 'judicial determination'. The court said at paragraph 32 of the judgment:

> "... and perhaps most importantly, it is the highly unusual circumstance that, for obvious reasons, the question of the appellants' fate is so politically charged that it is hardly reasonable to expect any Government of Grenada, even 23 years after the tragic events of October 1983, to take an objective view of this matter. In their Lordships opinion that makes it all the more important that the determination of the appropriate sentence for the appellants, taking into account the progress as they have made in prison, should be the subject of a judicial determination."

The separation of powers doctrine therefore was alive and well, in that there should be no executive inference in the resentencing process. The Privy Council had indeed ruled that the accused should be resentenced, purely upon judicial principles; not any extraneous considerations or influences.

The resentencing of the accused men was now being brought to the fore, as the media again highlighted the possibility of the release of the accused, upon a resentencing hearing.

Despite the recognition of the Privy Council ruling and the politically charged nature of the case, the then Attorney General was quoted as saying:

> "... that the government would do all in its powers to ensure that the men remain in prison, and that even if the court frees

# Death sentence was unconstitutional

**CONT'D from previous page**

Cornhill said (at p. 870):

"Lord Diplock's salutary warning remains pertinent: a claim for constitutional relief does not ordinarily offer an alternative means of challenging a conviction or a judicial decision, nor an additional means where such a challenge, based on constitutional grounds, has been made and rejected. The applicant's complaint was one to be pursued by way of appeal against conviction, as it was; his appeal having failed, the Barbadian courts were right to hold that he could not try again in fresh proceedings [for constitutional relief]."

**24.** A similar point was considered by the Supreme Court of Canada in R v. Sarson [1996] 2 SCR 223. The appellant had been charged with murder under the felony murder rule then applicable in Canada and pleaded guilty. Eleven months later, the Supreme Court decided that the felony murder rule was unconstitutional. The accused applied for leave to appeal out of time, but the application was refused. He then brought an application for habeas corpus on the ground that his detention on the basis of an unlawful conviction was an infringement of his rights under the Canadian Charter of Rights and Freedoms. But the Supreme Court held that he could not use a collateral procedure to re-open the question of whether his conviction had been lawful. Even if a subsequent decision establishes that the law under which he had been convicted was constitutionally invalid, his guilt remains a matter of res judicata as between him and the Crown. Sopinka J said (at p. 237) an accused could rely on subsequent judicial authorities only if he was "still in the judicial system", that is to say, if an appeal was still possible. Otherwise, the decision of the criminal court was final.

**25.** The finality of the appeal does not mean that the convicted person is entirely without remedy. As in many jurisdictions, the Governor-General has a power to refer the case back to the Court of Appeal, which must then hear and determine it as if it were a fresh appeal: see section 60 of the West Indies Associated States Supreme Court (Grenada) Act Cap 336.

**26.** Their Lordships therefore return to the main submission, namely that the mandatory sentence of death was unconstitutional. Mr. Dingemans QC, appearing for the Attorney-General of Grenada, did not contest this point. It was so held in relation to the similar constitutions of other Caribbean states in Reyes v. The Queen [2002] 2 AC 235 (Belize); Regina v. Hughes [2002] 2 AC 259 (St. Lucia): Fox v. The Queen (2002) 2 AC 284 (Saint Christopher and Nevis) and Bowe v. The Queen [2006] 1 WLR 1623 (The Bahamas). The last case decides that upon the true construction of the Grenadian Constitution, such a sentence was unconstitutional at the time it was passed in 1986. The result is that section 230 of the Criminal Code must be interpreted to mean, and has meant since the Constitution came into force in 1974, that the death penalty for murder is discretionary: a person convicted of murder may be sentenced to death, but may instead be given a lesser sentence. The judge did not exercise this discretion and the sentence was therefore unlawful.

**27.** Mr. Dingemans submitted, however, that the validity of the sentence of death was just as much res judicata as the validity of the conviction. If, as the Privy Council held in Bowe's case, the sentence was unconstitutional by 1986, the point could just as well have been taken before the Court of Appeal in 1991. The appellants are no longer "in the judicial system" and their only remedy is to petition the Governor-General under section 60 to grant them executive clemency or refer their cases back to the Court of Appeal.

**Lord Phillips of Worth Matravers.**

**28.** In the ordinary way, there would be both logic and practical sense in Mr. Dingemans's argument. But this is no ordinary case. First, the application to this case of the doctrine of res judicata is somewhat artificial. The legality of the mandatory death sentence imposed upon the appellants has never been the subject of judicial decision. It is true that it could have been raised before the Court of Appeal in 1991 and the Board's decision in Bowe's case shows that if it had been raised, the correct answer would have been that it was unlawful. But that follows from the principle that judicial decisions on the meaning of the Constitution have retrospective effect. In practice, however, as was shown by the citation by Lord Bingham in Bowe of earlier cases before the Board, it is unrealistic to expect that the argument which succeeded in Bowe would have been entertained, let alone succeeded, before the Court of Appeal.

**29.** Secondly, the sentence in question was death. If the appellants were still at risk of execution, there can be little doubt that the Board would not allow the principle of res judicata to stand in the way of granting relief to prevent the carrying into effect of an unlawful sentence. But the validity of the life sentence substituted by the warrant of commutation is dependent upon the validity of the sentence of death. In the absence of such a sentence, the Governor-General has no power to order that the appellants be imprisoned for life and the appellants therefore remain held in detention without lawful authority.

**30.** Thirdly, there has never been any judicial contribution to determining the sentences which the appellants should serve. Byron J, correctly applying the law as it was understood at the time, exercised no discretion. And the appellants' present detention is solely by the authority of the executive.

**31.** Fourthly, there appears to be no adequate mechanism in Grenada for providing the appellants, even now, with the judicial sentencing procedure to which they were entitled. The only prospect of a review of the sentences is by means of the exercise of the royal prerogative of mercy, which depends entirely upon executive discretion. It is the Minister who advises the Governor-General on the exercise of the prerogative powers in section 72(1) of the Constitution. Before doing so, the Minister may, if he chooses, seek the advice of the Advisory Committee under section 74(2), but he is not bound by their advice. Alternatively, the Minister may receive advice from a Board of Review which he has appointed under section 2 of the Prison Rules Cap 254 to review the sentences of long-term prisoners. In this latter case, however, it appears that the machinery has failed to function. Section 3(b) of the Prison Rules requires that the Board of Review should review the sentences of all life prisoners after the first 12 months have been served and thereafter after four years from the date of sentence and then at four yearly intervals. When these proceedings were before Benjamin J, he said (paragraph 49) that the Board had either never been appointed or had not functioned: in either case the situation was "unsatisfactory and inexcusable". It would appear from the affidavit in support of the constitutional motion that between October 1999 and April 2000, all but one of the appellants were interviewed by the Board, but there is no evidence that any advice was tendered to the Minister. When the case was before the Court of Appeal, the Review Board had still not functioned and their Lordships were told that nothing further has happened. It may be that the reason for the failure to review the sentences is that the authorities took the view that the terms of the warrant of commutation precluded any possibility of release. If that was the case, then, as their Lordships have already indicated, they think that this was a misreading of the terms of the warrant.

**32.** Fifthly, and perhaps most important, is the highly unusual circumstance that, for obvious reasons, the question of the appellants' fate is so politically charged that it is hardly reasonable to expect any Government of Grenada, even 23 years after the tragic events of October 1983, to take an objective view of the matter. In their Lordships' opinion that makes it all the more important that the determination of the appropriate sentence for the appellants, taking into account such progress as they have made in prison, should be the subject of a judicial determination.

**33.** In Hinds v. Attorney-General of Barbados [2002] 1 AC 854, 870 Lord Bingham qualified the principle stated by Lord Diplock in Chokolingo v. Attorney-General of Trinidad and Tobago [1981] 1 WLR 106 with this observation:

"It would be undesirable to stifle or inhibit the grant of constitutional relief in cases where a claim to such relief is established and such relief is unavailable or not readily available through the ordinary avenue of appeal. As it is a living, so must the Constitution be an effective, instrument."

**34.** Their Lordships do not think that in practice, the relief sought by the appellants in relation to their sentences was ever available through the ordinary avenue of the appeal. They will therefore humbly advise Her Majesty that this appeal should be allowed and that it should be declared that the sentence of death imposed upon the appellants was invalid and that the case should be remitted to the Supreme Court of Grenada for the appellants to be sentenced in accordance with the construction of section 230 of the Criminal Code, which their Lordships have indicated, taking into account the progress made by the appellants during their time in prison.

*The Grenada Advocate, 16 February 2007*

Lawyers Cajeton Hood, Ruggles Ferguson, Keith Scotland and Derek Sylvester.

## Privy Council: The appellants' fate is politically charged

FREEDOM from Page 1
re-sentenced.

The lawyers are claiming victory in the face of comments in some quarters that nothing has been achieved.

"The warrant, under which these persons had been kept in prison, did say that they should remain in prison for the rest of their natural lives; and now the privy council has said, 'go back to a court and have a proper sentence'," Hood declared .

"The privy council has struck down that provision, whereby they were expected to remain there for the rest of their natural lives. So if that is not a tremendous victory, I don't know what it is," Hood added

According to the Privy Council ruling, "This appeal should be allowed, and it should be declared that the sentence of death imposed upon the appellants was invalid, and that the case should be remitted to the Supreme Court of Grenada for the appellants to be sentenced in accordance with the construction of section 230 of the Criminal Code."

More than 23 years after the killings at Fort Rupert, feelings across this tri-island state remain strong.

The relatives of those who were killed are opposed to the release of the Grenada 13. Government also appears reluctant to re-open old wounds by releasing the prisoners into what is a small society.

The Privy Council statement acknowledges this.

"The question of the appellants' fate is so politically charged that it is hardly reasonable to expect any Government of Grenada, even 23 years after the tragic events of October 1983, to take an objective view of the matter.

"In their Lordships opinion that makes it all the more important that the determination of the appropriate sentence for the appellants, taking into account such progress as they have made in prison, should be the subject of a judicial determination."

*The Grenada Advocate, 16 February 2007*

## Amnesty International welcomes Privy Council ruling on Grenada 13

Stories by Linda Straker

**WHILE the decision does not amount to a full retrial, Amnesty International has welcomed the decision by the Privy Council to have the accused in the Maurine Bishop cases be re-sentenced.**

Amnesty, in a news release, said that the latest move is a means by which the cases can finally be reviewed.

After years of concern about the fairness of their trial and convictions the international human rights organisation said that it has not taken a position on the guilt or innocence of the accused persons.

The British based Human Right organisation has long called on the Grenadian authorities to establish an independent judicial review of the convictions, a recommendation also made by the Grenadian Truth and Reconciliation Commission in a report in June 2006.

In its ruling the Privy Council stated that "the question of the appellants' fate is so politically charged that it is hardly reasonable to expect any Government of Grenada ... to take an objective view of the matter" even after 23 years. It ordered that the case should therefore be referred back to the Supreme Court of Grenada for a new sentencing determination "taking into account the progress made by the appellants during their time in prison".

After 23 years of incarceration, 13 remaining members of the "Grenada 17" former government and military officers convicted of the murder of former Prime Minister Maurice Bishop and others had their sentences overturned by the Privy Council on February 7, 2007.

The council ruled that the death sentences originally imposed in the cases were unconstitutional and that this also invalidated the process by which those sentences were later commuted to life imprisonment.

The 17 were detained by US forces following the US-led invasion of Grenada in October 1983. The invasion occurred after a coup in which former Grenadian Prime Minister Maurice Bishop, members of his government and other citizens were allegedly summarily executed by supporters of a dissident faction led by Bishop's deputy Bernard Coard.

In 1986, 14 former members of the Government of Grenada and three soldiers were convicted of the murders. The former government members, including Bernard Coard and his wife Phyllis Coard, were sentenced to death, while the three soldiers received long prison terms. The death sentences were commuted by the Grenadian authorities to life imprisonment in 1991.

In December 2006, three of the "Grenada 17" – Andy Mitchell, Vincent Joseph and Cosmos Richardson – were released after serving 23 years for manslaughter. Phyllis Coard was given permission to travel to Jamaica due to severe health problems in March 2000.

In 2003, Amnesty issued a report called "The Grenada 17: The last cold war prisoners?" in which the organisation concluded that the "trial of the Grenada 17 was fatally flawed and did not meet international standards. Among its concerns were their lengthy pre-trial detention following their arrest by US forces in October 1983, their ill-treatment under interrogation and the circumstances under which confessions were obtained. The report also identified irregularities in both the constitution of the court before which they were tried and in the jury selection.

*The Grenada Advocate, 16 February 2007*

## BISHOP'S KILLERS SEND BACK TO HIGH COURT

*Front page, Grenada Informer, week ending 9 February 2007*

# Bishop's killers to be re-sentenced

The remaining 14 from the original 17 convicted for the death of former prime minister Maurice Bishop and others in 1983 were given a Independence present by the Judicial Committee of the Privy Council when they ruled that "it should be declared that the sentence of death imposed upon the appellants was invalid and that the case should be remitted to the Supreme Court of Grenada for the appellants to be sentenced in accordance with the construction of section 230 of the Criminal Code".

Three of the 17 who received jail sentences were released - December 2006, after serving their prison term.

In an historical ruling by the Lord Lords, dated February 7th 2007, the Privy Council in a ruling said, among other things, that "the appellants' present detention is solely by the authority of the executive".

Here is an extract from the ruling.

"Their Lordships therefore return to the main submission, namely that the mandatory sentence of death was unconstitutional. Mr Dingemans QC, appearing for the Attorney-General of Grenada, did not contest this point. It was so held in relation to the similar constitutions of other Caribbean states in Reyes v The Queen [2002] 2 AC 235 (Belize); Regina v Hughes [2002] 2 AC 259 (St Lucia); Fox v The Queen (2002) 2 AC 284 (Saint Christopher and Nevis) and Bowe v The Queen [2006] 1 WLR 1623 (The Bahamas). The last case decides that upon the true construction of the Grenadian Constitution, such a sentence was unconstitutional at the time it was passed in 1986. The result is that section 230 of the Criminal Code must be interpreted to mean, and has meant since the Constitution came into force in 1974, that the death penalty for murder is discretionary: a person convicted of murder may be sentenced to death but may instead be given a lesser sentence. The judge did not exercise this discretion and the sentence was therefore unlawful.

Mr Dingemans submitted, however, that the validity of the sentence of death was just as much res judicata as the validity of the conviction. If, as the Privy Council held in Bowe's case, the sentence was unconstitutional by 1986, the point could just as well have been taken before the Court of Appeal in 1991. The appellants are no longer "in the judicial system" and their only remedy is to petition the Governor-General under section 60 to grant them executive clemency or refer their cases back to the Court of Appeal.

In the ordinary way, there would be both logic and practical sense in Mr Dingemans's argument. But this is no ordinary case. First, the application to this case of the doctrine of res judicata is somewhat artificial. The legality of the mandatory death sentence imposed upon the appellants has never been the subject of judicial decision. It is true that it could have been raised before the Court of Appeal in 1991 and the Board's decision in Bowe's case shows that if it had been raised, the correct answer would have been that it was unlawful. But that follows from the principle that judicial decisions on the meaning of the Constitution have retrospective effect. In practice, however, as was shown by the citation by Lord Bingham in Bowe of earlier cases before the Board, it is unrealistic to expect that the argument which succeeded in Bowe would have been entertained, let alone succeeded, before the Court of Appeal.

Secondly, the sentence in question was death. If the appellants were still at risk of execution, there can be little doubt that the Board would not allow the principle of res judicata to stand in the way of granting relief to prevent the carrying into effect of an unlawful sentence. But the validity of the life sentence substituted by the warrant of commutation is dependent upon the validity of the sentence of death. In the absence of such a sentence, the Governor-General has no power to order that the appellants be imprisoned for life and the appellants therefore remain held in detention without lawful authority.

Thirdly, there has never been any judicial contribution to determining the sentences which the appellants should serve. Byron J, correctly applying the law as it was understood at the time, exercised no discretion. And the appellants' present detention is solely by the authority of the executive.

Fourthly, there appears to be no adequate mechanism in Grenada for providing the appellants, even now, with the judicial sentencing procedure to which they were entitled. The only prospect of a review of the sentences is by means of the exercise of the royal prerogative of mercy, which depends entirely upon executive discretion. It is the Minister who advises the Governor-General on the exercise of the prerogative powers in section 72(1) of the Constitution. Before doing so, the Minister may, if he chooses, seek the advice of the Advisory Committee under section 74(2), but he is not bound by their advice. Alternatively, the Minister may receive advice from a Board of Review which he has appointed under section 2 of the Prison Rules Cap 254 to review the sentences of long term prisoners. In this latter case, however, it appears that the machinery has failed to function. Section 3(b) of the Prison Rules requires that the Board of Review should review the sentences of all life prisoners after the first 12 months have been served and thereafter after 4 years from the date of sentence and then at 4 yearly intervals. When these proceedings were before Benjamin J, he said (paragraph 49) that the Board had either never been appointed or had not functioned: in either case the situation was "unsatisfactory and inexcusable". It would appear from the affidavit in support of the constitutional motion that between October 1999 and April 2000, all but one of the appellants were interviewed by the Board but there is no evidence that any advice was tendered to the Minister. When the case was before the Court of Appeal, the Review Board had still not functioned and their Lordships were told that nothing further has happened. It may be that the reason for the failure to review the sentences is that the authorities took the view that the terms of the warrant of commutation precluded any possibility of release. If that was the case, then, as their Lordships have already indicated, they think that this was a misreading of the terms of the warrant

Fifthly, and perhaps most important, is the highly unusual circumstance that, for obvious reasons, the question of the appellants' fate is so politically charged that it is hardly reasonable to expect any Government of Grenada, even 23 years after the tragic events of October 1983, to take an objective view of the matter. In their Lordships opinion that makes it all the more important that the determination of the appropriate sentence for the appellants, taking into account such progress as they have made in prison, should be the subject of a judicial determination.

In Hinds v Attorney-General of Barbados [2002] 1 AC 854, 870 Lord Bingham qualified the principle stated by Lord Diplock in Chokolingo v Attorney General of Trinidad and Tobago [1981] 1 WLR 106 with this observation:

"It would be undesirable to stifle or inhibit the grant of constitutional relief in cases where a claim to such relief is established and such relief is unavailable or not readily available through the ordinary avenue of appeal. As it is a living, so must the Constitution be an effective, instrument."

Their Lordships do not think that in practice the relief sought by the appellants in relation to their sentences was ever available through the ordinary avenue of the appeal. They will therefore humbly advise Her Majesty that this appeal should be allowed and that it should be declared that the sentence of death imposed upon the appellants was invalid and that the case should be remitted to the Supreme Court of Grenada for the appellants to be sentenced in accordance with the construction of section 230 of the Criminal Code which their Lordships have indicated, taking into account the progress made by the appellants during their time in prison."

*Grenada Informer, 9 February 2007*

them, the NNP (New National Party) would ensure that they remain in prison; we have employed the best legal minds to ensure they remain there."

The above indication by the Attorney General was cause for concern and would be used at the appropriate time, to the benefit of the defence. Edward Fitzgerald QC issued a statement condemning the utterances as political interference with the process. This subsequently formed part of the defence deposition.

“Can the AG’s statement make a difference?”

*Front page, Grenada Informer, week ending 22 June 2007*

**Can the A-G’s statement make a differ-**

Statements made by Grenada’s Attorney General Hon. Elvin Nimrod days before the commencement of the re-sentencing hearing of thirteen convicted for the 1983 killing of former Prime Minister Murice Bishop and others are being given great significance at the trial albeit unfavourable to the Crown’s case.

Head of the defence team, Queens Council’s Edward Fitzgerald, told the Court the statement made by the Attorney General cannot be taken lightly and give greater credence to the defence call for the judiciary to determine the fate of the men rather than leaving it up to the Executive.

Fitzgerald said the statement placed a dampened spirit on the true spirit and objective of the trial and therefore any outcome would, in some way, hinge on the weight, if

prison.

The AG, the Court heard, went further to say that even if the Court free the men, the NNP would ensure that they remain in prison; they have employed the best legal minds to ensure that they remain there.

Fitzgerald said the statement is inappropriate, particularly to be coming from an Attorney General. It speaks to some level of political interference and therefore would form part of the defence deposition

as they lobby for the men’s freedom.

When asked whether there might be any legal consequences as a result of the statement made by the Attorney General, Director of Public Prosecution Christopher Nelson told reporters that the defence are making heavy weather about the statement and using it to their advantage. Nelson said the defence want the Court to believe that the prison review procedure and the exercise of the executive prerogative of mercy would not happen would not happen for the men and therefore they are urging the Judge to have a fixed sentence of

AG Nimrod

thirty-five years so that they to rely on the exercise of that state body.

Protest outside the Hearing

A group calling themselves victims of the martyrs waved placards outside the Court in protest against moves to have the men set free.

Among those waving their cards was Annie Bain, wife of slain Government Minister Norris Bain together with her son.

The group was lead by Peggy Nestfield a former activist in the People’s Revolutionary Government of 1979 to 83, and included scores of other persons many of whom would have lost family members during the October 1983 massacre on Fort George.

...topher speaks to the media

*Grenada Informer, 22 June 2007*

In the interim, preparation was underway for the resentencing hearing. There was a total of thirteen accused to be resentenced. The depth of the material was voluminous, in that numerous affidavits, reports and assessments had to be conducted in aid of resentencing. It was agreed that different lawyers would be responsible for the resentencing hearing of the accused persons. Cecil Prime had since in or about 1998 requested my representation. He got his desire. There was a total of fifteen (15) lawyers for the accused men.

We received notice that the hearing would be conducted at the Grenada Trade Centre in the parish of Saint George, which was very spacious. It was a site where cultural and other like activities were normally held. It could accommodate numerous persons to witness the resentencing.

Justice Francis Belle who once sat as a High Court Judge in Grenada, was appointed to conduct the resentencing hearing. The hearing and delivery of the judgment was conducted on 18th – 27th June and 25th July 2007.

The team of lawyers selected for the accused included:

1. Edward Fitzgerald QC
2. Howard Hamilton QC
3. Keith Scotland
4. Celeste Jules
5. Jacqueline Samuels-Brown QC
6. Cajeton Hood
7. Earl Witter
8. Jomo Thomas
9. Ruggles Ferguson
10. Ashley Bernadine
11. Rajiv Persaud
12. John Heath
13. Derick Sylvester
14. Anselm Clouden
15. Daniel Khan

The State was represented by Mr. Ramesh Maharaj SC, Christopher Nelson QC and Dionne Lawrence.

*Left to right: Rajiv Persaud, Edward Fitzgerald QC, Ruggles Ferguson, Howard Hamilton QC, Earl Witter QC, Celeste Jules, Jomo Thomas, Keith Scotland, Derick Sylvester, John Heath, Jaqueline Samuels-Brown and Cajeton Hood*

*Standing (left to right): Ashley Bernadine, Cajeton Hood, Ramesh Maharaj, Edward Fitzgerald QC, John Heath, Jacqueline Samuels-Brown, Daniel Khan, Rajiv Persaud. Kneeling (left to right): Ruggles Ferguson, Christopher Nelson, Keith Scotland, Celeste Jules, Derick Sylvester*

CHAPTER SEVENTEEN

# TEARS OF A NATION: MAURICE BISHOP MURDER TRIAL PART 4 (Resentencing)

*"Earth has no sorrow that heaven cannot heal."*
SIR THOMAS MORE

The life and legacy of humans can never properly be written without documenting their struggles, triumphs and tears; for posterity and to serve as a guide to ensure history does not repeat itself negatively. The order of the Privy Council for the resentencing of all the accused men, who did not then have the opportunity to file documentation to mitigate their sentence and have a full judicial hearing, was now at the fore of not only the Grenada judicial system, but on the mind of every Grenadian. The resentencing was a hot button topic. There was the view that the men should remain in prison to die, and the other view, that after in excess of thirty three (33) years in prison, they would have been sufficiently punished. It was time for their reintegration into society. Fortunately, the above respective positions had no say or sway in the judicial process regarding the resentencing. It was a purely judicial exercise.

At the Grenada Trade Centre, during the resentencing both the Royal Grenada Police Force and Her Majesty's Prison ensured maximum security arrangements were in place since numerous prisoners had to be transported for the purpose of the resentencing. The duration of the resentencing was unknown, since it was a daunting task for any Judge to undertake. Despite the politically charged environment in Grenada at the time, the Judge, Justice Francis Belle, a Barbadian national who was currently sitting in another EC jurisdiction, was sent to Grenada solely for the purpose of conducting the resentencing hearing.

The preparation for the hearing involved voluminous material, as the depth of the trial at the High Court and preliminary inquiry had to be delved into for the purpose of examining the individuals' involvement

# Re-sentencing hearing begins

**The Grenada 13 appeared in front of Justice Francis Bell on Monday at the Grenada Trade Centre, which is being used as the Supreme Court for re-sentencing for the murder in connection with the executions that took place in October 1983 at Fort George - then called Fort Rupert - as ordered by the Privy Council.**

They arrived at the Trade Centre, well dressed and with smiles on their faces.

Leader for the defense team, Queen's Counsel Edward Fitzgerald, immediately called for a fixed term sentence of a maximum of 35 years, with time spent in custody on remand to be taken into consideration.

The argument was based on the fact that the upholding of the death penalty in July 1991, the near execution of the men in July 1991 when they came within days of being executed and were notified, their four and a half years on death row and the denial of review of their life sentences as required by law at four yearly intervals, were unlawful and should be looked at when deciding what sentence should be imposed.

Mr Fitzgerald argued that the imposition of a life sentence leaves the men to the mercy of politicians to decide their fate. Politicians, he said, who think it is appropriate to comment on what should happen when the court makes its final decision.

He said, "This is dangerous in such a highly charged case and it would be influenced by improper political considerations.

What happened on October 19, 1983 occurred within a short space of time in the context of an escalating crisis that got out of control on that particular day, resulting in bloodshed, something that was both unique and unexpected.

Director of Public Prosecution (DPP), Mr Christopher Nelson who is leading for the prosecution said that it is not the practice within the jurisdiction for the crown to be actively involved in sentencing, but this is an unusual case, in the legal history of Grenada, the OECS and the English speaking Caribbean.

He said that the case involves the highest number of deaths to have arisen from a single criminal enterprise.

In this context, he said that he was seeking his Lordship's leave to make submissions and representation in relation to the appropriate sentence to be handed down.

He said that the sentence should properly reflect the gravity of the crime, and great weight should be placed on the retributive aspect.

Fitzgerald pleaded for leniency on Monday for the 13. He said that they have experienced a "Spiritual Transformation" in prison.

*The defense lawyers*

The death sentences imposed in 1986 on former Deputy Prime Minister Bernard Coard and the other prisoners were thrown out in February by the London-based Privy Council, the highest court of appeal for the former British Territory.

"The defendants continue to maintain their innocence of the charges, but expressed their deep sorrow at the events of that day," said Fitzgerald. "They've also accepted moral responsibility for the tragedy."

Fitzgerald urged the presiding judge of the Supreme Court not to impose sentences of more than 35 years in consideration of the prisoners' "Spiritual transformation."

Defense lawyers read testimonials from other inmates, including a 17-year-old convicted thief who said the defendants taught him to read and write.

On Tuesday Morning, reports stated that Hudson Austin was complaining of stomach aches on returning to Her Majesty's Prison on Monday and was brought to the General Hospital for medical attention. It was said that he was returned to the prison and on Tuesday morning brought back to the hospital. Former General Austin is said to have problems with his prostate.

The Court was enlightened on Tuesday on who fired the first shot on October 19 1983, which triggered the tragedy on Fort George.

Mr Fitzgerald said that Court records as well as the testimonies of two persons showed that the first bullet came from the crowd of protestors.

He said that the soldiers' re-occupation of the Fort was met with violent resistance and that lead to a confrontation between soldiers and civilians.

He said that records show that civilians fired shots and the first victim was Officer Cadet Conrad Mayers.

Mr Fitzgerald quoted from Callistus Bernard's Statement, "As soon as we reach the bottom of the hill, some civilians opened fire ..... what happened afterwards was not justified or lawful but we were dealing with a civil strife where things went out of control."

Mr Fitzgerald also quoted from the statement of Angela Grant who in the original trial statement said that weapons were distributed to civilians at the Fort.

He said that there is evidence that they have changed. He noted that following Ivan in 2004 they remained in prison when they could have escaped. He noted that some of them are ill and some of them may die if brought back in prison. He said that we must look at the present and not the past. He is calling for the immediate release to return to society to continue the work they have been doing with fellow prisoners.

Fitzgerald's sumbissions concluded on Tuesday and he was followed by Attorney Keith Scotland representing Bernard Coard.

Mr Scotland spoke of the incident in 2004 when the island was ravaged and 95% of the inmates escaped, the 13 remained in prison and Mr Coard told the prisoners that at the time of disaster the law of the land came first and that he would not be part of an illegal act and leave the prison without the permission of the proper authority.

Scotland made reference to four institutions which continue to have a positive impact on Grenada even today. While in prison Coard, along with other inmates initiated a new education programme to help the prison inmates and other institutions outside of the prison.

Scotland said that since the 1990s Coard's area of concern was the youths. He made reference to one of the prisoners who said that Bernard taught him how to read and write and assured him that all was not lost.

Scotland pointed out to the court that before being convicted Coard was a man of good character. He said that time spent incarcerated, brutal torture and time spent on death row must be taken into consideration.

He said that a 100-watt bulb was burning

Please turn to page 05

*Front page, The Grenadian Voice, week ending 23 June 2007*

in the events of 19th October 1983. There were persons who were charged and convicted for the murders at Fort George, however they were not even present at the time of the offence. There were others who did not use any weapons. However, due to the legal nature of the offence of murder, the prosecution then threw a catch all net, and the jury at the time convicted each accused for the murders by a legal term referred to as joint enterprise.

The Defence lawyers all agreed to assemble at the Coyaba Hotel in Grand Anse, situated directly on the Grand Anse beach, since the Trade Centre was a stone's throw away, just a mere walk across the street. We drove to the Trade Centre. Upon entering I was flabbergasted when screams, chants and derogatory comments were flown at us; placards were held up against us. I was fully aware of the sensitivity to the whole situation, but the extent of the aggression by the protesters awoken me to the reality that the wounds were still fresh. There were photos of the deceased relatives being held up on placards along with calls for justice.

The vehicle soon stopped. As I entered the Trade Centre, which was lined with numerous police and other officers, I immediately dismissed what I just saw and focused on the task ahead. There was a large crowd inside, as the internal arena was divided into two sections. The back portion was for the public. There was a passageway or middle aisle. The frontal portion at the Centre was designed for the lawyers both defence and prosecution. The Judge sat elevated at the front. There was a designated area to the left for the members of the media.

Directly behind the lawyers, there were prearranged seats for the accused men. The lawyers were seated; the media and members of the public were anxiously waiting. The lawyers' backs were to the public so the security seating arrangement caused me some discomfort but I soon dismissed it. I immediately assessed three main exit points should there be any form of activity that necessitated my immediate self-preservation. I examined the exits to the left and right of me. The exit directly in front of me, the Judge alone was allowed to enter and exit. I deliberately positioned my seat to the left back of the sitting arrangement provided for lawyers. I had a 180 degrees view of the crowd if I turned slightly right. This was not paranoia, but having regard to the scene outside and the enormity of the task ahead, I was prepared for anything. Soon, the court orderly called the court to order; all rose as was requested. We sat thereafter. The room was so quiet then, you could have heard a pin drop.

The hearing was called to order. At the commencement of the court's sitting the prosecution made an application that Justice Francis Belle should recuse himself from hearing the matter. Two affidavits were sworn challenging the Judge's suitability. One by Grenadian, Nelson Louison, and another by a Barbadian lawyer, Robert Clarke. Their application failed. There were some concerns that they would have appealed the decision. However they did not.

The prosecution led its evidence. This included the facts as it occurred on the 19th October 1983 emanating from the deposition, victim impact statements from the surviving relatives of the deceased, and the effect the individual deaths had on their family lives. The evidence was copiously explained for full impact. Justice Belle's in-depth grasp of the submission was evident through his pointed questions and examination of the deposition. It was obvious that he had familiarised himself with every detail and was ready for the task placed on his shoulders.

While one of the prosecution lawyers, Dionne Lawrence, was reading the victim impact statements, there was some unusual rumble in the public

The three who were released last month with their lawyers.

**Government appealing court decision on Bishop Killers**

By Rawie Titus

THE Grenada Government is challenging the suitability of Justice Francis Belle who presided over recent re-sentencing hearings that resulted in the freedom of three persons convicted for the 1983 murder of revolutionary Prime Minister Maurice Bishop.

An affidavit filed in the Organisation of Eastern Caribbean States (OECS) Court of appeal is asking for leave to appeal the controversial decision by Justice Belle, not to recuse himself from the hearings, after Barbadian lawyer Robert Clarke and Grenadian businessman Nelson Louison questioned his suitability.

Reacting to the government,

COURT on Page 6

*Front page, The Grenada Advocate, week ending 27 July 2007*

domain directly behind me. I saw one of the relatives of a deceased walk from the public area and started advancing to the front. There was security everywhere so it was not a cause for concern. He advanced to the middle of the court. He slowly paused by a water dispenser that was placed in a strategic location for persons wishing to refresh themselves. My mind immediately started racing but he stopped there. I relaxed and looked forward as the statements were being read. I was alerted to look across to my right again. I saw the same person walking to where the accused men were sitting with a glass full of water. He dashed it in the faces of some of the accused men. I was stunned. There was an instant commotion from the public at the back but none of the accused moved. The accused men took their 'bath' in silence and not a word was uttered. I was not a beneficiary of the water blessing, because of my well-chosen sitting arrangement. The closest to the exit.

The behaviour of the accused men was commendable. We discussed it as a positive mitigating factor that even in the face of such abuse in the eyes of the court, they wiped their faces and

## Vater thrown at Coard Gang

ne 14 GRENADA TODAY Fri., June 22, 2007 LOCAL NEWS

: re-sentencing hearing for the remaining 13 olutionary prisoners in :nada was briefly interrupted on Monday when one of the slain victims son, Peter Bain, the son of Grenada's former Minister of Housing, Norris Bain, who was shot dead along with Prime Minister Maurice Bishop in October 1983, dashed a cup of water at the prisoners.

The incident occurred at approximately 3.20 p.m. while Crown Counsel Dionne Lawrence was reading statements to Justice Francis Bell, and taking the court through ten impact statements from the relatives of victims.

One of the statements was from Bain himself and it recalled the pain, hurt and fright the family members had to endure as a result of the 1983 bloody events in the Spice Isle.

At the time of the execution of Bishop and his Cabinet colleagues, Bain was studying in Cuba. The still grieving son is one of six children of Norris and Annie Bain.

The high court heard that Bain had left Grenada to go to Cuba to study two months before the tragic events.

He said on October 19, 1983, he heard that Bishop was shot, but that the injury was not serious.

In his impact statement, Bain indicated that he tuned into the Voice of America radio station when he heard that his father had died.

"I have no doubt that everything that happened on that fateful day was well planned and executed. My brother was on his way up to Fort Rupert, then came the armored cars and two trucks of soldiers. A soldier on one of the trucks cracked and pointed his gun to fire at him. He had to take cover behind a wall. Everything was well planned," he said.

Bain's own mother, Anne in her statement claimed that the murder of her husband did untold emotional damage to her children and that life as they knew it ended abruptly on October 19, 1983, with the death of her husband.

She said that they have waited 24 years for a day like this.

For Colville Bain, another son of the deceased Norris Bain, he had to leave his studies in the US for more than four years to return home to give support to his mother and his siblings.

He spoke of leaving behind his dreams and his belongings, and up to now it remains "an open chapter in my book of broken dreams".

As the statements were being read by the court official, Peter Bain got up and walked towards a water cooler which was placed approximately 15 feet from the prisoner's dock inside the courtroom.

He calmly filled a cup of water, and to the surprise of everyone including the lawyers, police and prison officers, hastily turned to the dock, and dashed the water at the men including Bernard Coard - the suspected mastermind of the palace coup against Prime Minister Bishop.

The officers on duty moved swiftly into action and were able to bring the situation under control.

Bain was grabbed and carried outside of the makeshift courtroom, as the high-powered team of lawyers sought to come to terms with what had happened.

Coard was seen relating to them the incident that had just taken everyone within the court room by surprise.

The attorneys have indicated that they will not be taking steps to have charges pressing against the "aggrieved son".

Bain's mother who was seated in the court room when the incident occurred, had to be consoled by other family members as she openly sobbed.

She told reporters after that her son's anger arose after hearing the statements read by the female Counsel.

She said that he's hurting inside and that his anger is now coming out.

Anne Bain together with family and friends who lost loved ones during the massacre have been staging a quiet protest outside the Grenada Trade Centre building (makeshift High Court) since the re-sentencing hearing began last week Monday.

The protesters have been calling for the remains of those who were gunned down on Fort Rupert (George) on October 19, 1983.

On Monday morning when the protesters turned up to continue their actions, they met the area cordoned off and were told that they were no longer permitted to stage protest action there.

According to Mrs Bain, she believes that her son's frustration also came out from the fact that the police had stopped them from protesting in front of the court.

Minutes after the incident happened, Peter Bain attempted to re-enter the building but security personnel prevented him from doing so.

He was informed that his action inside the court is regarded as contempt of court and that he could have been charged for the offence.

Bain was asked to leave the compound and not return. A similar order was laos issued against another well-known female protester against Coard and his gang, Peggy Nestfield for allegedly instigating violence.

But Nestfield told reporters that she had done nothing wrong and was amazed at the attempt to keep her out of the court proceedings.

She said that at the time of the Peter Bain incident she was not in the building itself and was at a loss to understand why she is being turned away.

The day's hearing continued with no further interruption.

*Grenada Today, 22 June 2007*

remained calm. Was it wisdom over the years, their deep faith or were they willing to accept whatever society or the court threw at them? Whichever it was, their calm in the face of that assault was a mitigating factor in and of itself.

The resentencing hearing lasted nearly two weeks. It ran from the 18th to 27th June 2007 and 25th July 2007. The media brought ball by ball commentary of every event which occurred inside and outside the court room. The resentencing was referred to as the hearing of the century, since it was the first time in our history pre or post-independence that quantity of persons had to be resentenced for an offence of that nature.

The defence team led by Edward Fitzgerald QC with fourteen local and regional lawyers, was allowed to address the court on behalf of their respective clients. Copiously, the mitigating factors were placed before the court, the individual accused's exemplary life while at prison, their academic growth, contribution to prison rehabilitation and its education programme among many other factors. Reports from persons who were affected were all placed before the Judge.

*Front page, Grenada Informer, week ending 22 June 2007*

## ...e-sentencing hearing for Bishop's killers continues

...urteen legal lumi-...ries from around the ...gion are battling the ...at a make shift ...urt in the Grenada ...rade Centre with a ...ew of freeing the ...maining thirteen pris-...ers convicted for the ...83 slaying of former ...ime Minister Mu-...e Bishop and other ...abinet Members in ...pid gun fire on Fort ...eorge.

...he team, headed ...e world renowned Queen's Council -Edward Fitzgerald from London, and including among others Trinidadian Keith Scotland, Grenadian Ruggles Ferguson, Anselm Clouden, Ashley Bernadine, Llyod Noel, Cajeton Hood, Derrick Sylvester, Celeste Jules, Jacqueline Samuel Browne, Howard Hamilton, Earl Witter, Daniel Khan, John Keith are advocating that the thirteen have made sufficient progress during their twenty-four years of incarceration, illegally so, to warrant their freedom.

Earlier this year, the Privy Council in London ruled that the death sentence handed down on the men in 1986 was illegal and unconstitutional, and ordered that the men be re-sentenced at the Supreme Court.

In a lengthy address at the start of the re-sentencing hearing on Monday, head of the defence team, Fitzgerald, asked the Court to consider a fixed term of sentencing of no more than thirty five years with consideration given to time spent be taken as time served.

This, in his view, would allowed the Court to make the type of deduction necessary that would be in sine with the many wrongs meted out to the men during the twenty-four year period.

Fitzgerald said that apart from having their constitutional rights violated, the men were held on death row for a period of over four years, during which time they came to within days of being executed.

Additionally, Fitzgerald told the Court, the men were denied review under the Constitution, and were the subject of inhumane treatment by their prison guards.

Despite all this, the QC went on to say, the men showed courage and made significant strides during those years, being role models to other prisoners, assisting in educational development programmes, among others that qualify them for big reduction in sentencing.

The QC told the Court that the men, after all those years, maintained their not guilty plea but have grown to accept that they were responsible for what would have give rise to the outcome of October 19th 1983, and for that they expressed great remorse.

Fitzgerald said that the imposition of any further prison term on these men would only amount to further violation of their constitutional rights.

The Court, he said, needs to give a sentence that would reflect the progress made by these men during those years of wrongful imprisonment.

Meanwhile, Director of Public Prosecution Christopher Nelson, who is leading the charge for the Crown, in his opening address to the Court said although the Court can no longer imposed the death penalty at this late stage, the sentence to be handed down must reflect the gravity of the crime. He urged the Court to consider consecutive prison term as an alternative.

Nelson said the case is a unique one and represents the highest number of deaths in a single incident leaving several families in grief up to today.

Nelson hinted that the State promised to do all in its power to ensure that justice in served. In fact if need be, the crown may make available to the Court victims impact statements including relying on evidence of key witnesses during the trial, among them Heny Bain, Lyn Creft.

The high profile re-sentencing hearing is expected to climax later this week and many look forward to the ruling that would be handed down by presiding Judge Ian Bell. Those to be re-sentence are Callistus Bernard, Lester Redhead, Christopher Stroude, Hudson Austin, Bernard Coard, Liam James, Leon Cornwall, John Anthony Ventour, Dave Bartholomew, Ewart Layne, Colville Mc Barnette, Selwyn Strachan, and Cecil Prime.

Phyllis Coard, who was also convicted on a similar count, is out in her homeland Jamaica undergoing medical treatment.

*Grenada Informer, 22 June 2007*

I addressed the court on behalf of Cecil Prime who was a soldier at the time of the revolution. The deposition evidence was clear in relation to him. I started with his minimal role as disclosed by the prosecution; his contribution to the prison development; his youthful life was spent in prison. Further, he was approaching the sunset of his life. His social inquiry report and psychological assessments were all very helpful in the process, including his academic growth while at prison. Even without the possibility of being released the accused developed himself.

The police had an arduous task of ensuring complete security for the inmates including their safe travel to and from Her Majesty's prison. The time for the court hearing was well known. So was the route to the court. However their task was completed with perfection. The time soon came for the judge to deliver his decision. There was anxiety in every quarter. The state, public, accused and respective lawyers laid their faith in the fact that we did all we were obliged to do legally.

## Arguments over in the Coard 13 resentencing

"If you are putting through significant violation of your constitutional rights, then the Court can reduce your sentence to reflect their violation".

Words from head of the defence team, Queen Council Edwards Fitzgerald as he challenged the Prosecution's case in a legal battle to free or not to free the thirteen, not labeled with the responsibility or causing the death of former Prime Minister, Maurice Bishop on October 19th, 1983 by firing squad.

In their earlier response to the defence case, one that cries for forgiveness and the opportunity of reconciliation having gone through their own suffering during those years.

In addition, one that calls for public sympathy given the fact that, as convicted men, they have accepted their role and responsibility for the events of October 19th and the death of several persons, many of whom have not received a Christian burial until this day.

Additionally, one can ask the public to see the progress made during those 24 years as sign of maturity and one that could work to their good.

The Prosecution claims, through Senior Council, Ramesh Lawrence Maharaj, that up to this day and despite the call for sympathy and forgiveness, these defendants maintain their innocence, they have not, Maharaj said, accepted their guilt

The high ranking Trinidadian lawyer said in his 40 years of practice, this case would go down in history as the most difficult one he would have had to deal with.

"I was hoping to here", Maharaj said, "from the accused, that they have accepted responsibility, seeing them going into the witness boxes and saying to the nation and to the victims that they are sorry".

Maharaj said, there cannot be acceptance unless there is acceptance and responsibility of guilt. From the inception, the prosecution member went on to say, there was no sign of remorse from the prisoners. In fact, he added, the position was that it was a war between themselves and the Bishop fraction of the revolution and casualties occurred, and for that they held themselves responsible.

In rebutting prosecution's case, Fitzgerald said, one does not have to plead guilty to show remorse, neither does one have to plead guilty to receive a reduction in sentence.

Fitzgerald said, there are lots of mitigating circumstances acting on the defence's behalf and asked the Court to give due consideration to all and impose a fixed term that would reflect those factors.

Among those sighted was the constitutional violation of the imposition of the death sentence, the exposure to the death by hanging in the last five days on an illegal sentence.

The absence of a review after 24 years:

A fixed term of sentence of not more than thirty-five years would allow the Court to make the necessary reduction and allow for the men's immediate release. This, he said, is not a matter of money, but justice.

Over the seven days trial, a number of related events happened. On day two, a police officer was thrown out of Court after his cell phone went off. On day four, a letter challenged the suitability of the sitting Judge, Francis Bell, to precede over the hearing, given his affiliation with a political group prior to 1983 that was linked to the Bernard Coard fraction of the New Jewel Movement.

Following the circulation of the letter, the prosecution brought a motion asking the Judge to excuse himself from the rest of the hearing. This motion was over-ruled and the matter went on.

On day six, Peter Bain son of Norris Bain – one of those killed on October 1983, threw a glass of water at the accused men. He had to be taken off the Court by Police.

Also on that day former activist in the People's Revolution, Peggy Nesfield, was also escorted off the compound by Police for what was dubbed unbecoming behaviour.

Argument from both sides came to an end on day seven with the Judge giving the undertaking that judgment would be given in point form on Wednesday to be followed by a written judgment in two weeks

Bartholomew

Cecil Prime

*Grenada Informer, 29 June 2007*

Justice Belle delivered his ruling, a detailed sixty one (61) page judgment. He examined in detail both the prosecution and defence theories, being guided by the decision of the Privy Council. He sentenced the accused men as follows:

> Cecil Prime, Christopher Stroude and Lester Redhead were sentenced to thirty (30) years, which meant they were to be released forthwith as they had served that time.
>
> The other accused were sentenced to forty years which was calculated so that they had to spend another three (3) to five (5) years in custody.

It was a day of relief for all the lawyers, and no less for those three men. The three accused including Cecil Prime whom I had represented throughout the process, Stroude and Redhead, as the order was that those three men be released that day. The lawyers for the three (3) men hastily retreated to Her Majesty's Prison. I proceeded to the

# THREE FREED

## Seven others jailed with hard labour for five more years

Mixed reactions greeted Wednesday's announcements made by re-sentencing Judge, Barbadian born Justice Francis Belle after seven days of presentations by prosecution and defence counsels. The Judge, who gave a briefing on what he accepted and disregarded from both sides' submissions, sentenced Cecil Prime, Christopher Stroude and Lester 'Goat' Redhead to thirty years with hard labor each. The others including Bernard Coard and Hudson Austin, Ewart Layne and Leon 'Bogo' Cornwall, John 'Chalkie' Ventour and Colville Kamau McBarnette have been sentenced to forty years with hard labor. Using the stipulated prison calendar where one year is equivalent to nine months, it means that the former three have already served their time and the other ten have about three more years in jail.

While the parents, sisters and brothers, children, relatives and friends of the victims shed tears of frustration that the release of all thirteen is imminent, Theresa Redhead, mother of Goat, said "Today is a blessing!" She openly thanked God for the release of her youngest son. Cecil Prime's daughter was seen sitting by herself shedding tears of joy and relief no doubt.

Meanwhile Prime Minister Dr. Rt. Hon. Keith Claudius Mitchell is reported to have stated upon learning of the Court's decision that this is a sad time for Grenada. He was at the time at a graduation ceremony in Happy Hill. He is said to have left to "...take care of business..."

For a couple hours, with defence lawyers, police and security officers making numerous trips into the prison, the fate of the three seemed uncertain. The media personnel gathered in the vicinity of Her Majesty's Prison discussed the possibilities, some noting that if the three among themselves were not out by four or five o'clock, then they couldn't come out on Wednesday.

Curious and conserned Grenadians wondered whether there would be a move form Prosecution for a stay of execution. In fact, on one occasion when asked about the delay, one defence lawyer told the media that there seemed to be some interference with the judiciary from members of the executive. He continued to say that the Commissioner of Prisons was instructed to wait for a call from the Office of the Attorney General before releasing the three men. That call, we were told, came just after four o'clock, when lawyers were considering alternative actions to deal with what they termed "an unlawful act."

Ruggles Ferguson, defence lawyer, told the media that the men would have to be compensated for each hour spent imprisoned after the issuing of the Court order.

Then at exactly ten past four o'clock, six hours, ten minutes af Court proceedings began Wednesday morning, the three walked the Richmond Hill Prison gates, free. They were surrounded by armed soldiers as they walked into the arms of their relatives and and lawyers.

As he walked to freedom Lester Redhead said that he is happy free and wants to get on with his life. He added that he wants to m reconcile with the victims' families. Cecil Prime said that it was feeling to be free again.

Of the ten, Bernard Coard, Hudson Austin, Liam James, Ewart Leon Cornwall, John Ventour, Colville McBarnette, Selwyn Strachan Bartholomew and Callistus Bernard, there would be reviews of the s ing of Hudson Austin because of the assistance he gave in the rebuil the Prison compound after the passage of Hurricane Ivan; John Vent Colville McBarnette because they are afflicted with cancer.

Meanwhile, Phyllis Coard's fate is unknown. She may have to atten on a future date when it is okayed by her doctors to be re-sentenced

*Front page, Grenada Informer, week ending 29 June 2007*

Commissioner's Office and later the reception desk. I was told the men could not be released as yet. This immediately brought a sense of concern. I was informed that the Attorney General's Office had instructed they wait prior to being released. The Defence lawyers started discussing the possibility of filing *habeas corpus* applications for their release and constitutional motions seeking damages for every hour detained beyond the court's order.

We later learnt that there was a move by the State to apply for a stay of execution of the oral judgment delivered. Leave was being sought for the stay.

It soon became obvious that the application did not get very far. I refused to depart the precincts of the prison. I took my notepad as I started documenting minute by minute my discussion with each prison officer, my client and every conversation I had for the purpose of his release. In the interim I was communicating with the other defence lawyers. These were tense moments for us all. The accused who were due to be

## Moves To Re-arrest Freed Coardites

P. 3

***The Keith Mitchell government in St. George's is making a bold move aimed at keeping members of the Bernard Coard Gang of prisoners inside the Richmond Hill prison.***

***Three of the prisoners - Major Christopher Stroude, Captain Lester Redhead and Lieutenant Cecil Prime - were released last month following a decision handed down by Barbadian-born high court judge, Justice Francis Belle.***

***The trio were among seventeen former government and military officials convicted in 1985 for the murder of Prime Minister Maurice Bishop and several colleagues in a bloody palace coup at Fort Rupert (George) on October 19, 1983.***

***The Privy Council in London deemed their original sentencing unconstitutional and ordered the high court in Grenada to bring back the prisoners for proper sentencing.***

***Stroude, Redhead and Prime were given 30 years jail sentences and because of the time already spent in incarceration were released from prison on June 27.***

***The remaining prisoners including ex-deputy Prime Minister Bernard Coard, former Mobilisation Minister, Selwyn Strachan, Army Commander General Hudson Austin and top army officers, Liam James and Ewart Layne are due for release in 3 years.***

***In light of the court ruling, the Grenada government has filed a motion in the high court seeking to challenge the Justice Belle ruling which if successful could see the freed prisoners back behind bars.***

***Following is the full text of the court action brought by the State against the Coard Gang of Prisoners:***

Application for leave to appeal

The Appellant, Director of Public Prosecutions, applies to the Court for an order that the Appellant be and is granted leave to appeal against the Oral judgment delivered by Justice francis Belle on the 21st day of June 2007.

The grounds of this application are as follows:

That the Oral judgment delivered by Justice Francis Belle on the 21st day of June was an interlocutory decision and the Learned Judge erred when the ruled that he had jurisdiction to adjudicate on the re-sentencing in this matter, having regard to section 8 (8) of the Constitution Order of Grenada and the affidavit evidence submitted to him.

An affidavit in support accompanies this application.

AFFIDAVIT IN SUPPORT OF NOTICE OF APPLICATION FOR LEAVE

I, Raulston Glasgow, Senior Legal Counsel in the Ministry of Legal Affairs, Grenada do make oath and say as follows:

(1). I am a Senior Legal Counsel attached to the Attorney General's Chambers, Ministry of legal Affairs, in the state of Grenada.

(2). I am authorised by the Attorney General's Chambers and the Director of Public Prosecutions Office to make this on his behalf.

(3). The facts stated in this Affidavit are within my personal knowledge except where I state the contrary.

(4). To the best of my knowledge, Justice Francis Belle delivered Oral judgment in this matter on the 21st day of June 2007.

(5). I am informed and verily believe by Counsel with conduct of this matter that the Oral judgment was interlocutory.

(6). I am also informed and verily believe by Counsel with conduct of this matter that in order to appeal this decision, leave is required.

(7). Further, I am informed and verily believe that the learned Judge erred when he ruled that he had jurisdiction to adjudicate on the re-sentencing in this matter, having regard to section 8 (8) of the Constitutional Order of Grenada and to the affidavit evidence submitted to him.

(8). I believe that the appeal has a reasonable prospect of success if leave is granted.

(9). I make this affidavit in good faith knowing the content to be true and correct.

(10). In the circumstances, I humbly urge the Honourable Court to grant the order sought by the Appellant.

*Grenada Informer, 29 June 2007*

released were unduly anxious. However, at 4.12 pm the men were allowed to depart the precincts of the prison as free men for the first time in thirty years.

The Judge ordered the Prison Review Committee be constituted in order to have periodical review of prisoners as mandated by law. The other accused men awaited their turn, as there was at least a date set for their release.

In December 2008, Hudson Austin, Colville Mc Barnette and John Ventour were released. They committed to contribute positively to the society upon their release and prove to the society that they were worthy of acceptance and reintegration. Their reintegration process commenced and continued unabated.

*'Soldiers Christopher Stroude, Lester Redhead and Cecil Prime as they walked through the gates of Richmond Hill prison on Wednesday afternoon to become free men once again in the society.'*

**Defense team is happy with outcome**

A high-powered team of defense lawyers who represented the "13" remaining revolutionary prisoners in Grenada are gloating with satisfaction following the release of three of the Gang who were charged with the 1983 murder of leftist Prime Minister Maurice Bishop in a bloody palace coup.

The defence team was led by QC Edward Fitzgerald of England and included Keith Scotland, Ruggles Ferguson, QC Howard Hamilton, Rajiv Persaud, Cajeton Hood, Anslem Clouden, Derick Sylvester, Earl Whitter, Jacqueline Samuels-Browne, Celeste Jules, John Heath and Daniel Khan.

The three prisoners - Major Christopher Stroude, Captain Lester Redhead and Lieutenant Cecil Prime were released a week ago at the end of eight days of a re-sentencing hearing that was ordered by the London-based Privy Council.

The law lords had earlier found that the original sentences imposed on the men of death by hanging and reduced to life imprisonment until the end of their natural lives were unconstitutional.

Fitzgerald told the media that although the defense team would have liked all 13 prisoners to be released they welcomed the ruling of high court judge, Justice Francis Belle to give the remaining prisoners a fixed term sentence rather than a life sentence.

The QC disclosed that the ten other prisoners will not be appealing the court's decision since they are due to be released in three years and two months.

"...This is an important step forward. They (the 10) have a sight of freedom, they have a real date (for) freedom and the others are free," Fitzgerald said.

Those who are to remain at Richmond Hill prison for the time being are former deputy Prime Minister, Bernard Coard, General Hudson Austin, former Mobilisation Minister, Selwyn Strachan, soldiers, Liam James, Calistus Bernard, Ewart Layne, Leon Cornwall, and Dave Bartholomew, as well as Colville "Kamau" Mc Barnette and John Ventour.

All the others with the exception of Bernard were members of the Central Committee of the New Jewel Movement (NJM) which is accused of ordering the execution of Bishop, three cabinet colleagues and several supporters at Fort Rupert (George).

The killings were sparked off by a bitter leadership feud among two warring factions within the NJM that seized power on March 13, 1979 in a coup d'etat against the elected Eric Gairy government.

The remaining C[...] Gang of prisoners [...] all sentenced to 40 [...] imprisonment by Ju[...] Belle but due to the [...] already spent in jai[...] due to be release[...] 2010.

*Attorney Derek Sylvester (l) is in the company of Lester Redhead, (law[...] Keith Scotland, and freed soldiers, Chris Stroude and Cecil Prime*

*Grenada Today, 6 July 2007*

# Remaining 7 of 'Grenada 17' recommended for early release

By Linda Straker

THEY are due to be completely released in 2010, but finally, seven of the famous "Grenada 17" prisoners are among a batch of 40 prisoners whose names have been forwarded to the island's Prison Review Committee (PRC) for early release.

According to Grenada's law, every prisoner who receives more than a four-year sentence should have their case reviewed by the island's PRC every four years for conditional release, based on behaviour in the prison and his/her ability to show proof of rehabilitation and willingness to change behaviour.

Attorney Ruggles Ferguson explains that inclusion of the names doesn't mean that they all will be released.

Ferguson, who has been one of the lawyers representing the 17, said that the Review Committee can only recommend the release.

He said, however, that the final authoritative voice is the Mercy Committee, who advises the Minister of National Security to release the prisoners.

The remaining seven, according to the judgment, will serve their time by mid-2010 and should be released.

The lot of 40 prisoners comprises inmates who have appealed their matters in 1979, but had changed procedure after Grenada declared its own High Court after the March 13th Revolution.

The seven are Bernard Coard, Leon Cornwall, Ewart James, Dave Bartholomew, Callistus Bernard, Liam James and Selwyn Strachan.

Former Army strongman Hudson Austin was among the latest group to be released from prison.

*The Grenada Advocate, 27 February 2009*

# Ten gone, seven more to go

## Austin and Ventour warming to new challenges

Free again (from left) Hudson Austin, John 'Chalkie' Ventour and Colville 'Kamau' McBarnette; former prisoners charged for the assassination of Maurice Bishop and colleagues in 1983

*Front page, Spice Isle Review, week ending 25 December 2008*

Attorney at Law Anselm Clouden who represented Selwyn Strachan, had urged the court to examine his client's record, contribution to the nation's development and ultimately his contribution in the prison while incarcerated. There was a demand then for the Prison Review Committee to conduct its hearing regarding the other accused.

The then shadow spokesman for planning and economic development Senator Kennedy Roberts called upon the Government of Grenada to use all within its powers to try and retrieve the remains of the persons who died on the 19th October 1983, since this had resulted in the inability of the families to have closure including a decent Christian burial. At the resentencing hearing the victim impact statements were plagued by the fact that the bodies of the victims were never discovered.

On Saturday 5th September 2009, the remaining accused were all released from the confines of Her Majesty's Prison. They were now all free men. Their freedom from prison was one aspect of their release; they were now faced with questions that were left unanswered. The public wanted to hear it from the men themselves.

John Ventour one of the released men, stated in an article that Fidel Castro tried to impose his will on the revolution hence the catalyst for its demise.

In an article reported in the *Grenada Today* newspaper of Friday 18th September 2009, Dr. Wendy C. Grenade requested that as the accused

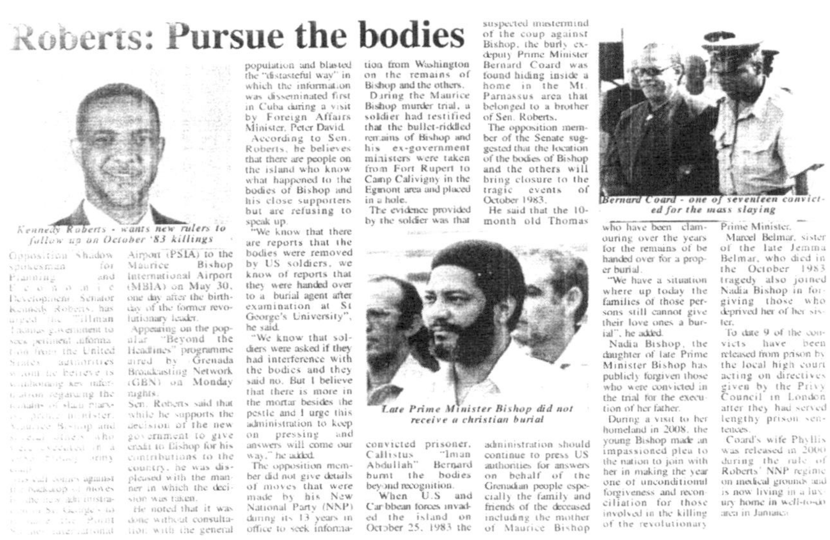

**Roberts: Pursue the bodies**

*Kennedy Roberts - wants new rulers to follow up on October '83 killings*

Opposition Shadow spokesman for Planning and Economic Development Senator Kennedy Roberts, has urged the Tillman Thomas government to seek pertinent information from the United States authorities whom he believes is withholding key information regarding the remains of slain Marxist prime minister, Maurice Bishop and several others who were executed in a [illegible] army coup.

His call comes against the backdrop of moves by the new administration [illegible] St. George's [illegible] the Point Salines International Airport (PSIA) to the Maurice Bishop International Airport (MBIA) on May 30, one day after the birthday of the former revolutionary leader.

Appearing on the popular "Beyond the Headlines" programme aired by Grenada Broadcasting Network (GBN) on Monday nights.

Sen. Roberts said that while he supports the decision of the new government to give credit to Bishop for his contributions to the country, he was displeased with the manner in which the decision was taken.

He noted that it was done without consultation with the general population and blasted the "distasteful way" in which the information was disseminated first in Cuba during a visit by Foreign Affairs Minister, Peter David.

According to Sen. Roberts, he believes that there are people on the island who know what happened to the bodies of Bishop and his close supporters but are refusing to speak up.

"We know that there are reports that the bodies were removed by US soldiers, we know of reports that they were handed over to a burial agent after examination at St George's University", he said.

"We know that soldiers were asked if they had interference with the bodies and they said no. But I believe that there is more in the mortar besides the pestle and I urge this administration to keep on pressing and answers will come our way," he added.

The opposition member did not give details of moves that were made by his New National Party (NNP) during its 13 years in office to seek information from Washington on the remains of Bishop and the others.

During the Maurice Bishop murder trial, a soldier had testified that the bullet-riddled remains of Bishop and his ex-government ministers were taken from Fort Rupert to Camp Calivigny in the Egmont area and placed in a hole.

The evidence provided by the soldier was that convicted prisoner, Callistus "Iman Abdullah" Bernard burnt the bodies beyond recognition.

When U.S and Caribbean forces invaded the island on October 25, 1983 the suspected mastermind of the coup against Bishop, the burly ex-deputy Prime Minister Bernard Coard was found hiding inside a home in the Mt. Parnassus area that belonged to a brother of Sen. Roberts.

The opposition member of the Senate suggested that the location of the bodies of Bishop and the others will bring closure to the tragic events of October 1983.

He said that the 10-month old Thomas administration should continue to press US authorities for answers on behalf of the Grenadian people especially the family and friends of the deceased including the mother of Maurice Bishop who have been clamouring over the years for the remains of be handed over for a proper burial.

"We have a situation where up today the families of those persons still cannot give their love ones a burial", he added.

Nadia Bishop, the daughter of late Prime Minister Bishop has publicly forgiven those who were convicted in the trial for the execution of her father.

During a visit to her homeland in 2008, the young Bishop made an impassioned plea to the nation to join with her in making the year one of unconditional forgiveness and reconciliation for those involved in the killing of the revolutionary Prime Minister.

Marcel Belmar, sister of the late Jemma Belmar, who died in the October 1983 tragedy also joined Nadia Bishop in forgiving those who deprived her of her sister.

To date 9 of the convicts have been released from prison by the local high court acting on directives given by the Privy Council in London after they had served lengthy prison sentences.

Coard's wife Phyllis was released in 2000 during the rule of Roberts' NNP regime on medical grounds and is now living in a luxury home in well-to-do area in Jamaica.

*Late Prime Minister Bishop did not receive a christian burial*

*Bernard Coard - one of seventeen convicted for the mass slaying*

*Grenada Today, 15 May 2009*

# Remainder of Grenada 17 FREED

*Bernard Coard*

On Friday September 4th, 2009, the Minister responsible for the Advisory Committee on the Prerogative of Mercy, pursuant to her powers under Sections 72-74 of the Constitution of Grenada, advised His Excellency the Governor-General, to remit the remainder of the sentences of 14 prison inmates and thereby effect their release from incarceration.

The names of the persons affected are: Winston Antoine, Dave Bartholomew, Callistus Bernard, Bernard Coard, Leon Cornwall, Liam James, Michael Jeffrey, Ewart Layne, Michael Louison, Keston Mc Queen, Ms Hilary Ogilvie, Joseph Paul, Selwyn Strachan, Kevin Taylor

These inmates have been in prison for periods ranging from 5 to approximately 26 years.

The advice of the minister represents the final act in the review process provided for under Grenadian law, specifically the Prison Rules.

In the case of the seven prisoners referred to as the Grenada 17, imprisoned since 1983, the review of their sentences was also in keeping with a court order, arising out of the resentencing hearing in June 2007, for their sentences to be reviewed within 2 years. Without that review order from the court, their sentences would have expired within one year.

The review process commenced in January 2009 with the submission of reports by the prison authorities on the conduct, attitude, industry and other relevant matters, of all inmates who had served beyond 4 years of their sentences. The reports were considered by the Board of Review which also carried out interviews with the prisoners and instituted its own background checks and investigations.

A total of 42 inmates had their sentences reviewed. At the completion of its work, as is required by law, the Board of Review presented its findings and recommendations to the minister of national security who, in the exercise of his discretion, forwarded the recommendations of the Board for action by the Minister Responsible for the Advisory Committee on the Prerogative of Mercy.

*Weekly newspaper, 2009*

# Ventour: Castro tried to impose his will on the Grenada Revolution

*Cont'd from page 08*

*John "Chalky" Ventour - the author of "The Missing Link that exposed Cuba's interference in the affairs of the once powerful New Jewel Movement (NJM) which created the 1979-83 Grenada Revolution*

cal/key aspect of Cuba's relationship to the NJM and the Grenada Revolution, which, in my view reflects what I would call their petty hegemonic aspirations/designs re our process and attempts to make us very dependent on them.

I think it is also necessary to give and share with you some background information on FC's (Fidel Castro) and Cuba's relationship to our P and the Grenada Revolution.

FC (Fidel Castro) and Cuba had absolutely no role in making the Grenada Revolution. Indeed, they did not provide any assistance in making the Revolution, despite requests for assistance by our P (Party), and despite pre-1979 visits to Cuba by Maurice and Unison on one occasion, Bernard on another, and Selwyn Strachan in 1979.

Basically, they did not believe our claims about being in a position to remove the neo-fascist Gairy. They were obviously wary of us and our claims since they knew little or nothing about our P (Party).

So FC (Castro) and Cuba were as surprised as the rest of the world when the Grenada Revolution was made on March 13, 1979. After that they came forward with massive assistance, and a hot love-relationship developed between Grenada and Cuba.

From the very early days of the Revolution Cuba attempted to influence our process in Grenada by getting involved into matters they ought not to have been involved in.

Consistently, throughout the 4-and-a-half years, they tried to, in improper ways, influ-

*Fidel Castro - accused of playing a divisive role in the '83 conflict*

*The late Maurice Bishop - was considered the "son" of Fidel Castro*

ence the placement and changing of personnel in the PRA, for example. This began as early as 1980. Then, to the annoyance of many in our P (Party) Leadership, including many Grenadian Army officers, Ambassador Rizo used to impose himself on meetings of Maurice and the High Command of the Army. It was a disgusting form of interference.

I remember a personal experience in September 1981. I had arrived in Cuba on a brief (4-day) visit re coordination of a Caribbean Trade Union Conference which was to be held in Grenada two months later – in November that same year.

Just weeks prior to my visit the NJM CC had unanimously removed Cde. Vince Noel from the Party Leadership. For almost one year before, Vince, who was also a member of the Political Bureau of the Central Committee at the time, had been criticised on several occasions for serious shortcomings re his work – failure to carry out Party tasks, etc.

Rank and file P (Party) members were now openly complaining about his poor work performance and questioning his leadership. It had indeed become very embarrassing to the NJM Leadership. As a result, George Louison tabled a resolution to remove Vince. It was supported by all in the CC, including Maurice, Uni and Kendrick Radix.

As was normal protocol, the Cuban and other fraternal parties had been informed of this development.

Now, here I was in the Jose Marti International Airport's VIP lounge, having arrived only minutes before, in discussion with a Cuban official who came to meet me. After I had politely answered some of his questions – explaining our P (Party) Leadership's rationale/reasons for Vince's removal, the official of the Cuban Communist Party had the gall to tell me that they (the Cuban Party) "did not agree!"

In very improper ways, also, they tried to change the way in which decisions were historically made by our P (Party) Leadership. Our P (Party) had always, from its inception, stressed Collective Leadership, with Maurice being the first among equals.

In that context the strength of all our leaders came to bear; and the weakness of Maurice in making decisions, in strategy and tactics, and in guiding and supervising the work of the P (Party), and later the Revolution, were overcome.

(Maurice himself, on more than one occasions, openly admitted to all these weaknesses). In that context (of our Collective Leadership), while Maurice was clearly perceived as the Leader, the first among equals, Bernard, because of his particular strengths in the areas in which Maurice was weak was looked toward for leadership, and in practice, therefore, it was Bernard who led the P (Party) in those areas, before and during the Revolution.

So it was an informal arrangement; one based on the years of experi-

*Cont'd on page 12*

*Grenada Today, 18 September 2009*

## Ventour: Castro tried to impose his will on the Grenada Revolution

*Cont'd from page 10*

ence in our struggle, and an arrangement which led our P (Party) to glory.

In Cuba, however, the form leadership takes in their P (Party) is obviously different: Their circumstances are different; their history is different; and FC (Castro) is FC (Castro). In Cuba, FC (Castro) is the Maximum Leader in all areas. And this seems to have always been the case in their struggle. It is their history.

In short, Leadership in Cuba was always more personalised, more individualistic, it appears, and to a great extent this is due to the incredible ability of FC (Catro). But in Grenada, Leadership had always been more collective. This was due to the tremendous qualities of Maurice and Bernard in different areas; and also due to their specific weaknesses.

So the emphasis on collective leadership was based on our history, and rooted in our history. It developed and took root on the anti-Gairy battlefields, and in the unforgettable days in laying the basis for the Revolution, planning the Revolution, and then its glorious execution.

But that history, (our history) Cuba did not know of because they did not know our P (Party) in any real way until after March 13, 1979.

Yet from 1979 and onwards, with ever-greater intensity, they attempted to influence Maurice into adopting FC's (Castro's) style of leadership; into becoming a FC (Castro). But Maurice was never, and could never have been, FC (Castro). They were different persons.

That interference by Cuba, again in many improper ways, for example FC (Castro) sending down persons to Grenada to tell Maurice that certain decisions are his prerogative; and that the NJM CC could not take certain decisions, etc., etc., made for and naturally did lead to friction.

This friction and its by-products, combined with other subjective factors, and with the objective difficulties inherent in the task of transforming a poor backward underdeveloped country, and especially having to do so in the face of the most hawkish U.S. Administration since the gun-boat diplomacy days of President Theodore Roosevelt, led to a profound internal crisis in the P (Party) and Revolution by August-September, 1983.

The JL (Joint Leadership) decision (which as I stated before was part of a package of measures to overcome our P (Party) crisis), however, went against the form of leadership Cuba had tried to promote and impose on us for the better part of 4-and-a-half years. And they were hell-bent on quashing it.

So Maurice, obviously convinced by those around him that the JL (Joint Leadership) decision was some kind of "conspiracy" to ultimately remove him as leader, was therefore in the correct psychological state to make a complete break with the historically based collective leadership, and to place himself above the Leadership and General Meeting of the Party's decision.

Outside of Cuba's interference, there was absolutely no way he would have done that. Given his personality he would have taken that step only under strong encouragement.

Indeed, even if he wanted to, the balance of forces within the P (Party) and the Revolution would not have permitted it – he would have recognised that the P (Party) and its organs were decisive for the future of the Revolution.

But with Cuba's backing and, indeed, encouragement, he had an alternative manpower and material resource base outside of our P (Party) to fall back on.

There is another critical/key aspect of Cuba's relationship to the NJM and Grenada Revolution – and how it directly affected the October '83 crisis.

In 1981, Cuba requested and received permission from the Party and People's Revolutionary Government to organise their construction workers at the Point Salines International Airport project into a reserve military battalion.

Over fifty (50) officers from the Cuban Armed forces (FAR) arrived in Grenada to lead them. Our P (Party) Leadership was only too happy to accede to this request because we were informed that this reserve battalion would assist our young PRA in the defence of Grenada, in the event of any invasion.

Months later, quite accidentally, while working together with Cuban Military Advisers, preparing defence plans for our country to be able to repel any military aggression, Lt. Col. Layne – the day to day Commander of the PRA – was told by the leader of the Cuban military mission in Grenada that the Cuban battalion would only respond to a request for assistance from the Commander-in-Chief (a position they imposed on us in 1981); not the P (Party) Leadership, not the PRG; but one man!

However, it was only years later, when the crisis unfolded, that the significance of this statement was fully realised.

Cuba's interference in NJM and Grenada's internal affairs is not unique. I have heard of several instances of their interference in the internal affairs of other Revolutionary Parties and Countries.

Among them:

(1) In the 1960's the Algerian Party removed Ben Bela as leader of their party. I don't know the reasons or the details; but I understand that Cuba objected to this and interfered, and this led to a strain in relations between the Algerian and Cuban Parties/Revolutionaries.

(2) In the 1960's, also, there was a debate on The Way Forward in the Venezuelan Communist Party. I understand that debate was centered around the issue of whether or not the party should pursue the path of armed struggle. FC (Castro) publicly condemned the leadership of the PCV, accusing them of "sitting on their doorstep watching the corpse of Imperialism pass by (rather than take up arms and make the Revolution)."

(3) In the mid-late 1970's, I also understand that the Ethiopian Leader, Mengisthu, threatened to expel Cuba's Ambassador to Ethiopia if Cuba did not withdraw him. The Ambassador was accused of interference in the Ethiopian party and country's affairs.

(4) Then, there is Angola. In 1976 or 77, I remember hearing and reading news reports that the number two leader of the MPLA (the Ruling Revolutionary Party in Angola) was killed because he was a CIA agent, and also because of some counter-revolutionary plot.

Several years later I learnt that a problem had arisen within the MPLA Leadership and the Cuban Military Forces in Angola intervened on behalf of the

*Cont'd on page 13*

*Grenada Today, 18 September 2009*

## Ventour: Castro tried to impose his will on the Grenada Revolution

*Cont'd from page 12*

then, late MPLA Leader, Agostino Neto, crushing a "rebellion" against him.

As a result, Neto Alves, the number two person in the Angolan Leadership, together with many of the MPLA members, several Angolan Army leaders and soldiers, had been killed by the Cubans.

I don't know the details of any of these incidents. And I am not concerned here with which side was wrong or right. Whatever, that did not give FC (Castro), or anybody else for that matter, any right of interfere in other People's/Party's affairs.

So with this history, on the night of October 14, 1983, Bernard Coard and Selwyn Strachan held a meeting with Cuba's Ambassador Julian Rizo and 1st Secretary Gaston Diaz. In the meeting, I understand, they asked Rizo and Diaz for clarification re the Angolan situation in 1976/77. All Rizo would say was that Cuban Forces intervened in Angola "upon a request from the Angolan Commander-in-Chief."

When asked how would Cuba respond if a similar request were to be made by Grenada's "Commander-in-Chief," Rizo refused to answer. An answer though was forthcoming.

Two days later the NJM CC received a reply from FC (Castro). He complained in that letter that we were impugning the integrity of Cuba, etc. When Ambassador Rizo delivered FC's (Castro's) letter he refused to shake hands as was normal with the CC Comrades present [illegible]

[illegible]

member of the NJM Leadership.

But that is not all. That letter from FC (Castro) to the NJM CC was signed: "Commander-in-Chief"! Highly significant, eh? Not 1st Secretary of the PCC. Not as President of the Republic of Cuba. Not as Prime Minister of Cuba. Not even as Commander-in-Chief of the Cuban Revolution; but just CIC! Commander-in-Chief of Grenada?

Anyone in the circumstances, then, would naturally have seen this as a deliberate insult to NJM and Grenada and, also, as a warning.

So given this background, and Cuba's interference in our P (Party) affairs; FC's (Castro's) support and active assistance to Maurice; Ambassador Rizo's movement of 30 Cubans to guard the Cuban Embassy; the placing of their Military Advisors and their workers at Point Salines airport site "on alert" from around October 13th (the workers comprised their Reserve Military Battalion; and "alert", in the military lexicon, is the first stage before a call to action); their continuing to recognise George Louison as a member of the NJM Leadership, even after he was expelled from the Party Leadership by the CC and the October 13th Extraordinary NJM General Meeting, our Security Forces were naturally gravely concerned about Cuba's intentions.

The combination of this and Maurice's role in originating and organising the spreading of the Rumour, and the consequent near violence of the rumour that same night (October 12th) at a Militia Station in St. Paul's (a suburb in St. George's) was discussed by the Security Forces with Maurice in a frank manner on October 14 thereabouts; and he was strongly advised to stay home for a few days and let things calm down in the country, and return to normal, while attempts were being made to resolve the crisis.

The objective also, I understand, was to deny Maurice access to the Cubans (until after we had resolved our internal crisis), about whom the Grenada Security Forces were obviously very concerned.

Maurice's moral position, was extremely weak for at the October 13th Extraordinary P General Meeting at which he and Errol George (deputy chief of his P.S. unit) and other spoke, he was exposed red-handed by the entire P membership present, as the person behind the fateful rumour that "Phyllis Coard and Bernard Coard (were) planning to kill Maurice Bishop."

I believe that FC (Castro) and Cuba's attempts to impose their form of leadership on us: (a) is a reflection of their genuinely held view that FC-type of leadership is the best – at least the best for this region; and (b) in their

*Sen. Chester Humphrey puts his hand on the shoulder of Comrade Coard minutes after he was released from prison*

view, provided the best mechanism for Cuba to wield influence and, indeed, control over the Grenada process.

With FC (Castro) adopting Maurice as his "son," and with Cuba's form of leadership, Cuba's control over the Grenada Revolution would have been complete.

I and all others here have the greatest respect and admiration for the man FC (Castro), as a Leader, and for the immense unquestionable contribution he (and his Party and Country) has made to the World Revolutionary Process.

Tremendous advances have been made under his great leadership for the people of Cuba. However, I would not be human if I don't feel angered – to put it mildly – over what I will describe as Cuba's act of great treachery of the Grenada Revolution.

After all these years, honestly, I want to sound dispassionate; but I'm sure you know that there are some things in life that one cannot forgive or forget. Despite its catastrophic consequences, it is still possible for me to forgive (but not forget) FC (Castro) for his interference in our affairs.

After all, one may argue that he thought he was doing the best thing and his decisions were based on incorrect information of the situation in our Party, etc., etc., etc. But let me tell you: I try to avoid thinking (and speaking) about this for it really hurts.

*Grenada Today, 18 September 2009*

men assimilate into society it was an opportunity to transcend their silence and write their memoirs as we sought to bring together the missing pieces of our historical puzzle. On the 13th September 2009, Bernard Coard conducted an exclusive interview with the *Trinidad Express* newspaper, highlighting the grave errors of the revolution. There is limited documentation on the revolution, either the persons with the in-depth knowledge were dead, incarcerated or others just buried it in the deep recesses of their mental abyss. The interview was in-depth. It had to be recorded in its totality for full effect.

The documentation of a nation's history is paramount. If it is not done timeously and accurately, its record would be superfluous, ineffective and the possibility of repetition would be inevitable.

## Exclusive interview with Bernard Coard

*Coard, the former deputy prime minister, was released from prison after serving 26 years for the killing of his former political colleague*

The following is being reproduced from the Trinidad Express newspaper dated Sunday September 13, 2009. The interview was conducted with Coard by veteran Trinidad journalist, Raoul Pantin.

Bernard Coard was 'in a meeting'. I was informed, when I phoned him in Grenada early Tuesday evening. I was asked to call him back in about an hour.

And when I did, I was given another phone number to reach him.

It occurred to me that only a few days after being released from serving 26 years in jail for the murder of Maurice Bishop and other members of the leadership of the New Jewel Movement (NJM) in October 1983, here was Coard taking up where he left off.

I could just picture him huddled with his old political cronies. But he quickly disabused me of that notion when finally I got on to him late that night.

Swearing that he will never get involved in politics again, Coard said he was meeting with someone 'who helped to save my life.'

Q: Tell me, Mr Coard...

A: Hey, Raoul! What is this 'Mister Coard' business? We go back too far for that. The only 'Mister Coard' I know is my father and he died a long time ago...

Q: Okay, Bernard. How does it feel to be a free man?

A: I'm elated. Just elated. That's the bottom line.

Q. And what was life like in prison for all those years?

A: The first eight years were really brutal. The man in charge of the prison at that time was from Barbados and he was really mentally ill. You didn't need a psychiatrist to tell you that. He could easily have run one of those concentration camps during World War Two. And the whole trial was a sham.

Initially we refused to cooperate because there were all sorts of wrong things going on. We were tortured...

*Bernard Coard and the last remaining members of the Grenada 17 walk to freedom from behind the the walls of the Richmond Hill prison*

Q: What kind of torture..?

A. We were sporadically beaten to force us to sign certain statements. Sometimes they would wrap a pipe in a wet towel and beat some of the guys on the stomach. I was not one of them. But medical reports produced in court testified to this kind of treatment.

Apart from that, in the middle of the trial, there were all kinds of irregularities. It was well choreographed. At one point, the judge decided that a new panel of jurors should be picked. There were certain rules to be followed in that selection.

And we subsequently discovered that at least 11 members of the new panel could not possibly have been on the jury. This was just one of some 200 irregularities that took place.

We refused to co-operate. We chanted them down....Then when (Trinidad lawyer) Karl Hudson-Phillips took over the prosecution he suggested a different approach to get us to co-operate. But the torture continued.

I was beaten about my head, my neck. I was bleeding from my ears. My injuries were superficial. But a medical report on my condition was three pages long. And in the cells, there were 100 Watt bulbs being used on a 24/7 basis. All the other cells had 60 Watt bulbs.

There was no sheet for the bed or blankets, there were no toothbrushes, the cells were full of cockroaches. We had no clothes, except the short pants and shirts we were wearing.

This went on for eight years. Eventually the man from Barbados in charge of the prison had a stroke and he returned to Barbados and subsequently died. Then a Grenadian took over running the prison and he was the best person. He made it one of the best-run prisons in Grenada, encouraging education and so on.

Q: Did you also face hostility from other prisoners, who were sympathetic to Maurice Bishop?

A: Initially. But this changed very quickly. Callistus Bernard (a former member of the NJM who was [illegible] imprisoned [illegible] a book [illegible]

Cont'd on page [illegible]

*Grenada Today, 18 September 2009*

# Exclusive interview with Bernard Coard

*Cont'd on page 14*

experience, titled, "They Can Only Kill Me Once". It's been published in the United Kingdom but isn't yet released in the Caribbean.

Q: So what are your immediate plans for the future?

A: I plan to write my memoirs...

Q: Tell me, do you feel any remorse over the killing of Maurice Bishop and other members of the NJM?

A: Oh Lord, yes! I've written a paper on this, titled 'Reflections And Apologies'. It was issued on February 8, 1997. In it, we apologised unreservedly to the Grenadian people. A lot of good things happened in the Grenada Revolution, the new international airport, people were being better educated. And so on. But we took moral and political responsibility for what happened. We did so.

Many things were wrong. And we've apologised. We don't apportion blame. We take collective responsibility for everything that went wrong. We accept full moral and political responsibility for all of it.

And I am still traumatised by it. It's not just a question of remorse. I've written 70 pages on this issue. Ask John 'Chalkie' Ventour to e-mail it to you...

Q: What, really, did lead to the split between you and Maurice Bishop? I believe you were deputy Prime Minister at that time...?

A: The seeds for what happened on October 19, 1983 (the day Bishop, among others, was killed) were sown by some of the things we did when we took power. People look on it as a 'split' but there were many, many dimensions involved. Any such catastrophe must have more than one cause.

A lot of media people in the Caribbean have consistently got it all wrong. And let me say this: you can take this as an exclusive interview because I have the highest respect for you. You are a distinguished journalist of the highest standing and the only reason I am doing this interview is because I have always respected you. You are the only Caribbean journalist I'm prepared to talk to...

Q: Well, I appreciate that but back to the question of the 'split', if that is what it was, that led to the breakup between yourself and Maurice Bishop...

A: We had taken a decision that there should be joint leadership of the New Jewel Movement (NJM). This was discussed at a Congress of the party and it was agreed that there should be joint leadership. But then there was the Cuban influence in which they insisted, based on their own political experience, that there should be a maximum leader. They sought to introduce that model in the NJM.

Bishop, who had contested the idea of joint leadership, said he wanted to give the whole thing some more thought. And despite the fact that it had been agreed on by a Congress of the party, we decided to invite the entire membership of the party to discuss it.

So a general membership meeting was convened. And Bishop was told 'we love you. We can't do without you.' But we also pointed out his weaknesses. We all felt that joint leadership was the way to go. It was a mistake. Because life is also about human emotions and feelings. And we failed to take that into account.

Bishop initially agreed to the idea of joint leadership. But he went on a short trip abroad and after passing through Cuba on his way home, when he got back he said he had changed his mind. And there were rumours circulating that we wanted to kill Maurice Bishop. And like the fools we were, we put him under house arrest. And the whole thing got out of hand...

Q: Well, that is putting it mildly. What subsequently happened amounted to a virtual civil war with murderous consequences...

A: Not initially. Bishop supporters demonstrated in the streets on October 12 right through to October 19 (1983). Apart from a couple traffic policemen, there were no policemen or soldiers on the streets during those demonstrations.

And anybody who was there will tell you that there was no lawlessness, no destruction of property. The demonstrations were highly vocal but they were disciplined. And the high command decided not to intervene because we felt that would only make things worse...

The first half of the demonstration for Bishop on October 19 was in the same vein: very vocal but very disciplined. In the second half, people found out where Bishop was being detained and they stormed the place and took him away. We thought, well now they'll call a general strike and heighten the protest. Instead, they headed for the army headquarters, seized the building and began to arm themselves and distribute arms.

Even at that stage, we were hoping things would calm down and we wouldn't have to intervene.

Q: But you did intervene!

A: When we realised that weapons were being distributed, we sent three armoured cars to recapture the fort. The armoured cars were meant as a show of force. There was no intention to use force.

One eye-witness said when he saw the armoured cars heading for the fort, there were soldiers sitting on top of the vehicles. That would not have been the case if their intent was to engage the demonstrators with arms.

The prosecution at our trial said the intent was to massacre the people. But that was never the intent. It was some of the demonstrators who opened fire on the armoured cars. The first people to die in that fateful day of October 19 were four soldiers.

Q: Were there any witnesses to this?

A: (The late Grenadian journalist) Allister Hughes was at the fort on October 19 and he sat in court during our trial and never said a word. But in his last days, he called in a few close friends, like Leslie Pierre, who swore to this in an affidavit that was presented to the Privy Council.

Hughes told Pierre that the crowd was the first to open fire. And after that happened all hell broke loose.

Q: But what about the execution of Maurice Bishop and Unison Whiteman, among others? Wasn't that a direct order?

A: No, no. American soldiers, with hundreds of years of military experience, have run amok in some countries. The British army, with a thousand years of military experience, has done the same thing. We had four and a half years of military experience in Grenada.

What happened was vengeance. It was nothing we ordered. And it can never be justified. It was a moment of revenge. Pure and simple. But everyone of us in the leadership take moral and political responsibility for what happened.

If we hadn't committed so many errors ... we were amateurs, we were arrogant and intolerant and all our mistakes came home to roost....

Q: I've seen it reported that you intend to give up politics. Is that true? Or are you going to get back in politics?

A: Are you crazy? Absolutely not.

Q: So what does the future hold in store for you?

A: I'm not sure yet. I'm going to spend some time catching up on my writing, working on my memoirs.

Q: I understand you plan to move to Jamaica?

A: Well, I am a Grenadian citizen. But my wife is a Jamaican and she is in very poor health. My son is also up there. My main duty and responsibility now is to her. (He explains that his wife got colon cancer while she was in prison, had been released because of this and had been receiving chemotherapy treatment which has affected her liver.)

It very successfully destroyed part of her liver for which she has to be taking a lot of medicine. She is also a victim of post-traumatic stress disorder. Tell me, is Ken Gordon still in charge at the Express?

Q: No, he's moved on, retired. The new CEO is Terrence Farrell.

A: Maybe I could become a correspondent for the Express.

Q: A political correspondent?

A: No, no. no. Perhaps an economics correspondent. I never want to have anything to do with politics for the rest of my life.

*Grenada Today, 18 September 2009*

CHAPTER EIGHTEEN

# SHARKS DO EAT SHARKS, AT LEAST THEY TRY: SHARK ATTACK

*"Plead my cause, O Lord, with them that strive with me: fight against them that fight against me ... Let their way be dark and slippery: and let the angel of the Lord persecute them ... Judge me, O Lord my God, according to thy righteousness; and let them not rejoice over me."*
PSALM 35

*"He that seeketh mischief, it shall come unto him."*
PROVERBS 11:27

When I was officially inaugurated into the legal profession and issued with my licence to practice, I had very high expectations for the legal ethos of the profession. In the speech delivered to the three lawyers who were about to be admitted to practice, the ethics of the profession was high on the agenda. The Judges were sure to express that our first and paramount duty was to the court. Our work should be a manifestation of diligence and nobility, qualities synonymous with the legal profession.

The manner in which attorneys should treat each other, devoid of malice, greed, jealousy and evil intent, was not part of the charge. As a legal embryo, the pasture appeared green to me. I had no idea then that there would be dark and bright days in the legal profession. That there would be summer, winter, autumn and spring. There were occasions when I was wounded but not defeated, battle scarred but yet I trod on. I knew the plight of the wounded was never to be defeated. It was my desire to practise my profession with the highest ethical standard. I was naïve when I entered the legal profession, but with each passing year my experience grew, not only in the law, but as it related to human relations and their thrust for power.

The seasonal nature of human existence is highlighted in the Bible. I had to draw upon that many times in my legal journey. I kept Ecclesiastes Chapter 3 verses 4 and 8 very close to my heart; it stated:

> *A time to weep and a time to laugh; a time to mourn, and a time to dance;*
> *A time to love and a time to hate; a time of war and a time of peace.*

There are many challenges along life's journey. I believe God allows these challenges to occur so as to make us stronger or be able to draw upon his teachings for propulsion in this life.

The years flew by in the legal profession. I focused on preparing for my cases as thoroughly as was demanded; sometimes many late hours, I would remain in office or stay up at nights. The appetite I had to be thorough, thereby leaving no stone unturned, became part of my DNA. I channelled every bit of my energy into my work.

The good old saying that time and tide wait on no man is true, the years spun on. The myriad of cases both civil and criminal were conducted by my law firm. By that time, it grew to the point where I had one associate attorney; later two associate attorneys. We developed the attitude that preparation was key and legal submissions must be properly researched, typed, paginated and presented. The rest should be left up to the judge. The preparation, research, writing and the adrenaline rush for the court presentation, seeing the law develop in written judgments were just wonderful. When one has found their calling, they experience true joy. True joy I did experience. My grandmother would say to me, "After joy is sorrow." And so, sorrow soon came.

During the latter part of 2016, the Registrar of the Supreme Court Lisa Telesford contacted me to alert me that she was in receipt of an email addressed directly to her from one named 'Arthur Frederick', alleging that I had an intimate sexual relationship with a female Judge who was then sitting in the island of Grenada. It was apparent that the email was sent to the Registrar because the author was aware of the relationship between the Registrar and me. The author of the email demanded that she forward the email to the Chief Justice, "... since there was a potential for the Registrar and the Judge to be fighting over a man." The email went further to say that the activities of the Judge and me were occurring around 4:30 am when the sentry left her house.

Authur Fredrick [atlasnappo@outlook.com]

You forwarded this message on 10/12/2016 1:17 PM.

**Sent:** Wednesday, September 28, 2016 3:19 PM
**To:** lisatelesford@hotmail.com

AFredrick

---

**From:** Authur Fredrick
**Sent:** Tuesday, September 27, 2016 6:08 AM
**To:** registrargda@caribsurf.com
**Subject:**

Dear Registrar,

I am writing to you in your capacity as registrar because of what is happening between Justice        and your boyfriend Derrick Sylvester. For a while now,, she has been sleeping with him. This has been the whisper around and no one has the guts to tell you. Most of their activity is around 4.30 am when I suppose you are asleep. This is when the sentry leaves her house. A few times he goes by during the evening and once or twice around 11 30pm or later.

I suppose this might be an embarrassing situation for you but I have to bring it to your attention because sooner or later it will bring the justice system into disrepute. People have been talking and it is said that is why she was so lenient on his clients. This is not to fair to you, and it is not right. It took me a while to write since I realise the effect it might have on you, since you have a duty to bring it to the attention of the CJ. Soon we will have a situation where a High Court Judge and the registrar will be fighting over a man. How would that look. I am giving you the opportunity to deal with it before it becomes further widespread

AFredrick

*First email sent to Registrar*

At first I thought it was a joke, but the Registrar was not one prone to jokes of that nature. Further, the Registrar and all the judges had a very close knit working relationship, by the very nature of their respective jobs.

Both the Registrar and I laughed it off. We felt someone was pulling a prank, so there was nothing to it. My work ethic or our daily routines would not have allowed the semblance of a thought in relation to the allegation. There was no reason to prolong the issue further. In my state of naivety I felt that was the end of the matter. That the obvious prank had ended just as it started.

I pondered to myself why someone would even attempt to falsely and maliciously bring into disrepute, not only my professional reputation, but also the administration of justice. The saying that 'idle hands were the devil's workshop' was probably at work, so I ignored it all and went on my business as usual, focusing on the daily tasks at hand.

On the 10th day of October 2016, directly twelve days after the first email, the Registrar contacted me again, this time indicating that a much more lengthy and detailed email was sent to the Chief Registrar in St. Lucia for the attention of the Chief Justice and copied to her. This time I was taken totally by surprise. I felt the pulse in my veins as if I had just run a 1500 metres. I saw my professional life flash before my very eyes. I stayed on the telephone in shock. It was the first time in my professional life I felt the pain and sting of a malicious rumour. I was determined to read the email myself.

The second email was longer in content, much more detailed and made spurious, libellous and malicious allegations against me, maligning my professional reputation. The email alleged that the Registrar failed to act on the first email because it was uncomfortable for her; the justice system in Grenada was being brought into disrepute that practitioners, staff members and onlookers were mumbling about it, that the female Judge was sleeping with the Registrar's boyfriend. It was creating a mess, and that I also influenced what the Judge's decisions were. The email went further to say, the Judge was very severe in her sentences regarding rape and murder, however my client Sheldon Payne got just over nine (9) years for murder. Further, that I was part of the Executive (being Chairman of the Public Service Commission). I was very influential in government. That I appeared before the Judge especially in civil cases. That I was compromising the independence of the judiciary. That I had cause to transfer one staff member who was working with the said Judge because she was uncomfortable with the relationship. Further, people in Grenada were talking about what was going on. The writer went further to say, he had proof of what he wrote because he saw it himself when I leave the Judge's house early in the morning.

This grieved me greatly. I felt lost in a world where I was an innocent lamb to the slaughter, but how could I prove my innocence. The Registrar and I immediately decided to contact the Royal Grenada Police Force to launch a full investigation into the matter including the sender of the emails. At that time the Registrar notified me that she had no option but to notify the Judge who it was alleged I had an improper intimate relationship with about the scandal. This tore me apart. The discomfort of having to appear before a Judge with an allegation that is false, malicious and poisonous was too painful for me to bear. I drew upon my grandmother's teaching, when she said, "You must pray in and out of season so you would catch the right season."

Authur Fredrick [atlasnappo@outlook.com]

You forwarded this message on 10/12/2016 1:15 PM.

**Sent:** Monday, October 10, 2016 4:19 AM
**To:** kphulgence@eccourts.org
**Cc:** lisatelesford@hotmail.com

Dear Madam,

Ive been advised to write to you since I wrote to the Registrar who is copied in, and no action has been taken, not even an acknowledgement of my email. I suppose it's uncomfortable for her, since the person involved directly relates to her.

There is some activity going on in Grenada which directly impacts the justice system and is bringing the justice system into disrepute. This is causing a stir among practitioners, staff members and onlookers who are mumbling about it and saying this should not be happening. Simple put, Justice is sleeping with the Registrars boyfriend Derrick Sylvester and it's creating a mess. Needless to say that he influences what is done by the justice. One does not have to look far to see what is happening. Let us take one example. If you look at her sentencing you will see that she is very severe on rape and murder. The public were appalled when she sentenced Sheldon Payne to just over 9 years imprisonment when this was blatant murder, only to find out what was going on between herself and Mr. Sylvester. Mr. Sylvester is part of the executive and very influential in the Government. Mr. Sylvester appears before her in cases especially civil cases. Her relationship with him has caused the independence of the Judiciary to be compromised. She should not be allowed to happen. Justice must always be seen to be done.

This situation has caused at least one staff member to be transferred recently since she was uncomfortable with the relationship. Grenada is a small place and nothing hides here.People are talking about what is going on. It is obvious what is happening and it is straining the relationship between her and the registrar, and between the registrar and her boyfriend. Parties are expected to be treated equally, not special treatment for Mr. Sylvester while others are treated like nothing. I would be grateful if this information is passed to the Chief Justice so that something can be done about. Clearly Miss Telford is unable to act.

I would be grateful for a response in this matter. I see what is happening and Im appalled at it. I write because I have proof of what I say. Ive seen the events I speak about on numerous occasions, especially late at night and in the early hours of the morning when he goes to her house.

AFredrick

*Second email sent to Registrar (Grenada) and copied to Chief Registrar (St. Lucia)*

This was a dark moment in my life. The face of my emotional pain was to be seen by me and the God I prayed to only. On mornings before I got to work I would pray as I normally do, however I descended deeper and deeper into prayer before I departed from my home. I kept wondering daily, who was the orchestrator of such malice, but it was left to the police to launch the investigation.

I could not sit still. I wrote the Commissioner of Police, requesting a full investigation. I was prepared to bear the cost of it. I had a meeting with the Commissioner of Police. He assured me that he would put his computer team to work on the matter expeditiously. This was a great sense of relief for me as I felt the perpetrator would be caught. I would be vindicated. That was a consoling thought, but the daily trauma of having to operate in an environment where you do not know who was about to stab you in the back became unbearable; however it only made me stronger and more prayerful.

I recall one night when I returned home from work, I went into my room and I prayed continually asking God for strength, peace, wisdom and character to deal with the untruth that surrounded me. There was no one I could speak to about this other than the ones directly involved with the investigation, so I resigned myself in my own sorrows. The author of the email was successful in causing me pain; and that he caused; but I called upon my God and prayed for vengeance on the perpetrator or perpetrators. I prayed Psalm 109 which says in part:

> *Hold not thy peace, O God of my praise; for the mouth of the wicked and the mouth of the deceitful are opened against me: they have spoken against me with a lying tongue. They have compassed me about also with words of hatred; and fought against me without a cause.*

I read that psalm nightly, but the pain never relented. I could not sit idly by, while my professional life that I worked so hard for was being dragged in the mud; I had to act swiftly. But before I acted, there were two untruths in the second email that were easily ascertained.

The first being that the learned Judge had sentenced my client to nine (9) years imprisonment. The accused was sentenced to eight years and ten months from the date the sentence was pronounced. However, he had already spent two (2) years and five (5) months on remand which totalled eleven point two five years (11.25) and numerous other sentencing conditions. For example, the accused had to undergo psychiatric treatment for the duration of his incarceration, counselling for anger management, ordered to take lessons in reading, mathematics and English, in default two (2) years in prison. Finally, the prison had to provide the court with a report after the accused would have served half his sentence.

The prosecution had appealed the sentence, however subsequently when the matter came on for case management conference and trial directions were given by the court, the prosecution's office withdrew the appeal. This was an appeal I was thoroughly prepared for as I had completed the submission just awaiting the date for hearing.

Secondly, the transfer of the staff member that was attached to the Judge's court. An investigation could have been launched as to the reason for her transfer. The request was made through the transferee's department and sent to the office of the Public Service Commission, wherein I was Chairman, with a five (5) member committee. There was no illegality or surreptitious motive. When there is a request for transfer, the Commission generally acceded, since it was a policy of the public service that officers could be transferred upon request to facilitate better efficiency of the service. So there was nothing sinister about that officer's transfer, once it was within the public service and the person transferred was in the same pay grade with the commensurate benefits they once had.

The investigation was now fully underway. I notified the police that I was willing to let them have unrestricted access to my computers at office, home and all my cellular phones including email access so as to determine the falsity of the allegations. I had also provided unrestricted access to my home. An examination of the surrounding video cameras for any period so investigated. It was my desire to prove my innocence. My house was in a central location, in the south of the island, perched in a 'T' junction with numerous neighbours in close proximity. Despite its residential nature there was visibility around my home. The Commissioner of Police gave me his commitment for an expedited police investigation.

As time went by, there was no word from the police. I again communicated with the Registrar. The computer where the email was sent was taken by the Criminal Investigation Department, Information Technology Unit. The IP and other addresses were being examined. I met again with the Commissioner of Police requesting continued assistance. He vowed to continue. However, I was informed that the files were sent to the office of the Attorney General. It was from that office the police was instructed to discontinue the investigation. When the Commissioner of Police notified me of same, it was as if the sword of Damocles was about to enter the left ventricle of my heart, piercing the aorta, thereby filling the pericardium with venomous blood, resulting in legal death. I had no idea my legal life would have been plagued with so much pain. I bore it silently. For I always said, I would prefer to suffer innocently, than be guilty, for if the latter, it would be deserved, but the former, my conscience would be lily white. I preferred a clear conscience, for then my nights would be peaceful.

I then had to decide my next move, as a chess player I had to be methodical. The Commissioner of Police was unable to act, as he was instructed by the office of the Attorney General not to. I discussed the matter with the then Registrar of the Supreme Court and I spoke to two most eminent and distinguished female attorneys, whom I had grown to respect, admire and appreciate. I decided to speak to them about the way forward in a matter of that nature as I had a plan that necessitated their presence and support.

Prearranged meetings were held with both Attorneys. My pain was raw as I spoke to them, they each recognised something was amiss because I was not my usual jovial self. I explained to them, that I was not contacted by the Chief Justice's Office, despite the email went there. The Registrar confirmed that she had spoken to the Chief Registrar in St. Lucia about the receipt of the email. I explained further, that I was considering writing the Court for an investigation and that all costs would be borne by me for it or to have an audience with the Chief Justice in St. Lucia. I did not want to breach any legal protocol so I wanted the two most senior members to accompany me there. However, the wisdom of the two experienced officers suggested an audience would be the preferred route.

After I left the meetings which were held on different days, one was at my office with one attorney and the other was at the private home of the other, for in my darkest hour, they were my only glimmer of hope. While the innocent suffer, the guilty are allowed to roam the earth freely. Oh, what an unjust world in which we live; but I was reminded that, weeping may endure for the night but joy cometh in the morning. Morning was taking very long to come, for indeed the darkest and longest part of the day was dawn. I awaited the morn.

A letter was penned and sent to the Chief Registrar in St. Lucia requesting an audience with the Honourable Chief Justice on the matter at any place or country that she was amenable to, and to be accompanied by the two attorneys from Grenada who were also copied in on the written request. After the terms of the letter were agreed upon, it was dispatched to St. Lucia.

I have never prayed for vengeance, punishment or the befalling of the most catastrophic type of evil on another fellow human, except during that period of my life. The daily pain was too much to bear. I reminisced on what Bernard Coard said to me one day while I was visiting him at Her Majesty's Prisons. He said, "Don't hate, because it only destroys the hater not the hated." I looked upon the legal profession with tremendous suspicion, antagonism, sympathy, rage and in some cases empathy.

But I was reminded by the words of Izaak Walton when he penned:

> *Affliction is a divine diet which though it be not pleasing to mankind, yet Almighty God hath often imposed it as a good, though bitter, physic, to those children whose souls are dearest to him.*

I have many times wondered about the pain the Judge may have experienced daily, because it is always easy to know the depth of your sorrow, but the sorrow of others may be immeasurable when compared to your own. Sitting as a Judge in a strange land and having to face the malicious, false and bitter scathing attacks in a society where the legal norms do not allow them to speak publicly on matters, is like being a lamb to the slaughter, in what is sometimes the abattoir called life. My faith in God grew immensely by virtue of the allegations levelled against me, if there was one good that came out of it, it was my faith in God as I wait for his justice.

Having regard to the content of the emails I did not disclose it to anyone outside of the investigation. I said nothing to my mother, family and close friends. I had no idea whether the email rumour spread or not. I was just taking each passing day immersed in prayer and continued to do my job to the best of my ability. The pain remained with me. There is a Yiddish proverb, which was very applicable to my situation which says:

> *The greatest pain is the pain you cannot tell others.*

The letter was sent to St. Lucia. I was anxiously awaiting a response from the Chief Registrar as to whether the Chief Justice would have audience regarding our request. I had mixed feelings about it, but it was the only way I felt I could have dealt with the issue. In my capacity as Chairman of the Public Service Commission, the Commission had to deal with many like issues, be it allegations of misconduct, unethical behaviour or breach of statutory rules, it was always the Commission's duty to have full in-depth investigations to get to the bottom of the matters, so as to enable transparency. I have had instances where matters were under investigation and third parties would seek to speak, write or send messages to influence the Commission.

Then the time soon came, I was in receipt of a response from the Chief Registrar wherein the Chief Justice agreed to have audience with the team in St. Lucia. This brought a sense of elation. I immediately contacted my colleagues who I referred to as from that day forth my "knights in shining armour". I soon made travel arrangements so as to embark upon the journey to vindicate my professional innocence.

The profession I loved, that I longed to enter since childhood, its members had launched a vicious attack on my professional life. This was like a marriage once filled with love, now turned to bitter hate and whose relentless desire had transformed into intentional destruction.

CHAPTER NINETEEN

# JOURNEY TO VINDICATE MY PROFESSIONAL INNOCENCE

*"Is Christ thy advocate to plead thy cause?*
*Art Thou his client?*
*Such shall never slide*
*He never lost a case."*
EDWARD TAYLOR

The Attorney General's office had ordered the discontinuation of the investigation. I was left in a quandary as to what should be my next step. The only other step was to seek the audience that we hoped for. It was granted. The preparation for the journey was well organised, my colleagues and I agreed upon the contents and the presentation at the meeting. It was a demanding time for us all as we were embarking upon a journey wherein we could not anticipate the response we were most likely to receive. From my past experiences with the Chief Justice in court, Her Ladyship The Hon Dame Janice Pereira DBE was always methodical, well-spoken and exhibited the level of professionalism commensurate with the office. So, I was hopeful that at least we would be received with professional courtesy, and despite there were occasions when I wondered whether that was the best route to take, there were no other options available.

The arrangements were made. The flights were booked to travel to St. Lucia via Barbados. I secured the use of the executive lounge at the Maurice Bishop International Airport, so as to enable smooth and hassle free travel. I had my law office secure accommodation at the Bay Gardens Hotel, where I had stayed many times in the past, ensuring we had transportation to the office of the Chief Justice . It was our intention that we would not be tardy for any reason whatsoever. We agreed upon the presentation before the Chief Justice, the order in which we should speak, including who would do the introduction.

It was mentally exhausting. I was innocent of the allegations against me, however the malevolence that would have precipitated the production of the emails was incomprehensible. That someone could orchestrate a story as vicious and vile as that, tells the particular character of the relevant human being or beings. The act was puzzling as it was troubling. I have been a punctual, respectful and hardworking attorney before all the courts, I had a no adjournment policy, as my practice grew, the complement of lawyers also increased. The destruction of my professional life and character was therefore very high on someone's agenda. I recalled when I just entered the profession; my father and I had a lengthy discourse on the law, its practice and colleagues. He had forewarned me in those words, "As soon as you start making progress you better wear a bullet proof vest." I listened to him then, feeling it was just a mere warning to be mindful, while ensuring the ethics of the profession was maintained. But I never fathomed the extent of the wars I had to wage; I needed more than a vest but an armour.

On one occasion when angered by this entire fiasco, the bible passage came to me, "False witnesses did rise up; they laid to my charge things I knew not," and I relented into a state of normalcy. I had decided I would not let the evil of this world cause me to change either my character or personality, for when one is fighting against evil they should be careful not to become evil. That I was destined to refrain from.

My colleagues and I agreed to meet at the Maurice Bishop International Airport at the south of the island. We were met by the protocol team from the Ministry of Foreign Affairs who escorted us to the VIP waiting area. This courtesy was afforded me as I was Chairman of the Public Service Commission. I looked at my colleagues who were leaving their families, business and homes to champion my cause. I had repeatedly thanked them for accompanying me on that journey. I kept praying for the fortitude to deal with all the challenges that I had faced and will continue to.

At the waiting area we again discussed the manner in which we would present at the meeting with the Chief Justice. Soon, there was the announcement on the intercom notifying us of the arrival of our flight which would depart shortly. We hastily wrapped up our meeting and agreed the conversation would continue when we got to the hotel. I was experiencing a whirlwind of emotions. I was interrupted by a knock on the door and we were escorted unto the ATR aircraft destined for Barbados *en route* to St Lucia. The meeting was carded for the following day so the night was for preparation, discussion and prayer.

While the plane taxied down the runway and made its ascension I peered through the window where I was sitting and thought to myself why an island so small, with just over one hundred thousand souls, could engender so much hate to promulgate a rumour aimed at destroying the professional life of an individual. The short answer to that question was, not even the devil knoweth the mind of man. I relaxed in my seat as I continued to pray. I then pulled out the LIAT magazine and read until the fifty-five minute journey from Grenada to Barbados had expired, with an announcement by the pilot to the flight attendant. I reminisced for a moment, whether I would not have better served as a pilot, since I had once embarked upon that journey but terminated to follow my true passion, by then it was too late, I was already in shark-infested waters.

The legal profession had long been referred to as a profession loaded with sharks, but since to my mind it was a noble profession, I thought the phrase may have been coined by dissatisfied litigants. I recalled one day while at the lecture theatre in the University of the West Indies in Barbados, one of my favourite lecturers decided to tell a story before he started his lecture. It went like this:

> One day a ship sank, just off the shore. It was loaded with professionals. There were priests, accountants and lawyers. The priests tried swimming to safety; however, the sharks came and ate them up. The accountants tried swimming also and the sharks in like manner had them for lunch, however the lawyers all swam ashore safely. When interviewed as to how they were able to survive amidst the shark infested waters and the other professionals perished, the lawyers responded: "Sharks don't eat sharks, it's professional courtesy".

I did not understand the moral of the story until I had experienced shark infested waters myself. Supper time for me was imminent, so maybe I was not a shark after all. The moral of the story stayed with me. It was on occasions like these, the tales which were told bore relevance and significance.

We all disembarked the flight and exited to the waiting area, where we remained to board the connecting flight to St. Lucia. We again discussed, the ramification going forward and the negative implication the rumour could potentially have on my professional life. The protocol for the meeting was rehearsed so as to ensure we had no administrative or professional embarrassment, after all, we were appearing before the Chief Justice of the highest regional court and who saw it fit to grant audience to us, at our request despite the Court's busy itinerant schedule.

The moment soon came for us to embark upon the second leg of our journey, as we were escorted unto the aircraft this time from Barbados to St. Lucia. At that time I was feeling jet lagged despite the short journey, it was more of a mixture of emotions, nostalgia with a bit of anger. I was determined not to be consumed by any one of the seven deadly sins. My colleagues and I soon were on our way, as we all decided what our evening would be occupied with as soon as we landed at the George F.L. Charles Airport in Castries, St. Lucia. The flight from Barbados to St. Lucia I spent reading through the itemised documents prepared for the meeting. I had carefully prepared bundles of all the documents I intended to use, all tabbed from Roman Numerals I to XII. I had intended to speak to them in that order as it would make for easy reference, synonymous to a court presentation.

The aircraft started its descent into St. Lucia. No one needed any announcement to confirm that, as it was felt in flight. The plane soon landed. We walked across the tarmac to the immigration and customs department. Our immigration forms were all filled out and our luggage was small since it was a one day travel to St. Lucia, the purpose of the visit was only to facilitate the meeting, to at least deal with the issue concerning my professional innocence, and whatever assistance that may be rendered to ensure that the investigation, albeit thwarted, could be reopened with alacrity.

The taxi ride from the airport to Bay Gardens Hotel in Gros Islet was a normal occurrence for me. Since my first visit to St. Lucia many years ago, I had always looked forward to the ride. It was a soothing relaxing ride as the greenery, likened to that of Grenada, was a welcome change as it was a new environment. St. Lucia felt then like a breath of fresh air. I was away from a toxic environment. No matter how short, it was exhilarating. We arrived at our destination in the evening so there was not much time for preparation, we had agreed after dinner we would meet to finalise the protocol for the meeting. Our attire was nothing short of professional. Our demeanour had to be likewise. After supper it was agreed we would alert each other via the intercom to be ready extremely early the next day so as not to be victims of the early morning St. Lucia traffic. We were determined to be on time.

That night I prayed continuously. The bible I normally travelled with was my companion. I stayed up that night for a long time, thinking about my life and its journey, the trials, challenges, failures and successes. I wondered about the accused men whom I had occasion to represent, who may have been convicted wrongly, whether their pain could be measured to mine. Though I was not incarcerated, it surely felt that way. Life has taught me so many lessons, but I am constantly reminded that this world is not our permanent home, for we shall all soon fly away into the sunset, and we shall be judged for our deeds and misdeeds. For the evil that men do live after them; the good is oft interred with their bones. That constant reminder by Shakespeare consoled my drooping spirit; I looked forward to the sunrise in my life.

I enveloped myself in my own thoughts, as I went to bed and entered the realm of oblivion. Soon, I was alerted by the alarm on the phone, as we had requested a backup plan of having the receptionist alert us when it was time to get up. Upon receipt of the call I was startled; I leapt to my feet and answered, being gracious to the receptionist. I immediately felt a rush of adrenaline, as if I was about to receive the verdict from a jury. I calmed myself as I knelt and prayed; thereafter I called my colleagues. We finalised our meeting time at the lobby. I re-examined the well prepared bundle and after dressing for the occasion, I hastily descended the flight of stairs into the lobby.

We assembled for breakfast at the café. I thanked my colleagues profusely for being a part of my painful journey, being thankful and grateful was the least I could have done. The debt of gratitude I owe to them could not be expressed in mere words, for they are worthy not merely of earthly accolade but much more. I looked at them while being commuted and prayed for them, because they could have simply resisted my entreaty, when I requested their assistance. They both knew my work in the legal profession, and were convinced it was a malicious attempt to interfere with the administration of justice, of which I was a part, and ultimately destroy the professional lives of all involved in the email debacle.

Perception could be as damaging as the reality, for even if false, the tainted may be so scathed that after the truth is revealed the damage has already been done. I took comfort in the words of my two colleagues, when one of them said to me that these things happen to make you stronger and to every bad thing that happens some measure of good would evolve. There would be a greater good behind the mischief. As consoling as the words were, I could not fathom any good which may arise except pure destruction. I was determined to prove my innocence. I had already given the police in Grenada full access to my home, office and technological devices. I had also pledged my full financial support irrespective as to the extent of the investigation.

We soon arrived at the water front building in Castries, where the Chief Justice's office was located. The taxi driver was very polite as he pointed out the way, which was on the upper story of a building that housed the bank of St. Lucia on its lower floor. As we entered the building, we decided to congregate for the purpose of prayer; we needed that spiritual food for the brobdingnagian task ahead. We prayed together and ascended upstairs to have the meeting as pre-arranged.

As we entered the waiting area, we were greeted by friendly and courteous staff. It was welcoming. Despite they may have known the reason for our visit, it did not influence their dealings with us. I tried to examine every face that greeted us. Oh how I wished I could have read minds, but the smiles obliterated any thoughts or knowledge they may have had as it related to our visit. It was very painful and embarrassing for me, as I was there to defend my innocence, but the made up allegation was so sordid that the effect of its pain was indescribable. But I rested in comfort knowing, we all would be judged one day. Divine justice is what I await.

We sat comfortably. For the first time since the receipt of the emails I felt some measure of pious calm. My conscience was clear. I just wanted to make known that I was innocent and open to an unrestricted investigation. I was intent on cooperating fully, so as to not impede the process of investigation, be it local or otherwise. My colleagues assured me all would be well. We agreed upon the protocol, so as to allow for an effective meeting.

The Chief Registrar greeted us. We were soon escorted to the office of the Chief Justice. I walked into the room, seeing the sign on the door, and thinking to myself, what injustice and indignity I have to suffer at the hands of the perpetrators with malevolent intent. As we entered the room we were seated. I sat in the middle. The chairs were prearranged for us. The Chief Registrar sat to my extreme right. The Chief Justice welcomed us with utmost courtesy and professionalism, as Her Ladyship sat at her desk. She exhibited the professionalism likened unto the office. She immediately put us at ease. I guess her experience made our emotions transparent. The introductory remarks were done by one of my colleagues prior to the substantive meeting. It was a welcome meeting for me, as I embarked upon the reason for our travel in detail. The hearing was comfortable as I was allowed to make the presentation following on every page from the prepared bundle. I was at no time restricted in my presentation. I pledged my continued support to the Court as I had done since my inception in the legal profession. That I was committed to continuing. The discussion was varied and the continuation of the investigation was urged by me as well as my continued willingness to participate. The meeting soon came to an end and the depth and extent of the meeting left me feeling that I was at least given an opportunity to be heard. I was hopeful that the true perpetrator or perpetrators behind the scandalous email would be discovered.

As we departed the office, I again thanked my colleagues who accompanied me. It was a relief, even though the pain was still raw. My concern then was more about my professional life and not my professional future. It is oft said, that one's reputation is like an egg shell once broken it cannot be replaced. I was destined to protect mine at all cost. When we

*Outside Chief Justice Chambers upon completion of meeting*

left the office of the Chief Justice the weight that was lifted off, albeit temporarily, was a relief. The weeks of agonising pain of having to determine a way forward to deal with this matter, had taken its toll on me.

I continued to thank my colleagues as we departed the office of the Chief Justice. Thereafter we embarked on our return journey to Grenada via the same route through Barbados. The discussion between us was centred around the possible effects and draw backs of the trip, the manner in which the meeting was perceived to have been received, the effect of the allegation on my professional life and any possible negative consequences as a result of the above. I was absolutely elated that I was at least given the opportunity to ventilate my professional innocence. I have never ceased praying for Solomonic wisdom for the persons in the position of judicial authority since they need it most. Many times the message of the messenger is tainted with malicious lies, embellished for smooth consumption and ultimate destruction.

I have had occasions while sitting as Chairman of the Public Service Commission to deal with issues of allegations. I tried to allow all parties to be involved in the investigative process to ensure open transparency and justice for all. That way I ensured that any statement made, the person who made it should come forth and face their accuser with proof. Thereafter, the process of a full hearing could be embarked upon either by the appointment of a committee or the commission. My own experience had caused me to be fortified in my belief that the procedure I had adopted for some time now was absolutely the correct one.

My return to the practice of law was viewed now in a different light. I was prepared to accept a bullet in my back as there was no measured extent to which persons may go to attempt destruction. I have made myself ready for any further allegation or attack that may arise. The point I reached was, 'Let it be done'.

In my capacity as Chairman of the Public Service Commission, I was aware that I may have caused some discomfort among many, but it was a constitutional task I undertook with professionalism, being guided by the rules and regulations of the Public Service Commission. The commission has control over its members including the power to discipline, appoint and transfer persons who are deemed public servants. The Commission has no power to transfer and or remove the following from office; Registrar of the High Court, any public office in the department of the Attorney General's office or Director of Public Prosecutions' office or Magistracy.

The authority for the above is vested in section 88 (1) and (2) of the Constitution and reads as follows:

> 88 (1)
> This section applies to the office of magistrate, registrar of the High Court and any public office in the department of the Attorney General (including the public office of the Attorney General) or the department of the Director of Public Prosecutions (other than the office of the Director) for appointment to which persons are required to be qualified to practice as a Barrister or Solicitor in Grenada.
>
> 88 (2)
> The power to appoint persons to hold or act in offices to which this section applies (including the power to confirm appointments) and, subject to the provisions of section 70 (4) of this Constitution, the power to exercise disciplinary control over persons holding or acting in such offices and *the power to remove such persons from office shall vest in the Governor General, acting in accordance with the advice of the Judicial and Legal Services Commission.*

It is evident therefore that the removal or transfer of the Registrar of the Supreme Court was solely the responsibility of the Governor General acting in accordance with the advice of the Judicial and Legal Services Commission, as implied from that section. When the Registrar was removed from the Supreme Court to take up an assignment at the Ministry of Legal Affairs it was widely reported that the transfer was at the behest of the Public Service Commission, where I was Chairman.

The falsity of the allegation was either as a result of the limited depth of legal knowledge possessed by the newspaper writer, or a dire concerted attempt to desecrate the cogency of the operations of the Public Service Commission.

My return to Grenada generated a heightened sense of urgency to get to the bottom of the email scandal. The thwarting of the investigation was disconcerting to me. I had constant dialogue with the Commissioner of Police. Since he was duty bound to take directive from the Attorney General's office, I had met a dead end. I awaited the moment when there would be a change of the tide in that department, and with the transition

## Lisa Telesford removed as Registrar

Registrar of the Supreme Court, Lisa Telesford has been removed from the position.

According to a well-placed source, Telesford, an attorney-at-law, was transferred as part of a backlash from the November 24 Referendum on Constitutional Reform.

He said that the Registrar has been directed by the Public Service Commission (PSC), headed by barrister-at-law, Derek Sylvester to pick up another assignment in the Ministry of Legal Affairs.

The source pointed out that the political directorate was unhappy with the manner in which Telesford handled a court case that was filed by former Attorney General, Jimmy Bristol to challenge the legality of the process used to facilitate the referendum.

He spoke of the government wanting the matter to be assigned to high court judge, Justice Shiraz Aziz but the Registrar choose instead to place the matter before a female high court judge, Justice Adrien Wynante-Roberts.

Aziz is assigned to the high court in its

*Attorney Lisa Telesford*

Criminal Jurisdiction while Roberts concentrates primarily on civil matters.

Legal officials have told this newspaper that the Br stol matter went before the "right judge" since Roberts is the one who does civil matters.

However, the State won the case with Justice Roberts ruling in favour of the arguments put forward by Solicitor-General, Dwight Horsford.

*THE NEW TODAY* has not been able to speak to Telesford on whether she will accept the new assignment.

The person selected as replacement for Telesford is Alana Twum-Barimah, the current Deputy Registrar who is the daughter of Dr. Bert Brathwaite, a well-known associate of the ruling New National Party (NNP) government.

*The New Today, 20 January 2017*

of the appointment of another Attorney General, I immediately sprung to action as I again wrote him and copied the Commissioner of Police requesting the continuation of the investigation, together with my personal commitment to pay the cost if any associated with the investigative process.

In very short order I received a response from the Attorney General wherein he instructed the continuation of the investigation. This was a great relief as the investigation had resumed. I awaited the outcome of it. I look forward to the outcome of the investigation for it to reveal the recalcitrant or recalcitrants whose intentions are best known to them. But I leave them in the hands of the one who said since the ages began, "Vengeance is mine."

CHAPTER TWENTY

# PIVOTAL MOMENTS ALONG MY LEGAL JOURNEY

*"The value of experience is not in seeing much, but in seeing wisely."*
SIR WILLIAM OSLER

It is important to not only remember but document the many instances in my life, when I had to take a retrospective and introspective examination of my journey. The many experiences, challenges and circumstances that I had to deal with and endure, either through helping other persons or personal challenges.

The vicissitudes of life demand that it comes with challenges. The only constant in life is change; those challenges ultimately build character and prepare one for the future. Since the beginning of the ages mankind has had to face adversity, for it is a natural part of human existence. There are some challenges that can be avoided and some that cannot. I have made it my duty to alleviate burdens not exacerbate them, for the circle of life dictates that we may all be placed in a position where we may need help. The old adage which states, "When the shoe is on the other foot, it is then we would understand," equally applies in these situations.

The island of Grenada being so small, the level of familiarity is astounding. Rumours spread like wild fire. Some newspapers use the 'rumour mill' to generate sales, in that good news sell papers but a juicy story sells papers faster. On one occasion in the height of an election season, when speculation was at a boiling point as to who would most likely be the candidate to contest the general election in the parish of Saint David, I received a telephone call followed up by a face to face conversation with a newspaper journalist, who wanted to know first-hand whether I was likely to be the next candidate for Saint David. I was taken aback, since I never expressed any political interest. My love has been the law as long as I knew myself. I had no other interest. My response

## Denial from Derick Sylvester

"I know nothing of what you speak...No one has approached me. I am not that lucky."

Those were the words uttered Monday by attorney-at-law, Derick Sylvester when approached by ***THE NEW TODAY*** newspaper on reports that he is talking to the New National Party (NNP) to run as its candidate for St. David in the upcoming general election.

The categorical denial came amidst reports from legal sources that Sylvester has been "bragging" about getting the nod from the NNP to replace the current Member of Parliament for St. David, Economic Development Minister, Oliver Joseph.

One source quoted Sylvester as saying that the country should expect "a big announcement" in the next few days from the NNP leadership about his candidacy for St. David.

*Barrister Derick Sylvester – is denying reports of looking at St. David's seat for the ruling party*

According to the source, Sylvester who is from the village of Corinth, expressed confidence that he is well known in the Constituency and can easily win the seat for the NNP in the general election.

Speculation is rife that the ruling party has concerns about the constituency and the growing influence of the candidate from the main opposition National Democratic Congress (NDC), Adrian "Persuader" Thomas.

Joseph won the seat from Thomas, who is a top calypsonian as part of the NNP clean sweep of all 15 seats in the 2013 poll.

The ruling party has already announced 10 of its 15 "Caretakers" for the elections with St. David not among them.

In 2008, policeman Carl Caton had publicly denied being approached by the NNP to contest the rural St. Patrick East constituency in the upcoming election against former Prime Minister Tillman Thomas.

However, four hours later, Caton was on a platform of the NNP accepting nomination to contest the seat for the party.

With the NNP return to power in 2013, attorney Sylvester was one of three lawyers being considered by Prime Minister Dr. Keith Mitchell for the post of Attorney-general which eventually went to Cajeton Hood.

Sylvester landed the post of Chairman of the influential Public Service Commission (PSC).

He came under fire over the Claudius Coutain affair when the Commission took the unsual decision to give the embattled senior police officer all the leave due to him to take him up to the age of retirement.

Coutain was suspended from active duties after he was arrested in 2015 in connection with a driver's licence scam.

The case is still pending before the Magistrate's Court.

*The New Today, 23 June 2017*

was, "I know nothing of what you speak and no one has approached me." I then said sarcastically, "I am not that lucky." I was of the view that this was the end of the matter, but I was so wrong. On the week following my encounter with the journalist and despite the heading in the newspaper indicating 'Denial from Derick F Sylvester', the report went on to state, contrary to what I said, that I would be the next candidate and am boastfully confident of victory.

The political playing field has never piqued my interest. I was more intrigued by the legal mine field, wherein my passion rested. I have had many occasions where I dreamt I was in court, preparing submissions, discussing law and celebrating victories. There were occasions where I dreamt the contrary, but despite the many challenges faced I would not trade my profession for another. I felt as if I was entrapped with the 'legal Stockholm Syndrome'. Whatever it was, love and passion conquered all.

The legal field has never been short of excitement. On another occasion it was widely published that the Government of Grenada through a Cabinet decision had passed a resolution to confer silk or what is referred to as the title of 'Queen's Counsel' on me and another attorney. The report went viral in legal circles and there were weekly reporting in the newspapers. The issue arose as to whether the State could confer this accolade without the application through the Silk Committee that would examine the application after payment of a non-refundable fee of six thousand dollars. No application was made by me. I had no intention of making one. I kept quiet on any matter that related to me unless it was concerning one of my clients. I spoke without reservation. I likened myself to the tailor who had no proper pants or the fisherman who refused to eat fish. During that epoch a journalist made enquiries as to whether I would accept the conferment of the title emanating from the State's recommendation or approval. I was determined to stay silent, remembering the prior discourse I had with the journalist when my words were completely twisted out of context. I would opt to not have a repeat, so I declined to comment. The print media then published an article which stated that my eyes were set on becoming QC despite my declining to comment. However, I had come to realise a long time ago that criticisms, untruth and innuendos were all part of public life.

The appetite I had for the law would not enable me to do or be a part of any exercise which would besmirch my professional image or reputation, in the eyes of the Judiciary, my colleagues or any quasi-judicial body affiliated therewith. My professional reputation was what mattered most. My calling in the profession was catalysed by a quest for justice, fairness and equality for all, also being able to champion the cause for others.

There were many occasions when members of the judiciary were under attack by members of the public who were either devoid of the understanding of the workings of the legal principles of sentencing or how the court system operated. On these occasions, judicial officers may be maligned, verbally abused, threatened and in extreme cases physically attacked. On one occasion a magistrate of the eastern district was allegedly threatened with death by someone. It was indeed a serious

# CJ invites lawyers to apply for QC

Chief Justice of the OECS Supreme Court, Dame Janice Pereira, has given a slap in the face to Prime Minister Dr. Keith Mitchell over his ambitions to appoint local attorneys to Queen's Counsel Status.

Eyebrows were raised in the local legal profession when government on the recommendation of Prime Minister Mitchell approved attorneys Ruggles Ferguson and Derek Sylvester for elevation to "silk" which is worn by Queen's Counsel.

The decision was made despite advice to the contrary from then serving Attorney-General, Cajeton Hood and Solicitor-General, Dwight Horsford that government should be weary to single out lawyers in private practice for QC designation.

Derek Sylvester – eyes set on becoming a QC

Ruggles Ferguson – identified by government for QC status

The government's own legal advisors indicated that the administration is limited to making recommendations from among attorneys working for the State like the Director of Public Prosecutions, Attorney-General and Solicitor General and should be cautious of incursions into the private bar.

The Chief Justice has reacted to the apparent breach by government by putting out a notice asking attorneys who want to become QC to apply to the "Silk Committee" that falls under her jurisdiction.

The notice reads as follows: "PURSUANT to Section 6.1 of the Eastern Caribbean Supreme Court, Queen's Counsel Appointment Protocol dated 26th November, 2010.

"The Eastern Caribbean Supreme Court is presently receiving Applications for Silk in accordance with Section 4.1 of the Protocol.

Your application, if it is to be considered, must be submitted together with your curriculum Vitae and the application fee of $5000.00 in your currency. Application Forms without the fee will be treated as invalid.

"Typed applications are to be submitted to the Office of the Chief Justice, Eastern Caribbean Supreme Court, 2nd Floor, Heraldine Rock, Bldg., the Waterfront, Castries, Saint Lucia in hard copy no later than 4:00 pm, on 15th January, 2018.

"Application Forms and the Guidance Notes for Applicants are available on the Eastern Caribbean Supreme Court website.

The Chief Justice also released the names of the newly appointed members of the Silk Committee to serve for a period of two years.

The body will be headed by Court of Appeal Justice Davidson Baptiste and includes high court judge, Francis Belle and two current QC's, Michael Gordon and Delano Bart, as well as a lay member, Sir Howard Fergus.

A legal source told this newspaper that it is now open to Ferguson and Sylvester and any other local lawyer to apply to the Baptiste-led "Silk Committee" of the Chief Justice for QC designation and not using the "back door" approach involving government.

Ferguson has already indicated that he would not accept a government-appointed QC that was not sanctioned by the Chief Justice.

Sylvester has declined to comment on the issue.

*The New Today, 1 December 2017*

cause for concern, as the incident occurred close to the home of the judicial officer. The Bar Association immediately went into high gear, appointing a few lawyers to look after the interest of the officer. I was one of the lawyers. We attended the court proceedings where the accused was charged, looking after the interest of the Magistrate, and we did that task until the matter was completed. Since the judicial officer could not have spoken on the subject to the public by virtue of the ethics of the profession, the attorneys had to represent the judicial officer both in and out of court and provide clarification on the proceedings that was brought against the accused, for the benefit of all concerned. This was proof of the fact that the legal profession had to represent its own, in circumstances wherein it was necessary to do so.

## MAGISTRATE SEALES DEPARTS

Prior to Magistrate Jerry Seales's resignation from office after twelve years of service, he was faced with an issue concerning his vacation leave, pension and retirement. The Public Service Commission was tasked with the responsibility of approving the Magistrate's leave, be it supplementary family leave, sick leave, paternity leave or leave for urgent private affairs. When the issue of the Magistrate's leave came up for consideration through his lawyer's request in writing, the Commission was called to action.

The administrative procedure and practice has always been to allow the request to emanate from the Ministry of Legal Affairs with a recommendation for approval or non-approval with reasons for it. However, the ultimate responsibility and decision was that of the Commission. Upon receipt of the request from the Magistrate's attorney,

DEATH THREATS ON MAGISTRATE

Full story on page 12

**Death Threats On Magistrate**

The Grenada Bar Association (GBA) is moving quickly to have Judicial Officers protected.

The move by the GBA came as a result of a barrage of verbal attacks that were launched on Magistrate Tahyre Gellineau at her private residence.

The Magistrate presides at the Number Three Magistrate's Court in St. George's that primarily deals with traffic offenses.

THE NEW TODAY was told that the female jurist was hurled with insults and threatening language by Lincoln Marshall of Old Westerhall, St. David's who was armed with a cutlass.

There is no known conflict existing between the magistrate and the St. David's man.

Marshall, a 45-year old Landscaper, was later arrested by police and slapped with 15 charges ranging from obscene language to being armed with an offensive weapon.

The accused pleaded guilty to 14 of the charges when he appeared at the St. David's Magistrate's Court last week Friday.

Magistrate Nevlyn John, who heard the matters, sentenced Marshall to two months and two strokes each for two counts.

On the other 12 counts, Magistrate John sentenced the St. David's man to three months each to run concurrently.

Attorney-at-Law Anselm Clouden told the media on Monday that the GBA would now be lobbying government to have police protection offered to all Judicial Officers on a constant basis.

Clouden said President of the GBA, Dr. Francis Alexis, QC intervened and assigned attorneys Cajeton Hood, Derick Sylvester and himself to seek Magistrate Gellineau's interest, and to also signal the Bar's abhorrence and repugnance with such conduct.

He said they are baffled over Marshall's rationale for attacking the Magistrate since she has had no contact with him on or off the bench.

"She had no altercation, didn't sentence him, tried him or anything," he remarked.

Clouden said the intervention was also geared at giving the magistracy some level of comfort that the matter would be taken up with the highest level of authority so as to ensure that all magistrates in the State of Grenada are afforded 24-hour police protection.

"That is necessary because of the job the Magistrate does. Magistrates commit violent criminals to prison, and it is very conceivable as was the case in St. Lucia whereupon release... that person can threaten the magistrate's life and sometime takes the magistrate's life," he said.

Clouden recalled that a magistrate in St. Lucia was shot and grievously wounded.

He said the GBA would also like to see judges getting 24-hour police protection.

*Front page, The New Today, week ending 25 February 2011*

the Commission was duty bound to act, so as to ensure the system functioned fairly and efficiently, thereby obviating the need for a judicial review application that may or may not succeed, but would have resulted in time wastage for all involved. The Commission was called to action via a round robin decision; the leave was approved. Therefore, the Magistrate could not have been deemed to have abandoned his job, despite being away from office without the requisite permission. This in effect would have affected his salary, retirement benefits and pension.

After the retirement of Magistrate Seales, he publicly expressed his gratitude to the writer and his attorney for their involvement in resolving the issue concerning his retirement, which could have had a deleterious effect on his emoluments by having him declared, to have vacated his post without lawful authority.

## Magistrate Jerry Seales Retires After 12 Years of Service

*Magistrate Jerry Seales*

Magistrate Jerry Anthony Seales has retired from his career in public service as a Magistrate in Grenada. Seales who tendered his resignation on February 13, 2018, has taken his vacation leave until April 5, 2018 - the effective date of his retirement. A release from Mr Seales' office says he has served in the Northern, Southern, Eastern, and Western Magisterial Districts over the span of 12 years and is known for championing law and order in Grenada.

Magistrate Seales expressed deep gratitude saying, "First and foremost, he would like to thank the Almighty God for giving him the mental and physical strength as well as the wisdom to perform all these years. He also thanks the people of Grenada for giving him the opportunity to serve them "to the best of my ability".

According to the release, the retired magistrate is also grateful to all the members of the Grenada Bar Association for the strong relationship they have built over the years. He extended gratitude to all the Court staff, Prosecutors, and "my distinguished colleagues on the bench for the support they have extended to me during my tenure as a magistrate."

Magistrate Seales also expressed appreciation to Mr Derrick Sylvester, Chairman of the Public Service Commission and Ms Celia Clyne Edwards, QC for their support during his efforts to resolve issues of pension, vacation and retirement. He considers himself privileged to be of service to Grenada. Upholding law and order for the protection of the people he said, has always been the Magistrate's main focus and he never wavered.

"Magistrate Seales", the release said, "started shortly after Hurricane Ivan, one of the most challenging times Grenada has ever seen. The preservation of the country's peace and order could be attributed, in part, to his body of work as a Magistrate. He has adjudicated over 7,000 cases during his tenure".

"In May, Magistrate Seales will be marking his 30th year as a lawyer, an impressive milestone backed by a significant law career. Despite receiving some complaints about his hard adherence to the law, he is highly appreciated by fellow lawmakers who share his belief in implementing the law for the greater good and not compromising for the sake of the few. Though known for his strict sentencing, his preference in sentencing, in fact, was Community Service and engaged a wide cross-section of the Grenadian society to get involved. For instance, offenders were sentenced to perform services like cleaning of public cemeteries, painting and cleaning of public schools, assisting in beach cleanups, hospital cleaning and similar community projects.

However, behind Magistrate Seales's toughness is genuine concern and compassion. All the weddings he has officiated were done for free. He continues to make significant contributions of time and other resources to initiatives to help the elderly and children. He serves as the Honorary Consul for South Korea to Grenada facilitating diplomatic relations between the two countries.

Magistrate Seales plans to continue to serve his country and humanity in the areas of law, music, diplomacy, and philanthropy. Known for being a musical genius, he also plans to use his talents to help young people who are musically gifted.

As he passes the torch to the next magistrate, he hopes that Grenada will continue to thrive economically, politically, and socially, keeping peace and order as one of its core tenets to ensure the unbridled success of the country moving forward".

*Grenada Informer, 2 March 2018*

I have had for many years the opportunity to practice before the Honourable Jerry Seales in almost every Magistrate court in the country, even on the sister island of Carriacou. I have exhibited professional courtesy both in and out of court. The same was reciprocated. He has fulfilled his years of service and has moved on to another phase in his life's journey.

While I embarked upon my legal journey there were persons I met along the way, who had short conversations with me, gave advice, complimented or encouraged me and their words resonate with me to the present day. During the resentencing hearing of the accused in the Maurice Bishop Murder Trial, I met a media icon. He was about 6 feet 2 inches, Trevor Thwaites, renowned sportsman, cricketer and boxer. After I completed my submission at the trade centre in Grand Anse and the court was adjourned, he walked over and we had a conversation. He said to me, "I have always heard of you, you did excellently, keep it up, you are on your way." I expressed my thanks for his kind words, but I never told him the effect his words had on me but it had propelled me even further. That initial conversation we had was the start of a good relationship in that once we met a conversation was sure to be ignited between us.

Trevor Thwaites has left a legacy not only with me but also with the media fraternity and the sporting community at large. He departed this life leaving a positive impact on me. His memory will live on in the lives of the many he touched, encouraged and motivated, to which I am a beneficiary.

The legal profession has seen the entry and exit of many legal luminaries who sat as judges. They submit themselves to serving the public with arduous hours of work and their desire to ensure justice is meted out to all. The judges are in a position to call for positive changes as they experience first-hand the needs of the society. The accused, complainants, prosecution, jury and defence all have an impact on the trial judge who has to ensure the trial is fair for all concerned thereby maintaining faith in the judicial process. One of our legal luminaries Justice Paula Gilford, like her sister Justice Clare Henry, constantly called for change such as; better accommodation for the mentally challenged in our society since the prison was not the best place to keep them, the maintenance of certain values and mode of dress while in Court, the need for pro bono representation of unrepresented accused and a proper legal aid system to aid in the due administration of justice.

# MEDIA IN MOURNING AGAIN, Thwaites Passes

Less than two months after, and still recuperating from the loss of videographer and former employee of the Grenada Broadcasting Network Rollins Williams who died by drowning in attempt to save his wife in Barbados, in October, the media fraternity in Grenada is again plunged into deeper mourning following the sudden death of senior journalist and broadcaster Trevor Thwaites.

Thwaites alias Big T, former national cricketer, boxer and one of Grenada's most ardent sports supporters and writers died last Saturday at the General Hospital where he was admitted only days before as a patient.

Trevor would be remembered for his passion for sports, particularly cricket and his readiness to take on just about anyone who had a different view to his if he believes that he is on the right side.

Trevor's presence at the national stadium or for that matter any other playing field where cricket or football is being played is almost inevitable. And once there, no need to be looking for him, he finds you, with a tight embrace, or a light-hearted invitation to a quick boxing bout. If he did not find you first, his voice in some heated conversation would indicate that he is around.

Apart for representing Grenada at the highest level in cricket in the 80s, Trevor was a founding member of the Media Cricket Team, a member of the X National Cricket Team, Morne Jaloux Cricket Team, Grenada Masters Cricket Team and just about any other team that was willing to give him the opportunity to play the game

Management and staff of the Grenada Information Services where he last worked as a Senior Information Officer described him as an invaluable team player; one endowed with the spirit of magnanimity that knows no boundaries.

President of the Grenada Cricket Association Dwain Gill joined hundreds across Grenada and the region paying tribute too and extending sympathy to the Thwaites family.

According to Gill, as a journalist and broadcaster, Thwaites made every effort to cover local and regional cricket especially the exploits of youth cricketers. He added that Thwaites no doubt remains one of Grenada's, Windward Island's and the West Indies' biggest fan and therefore his loss would be great to all in the cricketing fraternity.

His loss to the media fraternity in Grenada came at a time when the profession still mourns the departure of a number of its members, among them Michael Noel, Wayne Modeste, David Blackburn and more recently Rollins Williams all within the space of sixteen months. Given Trevor's active involvement in media activities, his unwavering support and readiness to stand up in defense of members of the media, his loss would remain in the minds and hearts of those now charged with the responsibility to carry on the mantle for a number of years, and no doubt he would definitely be missed by all.

## GCA Mourns Trevor's Passing

On behalf of the Board of Management, staff and members of the Grenada Cricket Association, as well as players, well-wishers and supporters of cricket, I extend our deepest sympathy to family and friends of Trevor Thwaites.

We are indeed saddened by the loss of Trevor, a former national cricketer.

Trevor's love and affection were remarkable. As a sports broadcaster and journalist, he made every effort to cover local and regional cricket especially the exploits of young cricketers.

He remained one of the biggest fans of Grenada, Windward Islands, and West Indies Cricket. His death is a great loss to us in the cricketing fraternity.

May he Rest In Peace.

*Dwain Gill*
*President*
*Grenada Cricket Association*

## Remembering TREVOR THWAITES: THE LIFE OF A HEAVYWEIGHT!

The Management and Staff of the Government Information Services (GIS) extend deepest condolences to the family, friends, former colleagues and acquaintances of Trevor Thwaites our Senior Information Office who died on Saturday morning.

Trevor was not a conformist, but he was an invaluable team player and all will attest to that. He was endowed with a spirit of magnanimity that knew no boundaries and for that, he will be greatly missed.

We take this opportunity to extend our wholehearted support to his daughter Neisha McIntyre who also lost her mother Nadica McIntyre earlier this year.

We know that mere words are not enough to provide adequate consolation in this period of utter anguish and pain – a pain that we too, deeply share.

Nevertheless, be assured that our staff stands ready and willing to offer support in whatever way needed.

The GIS family, of which Trevor was an integral part for years, also expresses condolence to the sporting fraternity in Grenada, especially the Cricket and Boxing Associations, two sports in which he excelled and for which he flew the Grenadian flag proudly.

*The media fraternity, like the rest of the population who* knew Trevor and his exploits in media and sports, is mourning the loss of an amiable friend; one who in word and deed brought smiles to tense and pensive faces.

He was one who knew how to evoke laughter, breaking the silence in an otherwise icy room.

If we are true to ourselves, we will agree that the greatest lesson we have all learned from Trevor "Big T" Thwaites is that we should never take life so seriously that we cannot find enjoyment in living.

We therefore take this opportunity to invite the public to join us this Monday morning from 6.30 until 8am, when the GIS Spice Morning will pay tribute to Trevor Thwaites: The life of a heavyweight.

***It's Monday November 20 from 6:30 to 8:00 a.m...Trevor Thwaites: The life of a heavyweight!***

*Trevor at the recent launch of Waggy T Super Knockout Football Tournament*

*Grenada Informer, 24 November 2017*

Many other judges have voiced the importance of numerous changes in the legal system to foster the continued growth of the system of justice, including adherence to the code of ethics which regulate the conduct of lawyers and litigants alike. Justice Shiraz Aziz, who spent three (3) years in Grenada where he served as a High Court Judge both in its civil and criminal jurisdiction, was a forward thinker. Where the justice system was concerned, he was a reformer and demonstrated same in his numerous judgments; he was an agent for development of the jurisprudence. His professional, respectful candour both to lawyers and litigants alike was

## High Court Judge wants better accommodation for mentally challenged offenders

High Court Judge Paula Gilford

A senior High Court Judge operating in Grenada wants the authorities to put in place better accommodation to take care of mentally ill offenders.

Addressing the opening of the January Criminal Assizes on Tuesday, High Court Judge Paula Gilford said the time has come when the powers that be, need put in place better facilities to accommodate the mentally challenged offenders. According to her, the prison is definitely not the best place for them.

The judge added that in the same manner that the issue of juvenile offenders was handled, systems need to be put in place to take care of the mentally ill since most of the time those offenders are not in control of their actions.

The ten-minute address from the judge also touched on the importance of dress code for the jury. According to the judge, while the role and function of the jury are important for the functioning of the court, it must also be noted that the court maintains certain values and the proper dress code is one of them.

Also addressed by the judge is the number of unrepresented accused persons coming before the court. While judge Gilford commended the lawyers who avail themselves from time to time to provide Pro Bono service, she called on others to lend their support, according to her it's not always about how much money one can make but at times it has to do with how much one can help.

Judge Gilford is one of two High Court judges that would be presiding over criminal matters down for trial in the January Assizes, the other being Judge Shiraz Aziz.

*Grenada Informer, 19 January 2018*

## High Court bids farewell to Justice Aziz

*Justice Shiraz Aziz - poses for the media accompanied by Supreme Court Registrar, Alana Twum-Barimah*

"Stick to the code of ethics. We should all resolve to be honest and act with integrity."

Those were the words of advice given by departing High Court Judge, Justice Shiraz Aziz, as he addressed a packed special sitting of High Court No.2 on the Carenage, St. George's in his honour on Monday.

*THE NEW TODAY* understands that Justice Aziz is expected to depart to pursue undisclosed undertakings in the Turks and Caicos Islands (TCI), at the end of the month after serving in the jurisdiction for approximately 3 years.

Justice Aziz, who presided over High Court No. 5 on The Carenage in St. George's, was praised for his "fair and impartial" execution of justice to persons appearing before him.

Senior Crown Counsel in the Office of the Director of Public Prosecution (DPP) Crisan Greenidge, who often prosecuted cases before Justice Aziz, when he then served at the No. 1 High Court on St. John's Street up to his final stint at the No. 5 High Court on The Carenage, described him as not only a judge but also a "teacher and a friend, a hard worker (who is) well read, well-reasoned, well researched and shows extreme dedication" in the execution of his duties.

The female Crown Counsel also noted that Justice Aziz is one who "always reminded litigants of certain developments in law ..always willing to share instead of saying that you should know."

The departing judge was also commended for his efforts in the administration of fair justice, to ensure public confidence in the justice system.

Acting Attorney General, Dr. Lawrence Joseph, thanked Justice Aziz for his contribution to the local court, and was confident that he will continue to make significant contributions to the administration of justice in the Caribbean with his jurisprudence, knowledge of and skill in law.

Speaking on behalf of the Inner Bar, female Queen's Counsel, Celia Clyne-Edwards said she admired the will of Justice Aziz to function under the "unacceptable conditions," particularly, when he was stationed at the No. 1 High Court.

"In my over 30 years experience at the Bar, we have our judges working without proper chairs...and they develop back problems...we have judges sitting in offices with mold so slippery that judges and jurors slip and fall...and just outside the Court (in front of the entrance to the No.2 High Court) we have toilet water dripping...it is unacceptable," she declared.

"You (Justice Aziz) have served with competence, care and the patience of Job (and) the numbers here is evidence of the respect that you have earned in the relatively short time you have spent with us," she told the departing judge.

In bidding farewell, President of the Grenada Bar Association (GBA), Lady Avril Anande Trotman-Joseph said, litigants will remember Justice Aziz most of all, for his "humane approach and judicial courses.

"He has left a legacy of criminal jurisprudence...to be learned from and built upon," she said.

Justice Aziz in his response said: "It was my honour and privilege to come to Grenada and be able to do, what I call my daily job as best as I can".

The departing Judge stated that he was shocked to hear all the great attributes given to him by his colleagues in the profession.

Justice Aziz, who is a member of the OECS Sentencing Advisory Committee said, one of the things he has always remembered in the administration of Justice is that "there are people at the end of it and that people's lives were going to be affected," and urged all and sundry to always do the same.

Justice Aziz, took up a stint in Grenada on April 1, 2015 with a predominantly criminal law practice background after working for approximately 14 years in the United Kingdom.

*The New Today, 23 March 2018*

admired. Despite the physical conditions under which he had to work, he was undaunted in his pursuit to ensure the wheels of justice spun without ceasing. Justice Aziz's departure from Grenada to take up assignment in the Turks and Caicos Islands was met with some resistance from the lawyers. But his departure could not be thwarted as it was 'much ado about nothing'. We all accepted that our island's loss was another's gain, and everyone who spoke at the farewell for Justice Aziz was lucid in their admiration for his legal astuteness, impartiality, willingness to impart knowledge and his humane approach to all who appeared before him.

The departure of Justice Aziz was a stark reminder that to everything under the heavens there is a season, a time to come and a time to leave, a time to be born and a time to die. The journey is temporary but the destination is final.

CHAPTER TWENTY-ONE

# WHERE DO WE GO FROM HERE?

*"I am learning to trust the journey even when I do not understand it."*
MILA BROWN

In December of 2019, the world was awakened to the news of the emergence of a virus named, COVID-19. A disease caused by a new strain of coronavirus.

This virus became a pandemic, resulting in worldwide deaths and it placed serious challenges on the health care system of the countries of the world. Grenada was no exception. Luckily to date, Grenada had a total of twenty-four (24) confirmed cases of COVID-19. There has been only one fatality due to the virus to date.

When the island of Grenada confirmed its first case of the virus, the Government immediately put measures in place to curb both community and individual spread.

A state of emergency was declared by the Government of Grenada. The country was placed on a twenty-four-hour curfew, inbound international travel was restricted, legislation was passed and regulations were made to ensure wearing of masks in public, social and physical distancing, restricted movement, designated opening hours for essential businesses and an immediate termination of large social gatherings.

The pandemic put a halt on the operation of courts of law. Immediately, systems had to be put in place to enable the continued functioning of the justice system. Practice directions were issued by the Chief Justice, based in St. Lucia and the business of the court was able to continue in some limited way, with numerous matters being heard online via the Zoom video conferencing platform. Court documents had to be scanned, sent to the Supreme Court Registry for filing and forwarding to the Judge who would be presiding over the matter.

In the case of the hearings at the Court of Appeal, it seemed to be heading in a paperless direction. The Court of Appeal's itinerant sitting was now being conducted online as the Justices of Appeal were now able to conduct the hearings via the Zoom platform while located in different countries.

This new normal, as it soon became, did not come without its challenges. While the court system was well poised to press on, and systems were put in place to ensure that it did, lawyers were at pains to keep up. The immediate and unannounced shut down of the country meant that lawyers were confined to their homes with no access to their offices and their files. No exception was made for them, in the early weeks of the state of emergency, to gain access to their offices. This inevitably led to the adjournment of numerous court matters. When permission was eventually granted by the Commissioner of Police, and lawyers could return to their offices to conduct online hearing of matters before the Court, many were challenged further by their unfamiliarity with the technology. The process was sluggish at first, but over time things accelerated and I was able to have many of my matters heard by this medium.

In April of 2020, for the first time, the Court of Appeal of the Eastern Caribbean Supreme Court heard matters for the State of Grenada via Zoom. I welcomed the development as I had matters before the court. The 24-hour curfew was in force and therefore permission had to be sought from the Commissioner of Police, to enable us to access our offices for limited durations to retrieve files, scan documents and prepare for court hearings.

Not only was our livelihood affected, but lawyers were not categorized as 'essential workers' for the purpose of the COVID Regulations. So lawyers' movements were restricted by the curfew.

We were all required to join queues which stretched for very long in order to access essential services such as the supermarkets and gas stations. Not being able to visit with family members and friends took a toll on many of us, mentally and socially. I was, however, grateful for the time off and much needed rest. The challenges faced during this period allowed me to step back and introspect into the meaning and purpose of life. Many insights were gained, and the frailty of life became a stark reality. It was a humbling experience.

The COVID-19 pandemic resulted in us finding new ways to accomplish the work of the Court as well as going about our daily activities. It has had a profound and negative effect on the tourism sector which was brought to a standstill as the movement of people was restricted to limit the spread of the virus.

The island of Grenada has been blessed thus far. Some of the neighbouring islands were not that fortunate as they recorded fatalities due to the pandemic.

The future is indeed uncertain. But as the pendulum swings and the sand moves through the hour glass, one thing we know for sure is that, until death, there is no end to the trials of a trial lawyer.

# INDEX